T0328775

B. C. HALL AND C. T. WOOD ARE THE COAUTHORS OF
Big Muddy

OTHER BOOKS BY B. C. HALL
NOVELS
  The Burning Season
  Keepers of the Feast

NONFICTION
  Judgment Day (with Bob Lancaster)

THE SOUTH

A TWO-STEP ODYSSEY ON THE BACKROADS OF THE ENCHANTED LAND

B. C. HALL AND C. T. WOOD

A TOUCHSTONE BOOK
Published by Simon & Schuster

TOUCHSTONE
Rockefeller Center
1230 Avenue of the Americas
New York, NY 10020

First Touchstone Edition 1996

TOUCHSTONE and colophon are registered trademarks
of Simon & Schuster Inc.

Designed by Irving Perkins Associates

Manufactured in the United States of America

10   9   8   7   6   5   4   3   2   1

Library of Congress Cataloging-in-Publication Data
Hall, B. Clarence.
  The South / B.C. Hall and C. T. Wood.
    p.   cm.
  Includes index.
  1. Southern States—Civilization. I. Wood, C. T. (Clyde Thornton) II. Title.
F209.M15   1995
975—dc20   *94-43617*
                                                CIP

ISBN: 0-02-547450-2
ISBN: 0-684-81893-0 (Pbk.)

For James T. Whitehead

ACKNOWLEDGMENTS

For their support and assistance the authors wish to thank the following: Marie Hall, Belinda Claunch, Julie Speed, Harvey Young, Rhonda Noble Hall, Deborah Wilson, Marcie Studler, Mary Jimenez, Harvey Clinton, A. J. Bickerstaff, Jerry Mann, Roy Reed, Martha Lancaster, Bill Berry, and Tom Royals. The authors would also like to give their special thanks to John and Odessa Wood and Sissy Fluit.

CONTENTS

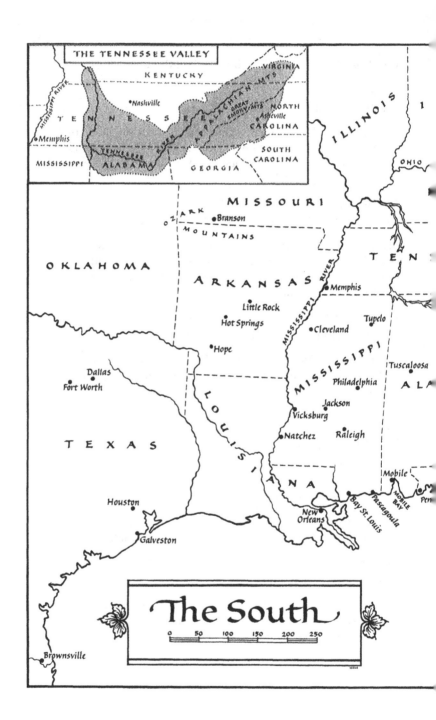

THE TENNESSEE VALLEY

KENTUCKY

VIRGINIA

MISSISSIPPI RIVER

TENNESSEE

•Nashville

APPALACHIAN MTS

GREAT SMOKY MTS

NORTH CAROLINA

•Asheville

•Memphis

TENNESSEE RIVER

MISSISSIPPI

ALABAMA

GEORGIA

SOUTH CAROLINA

ILLINOIS

OHIO

MISSOURI

OZARK MOUNTAINS

•Branson

TEN

OKLAHOMA

ARKANSAS

MISSISSIPPI RIVER

•Memphis

Little Rock

•Hot Springs

•Cleveland

Tupelo

Tuscaloosa

•Hope

MISSISSIPPI

Philadelphia

ALA

Dallas
Fort Worth

Jackson

Vicksburg

LOUISIANA

•Natchez

Raleigh

TEXAS

Mobile

Houston

New
Orleans

Bay St. Louis

Pascagoula

MOBILE BAY

Pen

Galveston

The South

0   50   100   150   200   250

Brownsville

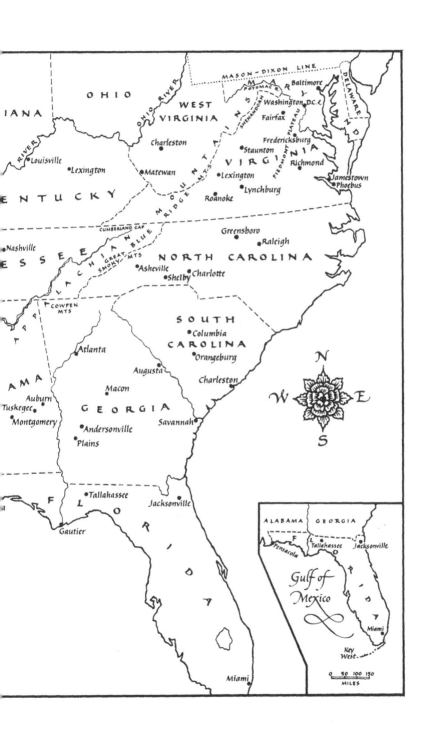

GATEWAYS TO THE SOUTH

AS TIME MOVES OVER the selvage of the millennium, America's South has had a life of some four centuries, and from the face of things— shining new cities, corporate fields, new social attitudes—the outside world may be thinking that the South is at last in the process of losing its identity as modernity imposes its will. Is the old sustaining, harrowing mythology about to give up the ghost?

The South has been such a stout entity in the world's imagination that any consideration of things "Southern" must begin with the question "What is the true nature of the South and does that nature still have a palpable existence?" To say that the South no longer exists would be to deny a cultural phenomenon that has been building up for twenty generations, and an influence that reaches now beyond the vague boundaries of the South into a good many parts of the American scene: transplanted Southerners still speak with syrupy drawls and practice Southern ways in parts of Delaware and Maryland; in the border regions of Indiana, Ohio, Illinois, and Missouri; in the projects of most major cities; and even as far away as Brazil, where thousands of descendants of Civil War refugees still hold on to their Southern allegiance (even though they speak hardly a word of English). Therefore, telling people in Dixie today that there is no South would be tantamount to having them believe they don't love their mothers or indeed don't have mothers to love.

In understanding the South, it would be well to remember that *Gone With the Wind* is no more relevant than *Birth of a Nation* or *Cool*

Hand Luke. In the same vein, the works of William Faulkner are no more relevant than those of Shelby Foote or James Dickey. Each face of the South provides no more than a random piece of the jigsaw puzzle that is the South.

As travelers pass through any one of the many gateways into the South, they begin to encounter a flood of thoughts, ideas, passions, peculiarities, angles, emotions, all streaming from the Southern consciousness in no particular order. It's as if a magic dust has been thrown into their eyes, obscuring the true character of the Southern psyche. They are bombarded with themes that live in the same shadow of a blessed or blighted lineage. Their senses are flayed by the reverence for loyalty, by the power of evangelical hokum, by the irony of the white man's world still holding on in a world ever more populated by people of color, by the ever-waving banner of Southern pride. They won't have traveled far at all into the South before they discover firsthand that definitions here are hard to come by.

With the modern world's tendency to label, it may be that the real voice of the South is that of the singer. After all of the historians, sociologists, and ethnologists have had their say, perhaps the final say-so comes from arguably the South's finest muse, Thomas Wolfe, who, like many another distinct voice of the South, drew his inspiration from the old songs and anthems of the common folk that best reveal the nature of the land and its people: ". . . We seek the great forgotten language, the lost lane-end into heaven, a stone, a leaf, an unfound door. Where? When? O lost, and by the wind grieved, ghost, come back again." The songs coming to the ears of those who travel through the gateways into the South form a bond, a linkage between the traveler and the South, its history, its people, its dreams. For the South is a concatenation of the souls of men and the land.

The first bonding was the most violent, the collision of continents some 600 million years ago when the present-day South was ocean floor. Not yet formed, the boundaries of the Deep South, of Virginia and the Carolinas, lay mired in troughs of mud and sand and fishy mass thousands of leagues deep. Florida was as sunken as Atlantis, as were Alabama and Georgia and even Tennessee. But nature was about to metamorphose up the Piedmont, the Blue Ridge, the Ozarks, the coasts, the Gulf, and dry out the Great Smokies, the Cumberlands, and the Appalachians, leaving the marshy Tidewater and letting nascent rivers fall down through borning plateaus to push out embayments with the richest soil on earth. The frangible linkage of the South had commenced, but the concatenation would have to wait longer, until European civilization had pushed its precincts into the primitive tropical zones of America.

The gateways to the South today are as metaphoric as they are geographic, for the South was born of myth. This myth is embodied within the illusions of Sir Walter Scott, D. W. Griffith, and Margaret Mitchell, entrenched in the enigmatic and complex panorama of the modern South. One might compare the character of the South to random pointillism in a full array of prime colors and subliminal hues. Put it all on an outsized canvas and the resulting picture will give rise to as many interpretations of the South as there are beholders. No other region of America can be seen in such a way; it's what makes the South not exactly a nation within a nation but the closest thing to it.

Not just one mind of the South exists, but many, each with a distinct lyricism that creates a seemingly unconnected cacophony—a harsh, blaring racket that can delight or frighten or horrify. The heartbeat of the South, that blaring racket, determines the pace of social patterns, standards, thoughts, and relationships. In his classic book, *The Mind of the South,* published more than fifty years ago, W. J. Cash recognized that there were many Souths contained within the one. Cash captured the essence of the heartbeat—the paradox between the legend and the reality of the South's cultural fabric. Cash's brilliance in explaining this paradox came in his analysis of the Old South and the continuity between the old and the new. Cash's delineation of the Old South was based upon three historic legends:

- the existence of an aristocratic, Cavalier-spawned Southern gentry;
- the idea that slavery was inherently beneficial to the black race;
- the belief that the "Cause" espoused by the Confederacy was a just one.

By far W. J. Cash's greatest contribution to historiography and belles lettres was his concept of the Savage Ideal. As defined by Cash, the Savage Ideal was (and is) dogged resistance to change of any stripe, plus the sanguine determination to fight all challenges to the existing order. The Ideal had its beginnings in white supremacy, demagoguery, and the off-center mentality of intolerance and racial hatred. It is a seemingly immutable theme, and as long as its roots exist in Southern soil, the South will exist.

Now half a century after Cash's landmark study, the question of the South's true nature remains. It is the purpose of this work to look at the South since Cash's day and to hear anew the conflicting lyricism rising from the South's class structure, psyche, and economy—to listen once more for the brazen racket of the Savage Ideal.

WE must all judge for ourselves whether the most recent "New South" is anything more than a mask. One has but to peel it from the collective face to see:

black farmers going it alone on the desolate Mississippi delta, fighting the odds against corporate agri-giants to put some brothers back on the soil;

gentle charity from feeling people feeding the homeless of all races in mission houses and shelters and storefront churches;

the KKK opening its new international headquarters in a double-wide trailer while skinheads and neo-Klanners try to rewrite the civil rights movement with white supremacists the winners this time;

a new breed of environmental watchdogs, late in arriving but coming now head-on at the spoilers with no quarter being asked and none given;

smug, anachronistic, two-faced towns of the old Deep South, once colorful and possessed of some character but now reduced to the seduction of *Fortune* 500 barons to keep these new white-flight capitals alive;

Indian tribes begging the government for some new lands and just a few houses for the homeless exiles of the forgotten Trail of Tears;

present-generation mega-heroes—rock stars, athletes, movie idols—rising from relative deprivation to the heights and leaving behind pity, compassion, and empathy;

new artists, writers, poets, and singers carrying on the traditions of not so much uplifting the soul as giving fresh voice to celebrate the light and spirit of life.

And the Great Speckled Bird of the Southlands (from the hymn by Roy Acuff). How it came to be or why is a question beyond answer, but the Great Speckled Bird, an aberrant symbol of the South, spreads its wings and circles like a carrion fowl, screeching out its discordant hymn. Though Christianity was born with Paul of Tarsus, for God-fearing Southerners it was truly born in the Great Awakening and reborn in the Great Depression. Then it was that the Great Speckled Bird hatched a passel of orphans: the splinter-berserker-shaker-snakehandler-self-whipping-hairshirt-tortured-acid-drinking-orgiastic-lunatic fringe of evangelicals on the Southern religious stage. When all's said, they are show people, snake-oil artists, God barkers, and Jesus hogs who'll sell you perpetual bonds in their savior's church, hawking prayer rags to be applied to the most afflicted parts of the body to cure cancer or diabetes, or blindness, or deafness, or even stomach ulcers, hemorrhoids, halitosis, and if you have them, rabies and leprosy, although these critical maladies require an extra bottle of genuine, double-rectified, Praise Jesus Jordan Water. Their church names reek with the holiness of the Pentateuch and the New Testament—from the Free Will Baptist and Church of God to the Four Square Tabernacle and the Church of God's Shield—all distillations from misreadings and ill-readings and no readings at all of the Scriptures. In these latter days they have bred even more down-and-dirty outlaw redneck tabernacles of Our Sweet Jesus' Blood scattered throughout the pitiful poverty burdens of the Southlands.

Myth, reality, and consanguinity are the three poles of the trinity holding up the South. Each of the three or any combination can provide a gateway into the South, though the traveler must tote along some thematic baggage beneath the gateway arches. Still, the South was born of myth. From the first moment settlers struck the pestilential coast that would be Virginia, the South was destined to be marked as an enchanted land. Those bold, ambitious, foolish colonists invented the myth: they portrayed the diseased land as "a delicious country" and the dreaded natives as "noble and angelic."

Thus it began, a confounding struggle between illusion and reality.

PART ONE

"STONES CUT BY SAXON, BRICKS MADE BY ROMAN HANDS"

CHAPTER 1

ANCIEN RÉGIME

Tidewater Virginia . . . Walter Raleigh and Jamestown . . . Nat Turner's Rebellion . . . The Cotton Kingdom . . . Maryland and the Chesapeake

THEY WERE ENGLISH, WELSH, and Irish. They came in tall ships on their passage to Paspahegh, the ancestral land of Powhatan and his brother, Opechancanough. How sweet and civil in name were these tiny vessels, the *Sarah Constant,* the *Godspeed,* the *Discovery.* Alas, these namesakes would prove to be the first of the South's many ironies. The passengers suffered miserably during the mean passage over. Some died along the way, more would die in the first days of 1607, most within the first year. More afraid of the dreaded Spanish enemy than any alien shore, they sneaked up a diseased river, the James, and hid. They tied the ships to trees along the malarial marsh to plant their doomed colony. It had its problems but it did survive.

Jamestown was successful, heralded as the first permanent English settlement in North America. From the first, like their conquistador cousins, the English were searching for gold, great chunks of it, just like the Spaniards had found in Mexico and Peru only a half century before.

If any European nation had a first claim to the lands called the South, it surely would be Spain. To sixteenth-century Spaniards, the lands now known as the United States east of the Mississippi River were called Florida, and there was no lack of suitably avaricious, ruthless discoverers to take possession. In Irish legend the mythical lands of the West that would become the Florida Sunbelt were called Brasil, and Alvar Núñez Cabeza de Vaca in 1528 was the first to make landfall and to crudely survey the jungles of the South (strong legend holds that Irish monks sailing in leather boats visited these shores as far back as the ninth century).

De Vaca and his boss, Panfilo de Narvaez, were following the fictive dreams of Juan Ponce de Leon, who began searching for the fabled Fountain of Youth in 1513. The first myth of the South, then, had been borne by this erstwhile governor of Bimini. De Leon's every attempt at exploration, discovery, and life everlasting was met by sound defeat at the hands of the Indians. De Leon died with an arrow in his throat and no magical drink of water could resurrect him. De Vaca didn't find anything but hard times in Florida, but his storytelling convinced Hernando de Soto to launch his famous expedition in 1539, beginning at Tampa Bay. This trek through nearly all of today's Southlands met with abject failure—after slaughtering thousands of Indians, de Soto wound up stuffed in a hollow log and buried in the Mississippi River to become food for the catfish.

Even with such initial failures, the South would become a come-ye-all cornucopia, a magnet to draw dreamers and schemers from every city, village, and hamlet in Western Europe. French Huguenots, running as far away from their sinister nemesis, Cardinal Richelieu, as their knowledge of the planet allowed, tried their hand in the Carolinas in 1562 with meager little colonies around Port Royal, Fort Caroline, and Parris Island (now one of two training bases of the U.S. Marine Corps, the other being Camp Pendleton, in America's other mythic paradise, California). By the summer of 1565 these French Protestants were starving to death, trying to survive on dewberries and palm roots. Almost mercifully, they were massacred by the Catholic forces of the Spaniard, Pedro Menendez de Aviles, who further gets the credit for founding the oldest permanent city in the United States, lovely St. Augustine. It may have been the oldest but it was sacked so many times that its age is difficult to tell. Freebooter, privateer, and purveyor of fine slaves, Britisher John Hawkins sailed up one day and burned wretched little St. Augustine to the ground before it ever reached its infancy.

Cap'n Hawkins made three triangular voyages to the New World in his flagship, the *Jesus of Lubec*. Hawkins's pathway was from England to Africa (where he stormed native villages and kidnapped hundreds of slaves); from Africa to the Spanish West Indies (where at gunpoint he forced the Spaniards to buy the slaves); and from the Indies back to England (where along the way he raided Spanish bullion ships). Hawkins captured so much silver he didn't have enough room on the *Jesus* to store it all. For all of his efforts John Hawkins was knighted by Queen Elizabeth I.

The first real British touch in America took place in 1587 at Roanoke Island, a desolate stretch of sand and rock and salt flats off the coast of what is now North Carolina. The first tangible wealth shipped back to England was the humble potato and a curious plant called sotweed. As far as its British ancestry is concerned, the South began as a martyred cause, symbolized by the death of an infant girl-child named Virginia Dare, America's firstborn.

The entire of the ill-founded, abandoned Roanoke venture disappeared from the face of the earth within two years. No one knows just what horrors these folks endured; they were mostly White Chapel gutter trash that Sir Walter Raleigh (standard Irish spelling Raleagh) had duped into sailing toward what they had been told would be a paradise. Their Christian names were typical for the era: John, Thomas, James, Henry, Ananias, Dyonis, Wenefrid, Audry, Agnes, Rose, Elyoner, Emme. Ananias and Elyoner were the parents of Virginia Dare. Dyonis was the father of Harvie, the second infant born in America. The mother's name is not known; the records only show boychild Harvie, his father's last name.

The lost Roanoke Colony comprised ninety-one men, seventeen women, nine children, two infants known to have been born in America, and two Indian natives who had been kidnapped to England in 1585 and brought back as guides and translators. No viable solution to the mysterious fate of the lost colony has ever been enunciated, though historians generally agree, despite any real evidence, that they were massacred by savage Indians. It seems far more likely that Roanoke was rubbed out by the Spanish. The colony was terribly exposed out on the North Carolina coastline and susceptible to almost every danger. And just as they tracked down and wiped out the Huguenots in the Carolinas, the Spanish would have delighted in ferreting out these English heretics. In fact, the Spaniards in the New World were under orders to do just that. It was, after all, the Age of the Inquisition and Spain was deadly serious about it.

• • •

BUT for a hurricane in the middle Atlantic in 1583, the trust and power and vision of one man might have defied the troubled destiny of the English colonialization of America and the South. This man's name was Humphrey Gilbert, and he, more than any other man of the age, had the right stuff for the New World. History, however, accords him but an obscure footnote.

Knighted for services to the Crown, Gilbert was an anomaly for an English gentleman of the sixteenth century. Although he was a successful soldier and the half-brother of Raleigh, Sir Humphrey had been educated at Eton and Oxford, and while other "gentlemen" were drinking and whoring, Gilbert studied. He could read and write, while most of his compeers couldn't. He had a superb grasp of his rapidly changing world; his *Discourse of a Discoverie for a New Passage to Cathay* was the first learned treatise on the outside world published in Britain. Unlike his more regaled brother, Gilbert had the personal courage to lead an expedition not predicated on instant profit or even escape from religious persecution. Sir Humphrey's aim was permanent empire. He was a man seemingly meant for the South, a Cavalier who dared brave the dangers of the New World.

Gilbert's plan for America was deceptively simple. He would first sail to the rich fishing grounds of Newfoundland and load up his five ships with vittles (dried cod and the sweet, fleshy bird known as the great auk, now extinct), enough to keep his expedition self-sufficient in the New World. Strangely, this common-sense approach to food supply had never been tried by any of the explorers before (nor was it adopted by the Jamestown or Plymouth colonies). Gilbert didn't waste his tonnage on iron and brass cannons; none of his five vessels were warships. Sir Humphrey came forth to settle and build, not to conquer and loot.

After loading his supplies in Newfoundland, he sailed for Virginia, choosing the smallest ship of his fleet as his flagship, the ten-ton *Squirrel*. He chose the smallest ship because it was "most convenient to discover upon the coast." He wanted to see firsthand for himself, and he led from the front.

Almost as soon as they lost sight of the Newfoundland shores the ships sailed into a turbulent summer storm that grew in intensity as the fleet drew farther into the middle Atlantic. The seas tossed and battered Gilbert's ships for days, and many of his sailors were lost to the crashing waves. Finally two of his vessels abandoned him, and only the *Golden Hind* kept faith with her admiral as the storm magnified itself into a hurricane.

At last the *Hind* somehow drew alongside the *Squirrel,* close enough to call out to Gilbert. The crew of the *Hind* saw him "sitting abaft with a book in his hand," seemingly impervious to the danger. They pleaded with Gilbert to save himself by transferring to the larger and safer ship. Sir Humphrey's response was that of a truly heroic Renaissance man:

"We are as near to heaven by sea as by land."

His little ship went down with all hands. And with it went Gilbert's dream and perhaps the better hope for the New World. Had he and his expedition survived and made landfall in Virginia, what would have happened? Of course it is speculative, but Gilbert was a different man from his half-brother Raleigh, and it is very unlikely that Sir Humphrey would have skulked up the James River like a pirate to hide from the Spanish. Gilbert would not have chosen Jamestown at all; he would have discovered the long, broad Chesapeake Bay where a clean, safe harbor offered every opportunity for colonization. With Gilbert's death, the seminal English colonies in the Americas were hardly equipped for even rudimentary survival.

No food, no skilled artisans, but plenty of guns. James Cittie was the first settlement, named after King James I. The ground on which it was built was called Paspahegh by the local Indians; it was founded in April of 1607 by slightly more than one hundred colonists. By far the greater number of these settlers were bond servants, men whose personal or family debts in England caused them to be sold into indentured servitude and transported thousands of miles across an uncharted ocean where they were to live in penury and misery.

The Jamestown leaders, the supposed "persons of quality," were incapable of planning or leading the colony set down by soldier of fortune Captain John Smith. These "persons" were the supposed Virginia Cavaliers of Southern mythology. In *The Mind of the South,* Cash popped this bubble with a derisive jab at the whole notion that Prince Rupert's Cavalier army even came close to the shores of Virginia, let alone anywhere else in America. But myths die hard in the South, and the whole world subscribes to the aristocratic bearing of some Southerners. As late as 1992 the noted Institute for Social Research at the University of Michigan declared that the South's habitual violence is an "inherited ancestral trait from quick-tempered Cavaliers."

This Michigan perception and scholarly conclusion is, alas, based on myth. More credence has been given to propaganda than to reality. There is, indeed, a propensity to violence in the South, different from any other part of the country, but it didn't come from invisible Cavaliers any more than it came from starving bond boys. It came from the "quality folk" who were the leavings of English primogeniture laws—third and fourth and fifth sons of an emerging English middle class who, since they couldn't inherit, had been forced to sally forth to make their fortunes in the New World. But the "quality" refused to work; they expected to be handed their food just like back at home. So here was the origin of the Savage Ideal in the South, the obstinate refusal to accept change or to adapt to new social circumstance. The so-called Cavaliers imported the crusty English social structure and they'd be damned if they were going to change it.

Of all those who claimed leadership at Jamestown, only John Smith made any pretense at fulfilling the role. His efforts were thwarted because the quality folk just wouldn't have it; they couldn't lead and refused to follow anyone who could. They rejected Smith because he suggested that they should break a sweat and hoe some peas and beans or at least help construct the shelters rather than tearing them down for firewood. In his later journal Smith dismissed the whole Jamestown lot with "They would rather starve than work." They believed, said Smith, that commodities grew "only for us to take at our pleasure."

Internecine bickering became so heavy that after only two years Smith was forced to leave the failing colony. He returned to England to become the chief propagandist for the Virginia Company in London. In a very real sense he became America's first spin doctor, a veritable child of calamity who could tell a yarn so convincingly that he would become the prototype Southern writer. Witness his descriptions of wretched Virginia as having "rich soil, balmy climate, lakes and rivers full of fish, huge timbers for lumber, ample game for hunting."

After its first two years the Jamestown colony was hanging on by its ragged fingernails. The Virginia Company sent out a troubleshooter,

Sir Thomas Gates, as lieutenant governor of the colony. Sir Thomas arrived at Jamestown in May of 1609 and was frankly appalled at what he saw: "The palisades torn down, the ports open, the gates from off the hinges, and empty houses rent up and burnt rather than the dwellers would step into the woods a stone's cast from them, to fetch firewood . . ." Gates gave up on the colony. He loaded the few survivors on his ship and sailed down the James River in June, intending to join the fishing fleets off Newfoundland to beg enough food to get them back to England.

Before Gates and his ragtag squad of deserters could get out of Chesapeake Bay they were overtaken by the newly arrived governor, Lord De La Warr. The good lord persuaded the wan deserters, no doubt at gunpoint, to go back up the vermin-infested James to resettle the town. The Virginia Company was soon to become unraveled, and not even the harsh governance of De La Warr or his successors could make Jamestown profitable. In 1624 the Crown took over the colony; the most immediate impact was to bring waves of willing settlers to Virginia in the hopes of success with a new crop called tobacco.

The tobacco that the world would come to know did not grow in the Virginia of the Jamestown colony. There was a native strain of the aforementioned sotweed, but it was odious to the European palate. The money crop developed by John Rolfe, the world's first tobacco baron, came from seeds imported from the Summer Isles. The new strain was so prolific that within a planting season the South had found its one-crop mentality. All of a sudden everyone was planting Bahamian tobacco. The streets of Jamestown were plowed under and sown with this new avenue to riches. The growing of tobacco was so successful that by 1629 the Crown imposed a poll tax not of money but of tobacco. This was the first tax in the South and would have an effect so far-reaching that it would actually define the South's identity: it would strongly touch the South's class structure, its economy, and its psychological makeup, and would be the causal force of the Savage Ideal. This poll tax distorted the social institutions of the South until the 1960s.

Since the medium of tax collection was measured in cured tobacco, the farmers—whether they owned twenty acres or twenty thousand—were institutionally forced to plant all or most of their land in tobacco. The pernicious nature of this reality meant that the relatively poor man couldn't grow food crops but had to trade what tobacco he had left after taxes to the proto-grandee plantation owner who could afford to plant some of his acres in food crops. This inequality simply reinforced the planter plutocracy that substituted for aristocracy in the South; it established the guidelines for the Southern class structure. Ironically the South expanded as more and more people moved deeper into the interior to escape the tax man.

Obscured by the passage of time comes a plea from the wilderness. In a letter home from a young bond boy named Richard Frethorne at Martin's Hundred Plantation ten miles downstream from Jamestown, the one believable voice bespeaking the true nature of the land and of the hardships suffered echoes through time from the spring of 1623:

> Loving and kind father and mother: I have nothing to comfort me, nor there is nothing to be gotten here but sickness and death . . . a mouthful of bread must serve for four men, which is most pitiful . . . people cry out day and night. Do not forget me but have mercy and pity my miserable case. If you love me as your child, release me from the bondage and save my life.

Of all those who died by the tens of thousands, Richard Frethorne's is the only voice heard today, and even he was forgotten and died a nameless, useless death like almost all of the bond servants. The white feudal lords would wreak a terrible vengeance, sacrificing their own poor and demanding death-for-death from the native tribes. Of these Tidewater Indians—the Chickahominies, the Occaneechees, the Ozinies, the Pamunkes, the Paspaheghs—none survived. They, too, died in the tens of thousands, from bullets, slavery, smallpox, cholera, typhus, measles, and chicken pox. In another of the ironies of the fledgling South, one of the first native products returned to Europe for profit was sassafras, a common root of Virginia that was hawked as a sovereign cure for the king's pox.

In August of 1619 a Dutch captain named Uwe Jope sailed his trading vessel to Point Comfort, a few miles downriver from Jamestown. Captain Jope unloaded "twenty and odd Negroes," exchanging them rather offhandedly for fresh water and a handful of provisions. This humble barter was the first act of the "peculiar institution" in America. So in the first few years of the South black slaves began working side by side with frail white bond boys. It wouldn't be long before the only hands working the fields were black ones.

FOR a while it looked as though James Cittie would become the London of the new Southern world. It was renamed Jamestown and became the capital; brick houses were built, a legislative assembly (of dubious worth) was established, and thousands of new settlers arrived through its port. Despite the fact that three out of four of the settlers died within one year of their arrival, by 1676 the population of Virginia had reached fifteen thousand hardy souls. And it was this seminal year that could have changed the face of the South yet again.

The Virginia frontier was in turmoil. The royal government that had been in office for half a century paid no attention to the needs of the common people. The only interest of the Crown and its governor was in gathering taxes and cheating people out of what little was left over. The colonists were not only subject to daily Indian attacks but were poor and unclothed, their only posterity a shallow grave and a naked burial (cloth was so scarce that the bodies of the dead were stripped of clothing to supply the needs of the living). The people knew the governor, Sir William Berkeley, and his cabal of advisers to be greedy, callous, and incompetent.

Under the leadership of Nathaniel Bacon, Jr., an English gentleman, the common people of Virginia rose up in revolt. Bacon had arrived in 1674, and because of his background (he was a landowner and had attended Cambridge) he was immediately admitted to the Virginia Council of State. He was shocked at the deplorable conditions of daily life on the frontier and was sympathetic to the complaints against the obviously corrupt governor. Under Bacon's name, what amounted to the first credo of the rights of the common man was published in Jamestown in August 1676. *The Manifesto Concerning the Present Troubles in Virginia* and *The Declaration of the People* brought into stark light the just complaints of the settlers against the "wicked and pernicious counsellors, aides, and assisters against the commonalty in these our cruel commotions . . . for having abused and rendered contemptible the Majesty of Justice, and of advancing to places of judicature scandalous and ignorant favorites."

Clearly something tragic and strange and maybe even wonderful was going on in Virginia. Conditions in England were not one bit better for the common man, but it was in the New World and the South that the protest was sounded. Try it in England and you'd be hung from the gibbet before you could grab your codpiece. More remarkably, here was the beginning of the Southerner's outlaw-individualism. One hundred years before Ben Franklin set loose archpropagandist Thomas Paine on the hated British, Nathaniel Bacon chose Oxford-educated and fellow Virginian Richard Lawrence to write these two original documents of American democratic protest.

In the end Bacon's uprising and Lawrence's rebellion only solidified the entrenched power structure governing the South. Bacon and his followers burned Jamestown to the ground, signaling the decline and death some twenty years later of America's first town. Bacon himself died of cholera, known as the bloody flux. About twenty of Bacon's followers were executed by a vengeful Governor Berkeley. Lawrence escaped hanging but lived the rest of his life as a hunted man in the Southern wilderness.

Bacon and Lawrence were young men full of the spirit of the New World; they were dismayed by the transfer of the old feudal powers to Virginia. These two free thinkers knew the nascent House of Burgesses to be a farcical denial of human dignity, and they risked their lives to challenge the old order rooted in Runnymede and now entrenching itself on the shores of the Tidewater.

JAMESTOWN today is a standard-brands tourist museum replete with gift shop, restaurant, and guided tours through a "living village" that the promoters here would have us believe is absolutely the same as the Jamestown of nearly four hundred years ago.

It's a sweet little village now, Jamestown is. A touch of designer squalor shows among the daubed and thatched cottages and the villagers working hard at playing their roles. They are locals, mostly young people glad to have summer jobs, though a few are perennials such as Pat Cavanaugh, in her thirties and making her living as Virginia's favorite potter. She's from Phoebus, Virginia, where her mother operates the first of the westernmost frontier Irish taverns in the South. She and her fellow Jamestown play-actors aren't supposed to, but in a lull they'll step out of character and talk a little. The pay is pretty good, better than minimum wage, and it's interesting work re-creating authentic history. Yet they all look fed, too well fed, and they all get along with each other, are too quick to smile. There's no smell to the village, no racket, no fuss. The object here is not verisimilitude but drip-dry pastiche.

One lone cannon squats in the center of the Jamestown settlement, its purpose back then to sound the alarm or to blast some charging Redskins. Captain Smith and poor old Chief Powhatan are long gone from these grounds, but on down toward the river, one can see the tall ships still there, moored to the wharf. They are beautiful, splendid facsimiles, the *Sarah Constant,* the *Godspeed,* the *Discovery.* All three remain under full sail and get taken out to sea on special occasions.

Standing on the aft deck of the *Godspeed,* one can only reflect that these miniature ships, once intended to capture the mystic wares and riches of fabled Cathay, Samarkand, Nippon, and the Spice Islands, are now rather pointed reminders of the folly of man. In a simple error of commission, the English landfall in the New World turned out to be about twenty thousand miles short of the mark. And not even Magellan's earlier circumnavigation of the unknown globe could convince the European dreamers of the futility of getting to the East by sailing to the West. Today's tourists purchasing souvenirs in the Jamestown gift shop find that they've bought coffee mugs, ashtrays, yoyos, Ping-Pong paddles, and Dacron jackets without much awareness of the irony that these articles of Americana came from the long-dreamed-for Orient.

Surrounding the settlement, the tidal marsh of the James River still rises to swamp the scrub cedar, pine, and oak masking these shores of Virginia. This vista is surely what the dispirited, seasick settlers beheld as they disembarked from their ships. Today a steady flow of wayward pilgrims washes up on this shore. They come in the rich vehicles of the modern world—tour buses, school buses, minivans, cars made in the New and Old World—to see what it was that made America in the beginning.

Standing in the center of the re-created triangular fort that once was Jamestown, one can almost believe in this bygone settlement now extolled as a living village. Just here are three outdoor settings: Powhatan's village, James Fort, and the pier holding the ships. Handsome white girls made up to look like Indian maidens work at washing and cooking near Powhatan's tepee; sturdy white boys parade in mock military muster. The visitor can walk inside the stockade and through the wattle and daub huts, homes, church, storehouse, and jail. People are encouraged to handle the stone and bone tools, bows and arrows, or the nautical equipment. You learn that the entire Jamestown complex was reconstructed with the same crude tools used by the first settlers. A lone scavenger bird that the early settlers would have known as a kite circles over these playful dioramas, searching for a feast in the surrounding marsh. A mockingbird chatters in a scrub oak that barely shades Powhatan's hut.

A modern brick-and-glass compound guards the entrance and exit to Jamestown. School kids on an outing crowd the long walkway where the state flags of the nation are displayed, arranged in the order of their adoption into the family of America. Of all the wondrous historical sights to see in the area, this beflagged walkway is the most engaging. People tarry here, curious to find their own origins. There's no doubting that the people love this country with faith and hope, and at Jamestown there's no real sense of division or reminders that it's smack in the heart of Dixie.

Simply by being, Jamestown is cherished by visitors, no matter what happened here four centuries ago. Much the same is true for Plimmouth Plantation in Massachusetts, though Plymouth gets far more play historically than does its Southern predecessor. The interesting question is why. Is the execution of witches and the scourging of hospitable natives down to the last puling infant any more distasteful than the abuse of bond servants and the arrogant use of black slaves? Jamestown made no pretense at fostering religious freedom; Plymouth, on the other hand, has been entered in the American Book of Ages as the repository of the nation's religious freedom and heritage. Until the advent of boosterism as an American way of life, Jamestown had been almost universally ignored save for the grandiose flights of imagination coming from Captain John Smith's lionization of his own virtues. The singular difference between the Plymouth and Jamestown colonies was philosophical, as would be demonstrated by the Lockeian precepts of law and political economy that came to govern the future Southern colonies of South Carolina and Georgia.

• • •

BY the beginning of the eighteenth century most everyone had pulled out of Jamestown and moved on to the rich plantation lands of the Tidewater. Jamestown burned and didn't live again until it became the tourist mecca of today. The James River is now a commercial corridor, just like its sister river, the York. Both are uncannily similar to the infamous Chemical Corridor along the lower Mississippi River stretching from Baton Rouge past New Orleans. *Fortune* 500 companies sprawl along the James and York river embayments. Most, if not all, of the petroleum and chemical biggies claim huge chunks of the rivers' channels in a ribbon of megatechnic industry that swallows up much of the Virginia coast and the famous Tidewater dominion. Business in the South has always had a clear run at despoiling the land and waters. The toxic scars on the landscape between the James and York rivers are nothing more than today's manifestation of the curious Southern approach to its own economy.

Waxed in among these industrial honeycombs, the storied plantation manor houses of Virginia remain. They've been painted and plastered and restored to the elegance of their old slaveholding days, and a steady flow of tourists passes through daily. The most common remark overheard from the visitors:

"Isn't it nice of these fine old families to invite us into their homes?"

The fine old families are no longer. What is not generally known is that the Tidewater estates for the most part are owned by big corporations and, aided and abetted by grants from state and federal governments, are turning handsome profits (the plum inside the pie is to be designated an historical landmark and to get on the National Registry, both fiefdoms provided by the good old boy solon and lobbyist).

Within a short driving distance of the Jamestown attraction, through scrubby coastal woods and vestigial tobacco and cotton fields, one can make the parade of the colonial estates, including the undoubted jewel, Shirley Plantation, the first and oldest in Virginia. Shirley was founded six years after the first landings at Jamestown and added to its laurels by becoming a supply center for the Continental Army during the Revolutionary War. It survived the Peninsula Campaign and many other subsequent operations during the Civil War. Anne Hill Carter, mother of Robert Edward Lee, wife of "Light Horse" Harry Lee, and matriarchal forebear of former

President James Earl Carter, was born here at Shirley Plantation. Many a famous man rode up the sandy loam bridle path. Among those partaking of Shirley's opulent hospitality were George Washington, the Marquis de Lafayette, Thomas Jefferson, James Madison, John Tyler, William Henry Harrison, and a late-nineteenth-century pilgrim, Teddy Roosevelt.

The land around Shirley Plantation has long since played out. Like all corporate fields in today's South, Shirley is still farmed, but only through the magic of chemistry. The plantation sits squarely in the middle of a soybean field, and the old Georgian manse seems to quake and shiver like some Southern Gothic version of the House of Usher. The only relief from this gloomy aura is the beckoning pineapple finial sitting atop the roof over the entrance of the main house. Now, there are a lot of things in the South with hidden symbolism and this decorative knob is one of them. Once upon a time it was only normal and prudent for a visitor to "hello the house" before coming within gunshot range. As a palliative to such frontier custom, Southerner plantation owners announced welcome and promised hospitality with the symbol of the pineapple carved in stone (the fruity finial is French in origin, dating to Louis XVI, a king noted for his love of good grub). Today one can find the pineapple finial decorating the homes, grounds, and dining tables throughout the South (and even as far north as New England).

A short way from Shirley sits the Berkeley Plantation, home of the infamous "hang 'em high" governor. Contrary to the popular fantasy about Plymouth Colony in Massachusetts, Berkeley is in the record books as the little-known but official site of the very first Thanksgiving in America, though there was precious little to give thanks for in the Virginia of 1619. A three-story brick mansion, Berkeley stands but a scant few hundred yards from the banks of the James River. The place was subsequently owned by the Harrison clan, whose children furnished a young America with Indian fighters, statesmen, and even Presidents. A scion of the family, William Henry Harrison, has the distinction of having made the very first presidential stump speech in American political history, attracting a crowd in the thousands. (Both before and after the speech Harrison's campaign workers passed out thousands of miniature whiskey barrels produced by the Booz Company of Philadelphia, hence the word "booze" in the American lexicography.) Berkeley is also noteworthy because the first pot-distilled whiskey operation in America was set up here in 1622. You can bet that the Puritan fathers of the Massachusetts Bay Colony would have looked upon this capital enterprise most disapprovingly—religious freedom carries its own responsibilities.

The right fork of the Virginia Tidewater is, in essence, the York River. To reach it, one must backtrack out the James River past the site of poor Richard Frethorne's purgatory at Martin's One Hundred plantation to reach old Point Comfort. Here Captain Jope landed the first slaves and the English built their first sea fortress, still defending themselves from a feared Spanish incursion. The emergent American empire built yet another fortress here two hundred years later to defend itself from a feared English assault, changing the name from Port Comfort to Fort Monroe.

If you're under five foot six, you can walk through the old casemate of Fort Monroe standing up; otherwise, much stooping is required to traverse the many tunnels of the nineteenth-century fortress. Fearsome thirty-two-pound cannons angle out to challenge any warship foolish enough to enter Chesapeake Bay. Memories of Fort McHenry and Francis Scott Key's musical eulogy were still strong in the 1820s when the fort was built. Fort Monroe never fired a shot in anger, even though a young West Point engineer named Robert E. Lee inspected the site in the 1830s and reported it fully capable of repelling any attacker. The fort did get to play host to the rebel leaders of two outlaw nations: Chief Black Hawk of the Sauk-Fox tribes and Jefferson Davis, president of the Confederacy.

Paramount Chief Black Hawk had been defeated by U.S. Army and militia forces in 1832; his last few warriors, along with women and children, were massacred in the infamous episode at Bad Axe River in Wisconsin. Black Hawk was himself taken prisoner by a young lieutenant named Jeff Davis, who treated the old chief with some Mississippi charm and civility. Black Hawk was later brought east by President Andrew Jackson, who had the Indian chief paraded from city to city in the manner of an ancient Roman triumph. But the American public received and treated Black Hawk with far more dignity than the Romans ever would have. The old chief was interviewed, photographed, painted in oils, and feted in Philadelphia, New York, and Boston. The Easterners who had long before rubbed out their own noble savages found Black Hawk to be charming and witty, something of a plains raconteur. Clearly Jackson's use of the chief to stir up his own popularity was backfiring, so for Black Hawk it was off to the crossbars of Fort Monroe where sympathetic eyes could not see. Less than forty years later, the same young lieutenant who had held Black Hawk prisoner in the Midwest would find himself incarcerated in this same damp, cold fortress. After Jeff Davis had been captured at the Civil War's end he was transported to the remote fastness of Fort Monroe; he spent two years in the tubercular stone fortress awaiting the pleasure of the vengeful, radical Abolitionists. Davis never did enjoy the patronage of Northern liberals as Black Hawk did; he was, however, spared the humiliation of a Roman triumph. Davis lost his health during his imprisonment and retired in ignominy to die in Louisiana in 1889, ignored by his native state of Mississippi and scorned by the putative nation he had led into hopeless rebellion. Black Hawk was humanely returned to his native Iowa, and after he died his skeleton was disinterred and put on display in the state capitol. At least Jeff Davis escaped this final calumny; neither was he hung from a sour-apple tree.

Just across the bay from Fort Monroe, a young black descendant of African slaves was to become yet another outlaw like Black Hawk and in exactly the same time span. Nat Turner grew up on a plantation in Southampton County where his white master, John Travis, recognizing his innate intelligence, took him into the big house and taught him to read and reason. For a black slave Turner led a privileged life and was encouraged, in part by Travis, in part by his mother, the archetypal matriarch of the South itself, to become the spiritual leader of the local slave community. Travis, too, was an archetype of sorts; he was an enlightened man and felt real guilt at the condition of all slaves. For Travis, Nat Turner became an offering on the sacrificial stone or, perhaps, insurance against the probability of damnation. Here was the ongoing tension that was creating the Janus-faced Southern psyche of love and hate, sin and atonement.

Inspired by his interpretation of the Holy Scriptures, Turner led a rebellion of Southampton County slaves. Here at last was the long-feared revolt that had so fostered the nightmares of the guilt-ridden white South. In light of two hundred years of slavery, Nat Turner's revolt actually amounted to less than a skirmish. Some fifty whites were murdered by Turner's zealous followers, including Travis and his entire family. The black slaves were put down ruthlessly with hundreds, perhaps even a thousand, being hunted down and executed. Turner and his leading confederates were captured, tried, and hanged. All save Turner were given Christian burials. Turner's cadaver was given to a Virginia doctor who peeled the fleshy envelope of skin and fat from Turner's body. The fat was reduced to an oil and the hide was used to make tobacco and coin pouches. The oil itself was used to cure the dried flesh. When the remaining meat and muscle of Turner's body had rotted away, the skeleton was displayed in the doctor's surgery, an item of curiosity like old Black Hawk's skeleton in Iowa.

Nat Turner had no idea in August of 1831 that some of the leading humanists of Virginia, the last remnants of the Jeffersonian branch of the Age of Enlightenment, had proposed a bill in the Virginia Assembly that called for the gradual manumission of slave chattels. Slavery was to be abolished from the very birthplace of the peculiar institution. Virginia's soil had been destroyed by more than two centuries of tobacco and cotton depletion. The largest commercial crop in the Old Dominion by the 1820s was homegrown slaves. Millions of dollars were made by Virginia's slave traders who were finding ready buyers in the emerging Jacksonian South of Georgia, Alabama, Mississippi, Tennessee, and Texas; in the two decades leading up to the Civil War more than 200,000 slaves would pass from Virginia on their way to the cotton states of the South.

Nat Turner's insurrection becomes a crucial point of understanding when placed in the perspective of its times. The rebellion and the vengeful savagery of its aftermath fueled radical Abolitionist thought in the North while awakening a slumbering xenophobia in Virginia and the still-developing Deep South. Although the insurrection had clarified the white man's worst fear of slaves rising up in the dead of night to kill their masters, a greater fear motivated the slave owners. That fear was of losing the massive capital investment it had taken to buy the slaves in the first place. When coupled to the profit that could be had from the retail sale of living black flesh, abolition was a doomed concept in the South. The slave-owning General Assembly in Virginia voted the manumission bill down resoundingly. Yet Virginia's enlightenment has never quite passed from the scene. More than a hundred years later a small group of young idealists at the University of Virginia would attempt yet again a new kind of manumission.

In 1954 the Supreme Court had just handed down its decision quashing the "separate but equal" schools in the South, and these young idealists came up with a plan to implement the full spirit of *Brown v. Board of Education.* The Virginia plan would not only integrate the schools of the state but would change the pharisaic face of the South. The state where slavery began would be the one to cauterize its last vestige and to become the model for the rest of the South and nation. But those young intellectuals at Thomas Jefferson's university had never come up against the likes of Harry Flood Byrd, scion of a first family of the Old Dominion, undisputed master of Virginia politics, and demagogue of the first tidewater. When word got around that some university eggheads were trying to trample on the old traditional order, Byrd moved quickly to stop this new manumission; he did more: he had the young idealists fired and run out of the state. The state of Virginia escaped the world's scorn; that distinction would be shifted to the back of beyond, to a place called Little Rock and Central High School.

THE first decades of the nineteenth century were critical ones, not just for the South alone but for the nation and the world—and it all hinged on the simple idea of a change of clothes. Until the nineteenth century, the great mass of the European and American population went through their adult lives in a single set of clothing. The rich could afford garments of silk and fine linen, and if stained or torn these could be replaced. The commonality had to make do with homespun wool or cured deerskin. Then came the cotton boom.

Cotton in the South up until Eli Whitney's gin was a mere luxury, almost a curiosity. With Whitney's new gin of 1793, cotton of the short-staple variety could be grown and processed throughout the South, not just in little parcels of moist soil on the Sea Islands off Georgia and South Carolina. Long-staple cotton disappeared, for there were new fortunes suddenly to be made, and people came streaming into the South's Black Belt by the hundreds of thousands to cash in. Whitney was not one of the "cashers," for Congress revoked his patent in 1812.

New businesses sprouted as rapidly as the new cotton in the fields. Shirtmakers and pants manufacturers bought the bolts of cotton cloth faster than the New England factories could produce them.

Little girls could have new pinafores and their mothers clean blouses and dresses. Men could change shirts every day if they were so inclined. Here was a true revolution. Cleanliness became the rage; Sunday-go-to-meeting wardrobes came into vogue. Easter bonnets and fancy cotton duds woven into colored designs gave a sparkle to the hard-time lives of the common clay. The vast growth of cotton down South coincided with the spectacular growth of the nation in the early nineteenth century, and it was no coincidence. All manner of subsidiary industries grew up around the cotton crop. Even soapmaking picked up and personal hygiene became a moral obligation—the Saturday night bath, whether one needed it or not, became a ritual. With the arrival of cotton cloth, it was your own fault if you stank. Overall, the real beneficiaries of the Southern cotton explosion were the New England and midwestern textile industries. America became wealthy, all because of cotton, but the South would always be the poor relation. Eli Whitney's cotton gin really began the division between the North and South, Jefferson's agrarian dream as opposed to the Industrial Revolution.

THE most colorful myth of the South is that there was an Old South at all. The Old South actually never existed for the simple reason that two centuries passed before enough people moved into the region to create a viable economy, a class structure, or even a myth. The Tidewater was there, Charleston rice planters were there, Chesapeake clam fishermen were there, and a handful of Creole French lived in the yellow fever swamp that was New Orleans. But before 1800 the South was an empty dream. With the demand for cotton outpacing the limited appeal of the tobacco crop, hordes of settlers clambered into the Southlands, and with them a new ruling class took control. They were a nouveau gentry, their roots not stemming from any mythical Cavalier seed. In a sense they were a self-defining order, and with the getting of cotton fortunes, they would create their own titles and antecedents, just as they would adopt the old feudal code. But the life span of the Old South outside Virginia can be measured in the scant forty years between 1820 and 1860. Millions of new Southerners moved into the cotton lands of Georgia, Alabama, Mississippi, Arkansas, Louisiana, and Texas. These new lands outpaced the moribund "Old South"; indeed this was the

first of the "New" Souths and would have become known as such if
the Civil War had not put a stop to the progress of the new region.

Today the most heavily populated section of the Old South, meaning Virginia and the ancillary coastal enclaves, is still the Tidewater
coastal zones. Certainly these zones are not the final redoubt of the
supposed old Cavalier class of "good families," though a lot of "good
people" live here. The Southern traveler will find it hard to move
any place in this red-clay peninsula of Virginia without stumbling
across something of historic significance.

A few miles up the road from Fort Monroe sits the bright little
town of Phoebus. A commemorative plaque tells that Phoebus was
founded before the Puritans landed at Plymouth Rock. The town
was in the middle of the fighting during the Civil War and at times
was held by both the Union and the Confederacy. The townspeople
once set fire to Phoebus to keep the Yankees from using anything
the town had. The highway into Phoebus becomes Hope Street and
leads to the best inn on the road, Sarah's, as Irish a bar as any that
can be found in Puritan Boston.

The long bar at the right in Sarah's would find immediate favor
with any professional Irishman. It's Ernest Hemingway's clean, well-
lighted place, Southern style, with lots of clothed tables in the center
of the room flowing over to old-fashioned leather-covered booths.
An interior partition at the entrance carries a truly catholic display
and tells you right off what Sarah's is all about—the great American
game of politics. Campaign posters festoon the whole wall; the faces
of pols, patriots, and bunk-peddlers, old and new, beckon to the patrons: Gary Hart, Jesse Helms, John Warner, Jesse Jackson, Charles
Robb, Doug Wilder, Bill Clinton, George Bush, Dan Quayle, Al
Gore, and a spatter of sad-eyed locals who never made it to the show.
The servers in Sarah's will tell you that most of the political figures
on the wall have spent some time in Sarah's. Prominent among the
faces is that of Jimmy Carter.

"Jimmy's been in here several times." He and Sarah are good
friends.

While Sarah's admittedly not a crusader for women's rights, she's
somehow the walking spirit of the movement. She's her own woman,
a solid pillar that can withstand the storm—ask anybody in Phoebus
and they'll tell you so. She might laugh at the accolade but Sarah is
the symbol of the new womanhood of the South. She draws her

quiet strength from the women who rebuilt these Southlands after its men had failed in the Civil War.

Sarah's place has an infectious quality about it, and one feels it by the presence of the South's diversity met here in this happy place— lawyers, business people, and politicians take part in high-spirited verbal donnybrooks with dock workers, merchant mariners, and off-duty army lifers. Sarah threw a victory party in her tavern for Bill Clinton's election in 1992. She had met Bill and Hillary Rodham Clinton back in the 1980s and was impressed with the break-throughs in education the Clintons had accomplished in the back-ward, poor state of Arkansas. Sarah's own cause is education.

"If they could do that in Arkansas, you have to believe it can be done here in Virginia. Once you get off the corridor from Virginia Beach to Richmond and D.C., we've got as much poverty as any place in the South. Folks would be surprised at how many people have so little in this state. The Byrd machine kept Virginia down on the bottom with Mississippi and Arkansas for so many years . . . now maybe we'll have a chance, and improving education is the only an-swer."

On the evening of November 3, 1992, Sarah's was a scene of cele-bration, yet as it became clear that her boy Bill was going to win, the party became oddly subdued, almost as if there was just too much riding on the result. Through the evening Sarah went among her guests, cornbread aristocrat Republicans and yellow-dog Demo-crats, with the same studied aplomb.

Sarah Taylor has no time for the old rigid class lines of the South. "You stand on your ability and your hard work, not on who your daddy is. Or at least that's the way it should be." She was born in North Carolina but has lived most of her life in Virginia. She loves her adopted state and would never move out of her Tidewater home.

"The old Tidewater is gone," Sarah says. "Oh, there may be some Byrds and Van Burens around, I don't know. I don't think about that. They don't matter anymore."

THE countryside from Jamestown up to Richmond is unremarkable except for the obvious reflection that these backwater lands are no different from the bayous that back up to the highways in Louisiana. This sad comparison between the two states escapes everyone who hasn't seen both places. The same wasted landscape punctuated by almost identical antebellum mansions is evident in the Tidewater and beyond just as it is on the corridor between Baton Rouge and New Orleans. The Chesapeake Bay has become the Atlantic Coast's version of the Dead Zone in the Gulf of Mexico. It becomes clear, passing through the Tidewater, that the Eastern branches of the petrochemical maze of companies from Louisiana are misusing and spoiling here with the same impunity. Seafood had been the specialty up and down the Chesapeake since Bartholomew Gilbert, son of Sir Humphrey, lost his life in a storm here in 1603. Yet today whether you go to fabled Ernie's Crab House in Alexandria or stand at the outdoor barbecues just across the street from Camden Yards in Baltimore and see the government warning signs concerning the consumption of local seafood, you have to think twice before ordering the crabcakes.

Along this historic silk stocking strip of Virginia, a series of signs directs tourists to such notable sights as Williamsburg and the Yorktown Victory Center. Yorktown is the site of Cornwallis's surrender ending the Revolutionary War in 1781. Williamsburg, the original capital of Virginia, attracts whole regiments of tourists to view colonial pageantry and the pomp and circumstance of Virginia's "good families," Cavaliers all.

A frantic network of highways pulls the traveler on into Richmond, the Southern city that paid the highest-ever price for the ground on which it stands. Back in 1865, just a few days before he was assassinated, Abraham Lincoln visited Richmond. He came to see the abandoned mansion that had housed Jefferson Davis. Lincoln toured every room, examining each artifact with childlike delight, whistling "Dixie" as he strolled about. Notwithstanding the Civil War and the soul of Robert E. Lee that condemned more than 200,000 Americans, North and South, to death or dismemberment in the city's doomed defense, not to mention the countless thousands of blacks who fell in the siege, Richmond today is no different from Cedar Rapids or Dayton or Albuquerque, except that Richmond has become the handgun and assault weapon retail-sales capital of the nation. Virginia's loose gun laws make it the gun-running center for lawless D.C. Some concerned Virginians bruited the possibility of modifying these Wild West laws, and just the whisper of such change was enough to bring out hordes of National Rifle Association zealots in a demonstration in Richmond larger than any civil rights demonstration or NFL football game. Richmond is also the home of the state Slugfest where children from across Virginia put their pet slugs on display—the biggest one wins the grand prize. So while the children slug it out with slugs (the straightest silver streak also wins a prize), the adults prefer to plug away with slugs that move at 1.5 miles a second, a silver streak indeed.

In nearby Fairfax sits a ghost town contaminated by the largest underground oil spill in U.S. history. Millions of gallons of black gold spilled into the soil, rock, and water table beneath fair Fairfax. Things got so bad, and the blame became so obvious, that Texaco was forced to admit responsibility in 1992, and to begin an unprecedented payout of up to a quarter of a billion dollars in damages to hundreds of families living over the spills. This type of wergeld doesn't even count the cleanup costs; the damage will extend well into the new millennium and real estate values have plummeted in the plague mentality that has gripped Fairfax.

Yet another slice of Virginia's opulent historical pie is served to the traveler in Fredericksburg. The Founding Fathers all gathered in this pretty little town on the Rappahannock River at one time or another. The Virginia "Statute of Religious Freedom," precursor to the American Constitution, was written here in 1777 by George Mason. Fredericksburg was all but destroyed by the four separate battles fought here during the Civil War, and 100,000 soldiers from both sides were either killed or wounded in these conflicts. The Union commander during the first battle was Major General Ambrose Everett Burnside, for whom side whiskers were forever memorialized as "sideburns."

America's great gray poet, Walt Whitman, served as a battlefield nurse at the first battle of Fredericksburg, and it was here during the winter of 1862 that Whitman began to lose his health. Questioned after the war as to whether he should have received a pension for his humanitarian work, Whitman responded, "Oh, no. I got the boys and I got the *Leaves.*" Walt also got his wonderful sequence of poems, "Drum-Taps," at Fredericksburg.

Just over the river that George Washington skipped a coin across sits Washington City, District of Columbia, now completely surrounded by an impossible series of concrete and steel highways called the Beltway.

George Washington donated this once-worthless marshland to the nation. Following the Civil War, Washington City became a huge refugee center for freedmen and their families; they had no work, no homes, no place else to go. For the biblical three score and ten (1790–1860) Washington had been a gateway into the frontier South. In the aftermath of the war, the District of Columbia became a floodgate, a sluiceway through which blacks sought the promise of Lincoln's Northlands. Today the descendants of these refugees still live here. One can find them off the frenetically beaten tracks of the herd, far away from the throngs of Americans come to see the monuments of their heritage. Strong ethnic neighborhoods have stayed alive in D.C. Urban renewal with its egregious high-rise projects tried to destroy all that, but it couldn't swallow up every last vestige of traditional life.

Neither geographers nor politicians will tell you this, but Virginia in the late twentieth century is two separate states. FDR's idealistically inspired projects during the Great Depression and the swarm of federal agencies these created have become the second state of Virginia. A military-industrial-bureaucratic complex extends from Virginia Beach through the Ancien Régime of the Tidewater and into the oligopolistic layers of American commerce. The masses who live in this corridor—the washed, faceless, and bleached souls of America's political functionary corps—could not be imprisoned by the D.C. Beltway. These happy folks needed *Lebensraum,* and the peasantry of Virginia and Maryland and Pennsylvania and West Virginia and Delaware had to make room for them.

Back across the Potomac lies the garden of stone, Arlington National Cemetery. More people than you know, match-flame sad but somehow proud, visit here. These rolling hills were once owned by Martha Washington's people, the Custis family, and later by Robert E. Lee. Walt Whitman strode these quiet grounds when the cemetery was first dedicated in 1864. Whitman's voice rides over these strange white fields as the mourners pass among the multitude of cross markers . . . *When you my son and my comrade dropt at my side that day.*

ON the other side of D.C. lies a state that has never seemed to figure itself in the Damn Yankee Sweepstakes. Maryland is as geographically diverse as its politics and perhaps therein lies the clue. The state includes the Appalachian Ridge and Valley, the Blue Ridge, the Great Valley, the Appalachian Plateau, Allegheny and Piedmont forests, and the Atlantic Coastal Plain. On top of all that, the Chesapeake Bay divides the state into western and eastern shores. No wonder the state is schizophrenic when it comes to the choice of being Southern or Northern. Maryland was a slave state, though (barely) nonsecessionist, and its sympathies for the most part were with the South.

Maryland was officially founded in 1634 as not only a refuge for disaffected English Catholics but as their North American stronghold as well; the state is named for Charles I's Catholic wife, Henrietta Maria.

Both generally and specifically, Maryland developed almost exactly as did neighboring Virginia; its workers were bond servants, it imported African slaves, it grew tobacco and then cotton, and it developed a plantation mentality. One doesn't usually think of Maryland as sharing in all the old banes of the South, but Lord Baltimore's colony had its intolerance, its heartaches, its Richard Frethornes, too. No diaries, no letters home survive to paint a picture of the travail of Maryland's bond servants, but archaeologists as late as 1989 unearthed the graves of eighteen indentured colonists on what used to be a plantation at Patuxent Point in Calvert County. Actually there were nineteen bodies found, for one woman had died with a baby still in her womb. These poor bond servants were buried in paupers' graves without markers or church records; they died in utter destitution more than three hundred years ago.

The archaeologists making the discovery turned the remains of the colonists over to Douglas H. Ubelaker, anthropologist for the Smithsonian Institution. In 1993 Dr. Ubelaker was able to read the bones and tell us some amazing things about our forebears, maybe more than American history has ever wanted to tell. Ubelaker's report discloses a wretched life for these people. They died of smallpox, malaria, or cholera; they all suffered from osteoporosis, a disease of aging, even though these colonists had an average age of thirty-one for the men and thirty-six for the women. Ubelaker determined that the bone disease was caused by starvation. All the remains showed signs of heavy physical labor, with many of them having had broken bones.

The plantation isn't there anymore, nor is the nameless graveyard. Blackeyed Susans used to run wild over the fields here at Patuxent Point, but they were all plowed under by the bulldozers come to make another housing tract.

EVERY schoolchild knows the names of Peter Minuit, Peter Stuyvesant, and William Penn. They are the equivalent of Founding Fathers. Grade-school teachers troop these hallowed names out around Thanksgiving and pin them up on bulletin boards next to the papier-mâché cutouts of tom turkeys and kindly Indians. Yet most folks don't know that all three men once ruled absolutely over princely, powerful, and proud Delaware, our nation's first state. Delaware borders Maryland, is across the bay from New Jersey, functions critically today as the water source of New York City, and somehow figures that it's still at least a small part of the South. The Delaware aqueduct system is part of the largest water supply system for any city in the world. Minuit ran Delaware as New Sweden between 1638 and 1654; Stuyvesant ran it as New Amsterdam until the British took it away from him in 1674. And William Penn, the sparest of all spare men, ruled the state as an appendage to his eponymic immortality. It wasn't until 1776 that the "three lower counties" of Pennsylvania were hived off to become Delaware.

Seemingly, the only thing that makes Delaware a "Southern" state is that it held slaves longer than any of the Confederate states. Delaware didn't free its slaves until it ratified the Thirteenth Amendment well after the Civil War had ended. Delaware more than sympathized with the Southern cause, mainly because of its stand on states' rights, and even after the war Delaware continued to vote with the solid-South bloc until sometime around the beginning of the twentieth century when this confused little blip on the coast of the Atlantic finally decided that it wasn't really Southern after all. Delaware does have its allowance of United Daughters of the Confederacy and a few hundred Delaware boys did get across to Virginia to fight the good fight, but the only real experience Delaware has ever had with war was an unheralded skirmish at Coochs Bridge against the British in 1777—the Brits had sneaked in while the famed Delaware Continentals were off fighting with Washington's army.

Regrettably, Delaware doesn't enjoy much of a national reputation for anything except being little. Still, it's the state that gave us the first Christmas Seals and the first nylon stocking, and once upon a time Caesar Rodney of Dover raced eighty miles to Philadelphia to break a tie vote so that Delaware's delegation could approve the Declaration of Independence. Delaware has the distinction, too, of being the first state to ratify the U.S. Constitution. Some of Delaware's towns sound Southern—Hardscrabble, Blades, Atlanta, Hickman, Viola, Angola, and Pine Tree Corners. The state has the requisite loungers and loafers in its little town squares, and one of them remarked, "Here in Delaware we know we're Southern because we still believe in myth and we love to dance."

The people down south Delaware from Dover to the Worcester County line use Baltimore as their big city, not Philadelphia. The city of Baltimore was first famous in American history for its defiance of the British in the War of 1812. Ever since the nation was founded the country reached deep into its pocket to build massive brick fortresses on its coastline. Fort McHenry just outside Baltimore has the distinction of being the only one of these forts to ever be attacked by a foreign power. Through the rockets' red glare the flag was still there, so the British marched into Washington City and burned it to the ground. The town of Baltimore didn't even get scorched.

Like the rest of Maryland, Baltimore never could make up its mind if it was Rebel or Yankee, yet once upon a time Baltimore could have become the true capital of the South. When Robert E. Lee set his army on the march in June 1863, the thinking behind the plan never considered fighting any Union army at Gettysburg. The whole idea behind the invasion was one of maneuver, not of battle. If the Yankee Army of the Potomac stayed to protect D.C., Lee's Army of Virginia would ravage the Pennsylvania countryside and capture Baltimore; if the Yankees sallied forth to fight the Rebs, then Jeb Stuart's ten-thousand-strong cavalry would threaten Philadelphia; in turn, if the Yankees chased Stuart, Lee would be free to come in and capture D.C. The whole brilliant maneuver fell apart when Lee unaccountably decided to fight a winner-take-all last battle at Gettysburg. Lee's more-than-able warhorse, General James Longstreet, tried to get Lee to stick with the plan, but to no avail. For his troubles, Longstreet has been blamed for all time by Vir-

ginia's historians for having lost the Battle of Gettysburg, no matter
that Lee was in command. Gettysburg cracked the South's spine and
paralyzed the cause. Though Gettysburg has been heralded as the
South's highwater mark, it was low tide for both sides. In three days
of fighting the South lost twenty thousand dead and wounded; the
North suffered twenty-three thousand casualties. The only thing that
lived after the battle was Lincoln's brief, inaudible address. Perhaps
fittingly, Longstreet outlived most every general on the field, though
he could never clear his name while revisionists on both sides made
Robert E. Lee a national hero. Baltimore was never threatened but it
never became the capital of anything, just a cog within the industrial
Northeast, with a baseball team called the Orioles.

Besides Francis Scott Key, many famous people have lived in Baltimore: Babe Ruth grew up here; H. L. Mencken made the *Baltimore
Sun* and his *American Mercury* forums for his acerbic wit and prejudices against American things boorish (the "Sahara of the Bozart"
started here); filmmaker Barry Levinson immortalized Baltimore's
founding district, Avalon; Edgar Allan Poe lived here and edited
Southern Literary Messenger, the South's leading publication before
the Civil War.

"Regionalism" has long been a convenient collator for anthology
makers, and under their guidelines Poe might readily have been designated as a regional writer of the South because he grew up in Virginia, went to college there, and became a leading author of his day.
Like many a Southern writer, Poe never had an easy time of it; he
was disinherited, never made any real money (he was paid ten dollars a week as editor of the *Southern Literary Messenger*). In the long
run Poe always was a Southern writer and in the same universal way
that Thomas Wolfe and William Faulkner were Southern writers. Yet
a dark mystique has always surrounded Poe; he was obviously a
heavy drinker and opium eater, and he died in Baltimore under
mysterious circumstances in 1849 at age forty. He was found uncon-
scious in a gutter outside a voting precinct, leading to speculation
over the years that Poe was a victim of a saloon sweep to pad the
polling boxes. He was buried in a pauper's grave with only a single
line of public notice in the newspapers. (Walt Whitman read the notice and made the journey from Brooklyn to Baltimore, where he
swelled the number of mourners to two, himself and the gravedig-
ger.) Including the darkness that forever surrounded him, Poe

wrote his poetry and his grotesque tales strictly within the tradition of the Southern storyteller. God told Poe to tell the truth, and Poe replied, "I'll tell you a story that'll stand your hair on end." Yet his poetry bequeaths a Southern legacy that only love and beauty can save humanity from despair.

FROM the time Sir Humphrey Gilbert's son, Bartholomew, sailed up the Chesapeake in 1603 seeking to fulfill his father's dream, the bay has been somehow caught up in the South's psyche. It was the first great obstacle for the settlers to conquer and tame, and it remained a prize until modern technology bridged it and tunneled it and used it as a conduit for commerce. Both sides of the oceanlike bay are lined with beaches, resorts, and fishing villages. The Jamestown colonists and the throngs that rushed in after them had come looking for profits, and here it was, perhaps the greatest freshwater reserve in the world, two hundred miles of it rich with fish, oyster, and crab beds whose supply was never ending.

Almost immediately the disputes began. Disputes over boundaries and ownership. Maryland is bounded on the north by Pennsylvania and the two states literally fought over a few leagues of land—until the Mason-Dixon Line was established in the late eighteenth century. To the south Maryland is bounded by Virginia, and the ever-erratic Potomac River would cause boundary disputes between Old Dominion and the Old Line State lasting well into the twentieth century. This dispute actually started with the first settlers and evolved out of the original grant to George Calvert, first baron of Baltimore (it was settled in the courts in 1930).

Chesapeake Bay has as dual a nature as the South itself: it can be bitterly cold on its northern reach and balmy toward its southern shore. Mostly the bay enjoys mild winters and warm summers. When Robert E. Lee's men crossed the Potomac heading for Gettysburg, they must have felt somewhat at home seeing the groves of loblolly pine and the flowering magnolias. Maryland itself had known a civil war before it became torn by the one between the states. In 1655 a holy civil war of sorts was fought here between the Puritans and the Catholics of the state; the Puritans won but it was only a matter of time before waves of Catholic immigrants turned Maryland's allegiance back toward Rome.

Maryland was not to be spared its allotment of Southern demagoguery either. It came in the person of Arthur P. Gorman, one of
the charter members of the Robber Baron guild during the Gilded
Age after the Civil War. Gorman got himself elected to the U.S. Senate and also gained control of the famous Baltimore and Ohio Railroad, the first rail line for public use in the country. Gorman's
political machine ruled Maryland until the turn of the century. Because of Gorman's rail lines, however, the state emerged as a dy-
namic crossroads between North and South.

Southern ways and sympathies persisted among Maryland's plantation class right up to the Civil War (records show that Maryland
had 87,000 slaves in 1860). The Southern sympathizers mounted a
vigorous campaign for secession; the popular state song, "Maryland,
My Maryland," written by J. R. Randall, was an unabashed emotional
appeal for Marylanders to preserve the Old South traditions by join-
ing up with Dixie in the coming fight. Maryland, of course, did not
secede, and in the war Marylanders fought on both sides while
singing "Maryland, My Maryland."

Chesapeake Bay was a crucial body of water during the Civil War.
But for that matter, the Chesapeake had always been crucial. It remained a prize, desired by both North and South in war and in
peace. In the beginning it had been a thing of beauty, though it was
soon to be a spoiled dream, a redoubt for the preservation of the
Savage Ideal throughout its eastern shore.

CHAPTER 2

LOST CAUSES, OLD AND NEW

Mason and Dixon's Line . . . Monticello . . . John Brown and Harper's Ferry . . . Woodrow Wilson and the Savage Ideal . . . VMI . . . Jerry Falwell and Pat Robertson . . . The Cumberland Gap

WHEN DID THE SOUTH become known as "the South"? Venerable scholars have searched for decades for a metaphysical answer. Could it be something philosophical? Perhaps a sociological peculiarity of people living in a subtropical zone? Or was it simply because the white man owned slaves in that ontological world known as "Down Yonder"?

We pedants have ignored the obvious that any courthouse loafer could have told us. It is 39°43′19.521″ north latitude. It's called the Mason-Dixon Line. The region is called the South because it is the country south of the Mason-Dixon Line.

Charles Mason and Jeremiah Dixon sailed from England to Philadelphia in 1763 to settle a wrangle between the colonies of non-conformist Pennsylvania and Catholic Maryland. The English astronomers mapped the strange-looking stars of this new continent, took their readings, and converted the results to terran geography. Mason and Dixon had no earthly intent of creating a confused mind-set that would last for centuries, but within the next generation their line would come to define America's division by creating all manner of lines—moral, political, economic, and finally battle.

Frontier Virginia set the style for the settlement of the South. The first significant wave of settlement along the rutted, tree-stumped tracks of America's first great highway, which swept from Philadelphia across the new Mason-Dixon Line and into the Shenandoah Valley. It was called the Great Philadelphia Wagon Road and along its length all the first towns of the South's interior were born. Beginning at the great port of the Society of Friends, the Great Philly Road first led to right about Gettysburg and then dropped into Maryland and the hamlets of Hagerstown and Harper's Ferry. In Virginia the towns of Winchester, Lexington, and Roanoke came alive with the traffic of the road; from there the road hewed its way into North Carolina, creating the villages of Salisbury and Charlotte. Finally the rough highway carved its way into the deep piney woods of South Carolina, ending at Camden.

All the settlements along this crude pathway were minuscule, random collections of lean-tos, one-room log cabins, Indian huts, and tepees. Hogs and goats and cattle and hundreds of dogs made their homes in the newly cleared fields, streets, and living quarters of the early towns. No amenities existed beyond the trading posts where grizzled frontier veterans, white and red, traded peltries for rum, powder, and shot. Somewhere in a darkened, smoky corner of these taverns sat a Royal land agent who sold "His Britannic Majesty's" patents to the highest bidder.

It was this prototype real estate agent who became the first truly corrupt "horse trader" in the South. No matter what Wall Street tells the world or Milton Friedman preaches to supply-side economists, the American free-enterprise system was always alien to the Southern way. Despite the success of Southern commerce, business in the South is based on a feudal system imported almost four hundred years ago. Southern businessmen were horse traders more at home in the bazaars of North Africa and Arabia than in the stock and commodities exchanges of the Western world. The Southern *suk* mentality inevitably led to the present condition of relative deprivation that so mars the Southlands. The economy of the South has traditionally depended upon the relative fairness of the horse trader's handshake, but that grip tightened so much over the generations that it has further split the social classes of the South.

In a very real sense the ruling class of the Southlands began here. At each land transaction it was "One, two shillings for the

King . . . one, two, three shillings for the land agent." From the accumulation of these silver coins came land speculation, moneylending, corruption, massive land holdings, and dynasties. Here were the true progenitors of the so-called Cavaliers: the robber barons, the good old boys, the first families—the self-rising nobility of the South.

These immigrants from north of the Mason-Dixon Line—the Irish, Scots, Welsh, English, and Germans—who came in succeeding waves to the New World and down the Great Philly Road could be likened to the hordes of Attila sweeping into a semicivilized Central Europe. This crush of new Southerners brought with them a brand of savagery unseen by the Indian cultures, and life for the white man and red man alike in the wildernesses of the South became a tribal cycle of kill and be killed. The result was all too predictable: the feral white warriors devastated the Stone Age red peoples, taking their land and exiling those few they did not slaughter.

The South's first great mythic figure, Daniel Boone, and his family were typical of the migrants who moved down the Great Philly Road. Boone's father, Squire Boone, who would prove to be one of the South's first founding patriarchs, had sold his property in Pennsylvania for the princely sum of £300 sterling. The Boone party consisted of Squire Boone, his wife, and the fifteen-year-old Daniel, plus eight unmarried daughters, two married sons and their wives, one married daughter, her husband and child, and two nephews. This migration was not one of idle loafers, trappers, or intrepid adventurers; it was a movement of entire families, and they brought their prejudices with them. Historian John Faragher notes in his book *Daniel Boone* that a diarist traveling the road at the same time as the Boones bought some hay from a Swiss, some kraut from a German, had a cup of tea with an Englishman, but made his camp "so as not to be too near the Irish Presbyterians."

The Blue Ridge mountain range to the west of the Shenandoah Valley confined the first great American land rush to the Southlands. There was no opportunity for westward expansion north of the Mason-Dixon Line. Upstate New York and western Pennsylvania in the 1740s were the preserve of the Indians and the French. It would be twenty years and more before the French danger would be eliminated and still another thirty years before the Ohio Valley really opened up. For perhaps the only time in its history the South stole a march on the North.

Outside of the populous corridor, away from the superhighways in the Orwellian world of D.C., lives the real Virginia, the superseded state that has little to do with the Golden Crescent that is D.C. Modern travelers are advised to get out of the open-air tunnels called interstate highways that mask the countryside. An interstate in Virginia is no different from one in Maine or Alabama. You get lulled by the sameness of these roads whose perimeters are lined with new-growth pine and some scrub hardwood so that the surrounding lands are obscured and the identity of its people and culture are homogenized. You can't see through this shallow gauze of the roadside to the real forests of the Old South, nor can you see the clear-cutting of the woodlands or the abiding poverty of the people. But get on a state or county road and you'll find the real South. Jack Cash's telltale tree with its age rings. Look closer still and you'll recognize those old Saxon and Roman churches that Cash evoked.

Love Virginia and be satisfied to live in a land of red clay. An excess of pine tells the tale of the land around the gently rolling timbered hills of Charlottesville: played-out red clay depleted by too many cotton and tobacco crops over the generations. But how those first families of Virginia loved their land. The Henrys, the Randolphs, the Tuckers, the Carters, the Byrds, the Van Burens, the Harrisons, the Custises, the Lees, the Jeffersons all poured their blood and faith into the lands they held. The land, the owning and holding of it, became the obsession in the South. In Europe only belted earls, dukes, and the like held title to the soil, whether for farming or running sheep or hunting deer or grouse or even for building a village or house. The milords owned it all and the commonality had to knuckle their foreheads and beg to lease. But in America anyone could hold land. A man and his family could survive and even prosper from the soil, and as the South confirmed its being as an agrarian society, the land became the singular focal point of its people. It was different in the North where industrialization started early, where jobs and wages could be had. A reasonable mix between farm and factory evolved in the North, but down South there was only the land.

Thomas Jefferson could have established himself anywhere; he was a man of means, family, and talent. He would have been a welcome addition to the intellectual communities in New York or Philadelphia or Boston. Yet Jefferson was a Southerner by birth and by inclination. He chose to build his life on the red clay at Monticello, his own version of Versailles, on his family's land just outside of Charlottesville.

Jefferson's magnificent estate perches on top of a diminutive mountain. The pleasure dome that Kubla Khan decreed became obsessed reality here. An architectural masterpiece (and slave plantation), this fairyland outpaced the opiated dreams of Samuel Taylor Coleridge and featured the very best of antebellum Southern indulgences: indoor running water, with many baths, toilets, and bidets; year-round ice with a conveyor to bring it into the big house; magazines and storerooms filled with culinary delights; dumbwaiters to satisfy midnight desires for wine and sweetmeats.

Unlike Versailles, Monticello featured an enormous library, the wonder of the day, and included, curiously, *The Book of Kings,* a privately bound six-volume collection of the scandalous memoirs of the French and English kings and their nobility. Hanging on the walls were copies of French paintings Jefferson had admired while ambassador to Louis XVI's court, as well as the stuffed heads of the wonderful beasts Lewis and Clark had brought back as trophies from their expedition. Even the bones of a mammoth found in the new Louisiana Territory had been reassembled and displayed in Monticello. And, of course, in the place of pride over the mantel, a portrait of Ben Franklin, Jefferson's great patron and mentor, gazed slyly out over the flamboyant dining hall.

The original cost of this sumptuous domain was astronomic even in those days. In one instance, the estate's private reservoir broke and caused some $30,000 in damages, which Jefferson treated as a minor irritant. Jefferson never worried about money; he took thirty years to build Monticello, going through both his own inheritance and his widower's dower in doing so. Yet years of careless spending finally forced him to part with his beloved library. An American myth spins the tale that Jefferson "donated" ten thousand volumes to start the Library of Congress. The truth is that he did start the library but he didn't donate the volumes—he sold them to meet the demands of his creditors.

It has become fashionable in some academic quarters to denigrate Jefferson, the man and his work. They tell us that he plagiarized, he dissimulated, he pontificated, and he consorted with females, slave, free, and otherwise. Back in 1800 Jefferson's detractors were leveling the same sort of charges. Federalist opponents called him an atheist, a political fanatic, a drunkard. Timothy Dwight, the president of Yale, augured that Jefferson would turn American wives and daughters into legal prostitutes; the *Connecticut Courant* proclaimed that "there is scarcely a possibility that we shall escape a Civil War. . . . Murder, robbery, rape, adultery, and incest will be openly taught and practiced." Some even say he stole the election of 1800, and unconstitutionally purchased Louisiana. But out of an age that gave the country James Madison, James Monroe, Alexander Hamilton, John Adams, Thomas Paine, Patrick Henry, Benjamin Franklin, and George Mason, Jefferson still stands out as the foremost thinker, humanist, and dreamer. In the American theater of the Age of Enlightenment, Jefferson must take center stage, for without him the nation would not have had its dream.

As minister to France, Jefferson completed Franklin's work during the Revolutionary War; he was the first American Secretary of State and the country's third President. He gave us the Declaration of Independence, the greater part of the Constitution, and, using George Mason's Virginia model, our Bill of Rights. Not bad for a Virginia country boy, no matter how privileged.

In his one published masterpiece, *Notes on the State of Virginia*, Jefferson left to posterity a state treasure of political concepts based upon humanity and timeless liberal thoughts. But his most overlooked gift to the nation might have been a small, obscure essay entitled "A Southerner on Slavery." In it were his impressions and profound apprehensions on the institution of slavery, despite the fact that he was a Southerner and held slaves. He condemned slavery absolutely as "a perpetual exercise of the most boisterous passions, the most unremitting despotism on the one part and degrading submissions on the other . . . I hope, preparing under the auspices of heaven, for a total emancipation. . . ." Jefferson lived in an era where such thoughts condemned him utterly in the eyes of his fellow Southerners and cast him as an eccentric in the North. Yet he had the courage to speak the universal truth.

In his retirement Jefferson roamed his fields and often wandered down to the manicured grounds of his university, keeping in touch with the students, their minds, and their curricula. In modern days symposia of select academics have met at the University of Virginia with the expressed purpose of revising and often reviling the Jeffersonian image. What disturbs these detractors is not so much the foibles of the man but the fact that they still have a hard time understanding him even after all these years. Non-Southerners and academicians have great difficulty in reconciling the Janus faces of the South.

Certainly by the time Jefferson came to the Presidency he was recognized as a "fiery Southerner." The polemic attitude of the country North and South was already an embedded reality. Although he was an architect, an inventor (to his credit was one of the very first copying machines), a philosopher, and a scientist, Jefferson would always be a Southerner first. And he was fully aware of his public and private image. Fifteen years earlier—when the nation was groping toward becoming a nation—Jefferson had just penned his "Statute of Religious Freedom," which the state of Virginia adopted, separating Church and State. At that same time Jefferson sat down and, curiously, sketched out something that surely must have come from his heart. He wrote about the differences between Northerners and Southerners, categorizing and even classifying. He said, "In the North they are cool, sober, laborious, independent, jealous of their own liberties and just to those of others." In the South, he said, they are "fiery, voluptuary, indolent, unsteady, zealous for their own liberties, but trampling on those of others."

Jefferson never worked these jottings into a formal essay, but it is clear that even in 1785 Jefferson was sensitive to the strict division of the country. He was delving the Southern psyche and at the same time probing his own, for it was also clear that he was writing about himself. He would later write his autobiography, but here was the most accurate self-portrait. Within the complex character that was Thomas Jefferson dwelt all these dual traits—he was, indeed, cool and sober and independent, while at the same time fiery and voluptuary and "without attachment or pretensions to any religion but that of the heart."

FROM the Shenandoah foothills surrounding Charlottesville, the worn-out land is scraggy with frail cedar and pine fit only for pulpwood. The richness of the old Shenandoah Valley is no more. The little farms nestled between the Allegheny and Blue Ridge mountain ranges are just whispers of the days when the Shenandoah was syn-

onymous with the word "bounty." Just over there ripples the Shenandoah River, flowing down from Harper's Ferry, a most unlikely spot
for the incarnation of a martyred cause.

In 1859 John Brown from Kansas came to Harper's Ferry wrapped
in the vengeful robes of John the Baptist; he came to steal weapons
from the arsenal and to start a slave rebellion that would create a
haven for blacks in the mountains of what is now West Virginia.
Brown was financed by the radical Abolitionists: capitalists, philanthropists, intellectuals, and preachers. The front men for Brown's
movement were Ralph Waldo Emerson, Henry David Thoreau, and
Horace Greeley. The so-called Secret Six who financed Brown's raid
were the core of New England intelligentsia: Theodore Parker, Ger-
rit Smith, Dr. S. G. Howe, Thomas Wentworth Higginson, George L.
Stearns, and Franklin B. Sanborn. To these men slavery was an
anathema that could not be purged with rosewater; it required
blood, all the blood of the Southern slavers. The prophet from
"Bloody Kansas" was to be their terrible swift sword.

John Brown was, even by noted historian C. Vann Woodward's assessment, "intermittently insane." He was also a known bully, wife
beater, drunkard, and murderer. Referring to the Secret Six, and indeed, to the emotional chaos surrounding this prelude to the Civil
War, Woodward says that "it is somewhat difficult to excuse such ignorance among intelligent men."

John Brown was arrested at Harper's Ferry by none other than
Robert E. Lee, then a colonel in the U.S. Army. Brown was taken to
nearby Charles Town and tried for treason. Brown's erstwhile New
England supporters openly prayed that he would hang so he would
become the martyr their cause desperately needed. They got their
wish.

Today the little town terraced on a mountainside reaching down
to the Shenandoah seems to breathe the same air of more than 130
years ago. Coming to Harper's Ferry one feels as if he has pierced
a veil into the equivalent of Elizabethan England. It's a downright
beautiful and charming little town, even including the City Hall
where the upstairs provides for town meetings and the downstairs
houses the police station and a liquor store. The Shenandoah River
flows to Harper's Ferry from the special little town of Staunton
(the *u* is silent). Woodrow Wilson not only slept here, he was born
here. Hardly anyone in America nowadays thinks of Wilson as a

Southerner, but he was, through and through. A small Woodrow Wilson industry hangs on in this little city. Travelers can stop at the home where Wilson was born if they've a mind to look upon the minutiae of his life. Wilson had a stroke while Henry Cabot Lodge and the U.S. Senate were repudiating Wilson's signature on the Treaty of Versailles. The last two years of his Presidency were run by his wife and his doppelganger, Colonel E. M. House, aide and confidant and biographer of the man who pledged never to entangle America in a European war. Perhaps with the invalid President in mind, Staunton is graced with a regional mental health center, named for Woodrow Wilson. It's the kind of place folks in the South used to call a lunatic asylum.

Wilson is another Southern President whom academicians and Northern intellectuals have trouble understanding. One of the little-known curiosities of Wilson's life was his friendship with the Reverend Thomas Dixon, Jr. Dixon had been a school chum of Wilson's and had become the premier racist novelist of the South. His writing success began with *The Leopard's Spots,* an archracist work condemning blacks as socially and mentally inferior. Dixon followed with the incredibly successful *The Clansman.* After Broadway stage productions this book was used as the basis of David Wark Griffith's monumental 1916 screen work, *The Birth of a Nation.* Although religiously opposed to films, Wilson asked to see Griffith's movie because of his long relationship with Dixon. After the screening Wilson remarked that it was "like seeing history written with lightning." Scholars and biographers have never been able to interpret this remark. It has nothing at all to do with the movie or Griffith's cinematic genius.

It has all to do with the Savage Ideal. While historians have adjudged Wilson's policies as the politics of reform, his acts were motivated by the most powerful theme in the South—blood guilt. The son of a Presbyterian minister, president of evangelical Princeton University, and governor of Bible Belt New Jersey, Wilson was just doing what came naturally, seeking repentance without the effusion of blood, as befitting some medieval fighting bishop scourging the infidels. The Savage Ideal was in Wilson's blood just as were the theses of white supremacy, special privileges for the special born, and Wilson's peculiar approach to the world of business—an approach born of a marriage between an evangelical house of elders and the horse trader's handshake. It was Wilson's intent to put the likes of

J. P. Morgan and Judge Elbert H. Gary in the stocks for moral turpitude whenever they sinned against the commonwealth. (Another Southerner and born-again Baptist from Georgia, President Jimmy Carter, whom we shall meet again in Chapter 4, would try almost the same thing with his "moral equivalent of war" thesis in the 1970s.) Wilson despised the immigrants coming to America with faiths other than Protestant; he derided Teddy Roosevelt's New Nationalism; he was a champion of states' rights. Standing in front of Wilson's boyhood home in Staunton, one is haunted with thoughts about this Southerner. He was to become something of a hero to schoolchildren all over the nation despite the way adults came to view the many paradoxes of his two presidential terms. Wilson's unfulfilled dream of a League of Nations captured the idealistic imagination of the children and they shared his heartbreak over its failure. His mysterious withdrawal from public life following the failure to ratify the Treaty of Versailles was viewed by the children as a tragic weeping for the world.

THE Valley of the Shenandoah takes its name from a long-vanished Indian tribe and means "Daughter of the Stars." This Indian totem was to have graced the land with richness, watching over her children protectively. Alas, this legend proved to be as baseless as the white Virginians' professed belief that the trees in the valley come to bloom on the anniversary of Stonewall Jackson's death.

Thirty miles on down the valley from Staunton, the town of Lexington does its fair share of keeping other legends alive. The town is the home of Washington and Lee University, founded in 1749, and of the Virginia Military Institute, established in 1839 (pretty much to soak up the spillover of Southern boys who couldn't get an appointment to West Point). VMI was just one of scores of military academies that sprouted up all over the South in the 1830s, almost in premonition of the fight coming a generation later.

The two colleges sit side by side and straddle a steeply rising ridge on the northern edge of town. The contrast between the two campuses couldn't be greater. Washington and Lee features stately colonial red-brick buildings with rich white porticoes and carpets of green lawn. Giant spreading oaks arch over cobbled walkways, offer-

ing an idyllic setting for a classic education, one guaranteed to preserve the aura of Deep South charm and elegance. Washington University became the retirement home for Robert E. Lee, who was flat
broke and dispossessed following Appomattox. The state of Virginia
in its wisdom and with the permission of the federal government
granted this pension to Lee, the man who would come to epitomize
the Southern ethic. The school even incorporated Lee's name and
traded on it to ensure its enrollment. (Lee's great adversary, U. S.
Grant, died in penury, the North having scorned him following his
two scandal-plagued terms in the White House—only Mark Twain
came to the aid of the general who won the war, publishing the auto-
biography that insured the future for Grant's widow.)

Visitors here can become lost in the surreal context as the Jekyll-
and-Hyde campuses merge without warning. If Fellini were alive and
here with his movie camera, he'd be struck a little dumb after moving through the studied gentility of Washington and Lee only to be
immediately confronted by the starkness exuding from the stone
archway proclaiming the territorial imperative that is VMI. Fellini
would see a naked ape in uniform with short back and sides and a
bloody bayonet.

Truly the architectural design of the VMI buildings is early federal
penitentiary: ominous plastered brick painted a banal yellow. Even
the trees along the parade ground look as if they've been doing hard
time. At the far end of the field looms the statue of Thomas J. Jackson, the great Stonewall himself, Lee's right arm during the war.
Stonewall died in questionable glory, shot three times by his own
men during the Battle of Chancellorsville. The great Jackson succumbed to blood poisoning soon after the battlefield surgeons
sawed off that same right arm, committing his soul to eternal re-
membrance by the expedient of quotable deathbed words: "Let us
cross over the river, and rest under the trees."

Jackson's statue, a good two stories tall, dominates the entire ambiance of the VMI encampment. Approaching the oxidizing bronze
hulk, visitors can't help but reflect upon the difference between the
totems that have lived in this valley. The bronze general glares down
with Cromwellian sternness upon the field where cadets grind
through the routines of deliberately mindless drill, guaranteed to
make them real men and soldiers of distinction. Behind the statue

broods the Stonewall Barracks, built to house aspiring soldiers in spartan discipline. The barracks seem to personify the credo of Leonidas of Sparta: "Come back with your shield or on it."

Jackson had been a tactics instructor at VMI before the Civil War. Far from being loved and revered, he was made sport of by his students; the ungainly, unlettered military professor sucked constantly on lemons and declined the use of black pepper at meals because he thought it made his legs ache. These and other eccentricities, along with his almost total inability to verbalize his thoughts clearly, virtually invited his privileged pupils to make fun of him. It did no good at all for Jackson's sister to spread the rumor that Thomas had cheated on his entrance exams to West Point. Perhaps it was fortuitous that Jackson married the daughter of the VMI president; Stonewall was not a good teacher, even by his own admission.

Although Jackson's character has been romanticized since the day of his death, many historians have been puzzled by this enigmatic figure. He was a strange, moody man much given to religious cant, yet thirsty for the blood of his enemies. When the war started, Jackson revealed his true nature. He wrote constantly, embarrassingly so, to Jefferson Davis advocating total war. Take no prisoners, kill them all. Jackson's military reputation was made as the defender of this very valley, yet in a single month of 1862 he executed thirteen of his own men for being absent without leave.

On late Friday afternoons both campuses are practically deserted except for a few stragglers waiting to be picked up by parents or friends. The cadets, *sans* uniforms and looking less haggard now that the week is over, mill around the broad circle drive and over near the statue of George Catlett Marshall, graduate of VMI, five-star general, chief of the army general staff and as Secretary of State the man whose name is forever synonymous with the rebirth of Europe following World War II.

The young VMI cadets of today seem steeped in the romance of military heroes, especially in the flame of Stonewall Jackson still burning brightly. He has been a hero since the First Battle of Manassas (Bull Run to the Yankees). Panegyrists have crowned Jackson's head with the nimbus of immortality. But the common soldiers may have always had a different opinion. Jackson's iron head won battles and winning battles creates the great captains of lore. He was that.

Yet the Stonewall eulogies have all passed on one obscure incident that holds more pathos than Jackson's last recorded words.

In the summer of 1862 a fifteen-year-old volunteer in Jackson's Valley Army fell asleep while on guard duty. A court-martial was convened and it condemned the boy to death. He was a local lad and his tearful mother came into the camp to plead with General Jackson for her son's life. Stonewall listened, denied her plea, and then confirmed the order of execution. The French have a phrase for it: *pour encourager les autres.* Jackson didn't mind if his men hated him so long as they feared and obeyed him. The general mounted his favorite horse, Little Sorrel, and rode away from the scene.

The boy's hands were tied behind his back and he was led to a tree-shaded field where, shivering, he was blindfolded. Jackson's chaplain, the Reverend Colonel Robert L. Dabney, read from Holy Scripture. The boy's mother pleaded to the very end and had to be restrained by orderlies. The firing party came to present arms. The officers of the court-martial stood by as witnesses for the record. The order was given: "Aim, fire . . ."

The westering sun casts long shadows over the VMI campus and the Shenandoah Valley. Visitors begin to stroll back across the parade grounds to Washington and Lee. The twin campuses are almost deserted except for a couple of regular army officers, perhaps tactics instructors at VMI. One cadet in dress uniform just coming out of the barracks walks in a leisurely, lilting style toward the gates. By his epaulettes one can tell he is the adjutant of the student corps.

" 'Evening, gentlemen. Enjoying your tour of our institute?"

The sociable timbre of his voice is obviously Southern.

"Whole lot of history here."

"Too much sometimes," the cadet responds, unable to restrain a chuckle.

As they walk across the grounds, the cadet tells the visitors that he's from South Carolina. He likes Virginia and VMI and his native South. He's a student of history and one of the volumes he carries is Douglas Southall Freeman's *Lee's Lieutenants.* He chats about the Civil War; it's his hobby. He says the war was about slavery, of course, but claims the root cause was money.

"Did the VMI cadets play a part in the Civil War?"

"A lot of the South's officers were trained here, many taught by

General Jackson . . ." He points back over his left ear to the statue.
"Any serve with distinction?"

"Oh, yes. But the school's finest hour was at the Battle of New Market. The corps marched from here up the valley to help stop the invading Union Army of General Franz Siegel. There were 226 cadets
and they charged right into the muzzles of a Union battery of artillery."

"Wish you'd been there?"

He gives a quick sidelong glance. "If I'd been there, I would have
been on the other side. It wasn't a good battle, you know. The cadets
were just kids."

"How old?"

"Fourteen, fifteen, sixteen."

"They win?"

"Lord, no. The Confederates did win the battle but the cadets
were bad shot up. There's a monument back over there that lists
their names. Ten were killed and forty-five wounded . . . twenty-five
percent casualties, ouch."

A somber hue surrounds the Washington and Lee campus at
dusk. Some fifty miles to the southeast, as the great speckled bird of
the South flies, sits Appomattox, Lee's last refuge. Lexington and
Appomattox remain strangely connected, and a melancholy irony
stings the air of both locales. Jackson lies buried in Lexington as
both conqueror and proud warrior, returned on his shield to his final resting place. Lee, too, had sought such a glorious end for himself, a soldier's death. As the war wound down to the South's
inevitable defeat, Lee had ridden into the firing line of several
fights, perhaps furtively seeking his death. Yet each time, his officers
and men had forced him to safety, shouting, "Lee to the rear! Lee to
the rear!" His men vowed to surrender rather than have their commander fall to enemy fire. Lee never took a bullet. Instead, he had
to endure early humiliation and late sorrow. Lee died in 1870 and,
though he had no inkling of it, the movement by his fellow Virginians to raise him to sainthood was already under way. Before the end
of the century Robert E. Lee would stand equal to his lifelong idol,
George Washington, as a berobed, laurel-crowned hero of the Republic.

Here in the Shenandoah, legends have lived for a great many
years. The people of this valley still want to believe that the trees

come to leaf on the anniversary of Thomas Jonathan Jackson's death. As he lay dying eight or so months after he had executed the young boy, Stonewall whispered out his famous last words, and everyone within hearing distance shivered.

Other folks in the valley will tell you that sometimes you can hear an urgent though doleful voice calling out with a bronze-hard, church-bell ring of finality over the Blue Ridge . . . *"Aim, fire . . ."* But the saddest legend of all is the sound of the mothers' cries borne through the trees by the mournful choiring of the cicadas, heard in the clear of day or in the stillness of midnight:

"All them boys, all them boys."

JUST out of the Shenandoah Valley, the town of Lynchburg sits on its seven hills just like Rome of yore. Lynchburg, where sad old Jeff Davis was fleeing on the last train from Richmond, is famous for lots of things. The great patriot Patrick "Give me liberty, etc." Henry's home is here; Thomas Jefferson's summer home is here; Randolph-Macon, the Southern belle finishing college, is here; Booker T. Washington's log cabin slave home is here. But mostly Lynchburg is famous because it was named for John Lynch of the Virginia Lynches. The legacy of lynching in the South dates from an earlier member of the family, the paterfamilias, Charles Lynch, a Virginia magistrate who initiated this truly Southern peculiarity by dispensing vigilante justice to Tory conspirators. Lynch gave name to the infamous "Lynch Laws" (an oxymoron if ever there was one).

In such a ruthless environment what measure of law and order could exist? And how was any sense of justice and civility maintained, let alone imposed? The answers did not lie with the Tidelands aristocracy or with carefully crafted political tracts and bills of rights as standard-brand history would have us believe. Such typical answers to these queries revolve around a sort of magical osmosis of the tenets of the Magna Carta. The myth holds that as families migrated, so too did the strongly held beliefs of these Englishmen. And as their communities grew, state and municipal assemblies passed laws and statutes that the frontier families were only too pleased to adopt, albeit sometimes at the point of a constable's gun.

Not so.

The South got civilized by one strong movement that couldn't be faced off with guns. The South got religion. Homegrown, evangelical, foot-washing Christianity. The civilized Anglicans built their temples amid the old colonial splendor of Baltimore and Richmond and Charleston. Out here in the real world it was hard-shell Baptist circuit riders who understood that these first waves of settlers were living in a state of wild nature. These men of the rough cloth weren't selling pardons or indulgences, for they were only just removed from a state of wildness themselves. They could pull a jug as easy as they could pull a pistol; they could stalk a bear, char it over a campfire, and eat it with their fingers. These preachers' totem magic lay in immersing their profane converts deep into a local creek or river, forcing eternal salvation upon their sorry good-fer-nuthin' white-trash souls, their universal cry being, "Are you washed in the Blood of the Lamb?"

The same crusading brand of eighteenth-century Southern justice and redemption still lingers in the real South of today. The old brotherhood still carries on in the hidden, out-of-the-way humble churches of Appalachia, the delta lands, and the hills of the South. One such voice is that of Will D. Campbell, author and practicing Baptist preacher who understands his forebears and the brethren from whom he sprung. Brother Will has served as spiritual adviser to Presidents and death-row inmates and country music performers whose songs carry the imagery of New Testament salvation. Campbell has declared on more than one occasion that all men are not good and decent, no matter how deep you look inside them. "All men are bastards, and God loves them anyway."

Though the official voices of the histories would not have it so, it was this canon of theology that brought law and order to the South-lands. It was here with this fundamental, knee-jerk spirit of dispensation from worldly sin that the South truly began to develop its identity. The tradition of rough frontier religion hollered out by hammer-tough preachers in the backwoods South also evolved over the years and gave us such stem-winders as Mordecai Ham, Cyclone Mack McClendon, Gypsy Smith, and Billy Sunday—all the way to Billy Graham, the single most successful evangelist in American history. Graham became the fundamentalist seed in the mid-twentieth-century South, and from his preachifying would sprout yet another brotherhood of reborn, charismatic Christians. While southwest Virginia was merely the first stop along the way in the evolution of the frontier Southern psyche, the town of Lynchburg today has become the spiritual shrine of the South's savage religious dogma.

In the past, people would pass through Lynchburg only to get to Appomattox. Today, Lynchburg is best known as the seat of the Reverend Jerry Falwell's Moral Majority. Of course no one is fooled into believing it's a majority, not even Falwell himself. All he and others like him have done is to resurrect the savage old brotherhood of a bygone age. Falwell's unruly TV throngs in their pin-striped suits and makeup are really nothing more than the latest version of the Savage Ideal, or as Jack Cash put it in *The Mind of the South,* "a place where dissent and variety are completely suppressed . . . where men become virtual replicas of one another."

Lynchburg is an old tobacco and manufacturing town squatting on the first rise of the Blue Ridge foothills. The headwaters of the James River flow through here and close by Falwell's Liberty University, and though Brother Jerry might think of some full-scale baptismal dunkings in the James, he won't ever get the chance because the river's just too polluted. Arguably, Falwell's college was named for Patrick Henry, though the faithful should know that Henry never put himself in harm's way. "Or give me death" was merely rhetorical; Henry was referring to some other patriot and mostly interested in becoming the first Revolutionary governor of Virginia.

One would think that one would have to travel far afield to find as rare a seat of religious power as Jerry Falwell has built for himself here in humble Lynchburg. But you don't. A simple float trip along the same route that the cured tobacco took down the James will bring the floater to another evangelical stronghold, that of Pat Robertson's Regent College in the populous, neopopulist Virginia Beach. Where Falwell has opted for the rural and grass-roots approach, Robertson has chosen the massed urban corridors of the Atlantic Coast for his media ministry. Similarities do, however, exist, between these two Godmen. In their proselytizing and faith healing they have always beat on the same old dead hoss of Calvinistic fundamentalism, trying to revive the imperfect logic of Jonathan Edwards's *Freedom of the Will* that dominated almost two centuries of American religious disposition.

The Falwell-Robertson tandem and their ilk should spare a moment to trace their roots by reading "The Deacon's Masterpiece," a poem penned in 1858 by no less a personage than Oliver Wendell

Holmes. Holmes's satiric one-hoss shay (Calvinism) fell apart in the nineteenth century, its system of "perfect" logic collapsing for the undeniable reason that its premise was false. Though Calvinism would fade in Holmes's New England, it would live on in the cloud-cuckoo-land of the South. Ironically, Calvinism didn't shift from the North to the South—it was already there and had been since the Great Awakening way back in the eighteenth century. It all began with America's first true evangelist, a virile, fire-breathing former rowdy named George Whitefield.

Whitefield was twenty-four when he came over from England to set the South on fire with a new style of preaching. He didn't just tell the masses who flocked to see him that their souls were going to burn in hell, he literally showed them how it would happen. Jumping down into the crowd, he tore at his clothes, his hair, his body. He writhed on the ground and leapt up in anguished rapture. He worked his crowd into hysterics, gaining thousands of converts with each of his revivals. He traveled from Georgia up the Carolinas and into Virginia (before taking on a more sedate New England). He touched the lives of many thousands, rich and poor, and taught them to lose their sins by writhing in the agony of their wrathful Maker. In short, Whitefield gave a new term to the South, "Holy Roller."

All that awakening took place in the late 1730s and early 1740s. Whitefield and the Wesley brothers later founded the Methodist Church, which in the South was pretty much a rival to the Baptists, who had already made strong inroads in the frontier mountains. Although Holmes's New England deacon would have to settle for cold-tater leavings of this new divinity, a fresh breed of journeymen—call them Dixie Deacons—took possession of the South's soul, and perfect logic be damned.

Only in the cloud-cuckoo South could such a phenomenon live on. The Dixie Deacons and their moribund theology not only survived, they found a new way to thrive. In the little towns and brush arbors all over the South they mustered up lusty throngs of the faithful with their pig-iron voices that mimed Whitefield and the kingfishers that followed; they aped the Apologues of Jesus of Galilee while strutting the towns with some free election-year barbecue or flapping the revival tents or rolling the whiskey wagons and voting the graveyards one more time. The trinity of the New South—the

Good Old Boy, the Seersucker Demagogue, and the Jerkleg Preacher—began to rule like latter-day Caesars. They found a single voice and kept prating against a common enemy, the nigger-loving agitators and Yankee one-worlders. Their brotherhood came to stand for more than champion and messiah—they were the final evocation of the South under siege.

The Savage Ideal is very much alive in today's South, though it is ensconced behind such getups as the Moral Majority and Pat Robertson's American Center for Law and Justice. Virginians Falwell and Robertson have a firm grip on Jack Cash's Ideal; both keep alive the essence of the Old South that gave birth to the Savage Ideal.

To enlightened and liberal audiences both North and South, Falwell and Robertson are easy targets and come in for some heavy-handed, even vituperative attacks, not the least for a high order of perceived hypocrisy. Well, it's only natural, for Godmen in the South have always been good targets. What these doubters simply don't understand, however, is that Falwell and Robertson (and their mentor, Billy Graham) are perfectly and honestly sincere. They are the true defenders of the faith and they just don't like transgressors, people who break the rules of the Ideal. In the end these new brethren of the blended silk and wool cloth play out to be sad, disappointed men searching for perfection on earth yet knowing that fulfillment can only be had in heaven. They are not hypocrites because they don't know it. Their real crime is that they've turned loose on the world ravening packs of TV messiahs on pogo sticks, false prophets whose only interest is profit. Pat and Jerry may be fools, but they're Southern fools, and as Julia Sugarbaker has said, we'll keep them in the living room.

LOVE Virginia and mourn her loss, her reversion to modernity through the theft of her charity. Gone are the rich fields of the Tide-water that so many died to plow, lost is the bounty of the Chesa-peake, sacrificed were the visionaries who would have created a clearer order of life, forfeited are the humanists who tried to give decency to the savage land, disinherited were the simple natives who took from the land only what was needed for a season, forgotten are the bleak coal hills worked by men in despair, bereaved are the songs of the dead, never to be heard.

Strange indeed it is that the state that produced Jeffersons and Madisons should end the millennium led by preachers and fools. What can the answer to such a riddle be? How could a society transform itself from the enlightenment of its beginnings, the old order, into a cause that has been lost since its inception? After the historians, anthropologists, ethnologists, and all the other scholars have piled their documents on the table to fully absorb what's been happening, one still has to delve deeply into the Southern psyche through the eyes and voices of the South's seers in search of the answers. Richard Frethorne, perhaps the South's first tragic muse; Annie Bethel Scales, known as Anne Spencer, the young black prodigy who should always be remembered for her stand on racism in the Jim Crow South ("I have no articulation for the things I hate"); Ellen Glasgow, who did articulate the plight of the Southern woman learning to live without joy; James Branch Cabell, lost now in the cloud of the cuckoo, yet before Faulkner the first practitioner of magic realism; Julien Green, who, even though a true Virginian, wrote his remarkable novels in French; and William Styron, whose uplifting visions prove that the shaky old verities somehow still breathe in the South.

Abraham Lincoln's family was caught up in the fever of migration along with thousands of others traveling the Great Philadelphia Wagon Road down the eighteenth-century Shenandoah Valley. It's interesting to speculate on the Great Emancipator's career had the Lincolns settled in Virginia. Would Abe have been able to use his homespun wit to advantage in the pristine and privileged world of the Tidewater grandees? Would he have turned his eloquence to the defense of states' rights? Could he have mobilized the old Whigs into the White House? All fascinating stuff made moot by the wanderlust of the Lincoln family.

There's a little town not far off the D.C. Beltway and the hustles of upscale America. It's named after Lincoln but it's called Goose Creek. Doubtless Abe Lincoln never set foot in this, his namesake town. Lincoln is a quiet, unassuming little community that has somehow managed to keep its character alive. As Goose Creek it was right smack in the middle of the Civil War. Soon after the surrender, Goose Creek, desperately trying to reconstruct itself, sought some sort of federal assistance. The town leaders thought of a post office, but they could get nothing from a Union government determined to keep the South on its knees. So the clever folks of Goose Creek came up with a cagey idea. They applied for postal incorporation under the name Lincoln. The ploy worked.

From the sweet pace of things here in Lincoln one would think that Honest Abe's fitful, troubled soul would have benefited from the occasional dose of these folks' gentle approach to life. A fair-sized Quaker community still thrives in Lincoln, and the Friends continue to call their meetinghouse "Goose Creek." The forebears of these savvy folks maneuvered the Feds into putting Lincoln on the map, and just because it's not called Goose Creek anymore doesn't mean it's not still there.

The Quakers didn't have a good time of it when they first came to Virginia in 1656. The advanced missionaries of this new sect who called themselves "The Society of Friends" ran into Governor Sir William Berkeley. He was an ardent Anglican and an autocratic administrator for the Crown. Berkeley forced an act through the Virginia Assembly calling for the suppression of these "unreasonable and turbulent sorts of people called Quakers." The Friends were persecuted and hounded into the deep backwoods of Virginia, to places like Goose Creek.

The people of Lincoln today are living in two worlds. They feed off the demon incomes of the Beltway, yet they have made a separate peace with themselves when they come home to the sweet country "somewhere 'tween the Blue Ridge and Wasatch Range." The demons disappear with the soft click of swaying grain growing in the fertile fields, and as the dry trees ring with cicadas. Down here old-timers and respectful newcomers have learned "to take their pain to the woods" and to settle down, cultivating "the knack of dying slowly." Here are the real aristocrats of the South, folks who have somehow managed to beat off the assaults of the Savage Ideal and to survive with grace.

A pretty fair country poet lives in Goose Creek like his father and grandfather before him. His name is Henry Taylor and in his poetry, his choice of place, and his seer's standpoint, he seems to exemplify the better qualities of the true New South. He's a poet all right and has a Pulitzer Prize from 1986 to prove it. He makes his living teaching English and writing at American University in D.C. Taylor has imbued his Virginia home with the cadence and light of the family's old homestead. He drives the forty-five miles into the city on teaching days and spends the rest of his time in Goose Creek working on his poems, which are mostly good stories with rural Virginia settings. Taylor is athletic and loves to ride horses. Riding is his passion, as the cover of his prize-winning volume, *The Flying Change,* reveals—a crowded field of steeplechase ponies. Acknowledged to be an Olympic-class equestrian, this poet understands that he could have performed in such an arena, but he has no illusions about that kind of glory. Deferred dreams are not part of his poetry.

What the reader finds in Henry Taylor are poems about the way a man teaches a horse to move beneath him, reminding the horse of how it moved when it was free. Or about learning how to speak to hawks (you do it by screaming through a blade of grass gnashed between your teeth). Or about a welder's wisdom of knowing which pieces of hot drops of steel to pick up first. Or about a crotchety heartburn that leads one to ponder some plausible answers to questions that can't even be thought of. But mostly about such simple things as porch lights left on to show you the way home, which shine right in your eyes so you can't see a thing, but you know you'll get there.

Taylor's father was not to the manor born, as they say in the South, but a dairy farmer who sold his herd to become a high school English teacher. His father was a pacifist and a conscientious objector in World War II, like all of the Quaker Taylors in all of America's wars. On the surface of things, the Society of Friends has always appeared to be a benign group, yet there's a crustiness, an intemperance to the sect that gets little notice. Long before Taylor's forebears settled in Virginia, an example of the brusque way Quakers sometimes manage their community came to light in an episode involving Daniel Boone's father, one of the founding Pennsylvania Quakers. Squire Boone had been roundly condemned by his Quaker community because his daughter had kept company with a non-Friend. He was forced to apologize for his daughter and to abase himself before the elders. When a second daughter transgressed similarly, Squire Boone refused to recant; he moved his family down the Great Philly Road through Virginia and into the Great Smoky Mountains.

Poet Taylor's father and explorer Boone's father seem to have a lot in common, principle and the refusal to buckle under to pressure. "My father doesn't suffer fools gladly," Henry Taylor affirms. "Not at all in keeping with the Quaker faith."

Taylor still loves riding to the hounds, a tradition in Virginia that simply won't die, even though the bluenoses won't permit thoroughbred racing. Riding stables abound in the countryside and riding is a serious sport. Taylor tries to get in the saddle at least once a week, more often if he can. The antiblood sport trend is growing throughout the country, but not in Virginia or most of the South. Taylor shows signs of his father's nature when he says that "there's not a goddamn one of those bleeding hearts around here."

Taylor was a French major at the University of Virginia. His prep school teacher had taught him so well that he was advanced into graduate French courses when he was only a freshman. He was able to pursue a classic education, and among his accomplishments was the translation of Virginia author Julien Green from the French. It is perhaps Taylor's remarkable aptitude for languages that gives him a special voice. He has a poetic photographic memory with thousands of lines of poetry at his command. He can call up whole poems, not just abstracts, from the great and obscure. Put Taylor in congenial company with a dash or two of Southern Comfort, and his inner voices sing with the commingled vision of Luciano Pavarotti and Hank Williams.

Henry Taylor has an omnivorous appetite for thoughts and words and a deep reverence for all things proud and profane about the South. He can readily call to mind the full five verses of "The Great Speckled Bird," and while admitting to being unable to sing, he teamed up with a couple of crazies from off the road and they joined in singing the mad anthem of the trashy South, sounding like tone-deaf crows trying to warble out three-part harmony:

What a wonderful thought I am thinking,
Concerning a great speckled bird . . .

THE Shenandoah Valley disappears past Roanoke as the lands climb up to the Cumberland Plateau. The landscape is foothills where red clay meets red clay. Ellen Glasgow had it right—this is barren ground. Not even the grass seems to grow very well here and travelers can see cattle grazing amongst cornstalk stubble. The texture of the land does not meet the stereotyped expectations of the South.

It's still Old Virginny but there are precious few cotton and corn fields or tater patches in this corner of poor mountainous land.

Daniel Boone's famous gap is close by, near the Jefferson National Forest. Boone didn't discover the wind-eroded Cumberland Gap, though history gives him the credit; Indians had used the Gap for centuries and Dr. Thomas Walker of the Royal Land Company of Virginia had actually recorded it as early as 1750. Yet the act of Boone, family, and friends moving through the Gap and along the Wilderness Road to settle in Kentucky did open up the Appalachian South. It also sounded the death knell for the Tidewater aristocracy, though it would take the Civil War finally to lay those old pretenders in their graves. Just as no English aristocrats had chosen to brave the New World at Jamestown, no mock-Cavaliers from the Tidewater chose to venture into the unknown frontier west of the Appalachians. It remained for the poor European immigrants, having nothing to lose, to brave the wild Southlands that lay before them.

The people of the southwest quadrant of Virginia have no more in common with northeast Virginia's Golden Crescent than chalk has with cheese. The plush-bottomed bureaucratic corridor isn't really a part of the South anymore. But here in the ragged hills and mountains of Virginia close on the Kentucky and West Virginia borders, the soul of the Frontier South defiantly lives on. This region has been exploited since the wake of the Civil War when ex-Confederate generals John Cabell Breckinridge and John Daniel Imboden became coal magnates and millionaires, writing their memoirs and extolling the virtues of the Lost Cause while they oppressed the people of this impoverished region. Breckinridge, former Vice President to James Buchanan, was the Southern commander who ordered the VMI cadets to their slaughter at New Market; Imboden had the duty of escorting the eight-mile-long wagon train of Confederate wounded out of Gettysburg.

To the casual passerby the little coal towns of Pound, Hurley, and Norton in Wise County, Virginia, have a quaint, almost picturesque look about them, a façade that won't give away the bitter old days. These lands have never been prosperous or much populated, and for more than a hundred years the economy of the valleys has been tied to the mines. The mettle of these people has been shaped by the mines for generations and hardened by the disasters that have trapped the menfolk hundreds or thousands of feet below the hills and ridges of this remote, severe, beloved land. The South Mountain tragedy that claimed eight lives in 1992 is hardly an isolated incident. If you live in a mining community you expect this, just as the people who live along great rivers expect floods and devastation—this foreknowledge of disaster has always seemed to breed a fatalistic but strong character of people unknown in any other walk of life in America. Every one of the thirty-nine thousand people who live in Wise County knew at least one of the men who died at the Number 3 Shaft at South Mountain.

"The people of these mountains are throwbacks to a better age," says Jenay Tate, editor of the *Coalfield Progress* in Norton, "especially in these indifferent times. They're kind and loving and compassionate. They truly believe that the death of anyone lessens their community and they feel the loss intensely . . . the national TV cameras that came here in 1992 could never hope to capture that."

Jenay Tate is herself something of a throwback to the hard-nosed old newspaper days. She's knowledgeable, she's tough, and she's good for her words. She's been in all the union halls and churches and knows everyone and every family. "Working in the coal mines today isn't like just after the Civil War or during the Depression when the people in Wise County had to put up with bad wages and company stores and tract houses just because they couldn't get any other work. Today men work in the mines because they want to. No one blames the mine owners for disasters. They accept the risk as part of the job."

South Mountain Number 3 was reopened but the permit went to a new company, and a state grand jury investigated possible criminal wrongdoing in the deaths of the eight men. The company was cleared of any wrongdoing, but the state of Virginia has changed its mining laws because of the South Mountain tragedy. One has to wonder if the legal changes would have come about if it weren't for the national spotlight that shone on Wise County for a few days. No matter. The real cause of the coal-pit deaths is the system that took control after the South had been beaten down and the people had to "accept the risk," any risk, just to survive.

In the South this kind of negative determinism—Southerners being the masters of their fate—has always hidden behind the mask of rugged individualism where the workers would rather sustain "right-to-work" laws than join a union (50 percent of the miners in Wise County refuse to belong to a union). It's the New Lost Cause of the South, little known and little understood. And the vision is a clear and hurtful one: the people of the South who banded together as brothers to fight the Civil War were so traumatized by the utter defeat that they created a mythic world to feed their spiritual needs.

PART TWO

A COSMIC CONSPIRACY

The country is one of extravagant colors, of proliferating fo-liage and bloom, of flooding yellow sunlight, and, above all perhaps, of haze. Pale blue fogs hang above the valleys in the morning, the atmosphere smokes faintly at midday, and through the long slow afternoon, cloud-stacks tower from the horizon and the earth-heat quivers upward. . . . I know there are days when the color and the haze are stripped away, but these things pass and are forgotten. . . . the influ-ence of the Southern physical world is itself a sort of cosmic conspiracy against reality in favor of romance.

— WILBUR JOSEPH CASH, *The Mind of the South*

CHAPTER 3

NEW MAGIC IN A DUSTY WORLD

*North Carolina's Triad . . . Daniel Boone . . . Biltmore and the
Vanderbilts . . . Thomas Wolfe . . . John C. Calhoun and Jesse Helms . . . Junior
Johnson and NASCAR . . . Tobacco Road*

A DESTINY THAT CAN cause an England to take a Dutch king is, as
Thomas Wolfe noted in the opening lines of *Look Homeward, Angel,*
strange enough, but a destiny that finds fulfillment in leaving England bound for Pennsylvania only to end up in the hills of Asheville,
North Carolina, is one that is "touched by that dark miracle of
chance which makes new magic in a dusty world."

If Wolfe was touched by that dark miracle, then Daniel Boone was
positively sledgehammered with his scrambled peregrinations
through Kentucky and even up into Missouri (this done before the
Louisiana Purchase). Boone's Cumberland Gap wasn't as easy to get
through as the frontiersmen of the era figured, and it didn't have
anything to do with the legendary high winds. The Shawnees, the
Cherokees, and the Mingos had been using the Gap for centuries
and were determined to defend it and the land of Kanta-ke against
the invading whites. The tribes fought better here than anywhere
else in the South. Boone himself proved to be an inept Indian
fighter despite the reputation made for him by eighteenth-century

writer John Filson, a frontier historian using the techniques of a dime novelist.

The Great Smoky Mountains loom up in this western wedge of North Carolina. They are huge, daunting, inspiring. They're beautiful and wistful. They put anyone who might gaze upon them into a subdued reverie. Their vision and being, the faraway crying of hounds and the nearby mourning of doves, are "of such sweet and inexorable opiates as the rich odor of hot earth and pinewood . . . of soft languor creeping through the blood. . . . it is a mood in which the imagination holds unchecked sway." Jack Cash recorded these perceptions of his beloved state in *The Mind of the South*. They hold true today despite a few reservations of creeping modernity.

These were the lands of Daniel Boone before the Gap. Potboiler John Filson never saw this land (though in the 1780s he did travel down the Ohio River to meet Boone in his tavern). James Fenimore Cooper, taking Filson's superman version of Dan'l Boone, would base his legendary Natty Bumppo character on the great frontiersman. No doubt this rugged wilderness did produce some bigger-than-life gallants, but these tale spinners overlooked a real-life figure who was the match for Bumppo, Chingachgook, and Uncas. That man was John Sevier.

Where Daniel Boon (the *e* was added by literate biographers later on) was repeatedly captured and beaten senseless by the Peaux Rouges, the premier Indian fighter on the Southern frontier was General John "Nolachucky" Sevier. The surest way to build a reputation back then was by fighting and whipping Indians, and "Lucky Jack" Sevier, as he was known, did just that—over a twenty-year military career, he never lost a battle. By 1777 the Cherokee Nation had ceded everything east of the Blue Ridge to the Colonials. In 1782 Sevier destroyed the Chickamaugas just outside Chattanooga; in 1794 Sevier eliminated a combined Cherokee, Creek, and Shawnee army at Lookout Mountain. The North and South would meet at both blood-drenched places many years later.

Sevier's reputation in history, however, doesn't depend on "mere" Indian killing. Few Americans today know that the proud roll call of our nation's states could have read ". . . Delaware, Florida, Franklin . . ." Franklin? Yes, Virginia (sorry about that), there was once a state called Franklin. It had an assembly, registered voters, a constitution, a freely elected governor. Sort of. The governor was the selfsame Indian fighter and massive landowner, Lucky Jack Sevier. In effect, Sevier founded America's first independent state (bite your tongue, Texas). Sevier's land-grab scheme, probably the largest ever attempted in the South, was quashed by the young Continental Congress because North Carolina claimed the lands called "Franklin" and wanted to pledge them against their Revolutionary War debts.

John Sevier had a fascinating life and career. He was arrested for treason by North Carolina but escaped during his trial. He ran back to Franklin and managed to get elected as the first governor of Tennessee (the new name for Franklin). Sevier was a noted duelist and had put many a rival down with his trusty barkers. In one of his most famous indulgences in the code duello, Sevier and Andrew Jackson stalked each other for five hours in a forest with neither able to get the drop.

Most of all, Lucky Jack Sevier is—and probably should be remembered as—the many times great-grandfather of Tennessee Williams, arguably the South's and the country's finest playwright of the twentieth century, who took his sobriquet from his outrageous forebear.

Once upon a time the Cherokee Nation was said to have started in this part of North Carolina, here on the embayment of the French Broad River. A much reduced reservation of some fifty-six thousand acres is all that remains. Three hundred or so Cherokee descendants wheedle out a living in the tourist attractions that have taken over the small town of Cherokee up in the Smokies. Here are parks and zoos named for Santa Claus, bears, and even one Cherokee. There are seasonal powwows, festivals, and an outdoor Passion play.

Out of urban Cherokee, other smaller reservation communities hide themselves just as their forebears hid in the 1830s to keep from being driven like cattle on the Trail of Tears (which will be viewed in more detail in Chapter 11). They live in clapboard shacks and shabby double- and single-wides. They eke out a living off the land, logging and hunting and fishing and making moccasins and trinkets to be sold down in the town of Cherokee. These places aren't towns, just clan settlements—Big Cove and Ela and Straight Fork—stuck up in ravines and gorges that rage with fifteen-foot-high walls of floodwaters every other season, washing away homes, vehicles, and meager possessions.

Travel these ancient hills, stop to pass some time, and these folks will tell you what it's like to live as Indians, for that's what they call themselves. Indians. Not Native Americans in a white man's world. They can't get bank loans, they don't qualify for medical assistance or unemployment or Social Security. Indian soldiers who have served in the armed forces and go back to live on the reservations don't qualify for GI loans. Education for Indian children is a nightmare. Whether by nature, nurture, or culture, Indians refuse to be individually competitive, and that's the name of the game of American education. The Indian kids are intelligent; they score well on aptitude and entrance exams. But they're uncomfortable on white campuses. Less than 9 percent of America's adult Indians have finished a college degree.

But at the height of its power by the start of the eighteenth century, the Cherokee Nation covered close to forty thousand square miles. These tribes once had a unique family culture built upon seven clans. No intermarriage between members of different clans was allowed, and the primacy of each was based upon the women who bore the children. The mothers owned the homes and the fields of corn, and it was from the mothers that the male children inherited, not their fathers.

The Cherokees had known defeat. The Iroquois ran them out of the far Northlands centuries before. No mean warriors themselves, the Cherokees then carved out an impressive empire down South. Their nation was made up of almost twenty-five thousand people when they were attacked and routed by an even fiercer foe than the Iroquois—the settlers swarming down the Great Philly Road. It was inevitable that the white Europeans would win, for the Indians had no concept of total war. Tribal champions always met in the open field and slugged it out, ending the battle without a bloody melee and sparing the men of both sides. Wilma Mankiller, retired chief of the Oklahoma Cherokees, will tell you that this was the women's influence. But when the Old Testament patriarchal white men went to war, their women had no such influence; the whites would sacrifice themselves and their sons just to win. The pantheistic Indians would do no such thing. This clash between opposing family structures, between the patriarchal willingness to sacrifice all and the matriarchal compulsion to conserve, would come back to haunt the South in the crippling aftermath of the Civil War, for it was the women of the

Confederacy, the mothers and daughters and sisters of the dead, who picked up the pieces after the war and rebuilt the South.

As travelers glide down the steep inclines of the Smokies and into the habitable foothills surrounding Asheville, they'll see something right out of the Loire Valley of eighteenth-century France. Dominating this declining town of around 100,000 is the Biltmore Estate, outdoing a dozen Vaux les Vicomtes. It makes Elvis's Graceland look like an outhouse or the Hearst castle nothing more than a disused brickyard. Biltmore is easily the most pretentious estate in the whole South. It is conspicuous consumption on such a scale that even at the highwater mark of the Robber Baron Age in which it was built it must have been embarrassing.

This realm once comprised 125,000 acres. Its main house rivals the Palace of Versailles. The château of châteaus contains sixteenth-century tapestries, original Dürer prints, rare Meissens, Pelligrini canvas ceiling paintings, china by Minton and Spode, crystal by Baccarat, and a three-story one-ton chandelier, all surrounded by grounds designed and laid out by Frederick Law Olmsted, the renowned landscape architect and builder of Central Park in New York. Biltmore was the country home of George Vanderbilt, grandson of the infamous old commodore. The price of admission just for walking-around privileges is over twenty bucks.

Down the crest of the hill toward town from Biltmore, a modest frame house sits in marked contrast to the staggering opulence of the Vanderbilts. It is the Old Kentucky Home, birthplace of Thomas Wolfe, run originally as a boardinghouse by Miss Julia, Wolfe's mother. Wolfe's *Look Homeward, Angel* might be considered out of vogue today, but it remains a celebration of the South because it extols family, the sine qua non of all the Southlands. Stand on the front porch of Miss Julia's Old Kentucky Home and you will begin to understand something of the importance of consanguinity in the Southern way. It's not that Miss Julia gave a folksy name to her boardinghouse just to attract paying customers; she was proud of her place, thought it was special. It was home to wayfaring strangers, that same stock that had settled Asheville, some going on to find the hills beyond or the meadows of Kentucky and Tennessee. So when

Wolfe wrote in *Look Homeward, Angel* of a dark miracle of chance be-ing "destiny," he was saying intuitively something as well about the consanguine spirit of the Southern trinity that holds up the South and continues to give it "identity."

You can spring for a double sawbuck at the Biltmore or pay a bit of change and walk through the home of the man who first and per-haps best expressed the tortured vision of the Southerner's life. You can stand in the room where Wolfe's brother Ben died or sit in the front-porch swing and conjure up old Gant's angels "frozen in hard marble silence" and look out onto the town square and hear "a rattle of lean wheels, a slow clangor of shod hoofs." *O waste of loss, in the hot mazes, lost . . . and by the wind grieved, ghost, come back again.*

These haunting lines from *Look Homeward, Angel* drift on the high winds swirling through the Smokies, calling all the old ghosts back home. Such a lofty vantage is needed to see and embrace all the dis-parate particulars embedded in the lands below: Asheville hungry to give up its Old South ways by succumbing to the mystique of the new age, with the cryptic melodies of a spectral Southern bard hovering all around; the unearthly splendor of a French Gothic château whose spires curse the destitution of the poor laborers who built it; the tumbledown shacks of the oft-slurred hill folk stuck randomly in the hollers of the mountain range; and a last glimpse from this soar-ing vista, the remnants of a once-proud Indian nation now subsist-ing on the untillable acres of a reservation whose size is less than half of the castle grounds.

The forbidding yet lovely mountains of the Smokies blend slowly and easily onto a plateau that extends all the way from the Hudson River Valley in New York to central Alabama. It is the Piedmont, the first region of the interior South to fall to the Industrial Revolution. More than a century of cotton and tobacco crops killed the fertility of the Piedmont. After the Civil War, not even the brutal system of sharecropping could turn a profit in the region. So the mills were brought to the fields, not because of any enlightened concept of effi-ciently growing cotton and milling cloth at the same location, but to exploit the cheap labor of tenant farmers without jobs. The cotton for these new mills came from sharecropped fields in Alabama, the lower Mississippi delta, and the blackland plantations of Texas. A new wave of capitalism hit the South. It was hard Yankee capitalism that rejected the tradition of the horse trader's handshake and impoverished the spirit born of the land. The only tradition, in fact, that was maintained was the segregation of the black and white races.

The quality of life for the mill workers and croppers, black and white, was kept as low as bare subsistence would allow. And even though peonage was imposed in both workplaces, it was this divisive mill system that did more than even the Jim Crow laws to set white against black. Textile mills sprouted up like bitterweeds throughout the Piedmont. By the beginning of the twentieth century, more than three hundred mills surrounded Charlotte alone, and mills numbered in the thousands in Virginia, North and South Carolina, Georgia, and Alabama.

The mills did begin to employ black laborers, but North Carolina itself had never had a substantial black population, and those blacks the mills did hire were kept in their own walled-off Astoria called Niggertown. Whole towns were owned by the Yankee textile magnates, many if not most of whom had been ardent Abolitionists. The poor white trash lived in row houses on the other side of the new railroad tracks bringing in the cotton from the Deep South.

The textile industry swept past Charlotte (today no longer smothered by the smoking chimney stacks) and on into South Carolina where the mills choked down little farming towns like Chesnee, Cowpens, Mayo, and Gaffney. W. J. Cash was born in the mill town of Gaffney and grew up in this state-line vicinity. Cash spent his summers at his grandparents' home in Boiling Springs, just over the line in North Carolina. He was called "Sleepy" by his family and friends, and perhaps these sylvan summers were the only carefree times of his tortured life, a life ended by his own hand in Mexico City on July 1, 1941.

Cash worked in the mills during the boom times of World War I and the early 1920s. Perhaps this experience in the good times explains Cash's benign attitude toward the mills in *The Mind of the South*. Money wasn't tight during the boom and labor unions were nonexistent. Cash grew up accepting the closed, segregated society around him; he once refused to sit next to a black student in one of his classes at Valparaiso College (he told this story on himself). He excelled later at Wake Forest and soon after became an outstanding journalist and editorial writer for the *Charlotte News*, one of the South's leading liberal newspapers.

As a young man and budding intellectual in his mid-twenties,

Cash came under the direct influence of two major figures in American letters, Sherwood Anderson and H. L. Mencken. He knew Anderson when both were reporters on the *Charlotte News*. Cash's
editorials were so strong that he soon became known as the "Pundit
of the Piedmont." His essays on Furnifold M. Simmons, the white supremacist senator from North Carolina, came to the attention of
Mencken, who published Cash's anti-Simmons essay under the title
"Jehovah of the Tar Heels" in the *American Mercury*. Cash's career as
the true voice of the South was launched.

"Doc" Simmons had maneuvered the white supremacist coalition
of the South into blocking Al Smith's nomination at the Democratic
Convention of 1924. When Smith got the nomination in 1928, Simmons and his wolf pack did their best to undermine the liberal
Catholic candidate from New York, ensuring Herbert Hoover's election. In his editorials Cash lashed out not only at Simmons and his
Ku Klux Klan mobs but at Hoover's conservatism. Cash predicted
that the Republican Party would soon raise the standard of white supremacy throughout the nation; he also observed that the only possible challenge to this emerging balance of conservative power was
the vote of the blacks, a trenchant vision for any American writer in
1928, whether white or black, Northerner or Southerner. It took a
Southerner to predict the vicious civil rights conflict that would tear
the South apart in the coming decades.

Bruce Clayton, Cash's biographer, notes that folks around Boiling
Springs "wondered what on earth could have gotten into John and
Nannie's boy . . . he surely did not get those ideas at home." No,
Cash didn't get those ideas at home. He got them from an inborn,
tragic sense of the South's dilemmas. What had gotten into Jack
Cash was a penetrating insight into things right and wrong. By
speaking his outrage, Cash condemned himself to the calumny of
his homeland that seemed forever steeped in the Savage Ideal. He
could have escaped to the safety of Mencken's North but he chose to
stay and fight in the brutal, hostile environs of his native North Carolina. Cash's second essay in *American Mercury* was entitled "The
Mind of the South"; that essay served, through the good offices of
Mencken himself, as an introduction to publisher Alfred Knopf,
who advanced Cash the lordly sum of $450 to begin the book that
would become a classic work of both history and literature.

"*The Mind of the South* is actually Jack Cash's mind," says biographer

Clayton. "The book is not only a record but a confession, objective and idiosyncratic, daringly imaginative, brilliantly written. Its message flows from sorrow. All of it flows from a profound sense of tragedy."

More than other biographies on the man, Clayton's work makes it clear that Cash was a native son of the crazy-quilt land that people called the South. There should be no great surprise that Cash and his work reflect the madness of this cloud-cuckoo world.

"Cash's reputation," says Clayton, "hinges largely on the validity of his notion of continuity . . . that the South remains not quite a nation within a nation, but the next best thing to it." In short, the Old South and its savage ways are still with us. With the exception of noted Southern sociologist John Shelton Reed, Clayton's colleagues in the academic guild believe the opposite to be true. "They would firmly believe that the Old South is dead, with the New South rampant on the flag of industrial growth."

Whether Cash is right or wrong about continuity or any Southern theme, his book, says Clayton, "has been a stick of dynamite, one of those explosions of art posing as history that keep the waters of the mind from freezing. . . . it is one of those books that make us crane our necks to see through time, not because we want to, or can, but because, after reading Cash, we must try."

Cash always considered Shelby, North Carolina, to be his home. Hardly anybody in Shelby today remembers Cash, even though some Cashes still live here. People do know where Sunset Cemetery is located, and it's easy to get directions: "Go over the railroad tracks from the town square and turn at the Anglican church." The cemetery blankets the hill behind the church and falls into the little valley below. Wilbur Joseph Cash's grave is hard to find. It's marked by a diminutive flat stone; no one trims the grass in high summer and certainly no beaten path leads the way here. The cemetery, founded in 1841, is a lovely, tranquil setting of narrow lanes, great oaks, and flowering trees. Cash's proud folks had wanted to erect a granite monument for their boy, but they were poor and knuckled under by the Depression.

A goodly number of Beams are buried here in Sunset Cemetery. A body would like to think that old Jack Cash is in good convivial company among these early settlers, lifting the occasional glass of store-bought whiskey to pass away eternity. Most of the gravestones have carved epitaphs, and by far the best one is close by Jack's—it reads

"In memory of a loving mother: Fair as a star when only one is shining in the sky."

Coming out of the graveyard along Martin Street, the visitor finds his sense of solace being invaded by an odd feeling, perhaps the imp of the perverse taking hold. Just over there in a grove of maple trees looms a gaudy, six-foot granite eyesore. It marks the grave of Shelby's true favorite son, Thomas Dixon, Jr., Baptist preacher, chum of Presidents, and, as we have seen, author of the worst kind of filth.

Senator Furnifold Simmons might have claimed to be the second father of the KKK—Confederate general Nathan Bedford Forrest, of course, was the first—but such misplaced pride is humbled by the specter of Tom Dixon, best-selling racist novelist. His books were the popular rage of readers at the turn of the century, North and South. We have seen Woodrow Wilson's response to *Birth of a Nation;* when Jack Cash saw D. W. Griffith's screen version of *The Clansman* he described his reaction as "alternately bawling hysterically and shouting my fool head off." A journalist contemporary, Hodding Carter, witnessed the same film in New Orleans as a nine-year-old amidst a crowd of Confederate veterans "who screamed the Rebel yell from the opening scene on." The hopelessly romanticized film gave renewed impetus to the hydralike rebirth of the Ku Klux Klan. In the 1920s and 1930s more than five million new members swelled the ranks of this secret vigilante army. Cross burnings, beatings, dynamitings, stompings, lynchings, drownings, and auto-da-fés swept the Southlands and flared up in all parts of the nation.

In his biography Bruce Clayton reveals that Cash's temperament belied his quiet, shy appearance. Cash was a fiery prophet in the best tradition of the hard-edged Fourth Estate; he took his Sunday school–Wednesday night prayer meeting–Baptist foundations seriously; he was determined to do and say right no matter the cost. He was a young man when he found his true voice, yet he set the standard for those few other lonely voices in the South who told off the fundamentalists, KKK, politicians, and preachers who had taken over the South. In Cash's time others like him were taking up the tocsin: Hodding Carter in Mississippi, Gerald W. Johnson and Nell Battle Lewis in North Carolina, Virginius Dabney and Louis Jaffe in Virginia, Julian Harris in Georgia, J. N. Heiskell in Arkansas, and Grover Hall and Carl Carmer in Alabama.

Pariahs all. It seems unlikely that most anyone outside of the closed society of the South even today could understand the magnitude of Cash's choice to both criticize the Southern way of life and to continue to live in the South as a "loyal son." A man who breaks the chain of Southern tradition and challenges the tension of the Savage Ideal becomes a stranger in his own land.

Jack Cash would hardly recognize his old newspaper stomping grounds in Charlotte. It was a wealthy town even in the Depression and over the boom years since then more textile millionaires have sprouted up than there were boll weevils in the cotton fields. For a few decades the only spectacle here was Billy Graham and his crusades, but in coming full circle, Charlotte's golden web has caught the prize fly of all—two major league sports franchises, the Charlotte Hornets of the NBA and the Carolina Panthers of the NFL. No one thinks of Charlotte as a "big" city, let alone major-league territory. It's just that Charlotte has too many millionaires to be ignored.

DANIEL Boone's famed Yadkin Valley in the western part of the state was the focal point of eighteenth-century expansion in North Carolina. The coastal settlements, especially Wilmington, served as seats of colonial government but had virtually no political control over the masses moving down the Great Philadelphia Road into what is now the Triad of Winston-Salem, Greensboro, and Raleigh. When the authority of the Crown or of the emergent state of North Carolina tried to exercise its will, the settlers in the western part of the state rose in rebellion scores of times during the last half of the eighteenth century, defying tax collectors and rejecting unwanted laws, and the central government backed off in the face of rapidly forming Southern individualism. In the coming generations this individualism would evolve into a states' rights issue on a national scale. Specifically, South Carolina under John C. Calhoun would learn the hard lesson of attempting nullification of federal ordinances. Once the immigrants moved down through the Yadkin Valley from Virginia into North Carolina, they metamorphosed almost magically into the reality of what would come to be known as the South.

Citizens of North Carolina have long considered their state to be a "vale of humility between two mountains of conceit." The accused states of Virginia and South Carolina had aristocratic pretensions since Colonial days. North Carolina never suffered from such conceit; it was redneck-cracker-tarheel frontier rubes and jays. And proud of it. Writing in *The Mind of the South,* Cash had some doubts about the origin of the South's much-prized and ballyhooed aristocracy. Cash guessed that the whole bunch of them could be numbered at less than 250; he firmly stated that "any bright schoolboy can tell you offhand the names of all the important ones among them." Cash posed, however, the critical question of how to account for the emergence of the ruling class of the real South. His answer was manifestly "from the man at the center . . . the strong, the ambitious, the pushing among the old coon-hunting population of the back country."

Cash's thesis was that a few of these coon hunters settled down, cleared some land, and started farming. As the years passed, they made some money that enabled them to buy more land and bring in some slaves. By the time they reached old age, they had accumulated relative wealth, had seen their daughters married off to the younger sons of other nouveau bluebloods in need of generous dowries. Here was the synthesis of the true Southern aristocracy. When the old patriarch died, he would be praised in church and in newspapers as "a gentlemen of the old school and a noble specimen of the chivalry at its best." All of his progeny believed it; they created coats of arms to proclaim their glorious heritage, and imitated the real origin of aristocracy by hiring genealogists to trace their roots to William the Conqueror or Ethelred or even Artos, the Dux Bellorum, the once and future king.

The modern-day equivalent of John C. Calhoun who stands as the epitome of the legendary "Man at the Center" can be neatly summarized in the persona of Jesse Helms, senior senator from North Carolina. Brother Helms, a lay Baptist preacher when it suits his psyche, has never missed a chance to blow hard on the fires of intolerance. Helms springs from the Daniel Boone–Yadkin Valley–"man at the center" stock. His daddy, Jesse Sr., was a small-town cop in Monroe, North Carolina, who made his reputation soaping up to the rich, rousting the drunks, and terrifying the white trash—so postulates author Ernest B. Furgurson in his book *Hard Right: The Rise of Jesse Helms.* Jesse Jr. seems to have picked up where his old man left off. Furgurson puts Helms into perspective by quoting a fellow traveler, James J. Kilpatrick: "There is never any question of where Helms stands. He stands slightly to the right of John C. Calhoun."

Helms began his career as a yellow journalist in Raleigh, the fine old town where Barney Fife used to spend his vacations at the YMCA. Barney finally got on the state police just like Jesse got himself up to the conservative trough as a TV commentator. Helms got elected to the U.S. Senate in 1968 on Richard Nixon's coattails and has soaped and waxed eloquent ever since.

Helms may be the heir to the efforts of Tom Dixon, Jr., and Doc Simmons, but he is not the only voice in North Carolina speaking his piece; there is a fairer side to the South's Janus-faced heritage. Perhaps the clearest voice of reason to emerge in the early-twentieth-century South was that of Frank Porter Graham, president of the University of North Carolina. Graham was much more than just a college administrator and academician. He was, according to Josephus Daniels, "the most militant liberal of all educators in America." Graham fought for academic freedom on his own campus, was a champion of humanism, defended labor unions and their organizers, crusaded against racial discrimination in education, and spoke up for the civil liberties of all. "Thank God for the University of North Carolina," said Clark Foreman, a chief adviser to President Franklin Roosevelt. Under Graham's leadership the university became the premier institution of the South. According to Howard Odum, himself a legend among educators in the South, Graham was "the conscience of North Carolina." One might add in retrospect that Frank Porter Graham was the conscience of the South.

In his book *In Search of the Silent South,* historian Morton Sosna tells a story that reveals Frank Graham at his best when under fire:

In 1936 an English teacher and disciple of Graham's at the University of North Carolina, E. E. Erickson, electrified the state by dining publicly with James Ford, an invited speaker at Chapel Hill. Ford was the vice-presidential candidate for the Communist Party of the United States. Ford was also a black man. The bigots of the state were in an uproar, virtually apoplectic. Erickson's dismissal was the very least of the demands brought to bear on college president Graham. The pressures on Graham were so heavy that his best friend, Ambassador Josephus Daniels, had to rush home from Mexico to help in the fight, for it was clear that the attack was really against Graham; the rabble had simply found an opportunity and seized upon it. Graham refused to fire Erickson, saying, "One has to act in the spirit of Christian wisdom." That spirit prevailed, Erickson wasn't forced out, and Graham served notice that he would never lie down in the face of racial aggression.

Graham served as president of UNC from 1930 through 1948. In March of 1949 a newly elected North Carolina senator died and the state's progressive governor, Kerr Scott, confounded the riffraff by appointing Graham to fill the position. Graham ran for reelection in 1950 and was opposed in the Democratic Primary by Mc-Carthyites posing as Dixiecrats; he was badly beaten by a smear campaign that accused him of being everything from a Communist to a "nigger lover."

"WAKE UP, WHITE PEOPLE," went a campaign broadside. "Do You Want Negroes Working Beside You, Your Wife and Daughters? Using Your Toilet Facilities? Frank Graham Favors Mingling of the Races."

The éminence grise behind the smear tactics used against Graham in the 1950 senatorial campaign was none other than a young, ambitious plotter named Jesse Helms. When the newly elected senator, Willis Smith, went to Washington, he took Helms along as his ace media adviser. Next door to Smith's office was the lair of the newly elected senator from California, Richard Milhous Nixon, the maître d'éminence grise. Now in his fifth term in the Senate, Helms will apparently be the last Nixonian.

IN North Carolina there are triads and triangles, but the troika of this state is an industrial belt that comes close to surpassing anything the industrial East or the Silicon Valley of California can offer. What one sees throughout the Tarheel State's Triad are matrixes of high-tech manufacturing firms producing the stuff of our daily lives. Gone is the old sooty, smoke-stacked image of mills and attendant poverty. North Carolina is by no means a service-oriented state like many of its sister states of the South, and one need mention only the industry here to prove the point: North Carolina in the 1990s is producing up to 90 percent of the country's furniture. From one angle of the Triad to another, this compound of progress with its *Fortune* 100 hum of activity gives more the appearance of resorts than the rather deplorable picture of these environs just three or four decades ago. The Triad today is the consummation of a long-deferred New South dream first conceived by Southern visionary Henry Grady (whom we shall meet in Chapter 5).

"Coliseum Next Right" is the common road sign throughout the metroplex area known as the Triad. North Carolinians succumb to this signal with more fervor than charismatic Christians celebrate "Jesus Is Lord" bumper stickers, but the Tar Heels, the Wolf Pack, the Blue Devils, and the Deacons are the lords of North Carolina. While collegiate hoops are fine and generate megabucks, the true blood sport in North Carolina and throughout the Deep South is stock car racing. It is the unbridled passion of the Dixie way of life. While fifteen to twenty thousand may turn out for roundball, and eighty to a hundred thousand for football, these subdued gladiatorial contests can't create the vicarious blood ardor in the mobs that swarm to the car races. A quarter million bellowing fans, men and women and children, vie for the best view of old road warriors like Earnhardt, Yarborough, Allison, and the legend of legends, North Carolina's own Richard Petty.

The South has bequeathed many an anomalous gift to its people: beautiful sultry women, romance, good old boys, corn whiskey, Cajun crazies, Brobdingnagian demagogues, snake handlers, coon dogs, bizarre genealogies, outrageous mythologies. By far the spookiest of all these gifts is the phenomenon of hot-rodding on a circular asphalt track—the 360-degree existential nightmare. The huge crowds roar at every turn, lapping it up and praying for a ten-car crash with fire and blood, wanting it and not wanting it at the same time. It's shivering, it's soul-stirring, it's bewildering, it's intoxicating, it's concupiscent.

The racing of finely tuned, Goldbergian-modified automobiles got its start when good old boys like Junior Johnson and his kin up in the backwoods and hollers of Appalachia were thunder-roading moonshine down to the bootleggers in the flatlands. Johnson got so good at lapping the Revenuers that he just had to take his act to a dirt-track circuit. When this sport began, the drivers were their own shade-tree mechanics; they became the greatest combustible engineers ever to appear on the planet. The old flivvers cost maybe hundreds and any crew consisted of a cousin or outlaw uncle who worked for a few beers in the evening on the motors propped up on cinder blocks and Pepsi crates (today's sport employs thousands with sponsored budgets in the millions).

Despite Junior Johnson's appeal, the driver "give up" to be the all-time best is King Richard Petty. In his autobiography, *King Richard I,*

Petty allows as how "not all race drivers are tough, but they'll do anything to win." Petty says his daddy was tough, "probably the toughest I've ever seen. If he could win without denting up your car, he'd do it; if it took beating on you, he'd do that too." Petty claims that Junior Johnson was tough too, that he could win with any kind of car, and that Junior would beat on you during a race, "just because he liked to."

No wonder that Johnson was one of the greatest heroes on the circuit. He gave his fans what they needed, a brash Southern champion whose outlaw blood would drive him to crash into any car that even looked like it was trying to beat him. There's a special breed of Junior Johnsons in these Southern hills. Their first feel of a fast car was as eleven- or twelve-year-old boys riding shotgun in an uncle's black Dodge coming down dirt and gravel roads at ninety miles an hour, keeping their eyes peeled in the dark for another pair of headlights striking like some shooting star off the crook of a forking logger road, government agents with rifles or rival bootleggers with sawed-off shotguns that would spur the uncle into kicking in the other barrel of the Dodge's carburetor just at the right moment to save their ass. And no matter how much NASCAR glory or money or fame or beautiful women they'd ever get, they'd never quite be able to recapture this thrill.

Outlaws in the South are special folk heroes, unknown in any other part of the country. It's a reflection of the rugged individualism particular to the Southlands since those folks came down from Daniel Boone's Yadkin Valley. They aren't villains; they're Robin Hoods such as Jesse and Frank James, the Younger Brothers, the pirates John Murrell and Jean Lafitte, Belle Starr, and the modern era's Bonnie and Clyde and Pretty Boy Floyd. They all spring from the blood of the English rebel Wat Tyler, whose fourteenth-century uprising condemned to death anyone who could read or write—such literacy automatically meant that these condemned articulates were the scum of the earth, lawyers and tax collectors. The very spleen and spirit of Southern rebels emanated from Tyler's peasant rebellion.

There are a lot of crops growing in the South besides tobacco and cotton. Peaches, watermelons, cantaloupes, pecans, peanuts, corn, lodge-pole pine. But the number-one cash crop (unofficial and untaxed) is reefer. Boo, shit, weed, marijuana to the narcs, and "let's fire up a bull" to the aficionado. The endemic hatred of narcs funny-fingering with a man's right to make a living off the soil keeps its relevance in today's South. If you travel just a little ways off the beaten path of the industrial and population centers of North Carolina, you'll find some of the finest crops this side of the Golden Triangle (of course, you'll be taking your life in your own hands if you venture too far into this forbidden garden, but adventure to Southern boys creates a rush that clears out the veins and arteries).

A new theme song has taken root in these hills. No longer is it "Dixie" or Merle Haggard's two-faced "Okie from Muskogee" ("We don't smoke marijuana in Muskogee and we don't take our trips on LSD"). It's Steve Earle and the Dukes' "Copperhead Road," an infectious, deep-beat paean that keeps alive the continuity of Rebel independence between running shine and running dope. Certainly the image of the law-abiding, Christian, conservative Southerner (for those who subscribe to such an image) doesn't jibe with the Copperhead Road, but just as certainly there are as many dopers in the South as there are conservative Christians, law-abiding or not—the "nots" you'll meet at church on Sunday. Smoking dope is not just an urban issue; country girls and boys smoke and rope dope with the same studied aplomb as their citified cousins.

SEEING all the splendor of North Carolina's Triad, one wonders how all these affluent folk got where they are. We know the eighteenth-century migration brought their forebears down the Great Philly Road, but how did the next generations fare?

The upper-class Carolinians (those whose warrants for land grants held up against the cross-claimers) did all right. Their cotton and tobacco plantations spearheaded the economic growth of the South and provided the raw materials for the industrialization of the North. These Carolina plutocrats held thousands of slaves, and their homes were not one bit less pretentious than the estates of the gentlefolk living in the two mountains of conceit.

The yeoman middle class were small landowners. They had homes, usually log cabins, that were occasionally chinked but more often not. The windows to these cabins were open to the elements, sometimes with oil paper to keep out the drafts and vermin, but no glass; the coming of the glassmakers was the first true sign of affluence in the Piedmont. Inside these rough cabins, one could find a few pieces of old-fashioned heirloom furniture. The yeoman and his family lived off kitchen gardens where the common veggie was the humble collard green (cole warts). They kept larger clearings for the growing of corn, whose meal was the staple diet. Packs of tame dogs trailed the grounds on the fringes of the pine forests, and hogs lay in wallows near the front stoops. The cash crop for these farmers was turpentine, but their wealth was measured in the number of slaves they held. The yeoman slave was actually better off than the slaves of the wealthy; these middle-class slaves worked side by side with their masters rather than being driven by overseers on the cotton and tobacco plantations, and as a consequence got the chance to learn and to excel as carpenters, blacksmiths, masons, cobblers, horse trainers, and wheelwrights.

No safety net existed for the lower-class white trash. These poor folks greatly outnumbered their privileged white brothers. They were "entirely uneducated, poverty-stricken vagabonds," relates Frederick Law Olmsted in his book on the South, *The Cotton Kingdom* (copyrighted in 1861). A New Yorker and a staunch Abolitionist, Olmsted was unique among travelers in the South during the quicksand years leading to the Civil War. He journeyed into the states that would become the Confederacy and he recorded his impressions of the people, their way of living, their beliefs. Though *The Cotton Kingdom* remained out of print for a hundred years, it stands as the most valuable sourcebook on the nineteenth-century South.

Olmsted's chronicle of North Carolina began in 1855. He observed that the majority of poor whites were held in thrall by their own ignorance. "They nearly all believed implicitly in witchcraft and attributed everything that happened, good or bad, to the agency of persons whom they supposed were possessed of evil spirits." A thin, civilizing coating of religion barely hid this ingrained superstition. The infighting among the religious sects created a mendacious dogma that preached against the new and solidified the eternal nature of the old. Here was the Savage Ideal in full flower. Olmsted was especially amazed at the vicious, even sanguine warfare between the hard-shell and soft-shell Baptists, those who take the Old Testament literally versus those who will abide a bit of interpretative balm in Gilead. He admitted that he did not understand the nature of the conflict, yet he reflected that it "curiously indicates how the terms

Christianity, Piety, Etc., are misapplied to partisanship and conditions of the imaginations."

Were Olmsted to travel the South today, he would find the same unremitting conflicts going on within the Baptist Church, buttressed by similar superstitions of 150 years earlier living on in unwavering fear and ignorance. The Papists of Rome and the Southern Baptist Convention based in Nashville have found they have something in common—their negativity. Neither dogma can stomach women's rights, gay rights, or the right to abortion. Both sects proclaim that God is definitely macho, just as both are determined to abrogate the separation of Church and State, even though both sides believe the other to be drunk with apostasy. Every Sunday down South the Baptist preachers and Sunday school teachers go out of their way to find something bad about the Romanists. Back in the 1940s the Baptists jumped President Harry Truman so viciously that he stormed out of the church and never went back (and that was just because Truman shook hands with the Pope). At the end of the twentieth century, the Southern Baptist Convention has done the same thing to President and Southern Baptist Bill Clinton, not so much for meeting the Pope or even shaking hands with him as for daring to send an ambassador to the Vatican (the first such since Henry Cabot Lodge fulfilled the same role for John Kennedy). So if Olmsted were in the South today, he would find his bemusement deepened. The Baptists have added a few more coats of lacquer to their tortoise shells. The bumpers of their step-up pickups and Lincoln Town Cars are plastered with stickers announcing "Abortion Stops a Beating Heart" right next to "The NRA Is Us." No wonder Olmsted gave up travel writing and returned to New York to become a landscape architect; the smooth natural lines of his gardens and arbors were a good deal more soothing than the labyrinthine excesses of Southern religion.

MOVING across the Piedmont Plateau, most travelers don't sense the subtle changes taking place. Make no mistake, this is flatland, and the cultural differences between the hills and plateau are enormous. Hill people have the reputation of being the most deliberately unprogressive in the United States; they are secretive and independent and have little desire to associate with anyone outside their own kind. North Carolina was the last state to secede from the Union in 1861, and most of the hill clans wanted nothing to do with the rebellion on either side, any more than Daniel Boone and his people wanted to fight in the Revolutionary War. The hill people of both centuries looked upon the flatlanders as their traditional persecutors and saw no advantage to helping them in a fight. Many moved west through Kentucky all the way to the Ozarks to find new sanctuary for their peculiar individualism.

It was down in these flatlands then that the plantation mentality took hold, where feudalism would find a home and would reign. Commonality in the hills was (and still is) limited to clans, but on the flatland, ideology took control and it was here that connections with the past were the strongest and most virulent, and where the aftermath of the Civil War would leave its indelible mark.

Not twenty minutes from the campus of Duke University stands the Bennett farm, where in 1865 the South's dreams of glory vanished like the dew on the meadow of wildflowers below the old Bennett place. On April 9, Robert E. Lee had surrendered to U. S. Grant at Appomattox, and General William T. Sherman, who had already finished his infamous march to the sea, was closing in on the remnants of what was left of the Confederacy. Here on April 26, General Joseph E. Johnston, defying Jefferson Davis's desperate order to keep the war going, surrendered the last Confederate field army. President Davis, his generals, and the people of the South had known since the summer of 1864 that the cause was hopeless. Davis's Secretary of War, James Seddon, had long argued for capitulation, hoping to stop the massive shedding of blood. Seddon resigned after Davis, Lee, and others took what can only be called a Samurai oath to fight to the death.

Joe Johnston of all the Southern generals was unwilling to sacrifice his men for this vainglorious death wish. Unlike most commanders on the battlefield, Johnston refused to execute his own soldiers just to encourage discipline. He was the favorite of the Rebel fighting soldier, the Omar Bradley of the Civil War. But more than 100,000 Confederate soldiers true to their oath died in the last stages of the war. Joe Johnston became one of the lost personalities in this much romanticized epoch. Before the Civil War he had a higher reputation among his native Virginians than did Robert E.

Lee, yet after the war Lee was canonized while Johnston was forgotten. During the conflict, Johnston would have nothing to do with the suicidal frontal attacks so dear to the hearts of his brother generals. The carnage in Lee's so-called victories alone was greater than all the casualties suffered by Southerners under Johnston's command.

Joe Johnston led the last army of the South onto the modest Bennett farmstead. His men were bone-tired, starving, shoeless, shivering with the cold, virtually without ammunition. They were outnumbered ten to one by Sherman's veteran troops, with Grant's massive army closing in following the victory at Appomattox. Had Johnston followed Jeff Davis's order to fight on, a bloodbath would have enriched the soil of the farm for generations. Unlike Lee at this point, Johnston refused to succumb to any futile sense of Southern honor. His compassion for his men transcended all delusions of glory in a just cause. So it fell to Joe Johnston to put an end to the madness. He quieted the raucous battlefield and brought curing peace to the South. Here was the final stillness, not at Appomattox.

The Bennett farm today is on a memorial road just outside the city of Durham. The quaint old farm buildings enclosed by split-rail fences are preserved as a tourist attraction, though they really stand as an object lesson. The homestead was built in 1846 and provided a subsistence living for Bennett and his extended family. His sons, Alphonso and Lorenzo, and son-in-law, Robert, might have made a go of the farm, but all three were killed in the war. Father Bennett kept going by raising a little wheat and oats, potatoes, and corn. He sold horse feed, tobacco plugs, and corn whiskey to help ends meet. In the Reconstruction, ends never met and the surviving family was reduced to the lowest level that poor whites could sink, sharecropping. The land beat Bennett down and he died in 1878. Somehow a strong sense of family kept the place going; Bennett's grandchildren carried on the sharecropping until they were literally starving. They exchanged their peonage on the land for a similar one in the textile mills of Durham.

For some unknown reason posterity has seen fit to preserve the Bennett place, but no one comes here much, certainly not for the historical incongruity of another Confederate surrender. Nor do tourists flock in just to see the deserted fields where the Bennetts tried so desperately to hold on. The land hasn't been worked for years now and despite the calm that surrounds the farm, an eerie feeling grips one here. The fields want to be worked, to feel the plow, to support a family again.

The life the Bennetts suffered through at the end of the war was pretty common for North Carolina. It stands as a shameful model for millions of poor whites and freed blacks all across the South. A full 90 percent of the Southlands were put into sharecropping by the federally mandated parole called Reconstruction. The Yankees wanted their pound of flesh and they got it by the wagonload. The entire South in the North's eyes was a land of convict labor. There was in the South still a genteel element, but it became as threadbare as Joe Johnston's defeated army. Just as the Confederate generals forgot the soul of the Bonnie Blue flag, the leaders of the post–Civil War New South forgot their soul. The people of the South had been betrayed by their leaders, military and political.

The emotional treachery that had duped men and boys who had never owned a slave into fighting a war for slavery would be compounded into a new hatred of the blacks simply because they had been set free. Jack Cash wrote in *The Mind of the South* that even though "this war had smashed the Southern world, it had left the essential Southern mind and will . . . entirely unshaken." In this Cash was writing from the heart, out of hurt pride as a loyal Southern son. In truth, the Southern mind and will were not only shaken, they were destroyed, and from within. This prideful Southern will had betrayed itself, and no need to blame the Yankees here. The old paternal order had simply gone mad by reenacting the Old Testament ritual of filial sacrifice. The only way the discredited leadership of the South could regain power was to lay the blame on the Yankee and his freed, unwanted, and unloved slave. Like Pontius Pilate, the Southern hierarchy washed its hands of the whole embarrassing affair and retreated under the shadow of pretended gentility. That shadow would deepen with the progression of the generations, yet would offer little shade or comfort to the Bennetts, the poor whites of the South.

The grandchildren of poor-white Father Bennett had been reduced to eating their seed corn before finally giving up and going to work in the mills. The poverty was so deep that most families in North Carolina and throughout the South could not afford new seed and, more importantly, were unable to buy the guano needed to bring new life to the played-out soil. It would have been little consolation to the Bennetts had they known what would happen to these fields in less than one generation following the war. What these depleted lands worked out to be is one long tobacco corridor stretching from modern, bejeweled Winston-Salem through Greensboro and Durham into Raleigh, then drooping all along this line as far down as Charlotte. This is the Triad, the empire built by the Dukes, the family whose name graces one of the South's finest universities.

The fortunes made from the "evil weed" owe an everlasting debt to the Duke family: Washington Duke, the paterfamilias, and to his youngest son, James Buchanan, called "Buck." Washington Duke started up after the Civil War as the archetypal Southern horse trader, bartering flour for bacon, bacon for tobacco, tobacco for cotton, and cotton for gold. "Wash," as he was called, started growing brightleaf, a new variety of smoking tobacco; in the 1880s Buck Duke would revolutionize the industry when "Duke, Sons and Company" started making store-bought cigarettes already rolled and packaged. By the 1890s Buck had organized the American Tobacco Company, a cartel that controlled cigarette tobacco not only in the United States but all over the world.

"Where can a man get as much fun out of fifteen cents as buying a package of cigarettes and enjoying them?" Thus spake Buck Duke just before his demise in the 1920s. Buck was reflecting on his life's work while traveling in his luxurious Pullman car on his way to Canada to take over Alcoa, the aluminum giant. He was keeping high company with some of the Northern Hemisphere's most notorious Robber Barons, including the Secretary of the Treasury, Andrew Mellon. While Yankee moguls such as J. P. Morgan, Jay Gould, and Henry Ford had more than just some passing interest in the Southlands, Buck Duke was the first of their kind born in the South.

Despite his father's pious compulsion for things and deeds Methodist, Buck Duke had few such compunctions. He fixed prices, cornered markets and patents, coerced rivals, outlawed labor unions, gouged his workers and the public, and literally owned enough key members of Congress to secure the largest subsidy ever granted to private industry by the federal government. He also formed the world's first truly international combine through British-American Tobacco (BAT). Duke did all this by virtually waging war on his competitors. The famous "Plug War" in the 1890s was over nothing more than Duke's wanting to control the plug chewing tobacco market, and he did that, too. Teddy Roosevelt in his fabled trust-busting episode did his best to break up the Duke empire. But Buck went to his grave a very rich man and believing that he had given "the poor man a lot of pleasure."

The Dukes also owned textile mills, railroads, banks, and the entire hydroelectric power systems of North and South Carolina. The Dukes cached the gold into the scores of banks that they owned. The extent of Buck Duke's wealth can perhaps be measured best by the fact that he not only bought a university but built it from the ground up and endowed it beyond the wildest dreams of any educator in the twentieth century. The joke of the times was that Buck had tried to buy Princeton, then Yale, but had to settle for Trinity, which on the seventh day he caused to be named Duke. When Buck found the building stones he wanted, he bought out the quarry and hired Frederick Law Olmsted's sons to design the grounds (what was good enough for Central Park and the Vanderbilts was good enough for Buck Duke). All told, James Buchanan Duke bequeathed, donated, and spent more than $150 million on his Duke University.

Durham today is justly renowned for the academic excellence of Duke University. But out in the real world, the principal industry of the town is no longer tobacco farming or even cigarette making. It's fat-farming. Thousands of upwardly mobile obese persons pass through this new diet capital of the world. These diet and fitness centers situated in and around Durham are done up in splendid Greek or Roman architecture and stretch all the way over to Chapel Hill. Duke University itself has a thriving diet center in the middle of the fat-farm complex. Here is the home of the famous rice diets, water diets, grapefruit diets, even popcorn diets; and the leading centers—Structure House, Fitness World, Imperial Athletic Club, Diet Center of Research Triangle Park—have long waiting lists and have no trouble at all attracting affluent, Rubenesque men and women. One can only wonder what old Buck Duke would have made out of this new cellulite city.

IN the 1990s some new blood flowed into the Triad. The last thing these people were interested in, though, was dieting. They'd been hungry for decades, their children sick and emaciated, their grandparents just barely hanging on, the young husbands and wives suffering from snakebites, pellagra, and bullet wounds. These new immigrants were settlers from afar whose journey to North Carolina followed the metaphorical tracks of the Great Philadelphia Road but in 747s rather than in covered wagons.

They are the Montagnards, the last tattered survivors of a centuries-old culture from the highlands of Indochina. They had been the stalwart allies of the United States during the long war in Southeast Asia. When the United States pulled out of Vietnam in 1975, the Montagnards had been left behind with promises of help to keep the war going until we could come back. At the height of their culture they had once numbered close to 700,000, but centuries of persecution by the South Vietnamese, the North Vietnamese, and finally the Khmer Rouge had reduced them to a few hundred. They had fought for their American friends with absolute loyalty throughout the Vietnam War and had carried on alone for seventeen years, until they were reduced to the broken remnant found by U.N. Peacekeeping troops deep in the Cambodian jungle. The story of how the Montagnards found themselves in the world of the American South is one of mystery, intrigue, and betrayal.

Even though the Montagnards had been true to their word, the U.S. government didn't uphold its end of the bargain. While the TV eyes of America in 1975 were watching the chaos of the final evacuation of the ambassador's compound in Saigon, the policy gurus in Washington were stockpiling arms and ammunition up in the highlands to keep the war going. North Vietnam had triumphed by a guerrilla war; why couldn't we undermine their victory the same way? The promise to the Montagnards was a U.S. return to Vietnam to ensure the autonomy of the tribes in their native mountains. This story never got any media exposure. No reports, no in-depth TV analyses, no leaks. Nothing but the silent death of a whole culture.

In 1992 many devoted comrades-in-arms of the Montagnards flew to North Carolina from all around the country—from California and Texas and Michigan and Maine. Green Berets who had fought in the highlands of Vietnam with these embattled warriors came to lend comfort to the pitiful few survivors. They came also to pledge their personal loyalty to friends. Many Green Berets will testify to the closeness of the relationship between the Americans and the Montagnards.

Seventeen years after the fall of Saigon the Montagnards were being brought to Raleigh, North Carolina, by the U.S. State Department, thanks to the tireless work of the family services arm of the Lutheran Church, which sponsored the Montagnards' relocation to America. At the airport in Raleigh the Montagnards (known to themselves as Degas) were met by a group of family service workers: doctors, nurses, teachers and aides, people who would help them start the process of becoming Americans.

Among the welcomers at the airport was a young man named Chien Vu, a Vietnamese himself who had survived the killing fields of Vietnam and Cambodia and who knew the Montagnards' story. "I knew them not as the Degas but as *moi*... savages. They weren't. They were my countrymen and I came to help them." Chien himself is an extraordinary survivor. A native of Saigon, he spent seven years running and hiding after Saigon fell in 1975. He saw people fighting to lick up a few grains of rice spilled along the dirt roads; he saw villages burning and dead people with their hands tied behind their backs, and he saw children starving, heard their cries.

Chien was a high school math teacher in Saigon and was one of the few who got relocated in the 1980s; since coming to Raleigh he has completed his doctorate at North Carolina State University and is an analyst for IBM in Raleigh. He was at the airport to greet the Montagnards, to offer a few friendly words in their own language, and to interpret them for those who were bringing them into the American melting pot.

"You only got one chance in Vietnam," Chien Vu said. "In America you get two, three, four chances, as many as you are willing to try and to sacrifice for. The Degas will fit in here. They have a chance."

"They took care of us," said Paul Campbell in Raleigh as the first wave of refugees came through the airport. Campbell was a CIA operative attached to the Green Berets. "I felt safer with the Montagnards than I did with my own. I slept easy at night." The Green Berets will tell you that thousands of American lives were saved by these tribal warriors. The Berets lived with the Degas, protected their communities, and fought side by side with their men. Their combined operations put a heavy crimp into the NVA strategy. The Degas soon became the only reliable allies the United States had in Vietnam. When the United States pulled out, the North Vietnamese would neither forgive nor forget, and the Degas became a hunted people with prices on their heads.

Once safely in North Carolina, the Montagnards were taken to various relocation centers throughout the Triad. In Raleigh, Paul Campbell, who came out of retirement to take over the kitchen at the relocation center, saw to it that the tribespeople were properly fed. When Thanksgiving and Christmas came around, Campbell made sure they were treated not only to turkey with all the trimmings but also to traditional native fare, including the fermented sauce made from fish heads.

Campbell encouraged the tribespeople with common-sense advice. "You've just come out of the jungle," he told them, "but here you are in a concrete jungle and it's a hell of a lot worse than where you were." In effect, he was telling them that they'd get a chance, but they wouldn't get a choice.

Not all the people of North Carolina were as pleased as the former Green Berets and Chicn Vu to see the Montagnards. There was grumbling and innuendo in Raleigh, Greensboro, and Charlotte. A local TV station claimed that an outbreak of tuberculosis was raging through these refugees. "No telling what kind of filth and disease them people are bringing in here," went some of the local talk.

"The Montagnards will adapt better than any other Asians brought into this country," says Paul Campbell. It was, perhaps, a hope but one founded in certain faith.

Adapt the Degas did. They gained a working knowledge of the language in short order. They got sponsors and jobs and began to set up new households. Resentment existed, for this is the land of Jack Cash's Savage Ideal, and fermented fish sauce is sufficiently different from redeye gravy to raise redneck hackles. But not for long, a generation perhaps, and then we'll see Montagnards as new Americans hanging out in the malls of Raleigh and Greensboro and Charlotte. Already they've learned to eat KFC and pizza and even grits and pan-fried catfish with smoking-hot hush puppies.

Transplanted Yankees in the South eventually come over to turnip greens and cornbread and the South's vin de table, strong iced tea. So will the Montagnards. They've been stirred into the melting pot, Southern-style. They'll belong to churches and go to town meetings and block parties. Their children will become homecoming queens and running backs and Merit Scholars. Surely the Degas caught a little luck in being placed down in the South. Here they won't find themselves so isolated as in a big Northern town. Had they been thrown into Chicago or New York or L.A., their only hope for survival would have been to band tightly together into a defensible, hedgehog ghetto.

"Where you folks from?"

"We're from the South . . . the Deep South."

CHAPTER 4

THE GRANDEES OF GOD'S LITTLE ACRES

South Carolina and Georgia . . . Southern Language . . . Blood Sport and Cock-fights . . . Charleston and The Citadel . . . James Oglethorpe and Jimmy Carter . . . Augusta National Country Club . . . Erskine Caldwell

PEOPLE WHO MAKE THE study of the South their business—folk-lorists, ethnologists, and sociologists—have never quite been able to define just what makes the South the South. By the 1990s it's clear that portions of both Virginia and North Carolina have lost most of their Southern identity. Clerks and attendants at gas stations or bar-becue stands will say that curious travelers often stop to ask, "Is this the South?" But go anywhere south of the Blue Ridge down to the Sea Islands and you won't have to ask. The state of South Carolina is the absolute and unmitigated South, and to prove it, it's the last state in the South still officially flying the Rebel battle flag.

Events stretching back to the last decades of the seventeenth century and the first decades of the eighteenth can furnish reasons enough for why South Carolina has always been what it is—obstinate, haughty, disparate, and undeniably Southern. When Charles II awarded Carolina to Lord Ashley, the first Earl of Shaftesbury, in 1663, he likely cared little that Lord Ashley would ask John Locke to write the governing constitution for Carolina. At that time Locke had not yet risen to the heights that he would achieve as the leading philosopher of freedom and the father of the Enlightenment. Something was happening in England and Europe and it was the emergence of the middle class, and Locke was its champion. He wrote into the Carolina constitution certain guarantees, among them being "life, health, liberty, or possessions." Though his constitution provided for a distinct class structure and the incorporation of a feudal system, his ideas on checks and balances would profoundly influence Thomas Jefferson and would form the basis for the U.S. Constitution.

Inherent in Locke's legal writ for Carolina was his concept of empiricism, which relied strictly on sensory experience. Only that which could be seen, touched, and felt had merit, and these traits would become the guiding characteristics of the new South Carolinians, even to the point that the colonists would eventually refuse to ratify Locke's constitution. They might have accepted his precepts of the rights of property owners, but they were practicing a New World empiricism, one that would lead them to extend Locke's defense of rights and freedoms perhaps into their grandee sphere of business and commerce. Their first colony to thrive was at Oyster Point; by 1680 the plantation owners had established their own capital city, called Charles Town (later Charleston). Here began the luxurious period of wealth and culture that would ultimately make Charleston the envy of the whole South. Here, too, began the grandee arrogance. These Charlestonians, never forgetting the feudal privileges they had not ratified but assumed nonetheless, began to portray themselves as "grandees," imitating the nobility of Spain and Portugal. They saw themselves as the new proprietors of Carolina, on a level with the Earl of Shaftesbury himself. With the amassing of greater wealth, they controlled their own legislature and made their laws to fit themselves. They were Anglicans, and when other religious sects tried to move in, they denied them any religious liberty and tried to drive them off (until the English government had to intercede, in 1706). The grandee class stood up to the English over the parceling of new land grants, trying to keep out upland settlers, and they denied the uplanders access to representation and to law courts. And when it became economically advantageous, the grandees more or less bluffed their way into being a Royal colony.

From the very beginning, then, the grandee class asserted their will and widened the chasm between themselves and their upland fellow Carolinians. The settlement of South Carolina and Georgia would be restricted to the coastal towns of Charleston and Savannah up to the middle of the eighteenth century until the Great Philadelphia Wagon Road, chopped out of the wilderness by increasing waves of settlers, connected the first colonies to the hinterlands. Even though the Carolinas would be separated into two royal colonies in 1729, the grandees with their peculiar brand of Southern narcissism would resist change and see the new immigrants—German, Swiss, Irish, and Scot—as threats to their aristocratic culture.

The grandees made fortunes at rice farming along the coastal plains at the time of the Revolutionary War and they supported the Crown during that war. With the advent of Eli Whitney's cotton gin in 1793, the Cotton Kingdom and its plantation society were born. The grandees and their imitators across the South were elevated to the riches of Croesus, though the breach between grandee and uplander remained as a pronounced class distinction. They would only come together over the bigger issue of North versus South in the buildup to the Civil War, and even then there existed some divisiveness. South Carolina was the first state to secede from the Union, and it was the grandee class that stood at the forefront, just as it did when the first shots were fired at Fort Sumter over on Charleston Bay.

MODERN travelers retracing the old wagon road can readily detect the class lines that have prevailed in South Carolina since colonial times, and those lines basically demarcate three tiers: the uplands, the capital city of Columbia, and the rich coastal region. The upland tradition can be seen in such towns as Cowpens, Fort Mill, Catawba, Liberty Hill, and De Kalb. Though most Americans think that the famed old cattle drives first took place out on the Western frontier, the very first drives actually originated here in South Carolina. According to nineteenth-century historian Frederick Jackson Turner, the drives started at Cowpens and "dated back to Colonial days when animals were driven from the Southern cow pens to markets in Charleston, Philadelphia, and New York." Cowpens was also the scene of a major battle in the Revolutionary War when General Daniel Morgan, who had served with Benedict Arnold in the battle of Saratoga, came down from Virginia with his Rangers and soundly defeated the British, turning the tide of the war in the South.

Today the little towns of the uplands abide in an easy repose. One can sense South Carolina's class tiers by talking with the local home-spun philosophers whose seats of learning are the benches on the town squares. The state of South Carolina has the most impeccable claim of any state to represent the true Old South, and these old courthouse square codgers are erudite about it: "Cane chew see? This hull state is a poach on the garn for them that's Charleston bone." Translation of the above and other Carolinese can be had in Lord Ashley Cooper's (pronounced "Cuppa's") *Dictionary of Charlestonese.*

While Virginia and North Carolina have lost a lot of their Southern drawl, South Carolina has preserved in these out-of-the-way places the true old language of the South. "Can't you see? This whole state is a porch on the garden for those born in Charleston." Language in the South can change from county to county, but some spoken oddities remain constant whether one is in Virginia, South Carolina, Alabama, or Arkansas. The prime example is the transitive verb "fix," the heart and soul of all Southern speech. It's the Southern child's first word; it's his right of passage and safe harbor. "I'm fixin' to do it, grandma . . . just in a minute . . . but I'm fixin' to fall if I'm not careful." The word "fix" as used all over the South comes from the Old French, and nowhere else in the nation is this word used in all the variety of its meanings.

Down South the speech can be confusing. The drawl is supposed to be slow and syrupy, like molasses in wintertime. But Southerners speak as rapidly as anyone else in the nation; they just take a few pregnant pauses, sometimes between syllables. Individual words down here don't sound the same as outside of the South. Listen to the true philologists, the old codgers on the courthouse lawns: Abode? That's a wooden plank. Flow? What you stand on in a house. Hone? What you blow when a car pulls in front of you. Poke? Meat from a hog. Snow? Obnoxious noise your husband makes when he's asleep. Versions? Brides on their wedding nights. Wheel? What Captain Ahab chased all over the oceans. Idiomatic expression in the South is just that little bit more colorful than in any other region of the country.

Sit down with these old-timers and they'll explain how real talk in the South works. They will become your interpreters. They will tell you the story of the cross-eyed lady ("She was born in the middle of the week alookin' both ways for Sunday"). Or about the young couple who'd had a child soon after they were married ("They planted the corn before they built the fence"). Or about the man who couldn't play a fiddle very well ("That's the tune the old cow died on"). Or about the prettiest homily you could hear, concerning the girl who had just arrived at her womanhood ("Melissy is now in the rise of her bloom").

Still and all, there is a haunting quality to gentility in South Carolina. For all the sarcasm leveled at such a thing, a genuine sense of courtesy exists down here, romantically feudal in nature—Sir Walter Scott come to life on the tresses of Eleanor of Aquitaine. Perhaps Harvey Gantt, the man who broke the color barrier at Clemson University in 1963, expresses it best: "If you can't appeal to the morals of a South Carolinian, you can appeal to his manners."

The state capital, Columbia, is an Avalon perched on the edge of South Carolina's Sand Hill region between the Piedmont Plateau and the grandee paradise of the coastal plains. Columbia lies at the confluence of the Broad and Saluda rivers, which meet to form the Congaree. Brothels and slums once thrived there, along with the ramshackle hovels of cracker girls who slaved away in the Saluda factory making cloth for Confederate soldiers. When Sherman visited the city with his army in 1865, he looked down on the center of Columbia and marveled. He saw streets a hundred feet wide lined with magnolias and orange trees and palatial homes crowned with flower gardens full of jasmine, oleander, and solfaterre roses.

Sherman burned it all to the ground. Photographers following Sherman's march recorded the aftermath for the curious. Columbia resembled Dresden after the Allied carpet bombing during WWII. The town was leveled, littered with the bricks and rubble of collapsed buildings. The trees were scorched and stood burning to light the evening sky; the ashes of the flower gardens perfumed the air. Sherman even set loose on the terrified Columbians the inmates of the asylum for the criminally insane. The Civil War had started here in Columbia. The South Carolina legislature had passionately voted for secession in the old wooden state house that was now a pile of ashes. In April of 1861 this city had staged gala balls and let off an unprecedented fireworks display for its gilded citizenry when Fort Sumter had been shelled into submission. In 1865, with the Northern wolf at the door, the Columbians scurried away like frightened rabbits. South Carolina couldn't face up to the mess it had started; not one of its hotheads summoned up the gumption to resist the Yankees or even to try to negotiate the city's surrender.

Despite the wishful claims of its ruling class, no antebellum buildings remain in Columbia, unless you count those made from the brick of the burned and dilapidated structures. During the apocalyptic days of February 1865, some forty Union soldiers stormed into the state senate chamber just before they burned it and organized themselves as a new South Carolina legislative assembly. According to historian Charles Royster in his book *The Destructive War*, these soldiers "voted repeal of the ordinance of secession and passed a resolution of censure against John C. Calhoun." The new Solons then proceeded to trash the chamber, pelting the marble bust of Calhoun with spittoons.

Of all the descendants from the famed "Man at the Center" in the history of the South, the figure of John Caldwell Calhoun stands as the single most imposing proponent of the intolerance inherent in the Savage Ideal. Without doubt, Calhoun was the prototype of Cash's New South coon hunter ruling class, though Calhoun's father had seen to it that his boy was educated at Yale, smack in the middle of the Abolitionist North. When young Calhoun came home he immediately got into politics, joining the brotherhood of the Southern demagogic triumvirate—the good old boy (grandees), the politician (lawyers and judges), and the jerkleg preacher (rabble-rousers). Calhoun's career was so eclectic that he became all three. In politics he did and was everything: he was a member of the U.S. House of Representatives; he was the Secretary of State and of War; he served as Andrew Jackson's Vice President; and he was U.S. senator extraordinaire. He dominated the Senate so powerfully that even Daniel Webster, the universal voice of reason, was no match for his rhetorical excesses.

In spite of themselves, Southern historians have made Calhoun appealing in the same way they have helped to popularize Andrew Jackson, Theodore Roosevelt, Huey Long, and Harry Truman. In the process the demagogue and his laughingstock antics have become almost socially acceptable, especially to those looking for diamonds among the dross. Calhoun's tactics of belligerent obstruction became the pernicious model for all demagogues to come. He led the U.S. Senate into adopting one unworkable compromise after another, which drove the nation to its inevitable conflict between the slave and free states. In South Carolina most people still revere the memory of Calhoun. What they are expressing is perhaps what most Americans feel over the nation's greatest tragedy, when more than 600,000 soldiers died.

The bequest of Calhoun continued to pay dividends, if that is the word, long after the casualty figures from the Civil War had been finalized. In the bitter aftermath of the Civil War, when the brutish Nathan Bedford Forrest founded the invisible empire of the Ku Klux Klan, nowhere in the South was it more virulent than in South Carolina. In that state no white man could be convicted of a Klan-related crime. Such times called forth more than demagogues; they also called forth heroes.

President Grant's second attorney general, Amos T. Akerman, had fought for the South in the Civil War; he fought for civil rights in the South after the war. With a small group of federal marshals Akerman formed what could only be called the first Untouchables in the nation. Akerman, a native of New Hampshire, loved his adopted state of Georgia and despised the Klan and everything it stood for. Though he had to suspend the writ of habeas corpus to get the job done (Lincoln had done the same in the North during the war), his Untouchables secured six hundred convictions of Klan crimes throughout the South. By 1872 the Klan was broken. It stayed broken until, as we have seen, the 1920s, when the neo-Klan rode the popularity of *The Birth of a Nation* into a new era of racial hatred in the South. Akerman served until 1872; with his departure, the obvious happened. It was politics as usual in the South, and the egregious Jim Crow laws were upheld by a federal government in need of Southern votes.

Many of the same old prewar faces showed up in the state legislatures and constitutional offices; some were even returned to Washington as representatives of the New South. The brotherhood seems to live forever (unless they get freakishly shot down, like the Kingfish of Louisiana or the Fighting Little Judge of Alabama). The heritage of John C. Calhoun extended through South Carolinian despots like Ben "Pitchfork" Tillman and the twentieth-century Calhoun clone, Strom Thurmond, whose influence presses on toward the new century and millennium.

In 1856 the Abolitionist senator from Massachusetts, Charles

Sumner, was beaten on the Senate floor and left for dead by Congressman Preston Brooks of South Carolina. Brooks was expelled from the nation's capital but returned home and got himself elected governor by an adoring public. In the Jim Crow era, senator and demagogue sans pareil Ben Tillman had a fistfight on the U.S. Senate floor with a liberal senator who had disagreed with him. Tillman's good friend John William Thurmond (father of Strom) once killed a political opponent in a duel, and Strom himself twice tackled and pinned to the Senate corridor wall a fellow senator who was going to vote against him in committee. They have their own way in South Carolina, despite their strange sense of courtesy, of solving problems.

Politics in South Carolina today seems not a whit different from the old Reconstruction days when the same old crowd of cronies got themselves back up to the public trough. As late as 1992 state politicians proved that the pickings here are almost as good as those in D.C. An FBI sting trapped some seventeen of the state's lawmakers taking bribes. The legislators were all charged with taking backpocket folding money from promoters of greyhound racing. All but one ended up doing time in the federal crossbar hotel. The bagman luring the greedy "ledgers" was a former legislator himself; he publicly assured the people of South Carolina that at least half of the state assembly would have taken the bribes had the FBI not shut down the sting. One of the old town-square codgers had a thought about these corrupt lawmakers: "The do-gooders tell us that we ought to change things by a letter to our congressman. Only problem is, where to send the letter—to the assembly or to the penitentiary."

Columbia likes to think of itself as a beautiful, functional new city of the South. The children of the blue-blood stock mostly leave at the first opportunity. "There's nothing to keep young people here," said several students out at the university. "That is, if you don't have the right family connections. If you're from the old purple-ass crowd, you'll stay because you're vested and crested."

HALF-GROWN pines and scraggly underbrush try to disguise the exhausted, sandy terrain south of Columbia leading into the lowlands toward the coast. For anyone who still wonders what all the hoorah was about back at the time of secession, from here on down to the sea the population used to be upwards of 85 percent black. And that's what the flapdoodle was all about—field hands at $2,000 and more a head, walking capital that totaled into the billions in the Southlands.

About forty-five miles south of Columbia sits the humble little town of Orangeburg. To come here is to realize why the Civil War was fought, for Orangeburg was a market center for slaves and cotton in antebellum South Carolina. As cotton spread across the Deep South, the blacks on the coastal plain's rice plantations were herded into the interior of South Carolina, on into Georgia, and into the Black Belt of Alabama. Here was the genesis of the predominant black population and culture of the South.

Just about a hundred years after the end of the War of Secession, a new civil war broke out here in Orangeburg, a backlash from the racial hatred that had festered ever since Reconstruction. The leader of the whites was state police director J. O. Strom; the leader of the blacks was John Stroman, a young student at South Carolina State College.

On February 8, 1968, hundreds of South Carolina state troopers armed with riot guns muscled up and fired point-blank into an unarmed assembly of students on the college campus in Orangeburg, killing three young men and wounding others. The dead had been shot in the back as they tried to run from the sudden barrage of gunfire. In 1968 the counterculture movement was in full flight on the college campuses of the country, but the students at all-black South Carolina State weren't protesting the war, or burning draft cards or bras. They had been demonstrating a couple of days for the mundane privilege of going bowling at the only bowling alley in town.

Despite the recent civil rights legislation, the owner of the bowling alley had put up a "Whites Only" sign. John Stroman had never entertained ideas of leadership or protest. His passion was for bowling, and he was good at it, good enough to be a pro someday. Because some of Stroman's friends and fellow students at State accompanied him to the nearby bowling alley in an attempt to break the long chain of segregation, a tragic sequence of events unfolded.

According to Jack Bass and Jack Nelson, authors of *The Orangeburg Massacre,* Police Director Strom was known as "Mr. Law and Order" in South Carolina. He was called the J. Edgar Hoover of the

South, and to his credit Strom had sent the grand wizard of the KKK to prison. Here at Orangeburg, Strom overreacted. He massed three hundred state police in a show of heavily armed force to intimidate a bunch of kids. Strom also failed to control his vigilantes, and when one trooper lost his nerve as the students advanced against the police lines, the fusillade that followed knocked down thirty trying to run away.

Chief Strom served under three more governors, polishing his image. John Stroman finished up his degree and wanted to be a teacher but had trouble finding a position in his home area. Author Jack Nelson went on to become a nationally syndicated columnist for the *Los Angeles Times,* despite J. Edgar Hoover's open attempts to get him fired over the book. Strom's state police were never prosecuted for criminal acts; they were put on trial in a civil suit brought on behalf of the victims' families, but those who fired the weapons were exonerated. Frank Beacham, a member of the faculty during the crisis, wrote an award-winning radio play that has been broadcast nationally. In 1993 South Carolina Public Radio declined to air the show, stating as its reason that the play "criticizes state troopers and the former governor."

Each year on February 8, State holds a memorial service for its martyred dead. On that day in 1993 the new bowling alley on campus was pretty busy. It's a popular place and the very act of bowling constitutes a wistful alternative observance. Students came out of the bowling alley carrying their books for the next class. One young woman had a copy of *Gulliver's Travels.*

"I'm the world's worst two-handed bowler," she said, giving up the most delicious laughter you ever heard. "I took bowling because it's required . . . it was either that or field hockey."

FROM Orangeburg to the coast, the lands are known as the Low Country. At some time in the unrecorded past the seas inundated the region and created a fecundity almost unknown anywhere else in the world. The early European settlers inherited these unbelievable riches, and the rice plantations of the seventeenth century yielded fortunes, giving rise to the new class calling itself grandees. From the start, slavery was integral to the profiteering. The English first tried to enslave the Indian tribes, and when these natives rose up in rebellion, the Charlestonians began the importation of black Africans. How cunning and thoroughly ruthless these early grandees were. To fight off the warlike Indians, the grandees armed the blacks, and in turn when the blacks tried to escape into the interior, the grandees hired the Indians to track down the runaways. By the middle of the eighteenth century only the black Africans were left as slaves for the white man. The Indian slave catchers were replaced by bloodhounds. A display ad in the region's newspapers (revealed by Frederick Law Olmsted in *The Cotton Kingdom*) exposed the popular practice:

BLOOD-HOUNDS

**I have two of the Finest Dogs for
Catching Negroes in the Southwest
They can take the trail Twelve Hours
After the Negro Has Passed, and
Catch Him With Ease**

A pack of ten hounds trained for runaways brought the princely sum of $1,500, which was three times the annual income of the average Carolinian yeoman. Using bloodhounds to chase down slaves became so endemic that it evolved into a sport, and after the slaves were freed by Mr. Lincoln, the catchers simply substituted the raccoon for the black man. Here was the origin of the coonhound, and, with it, the sport of coon hunting, which rose to such popularity among the good old boys that today it rivals football, stock car racing, sipping sour mash, and chasing women. Many believe this to be the origin of the racist slur "Coon." But the history of this word is much older. When the first slaves were brought into America, they were penned together in rough stockades called "barracoons." The whites were terrified of the Africans and kept them locked up until some measure of fear could be beaten into them. Here is the origin of the word "coon," not to be confused with "nigger" (the world owes the Dutch for this universal indignity).

As much as it loves coon hunting, fishing, and its mamas, the Southern bubba class loves a good fight. All along the Low Country of South Carolina, right through the lands of the Sunbelt, specially bred and trained dogs and game fowl shed their blood for the entertainment of traditional regional enthusiasms. It's not for nothing that the University of South Carolina mascot is the "Fighting Game-cock," named for the practice that came over to America with the first English settlers. Southern writers have penned some powerful indictments of these blood sports, most notably Harry Crews's *Feast of Snakes*. Pit bull fights and cockfights are illegal, of course, but the bifurcated law doesn't stop them or even slow them down. It's legal to breed the game birds and even to sell them. Driving down country highways, one can see the charming little breeding ranches, each cock with its own miniature A-frame chalet. The cocks themselves are beautiful with splashes of red and white and yellow and black—they're like Paul Klee paintings. The birds would make gorgeous pets, if only people could think of them that way. Quite literally, though, hundreds of thousands of people in the back counties of the Southlands attend the fights. Sometimes the contests become family outings. Designer-built pits with refreshment stands and bleachers accommodate the blood frenzy. Betting is the point and the local cops often get their share of the take.

You'd think the cockfights might be hard to find, but they're not. Ask around in the small towns off the beaten track—at body shops, pool halls, honky-tonks, livestock sale barns—and people will direct you, if you don't look too much like a hardshoe from the state capital, because they're always on the lookout for fresh money and an easy mark. It's not a good idea to go alone, and you really need to know someone on the inside. It's a rough, mixed crowd; you'll find nicely dressed country women right next to road whores. The venue for a fight is usually a spacious old barn or a newly built prefab. There'll be dozens of pickups and late-model cars, little children playing alongside the arena. The guys who run the pits (and many of those who breed the birds) are generally ex-cons; you'll recognize them by the Aryan Brotherhood tattoos they got when they were in the joint. The crowds go crazy when the fighting cocks are faced in the sawdust pits.

"Twenty on the roundhead stag!"

"Ain't enough . . . fifty!"

"That Filipino slasher ain't been to test yet . . . can we get some good money down?"

"That's not a cock, it's a swamp rat!"

"Seventy-five on the Hulsey brood! It'll cut like a sewing machine!"

The fight is always to the death, though some cockers pick up their wounded birds and put the heads in their mouths to suck the blood from their throats, hoping to get them to face and fight again. At times when a cock is mortally wounded, its crestfallen owner will pluck it from the sawdust and bash it against the cinderblocks. The fights last way into the night, and at the end the sawdust and sideboards of the pits are greasy with blood.

As you pull away from the scene, the wild voices of the crowd meld into an eerie music and above it comes the shrill of the cocks crowing at a false dawn. You are hard put to make meaning from any of this freak show. The senses get numbed by such a madness until you are miles away and back in the sane world where there are cafés and people having coffee and talking about grandchildren and potluck dinners and life in the slowest of lanes. And the question keeps pounding in your head—why must they have this savagery in their lives? Could their lives be so meaningless that flecks of blood give them an appetite for living, and does it give them a reason to go to their redneck churches for benediction after a Saturday night bloodletting?

It may be a reflection of savage innocence or a self-hate so dehumanizing that it becomes a kind of exorcism. It may be sexual or psychopathic or a voyeur's way of drinking the enemy's blood or biblical poison. Or it may be akin to picking up serpents like the Holy Ghost people up in the hollers all over the South where they too dearly love their Saturday night bloodlettings. Maybe it's an obsession with ritual contest. It has to be. Pitting honor against chance, with the purpose the game itself, not the result and never the winner. It's the cracked-mirror honor of the South.

THE tides pull through the marshlands and into Charleston, almost into the sea. Charleston, founded in 1670, was to become the once and forever polestar of the grandees. Charleston is tourist-pretty but awfully cluttered. The town is house-proud that its library was established before the one in Boston. Today Charleston's intent seems to be to compete with New Orleans but in a more uptight fashion—no girlie shows, no jazz joints, no pimp fights. Until the end of the Cold War, Charleston owed its economic well-being to its favorite son, the now-deceased congressman Lucius Mendel Rivers. The pork-barrel economy of the city has been swabbed out now like the decks of obsolete battleships.

Inside the D.C. Beltway, old Mendel Rivers was known as "Sweet Finger" because he had it in every pie of our Republic. As the longstanding chairman of the House Armed Services Committee, Rivers caused Charleston to become the most armed-to-the-teeth fortress in the history of man. Before President Clinton's military cutbacks, Charleston had the following: an air force base, a navy base, a Polaris missile maintenance center, a naval shipyard and ballistic missile submarine training station, an army depot, a naval hospital, a naval supply center and weapons station, a marine air station, a marine recruiting depot and training center, a Coast Guard station, a mine-warfare center, and the Sixth Naval District headquarters.

Little chance of a girl going without a date in this town.

As of 1993 the annual payroll of these bases had reached $1,100,000,000—eleven hundred million of Mr. Lincoln's greenbacks. And that's not counting the billions it cost to construct these places. Even Mark Twain would have been staggered by the Gilded Age largesse of a Congress and a country so gulled by one man. Rivers was a congressman for more than thirty years and faced only token opposition whether running for office or holding it. There's no tedious democracy down here; political office is like a satrapy, held for life. Precious few names conjure up the debased image of Al Capp's Jubilation T. Cornpone better than Lucious Mendel Rivers.

Ironically, Charleston will never be remembered as the town that Mendel Rivers built because it's crumbling as we speak. Still it is a beautiful, romantic town and it would be hateful for America to lose it. We'd miss the carriage horses and their plastic diapers that keep the road apples off the cobblestone streets down by the harbor; we'd miss the rickshaw rides hauling folks to and from the elegant old hotels and restaurants where the city's claim to gastronomic delight, Key lime pie, cools the traveler off of an evening.

In a funny way, Charleston is Margaret Mitchell's city, because *Gone With the Wind* was the romantic tragedy of the grandees' fall from grace. Mitchell was a keen student of the Civil War and knew the details of all the battles. She got Rhett Butler's name from the last names of two South Carolina militia colonels, Butler and Rhett, whose troops lined the wharves right here in Charleston. Rhett Butler was Mitchell's fictional truth-sayer, her empiricist who while scooping up his contraband profits with both hands warned the grandees that they couldn't possibly win the war. But in the South no one ever paid any mind to the truth-sayers, for what's truth in the South but a secondhand emotion?

Even if the whole military establishment were to be pulled out of Charleston, the locals need have no fear, for The Citadel is near. Back in the 1840s, way before Sweet Finger, Charleston built its own military college. It's not as fierce looking as VMI up in Virginia. Inside the barracks quadrangle the floor is like a fancy checkerboard of red and white flagstone. The passerby can witness the scene of cadets on punishment tour down on their knees scrubbing the checkerboard with toothbrushes, becoming men. Not much fun goes on in The Citadel, no loafing, no sense of irony.

Novelist Pat Conroy, probably The Citadel's best-known graduate, wrote a scathing characterization of the school in *The Lords of Discipline*. Conroy, whose novels have been unofficially banned in South Carolina, has said that the plebe system here gave cruelty a good name. A president of the school resigned in 1980 over its inhumane policy. He was quoted in *Newsweek* as saying that the place "is locked in pre–Civil War concrete." Things haven't changed at all since then. The current president of the school, a three-star general, knows that the song "Dixie" is offensive to many students; he said as much to the cadet corps in 1992, yet the college won't ban the song or for that matter the waving of the Rebel battle flag at football games. Or, for that matter, its determination to bar the door to any plebe with two X chromosomes. In July 1994, a federal court ordered The Citadel to permit female students to take part in all the military school's activities; thus a further blow was struck against the old Savage in this most Southern of Southern states. (This ruling was still under appeal two years later.)

Depending on individual taste, Charleston's antebellum look is mostly authentic. The city was spared the total destruction suffered by Columbia at Sherman's hands, but as the march to the sea continued, the grandees got crafty and tried to run their valuables out of town. They put together a wagon train loaded with their finest wines and sent it to the nondescript little town of Cheraw, up near the North Carolina state line. The Yankees got there, too; they marched in after burning Columbia and had a field picnic, dinner on the grounds, with hundreds of crates of the grandees' best vintages.

Cheraw's sole claim to fame other than this Yankee bacchanalian guzzle was that it gave to the world the bebop pioneer John Birks Gillespie, the sweetest trumpet this side of the Angel Gabriel. "Dizzy" Gillespie was the youngest of nine kids in an impoverished black family. Not a lot of blacks got lucky in Cheraw, but Dizzy did—he fell in love with the trumpet at the age of eight and used it both as his ticket out and as a weapon against racial discrimination. Dizzy even ran for the Presidency against Lyndon Johnson and Barry Goldwater in 1964, and nobody can say he didn't give the voters a decent choice.

In the 1990s Charleston is proud to be a tranquil city. Compared to its bustling days of military installations, this resort city now has a ghost look, perhaps masking a bit of an old problem in Charleston that won't go away. "Relative deprivation is the shadow of the wolf's tail in Charleston," explains Dr. Michael J. Ohr, a sociologist who was on the faculty at the College of Charleston for several years. "The major problem is the sad juxtaposition of the rich living right next to the poor. This relative deprivation is a problem throughout the South and must be solved if the South is to have a future."

Regrettably, many areas of the South are still predicated on the ancient theme of the white man's world. "The old aristocracy hangs on to the notion that 'coloreds' are children who need to be carefully nurtured and cared for by indulgent parents." Ohr brings out that sociologists have always worked under this cloud of aristocratic racism in the South. "There's worse," he says. "There's a cloud of inequality, a democratic racism where the whites still claim superiority simply because they are white. And Civil Rights legislation has barely made a dent."

SEVEN generations ago an obsession gripped this exquisite city by the sea. In April of 1861 a mammoth fireworks display shook the skies and the land and the water for forty hours, sending a message to the world that America was going to war with itself. From that moment on the study of the Civil War became an industry, a major one, with thousands of studies and books on battles and glorious generals and dreams of what could have been. Be they abolitionist or secessionist or contemporary hobbyist, the industry's customers have all wanted a true piece of the cross.

What gets lost in all this is that the Civil War was a tragic misunderstanding. It is clear that neither side wanted a real shooting war and had no intent of ever really starting one. The idea was absurd. But players on both sides unknowingly collaborated in a freakish series of events that brought on four years of dementia. The chain of misunderstanding had links in Washington, D.C., in Montgomery, Alabama, on the wharf here at Charleston, out at Fort Sumter in the bay, and even on the relief ship bringing food to the starving men manning the fort.

The Confederate Congress couldn't communicate with the U.S. Congress; the South didn't know what to ask for and the North didn't know what to concede. The Confederate politicians didn't know what was being asked of them. The Union politicians didn't want to do anything that would provoke the South, but the Union officers weren't told not to upset the Rebs. The orders and counter orders on both sides were models of obscurity, indecision, and downright abdication of responsibility. Scholars do agree with the substance of these points, the details of which are available in most reputable histories. But the historians treat each point in such isolation that the general American public has never really understood how the war started or what it was all about.

The two military commanders facing off at Fort Sumter were actually both Southerners—for the Confederacy Brigadier General P. G. T. (Pierre Gustave Toutant) Beauregard from Louisiana, and Major Robert Anderson from Kentucky for the Union. Beauregard tried to cajole Anderson into surrendering and Anderson wanted to do so—he just didn't want the onus of giving up without orders. He never got them. What he did get was the promise of reinforcements that never came. What was sent was a food ship that Beauregard's cannons fired on when it entered the harbor. When they missed it, they started firing on the fort itself. The rest is melancholy history.

CHARLESTON is the axis of what has been called the Grand Strand, the built-up strips of land on the Atlantic Coast from North Carolina to Florida. The twin resort cities of Myrtle Beach and Hilton Head bracket a multibillion-dollar international development zone with marinas berthing million-dollar yachts for the neo-grandees where once John Teach (a.k.a. Blackbeard) preyed on coastal shipping. As recently as the 1950s both areas were underdeveloped homes to common folk; Myrtle Beach played host to cracker families in pickup trucks and Hilton Head was a row-crop and fishing community.

For a long time the magnolia tree has been the benign symbol of the antebellum South. The tree is graceful, its orchidlike flower sweet and pristine, though its dead leaves are a rare pain to rake up and mulch. There are perhaps more genuine flowering symbols of the Southlands—forsythia blooms are a sovereign palliative for the blues; honeysuckle is William Faulkner's emblem of Southern maidenhood lost; dogwoods and redbuds are both energetic panoplies of beauty; and the crepe myrtle is a gentle blend of colors and scents that brings a smile to your grandma's face.

It is for the crepe myrtle that Myrtle Beach was named. There are still a few of these flowering bushes and trees along the roads and byways bringing the throngs of revelers, stud puppies, and beach bunnies to the pure white sand. Myrtle Beach is also where the modern-day Southern wit and sage Brother Dave passed from this mortal coil in 1983.

David Milburn Gardner hit the big time in 1957 on Jack Parr's *Tonight* show with his stinging, vitriolic, evangelical voice. A native of Jackson, Tennessee, Brother Dave was born wanting to be a preacher, even went to a Baptist college for a while, but it didn't work out. He found his true pulpit on the stage, with a cigarette in one hand and a big-barrel glass of whiskey in the other. Brother Dave laid them, his beloved hearts, in the aisles with his irony, Swiftian imagery, and shit-kicker jive.

"Let's get rid of the poor folks," Brother Dave would start one of his incantations. "No, man, poor folks is good news. If everybody eliminated the poor, what would success mean? There ain't no such thing as poor folks in the South. And even if they are poor, they're rich in poverty." And with a lament in his voice, Dave intoned, "Poverty is good."

Dave Gardner was spectacularly Southern. He grasped the Southern psyche and gave it voice. But this regional tie left the national market for the slick, button-down humor of Mort Sahl, Shelly Berman, Bob Newhart, and the best of Dave's stepchildren, Lenny Bruce. Brother Dave was just too funny, too close to the Southern bone to stay on the top of the charts. He disappeared into alcoholic obscurity in the late 1960s. "I was *left* when the world was right," Gardner explained. He was trying to make a comeback as a movie actor in 1983 when he died of a massive heart attack here in Myrtle Beach. He was fifty-seven years old.

RIGHT from the beginning of the English settlement of North America there was a pronounced difference in the psychic motivation between the North and the South. Both Plymouth and Jamestown were mercantilist-inspired and operated, though Plymouth was run as a theocracy while Jamestown was conducted as a trading company. Within six decades of the founding of these initial settlements, the North and South were expanded by colonies in Pennsylvania and in South Carolina. William Penn founded his Quaker refuge in the 1680s, and Charleston was established by rice plantation owners in 1670. Thus the split between the worldly South and the theocratic North deepened. Strangely, John Locke had a strong influence on both the North and South, but in completely different ways.

In the South, Locke's empiricism became the acknowledged gospel of commerce; in the North his "corpuscles of matter" became the religious cant of an angry God through the Calvinist dogma of Jonathan Edwards. From these beginnings, empiricism evolved into rugged individualism down South while it developed into transcendentalism up North. It is odd to think of a brotherhood between Ralph Waldo Emerson's sweet reason and John Caldwell Calhoun's Savage Ideal, but both concepts grew from the same root.

The South did experiment with altruism, though, and long before Emerson was preaching serenity from his New England pulpit.

The settlement of Georgia in the 1720s came pretty much as an afterthought. The lands first claimed around Savannah were subject to the laws of Carolina, and the new colony was split off as part noble experiment and part hopeful flank support against the Spanish. The first part was the utopian dream of James Edward Oglethorpe.

A meager lot of philanthropists in England had been appalled at the results of all the previous colonial efforts—religious persecution, butchery of the Indians, peonage, slavery, and the constant quest for profit at any price. Oglethorpe and this small group of visionaries believed in giving the downtrodden in English society a second chance. In essence, they were the forerunners of Spencerian naturalism and the Fabian Society.

Oglethorpe was the leader, and if ever there was one, here was a man with both vision and mission. He was born into a wealthy, influential family much given to biblical duty and compassion. Theophilius and Eleanor Oglethorpe raised their boy James to have Samaritan purpose to his life. In his early career in England he became involved in the reform of debtors' prisons, the abolition of slavery, and the recognition of common-law rights for English sailors long ignored by an admiralty that impressed seamen. And always Oglethorpe was a generous contributor to charities. He was fighting a losing battle in England and he knew it. He sought the New World and a new land to foster his parents' dream.

Georgia has had the bad rap for centuries of being the Convict State. Oglethorpe didn't bring any convicts to America; he brought the victims of debtors' prison, small impoverished farmers, pensionless sailors, and penniless storekeepers. To these he added oppressed Protestant minorities, and the ever-persecuted Jews. Oglethorpe and his small band of altruistic followers were determined to give these poor devils a new opportunity. If ever there was to be a real class of grandees in the South, Oglethorpe and his conscience-stricken patrons should have been the foundation. Yet just twenty years after Oglethorpe's new colony was founded, this noble dream blew away on the winds of avarice and arrogance.

James Oglethorpe was a spare man. He forbade his colonists the strong waters that plagued the Virginia colony. English advertisements and handbills for the Georgia settlement came right out and declared that sickness was "dangerous to those who drank distilled liquors." The attempt at prohibition failed for the very good reason that rum and whiskey were handily available from the rival South Carolina tradesmen licensed by the Crown to deal with the Indians of Georgia. All that was necessary was to walk out of the temperance township of Savannah and belly up to the nearest tepee pub. Modern Savannah still ignores Oglethorpe's mania for temperance by rolling out barrels of its world-class artillery punch at every cotillion.

Oglethorpe also tried a few other idealistic bans. He and his trustees, like Shakespeare's Falstaff, had little use for lawyers and tried to exclude this priestly class from utopia. But in fact, Oglethorpe's intransigence in establishing even a rudimentary legal system exposed the early Georgians to an unlooked-for takeover by corps of lawyers and land speculators swarming in from Charleston. Most unfortunately, Oglethorpe's colony failed in its lofty attempt to outlaw slavery. The hard land and unforgiving climate of up-country Georgia wouldn't support an economy based on European labor, and Oglethorpe couldn't stop his own people from bringing in slaves to work the rice fields in the incredibly rich soil along the Savannah River basin and coastal plains. The grandees over in South Carolina were making fortunes from rice crops on land barely one-tenth as productive as that in Georgia, and there was no way Oglethorpe's gentility of purpose could survive in the face of England's ruthless mercantile mentality.

Oglethorpe's ideal for the Georgia colony crumbled from within and he retreated to his old home place in Godsalming, Surrey, where he lived to the overripe but disappointing age of eighty-nine. His was such a selfless life that he left us no diary or journal, no reflection on the bitter inner turmoil he must surely have felt during the last fifty years of his life. Oglethorpe's enemies and traducers gave him no rest, not even in his eighteenth-century kingdom of heaven, as the following anonymous lines of doggerel in a Savannah newspaper attest:

One hundred two! Methusalem in age,
A vigorous soldier, and a virtuous sage;
He found Georgia, gave it laws and trade;
He saw it flourish, and he saw it fade.

With the passing of the philanthropic charter for Georgia went the dream of utopia. Slavery was firmly ensconced, so much so that by 1860 Georgia had 466,000 blacks in a population of just over a million. Protestantism became the official religious dogma—no Catholics or Jews wanted. The Wesley brothers and George Whitefield began their hard-line proselytizing, the Great American Awakening, right here in Savannah in the 1730s. The Indian tribes were systematically eliminated, culminating in the theft of the Cherokee lands all the way up the Tennessee Valley.

The lawyers so despised by Oglethorpe had a field day. Georgia was ultimately gerrymandered into 159 counties, creating one of the South's fattest patronage systems of county judges, county sheriffs, county prosecutors, county land agents, county tax collectors, and all-around county corruption. Land speculation, the all-consuming sport of the Southern gent, grew to heroic proportions and gave rise to perhaps the most bizarre swindle in American history, the Yazoo Fraud. It rivaled John Sevier's State of Franklin and even John Law's infamous Mississippi Bubble.

Never think for a minute that the good-old-boy network so peculiar to the South is a recent phenomenon. Some of these early enterprising bubbas, esteemed members of the Georgia state legislature, hammered together an act in 1795 that claimed millions of acres of land all the way over to the Mississippi River. This real estate shuck, called "the Georgia Western Reserve," sold the better part of the rich delta lands in and around Vicksburg, Mississippi, to thousands of naïve investors. Then a new group of legislators nullified the law in 1796, leaving the land companies with their cash—more than $500,000—and the investors holding the bag. The scene shifted to the courts, where property rights were deemed to be the absolute center of the U.S. Constitution. Not until 1810 did John Marshall's Supreme Court rule that the original investors had to be compensated; they got pennies on the dollar. Here was the beginning of the conflict between the federal Constitution and states' rights, the precursor to the Civil War.

Somehow not all benevolence in Georgia died with Oglethorpe's dream. There is a spatial congruence of similarity in this state that is uncanny. How could it get so overlooked? Separated by more than 250 years are the personas of James Oglethorpe and James Carter. Both Georgians. One from Godsalming, Surrey, in England, and the other from Plains, Sumter County, Georgia. Both committed to a dream of justice in the face of meanness, hatred, and despair. Both with parents, particularly their mothers, whose visions for their sons went beyond any desire for power and wealth.

Journalists made fun of both Oglethorpe and Carter. Despite the venom from the pens of these erstwhile panegyrists, both men kept their commitments even in seeming defeat. James Oglethorpe was such a private man that we can only sketch out his personality from his works. We know of his pity for the families of the poor condemned to debtors' prisons, often for less than a dollar; we know of his concern for the rights of sailors shanghaied into service and kept in thrall until they died; we know of his charity to the homeless and the hungry, and we know of his utopian dream based on love for man.

Love and respect and children seem to be what the Carter family of Georgia is all about. The Carter Center is committed, says the former President, not only to the immunization of the children of Georgia, the South, and the nation, but to "all the world's children." Carter is an amicable man, one who can spend the time of day pleasantly with anyone. But when he speaks of his mission to prevent the needless death of babies, his voice quietens and becomes steely. "We're going to do it," he vows. If you say no, he gives the idea he'll bite your head off.

Jimmy Carter is involved in multifarious good works—the Carter Center itself is an umbrella for so many agencies and so many causes that they can hardly be counted. Like Oglethorpe before him, Carter has used his good name to round up rich patrons. Carter's dream may seem as hopeless as Oglethorpe's and may end with the same posthumous, satiric doggerel. Unlike Oglethorpe, Carter is an empiricist, one with a strong hold on his born-again corpuscles, and if one can suspend one's cynicism about politicians for a moment, it's entirely possible that Carter carries with him a sense of hurt at his failure in the Oval Office to get his good works into law and into the fabric of American life. If that's the case, the man has something to prove, and beware a Southerner with something to prove.

THE Great Philadelphia Wagon Road ends at the Savannah River just across from the town of Augusta, Georgia. The raison d'être for the city is its annual Masters Golf Tournament, played at the Augusta National Country Club. Once upon a time the site was an orchard. In 1857 Baron Prosper Jules Alphonse Berckmans came all the way from Belgium to establish the first nursery in all the South in Augusta. His 1861 catalog listed thirteen hundred varieties of pears, eight hundred of apples, three hundred different grapes, and a hundred each for azaleas and camellias. Sherman came through there on his march, and he must have been partial to fruit trees because his men didn't chop down a single one. It was left to golf's sainted Bobby Jones to lay waste to the baron's work.

The city of Augusta has a true native son that it doesn't make much about today, though in the 1930s and 1940s his works were considered to be at the forefront of American literature. That native son was Erskine Preston Caldwell, author of *God's Little Acre* and *Tobacco Road* among other works, many of them banned in Augusta, throughout Georgia, the South, and other parts of the nation. Caldwell's real tobacco road begins right here around the Augusta airport at the end of the Bobby Jones Expressway.

It's just across town from the country club, where some of the world's richest athletes compete, not for money but for the right to wear a green coat. But the south side of Augusta is a face of Georgia and the South that no one wants to be seen. It is a visage of abject poverty and despair. Abandoned cinder-block houses, beat-up cars, and boarded-up 1950s motor courts serve as a refuge for the poor whites of today's tobacco road. Young cracker girls right out of one of Caldwell's novels wash their tattered clothes in throwaway plastic buckets with the water from a drain pipe. Wearing ragged blankets sewn up to be coats, young kids play in the littered, grassless vacant lots next to slaggy, murky drainage ditches that stink of chemicals. There's lots of industry here—a newsprint pulp mill, the city's sewage treatment plant, a chemical factory, and support services for the airport—but few jobs for the people living here on today's tobacco road in much the same despair as Caldwell's all-too-real characters sixty years before.

Erskine Caldwell was born in 1903 in nearby White Oak, Georgia, the only child of Ira Sylvester and Caroline Bell Caldwell. His father had been a soldier in the Spanish-American War and had come home from Cuba to be a Presbyterian preacher. His father also came back with a mind full of liberal and social ideals. Clearly, Caldwell's father was the most profound influence on this major American writer's life. Moving from one poor little congregation to another all over Georgia and Tennessee, Ira Caldwell got the reputation as a champion for the causes of the poor. Indeed, the living conditions for a journeyman preacher and his family weren't much better than those of the crackers who lived down the tobacco roads of the rural South. Ira took young Erskine with him wherever he went and let his son witness firsthand the plight of the poor.

"My father knew the land and the people better than I ever did," Caldwell reflected in his later years. "He was always going out there, down those tobacco roads, taking people old clothes and food. He knew them all."

The elder Caldwell never attempted to force religion on his son. He did expose young Erskine to a variety of sects, taking him to brush arbor revivals (usually in groves used as makeshift shelters from the hot sun), Catholic masses, and Jewish synagogues, even to see "the holy rollers and footwashers."

"After I had seen it all, I decided I didn't want any of it. My father gave me permission to leave the religious community. He was a kind and tolerant man."

It was this background of gentle care and understanding, tempered by the harsh reality of the desperation poor whites and blacks were enduring during the Depression, that gave Caldwell his unique Southern voice. This blend of the bright and dark sides of the South in his personal life led to an abiding, universal vision in Caldwell's writing. During his early career he became one of the world's most popular writers, and yet he was accused of producing vile and pornographic works. Along with Henry Miller, D. H. Lawrence, and James Joyce, Caldwell managed to get himself on every banned list in America and Europe. It is exasperating that the man never fit the image—and he never once defended himself.

With the publication of *Tobacco Road* in 1932, Caldwell's remarkable career was launched. At first the novel seemed doomed to obscurity; it received hardly any reviews and failed to earn back Caldwell's modest advance. In the coming decade his talent and success would soar: he would write some of the best-selling novels of all time, lecture at the New School for Social Research, take a delightfully disastrous tour of duty in Hollywood, have a record-shattering play on Broadway, collaborate with famed photographer-wife Margaret Bourke-White on perhaps the finest documentaries ever published on American life, and as a war correspondent would cover almost single-handedly Hitler's invasion of the Soviet Union.

Erskine Caldwell wrote in a style of journalistic realism and described a raw, earthy South. He had no style other than honesty. If Caldwell didn't find favor with the critics and scholars, he did find it with his peers. Perhaps the greatest testimonial to his achievements was given by William Faulkner, who gave posterity his personal list of the five greatest American novelists in the following order: Thomas Wolfe, Faulkner himself, John Dos Passos, Erskine Caldwell, and Ernest Hemingway. Good company in any order and a list that stands the test of time, though Caldwell himself expressed no interest in rank or rivalry and if anything was embarrassed by Faulkner's praise.

One of Caldwell's finest works was his tour de force of the South, *You Have Seen Their Faces.* It's a book that never received much attention. Caldwell wrote the text and Bourke-White took the pictures. They traveled all over the South in the 1930s recording the poverty, the bittersweet joy and pain that had gripped the mangled Southland from the time of Reconstruction to the wasting of the Great Depression.

Caldwell explained his ability to portray accurately the poor Southerner by saying, "Well, you see, I'm one of them. I was just as poor as anybody, my family was. My father was not a moneymaking man. The sharecroppers didn't have much cash to put in the collection plate, a nickel or a dime maybe, but they didn't have the dollar bills. If it wasn't for the poundings—where the poor cracker folk brought the preacher a pound of this and a pound of that—we wouldn't have had enough black-eyed peas to go around."

He wrote *Tobacco Road* oddly not in the South but up in Maine. He met a lot of French-Canadians up there working in textile mills and living in squalid shacks. "It was a terrible place for any human beings to have to live in. The mostly two-story tenements were divided up like rabbit coops. There were constant fires and folks were getting burned up, children and all. I thought there was a better life in the United States, but I wasn't able to find it.

"I couldn't write about the conditions and people up there," he said. "But it helped me understand more about the South and what was going on down there. It was almost as if Maine gave me the push to write about Georgia."

Scribners editor Max Perkins published *Tobacco Road.* He told Caldwell the novel might be controversial and that most of his other editors had misgivings about it. "But we're going to publish the book and we're not going to change a word of it," Perkins told him. The novel became a classic, was adapted into a Broadway play, and gave Caldwell his entrée into Hollywood, an exercise in existential disaster and futility, by Caldwell's own admission.

Darryl Zanuck produced the movie of *Tobacco Road*. The director was John Ford and Nunnally Johnson wrote the screenplay. The cast was a good one, with Ward Bond and the all-time screen lovely, Gene Tierney. "The trouble was, even with these good people, Zanuck had to stick his nose into the business," Caldwell said with a shrug. "What he did was, he took over. He didn't like the ending in the play, he didn't like the ending in the book. I guess he didn't like anything. He had them shoot a new ending. Rather than having the cast walking down the road on their way to the poor house, Zanuck had a banker drive up in a big car, take a wad of money out of his wallet and tell the folks to take the money and go get themselves a good meal."

What the intellectual world—the critics, scholars, biographers, publishers, and editors—have never discovered is that Erskine Caldwell was a literary innocent. He didn't read books, cared nothing for literary movements or genres, and never developed a plot in his life. Caldwell was a perfectly intuitive writer and as such laid himself open to all the misunderstandings that his works have long suffered. He was a kind man and never a vulgar-spoken one, a true Southern man, and a product of his father's tolerance.

"If you're going to write a story and it's going to be true to life, you have to put the life of the people in it as life really is, no matter what. I guess that's why I ran into so much censorship trouble—because I was writing about what the people I had created would say and do. Not that I wanted them to, or approved of it, but that's the way it was. Not all in life is good."

Erskine Caldwell was an intensely private person throughout his life and career. He never thought of seeking out the spotlight, and perhaps this characteristic as much as anything contributed to the controversies surrounding his major works. But if you were to know the man a little, be able to speak with him in the comfort of his home and family, you couldn't help but carry away with you a sense of his indelibility, as is shown in a story he told about his father:

"My father was very much interested in what I was doing, in my writing. When *Tobacco Road* was touring, the play came to Augusta once. What he did, he bought up a block of tickets and hired a school bus driver and he went up and down one of these tobacco roads and invited anybody who wanted to go see the play to climb aboard. So he had a whole school bus full of crackers, took them in to see the play in downtown Augusta. And he said they hooped and hollered at every scene, yelling out, 'That's me right there! There you are, Clyde, that's you! There's every damn one of us!' "*

*The preceding pages are based on personal interviews and correspondences with Erskine Caldwell over a period of years. He died in 1987.

CHAPTER 5

"Just an Old Sweet Song"

Atlanta . . . Henry Grady . . . The Cathedral of the Holy Spirit . . .
W. E. B. Du Bois . . . Macon and Southern Rock 'n' Roll . . . Andersonville

Belief in mythology is still so thick in the South that it can be cut with a chain saw. Up at Stone Mountain a few miles north of Atlanta, the features of Robert E. Lee, Thomas Jackson, and Jefferson Davis are carved into the rock on this minor Civil War battlefield. It's all a passing strange memorial. The battle at Stone Mountain was just one in a series of encounters between Sherman's and Joe Johnston's armies in the encirclement of Atlanta. Robert E. Lee never saw Stone Mountain; Stonewall was dead before the set-to; and Jeff Davis was a figure of ridicule in the whole state of Georgia. But perhaps it's not so strange at all that the countenances of these three Southern demigods were carved into the basalt of Stone Mountain, considering that myth has always been at the cornerstone of the South's belief in itself. In the case of Stone Mountain, the myth went national; Calvin Coolidge authorized the minting of a Robert E. Lee half dollar to fund the great outdoor sculpture.

Before the Civil War, religion in the South, a faith as close as this region ever came to philosophy, taught that a just God would defend a just and righteous cause. The political rhetoric throughout the war depended on just such an ethereal commitment. The people believed it, the troops believed it, the generals and the politicians believed it. Even before Stone Mountain, Joe Johnston and most of his generals literally got the call to the cross. Historian Thomas L. Connelly reported in his *God and General Longstreet* that Episcopal bishop Leonidas Polk baptized almost everyone in the upper military echelon of the South. The Confederate generals rounded up their troops and had many thousands baptized in rivers and creeks. "In Virginia," wrote Connelly, "whole brigades stood barefoot in several inches of snow to hear chaplains warn that the military reverses prove that Jehovah was angry with the Confederacy." Southern war nurse Kate Cumming wrote in her diary: "Our sins must have been great to have deserved such punishment." Connelly summed up the Southern attitude: to Southerners, the belief in the superiority of their military prowess and faith in Divine Providence were inseparable.

The Confederacy had managed to withstand the early defeat at New Orleans, the blockade of her other seaports, and the loss of the Mississippi River. Her faith in the great Cause was undiminished. But with the fall of Atlanta, the faith began to unravel as the Cause crumbled. After Appomattox the defeated South sued for penance with its angry Old Testament God. Just as in the Greek mythologies when the noble hero fell from grace because of his false pride, so was the South cast into the pits of malebolge, the evil, ordure-filled confines of Dante's Hell. The South's faith had been lacking, its hubris too heavy for its soul.

The fall of Atlanta was not just a mortal blow to the military cause of the Confederacy—it was the war's climax, the thrust to the heart of all the Southlands. Appomattox was nothing more than a denouement. Margaret Mitchell was clever enough to set *Gone With the Wind* not in Charleston or Richmond or Montgomery but in Atlanta, the spiritual capital of the defeated South. After innumerable defeats, the South had forged Atlanta into its citadel, the final bastion of defense against the encroaching Yankee armies. When Sherman burned Atlanta, he set fire to the South's soul, an auto-da-fé of the South's own choosing. The mere fact that the interior of the South could be penetrated and suffer immolation raised the town of Atlanta to a level of Southern martyrdom in keeping with the military religious revival that had begun in the spring of 1864.

· · ·

ATLANTA has fed off its martyrdom ever since Sherman burned it down in 1864. The city had been founded almost incidentally as the westernmost terminus of a railroad in 1837. As it happened, the location of the town was geographically suited to the needs of the mid-nineteenth-century South in general (the same sort of coincidental good fortune would fall to Atlanta again in the mid-twentieth century). At about the time the town was founded, a gold rush in the hills and valleys to the north erupted, bringing in thousands of fortune seekers and making Atlanta something of a boomtown. The hunt for gold added emphasis to the need for a railroad supply center and rapid transport for the U.S. Army. The troops were needed because the gold had been found on ancestral Cherokee lands, and the tribe was peeved over the influx of all those crackers carrying picks and shovels.

Atlanta never really had any ties to the old grandee South; it's been cracker all the way. It was a classic frontier town featuring lean-to flophouses, grub under the tents, barrelhead saloons, and bordellos set up in boxcars, livery stables, and in the back rooms of gambling halls. Those lucky few finding gold up in the hills would come back to Atlanta to exchange their yaller dust for supplies, whiskey, and the one- and two-dollar wooden tokens called "screw pieces," universally accepted as bona fide currency by Atlanta's working girls.

By 1860 Atlanta had a population of ten thousand, and it had not only carved out a reputation as a thrust-and-go town but had begun to assemble the wispy, cloudlike pretensions of Southern pomp and gentility. The Civil War added to the luster of Atlanta in two ways. First, the Southern armies fighting up in Tennessee were so incompetent that Atlanta had to become the last resort for the defense of the South's interior; second, with Sherman's easy victory, Atlanta had to be cast as the martyred capital of the South.

The emotive scenes in *Gone With the Wind* depicting the burning of the city aren't quite true. The movie's scene of the gallant wounded Rebel soldiers laid out in the railroad marshaling yard is one of the landmark achievements in cinematography, but it just didn't happen that way. There was no real combat around Atlanta for the simple reason that the Confederate armies were in headlong retreat (John Bell Hood, the newly baptized defender of Atlanta, had already scudded off to Alabama). Atlanta burned, but as the result of explod-

ing shells, not by Sherman's men torching the buildings. Had the
City Fathers surrendered, there would have been no wasteful fire.
Still, the fire turned out to be something of a godsend because it
eliminated all the dilapidated, first-generation tinderboxes left over
from the gold rush days. By 1900 Atlanta had rebuilt itself into a metropolitan showcase boasting a population of a million people. The
martyred city had transcended the rhetoric of myth to become a
sprawling reality (never mind that at least half the population consisted of black refugees, ghettoized in one of the worst slums in the
country).

This regenerated symbol of the city belonged to one man and his
vision. A statue of him graces the very heart of downtown Atlanta at
the corner of Forsythe and Marietta Streets. His name is Henry
Woodfin Grady. He is cast in bronze and stands a forlorn watch over
a dream that never was, the emblem for the riddles of Cash's cloud-
cuckoo-land. Grady was the post-Reconstruction voice of the South
whose rhetoric told his countrymen how to save their homeland
with an unlikely combination of Jeffersonian farmsteads and Yankee
industrialization.

In 1886 Grady made a speech to the liberals of New York and New
England that set them on fire. A boy-wonder orator turned crusading editor of the *Atlanta Constitution,* Grady proclaimed that his New
South had set aside racial hatred as well as its bitter quarrel with the
North, and that the only ingredient lacking to bring the South into
the Gilded Age was Yankee investment in factories (to be built right
next to abundant Southern fields of cotton, corn, and tobacco).

"A hundred farms for every plantation, fifty homes for every
palace, and a diversified industry that meets the need of this complex age." With these words Grady described his hope. He had a
dream, all right, but one where the facts didn't fit the puzzle. Overt
democratic racism and patrician rogues running the state capitals
blocked any real chance for changing the traditional culture of the
South. In spite of this Grady's rhetoric was turned into a tortured reality. Atlanta grew but not on the back of agrarian reform financed
by benign industrialization; it grew on the backs of the poor. Without knowing it, Grady was ushering in the cruel Sunbelt myth of a
Southern economic renaissance. He died in 1889, still a young man
and unaware of the darker side to his dreams.

Atlanta today has sculpted for itself a new image, even though it's nothing more than a warmed-up bit of Henry Grady rhetoric. "Atlanta, the city too busy to hate." That's kind of like saying, "Zeus, the god too mighty to lust." If the wayward traveler is searching for brotherly love, he's not likely to find it here any more than he could latch onto it in Philadelphia. Hotlanta still has its share of hate, and whole industries here are devoted to lust.

Of an evening at quittin' time, thousands of Y.E.S. men (Young Executive Studs) emerge from their *Fortune* 500 hives and crowd into watering holes stretching from downtown out Peachtree to Lennox Square, where singles' bars like Cheaters and Rupert's are bedecked with money, state-of-the-art cocktails, airline stewardesses, college sweethearts, and working girls. The joints are jumping wall-to-wall with people in heat.

You can talk all you want about the major centers of the South—cooled-off Dallas, nasty New Orleans, strangely hip Memphis, staid-Baptist Nashville, or cocaine-colada Miami—but Atlanta is the pulse of the South. It's a city of indeterminate age. It's an international city and gets more flights from Europe than anywhere else in America. Bond daddies jet down from the Big Apple just to hang out at the Gold Club, a rigidly bright, Bauhaus steel-and-glass-and-mirrored teatbar, the fanciest in the world, and that includes the Crazy Horse in Paris. The talent inside the Gold Club is beyond the ken of mortal man. Before 5:00 P.M. entry is free; it costs five bucks after that, and no screw pieces allowed. It's as if the old gold rush days have come back to life, beating out the pulse of the new city: money, money, money. It's table dancing in the honest-to-God buff; the unabashed pubic hair is coiffured in all manner of snatch-patch do's, Mohawk and isosceles and shaved and high hirsute.

The overwhelming imagery here is of corporate eyes, steady and thin gazes like diaphanous shields camouflaging emotions the same as in the boardrooms. Around town the execs are known as Hardshoes, and they're all college men versed in the liturgic ways of the Greek fraternities. In keeping with the tradition of Southern myth and metaphysics, the Hardshoe behavior these new Greek temples have taken on has the quality of ritual much like the rites described by Carl Carmer in *Stars Fell on Alabama:*

"Young men march in carrying flaming brands. At the end of the procession four acolytes attend a long cake of ice . . . the leader lifts a glass cup of water and begins a toast: 'To woman, lovely woman of the Southland, as pure and chaste as this sparkling water, as cold as this gleaming ice, we lift this cup, and we pledge our hearts and our lives to the protection of her virtue and chastity.' "

There's no softness at the Gold Club. It's a safe house. The Hardshoes count coups with the stewardesses, kindergarten teachers, and working girls. They're all looking for performance, for glory, for the fuck of the century. And it's all to the beat of the ten million a year the club pays in tax revenues. The rule in the club is simple: No Touch, No Feel, Voyeurs Only Need Apply. In all of Atlanta, it's only in these glorified B-joints that the laying-on of hands is forbidden. The Hardshoes are not the only group in Hotlanta given over to horny ritual.

The charismatic hard-shells have a better claim than the Hardshoes to hands-on experience. The word has been out in the South for some time that Atlanta is the home of spiritual healing, where the "laying-on of hands" is the prime medium for the cure. Today's trendy evangelists have hidden themselves behind the mask of "charismatic ministry," but it's the same old dodge of discredited faith healing. The Swaggarts of Louisiana, Robertses of Oklahoma, Tiltons of Texas, and Bakkers of North Carolina. To this list must be added the Paulks of Georgia, whose Atlanta-based "Cathedral of the Holy Spirit" once claimed 12,000 tithing members in Fulton County alone. Former President George Bush once joyously proclaimed Bishop Earl Paulk's church to be "a shining example of the thousand points of light."

But the night the lights went out in Georgia for Bishop Paulk was when he was disgraced before his congregation. Through the miracle of TV his humbling reached millions. Sadly, a number of the female members of the cathedral charged that the Paulk clan (Bishop Earle, his brother, Reverend Don, and their two apprentice-apostle nephews) laid on more than just their hands after the curtain had closed on the services. The allegations charged the four Paulk preachers with pressing the women into having sex by telling them they'd be serving God. The Paulks have denied the charges. What the disgraced church ladies and their supporters desired was to get a law on the books to punish the clergy for coercing sex with the women of their congregations. The spirit of this law would go much further; it would put under public scrutiny the operations of the charitable corporations calling themselves churches and perhaps even add a modicum of control to the intent of charity. At this writing, this revolutionary notion is still under judicial review, and according to a young lawyer in the Fulton County courthouse, the chance of such a law being passed is about as good as the Cherokees' getting their Georgia land back.

In downtown Atlanta it's hard to find what Mark Twain would have called a Hannibal layabout; few courthouse loungers and even fewer cracker-barrel philosophers hang out in this busy city. What few talkers you find are friendly and willing to pass the time of day with strangers, whether they're just off the turnip truck or a 747 from Tokyo. Plenty of up-market hotels punctuate the city center, but if you're lost and looking for help, you won't get it here. The concierges preening in their swallowtail coats and thunder-and-lightning pants are too busy fawning over their monied guests. The man who comes to the rescue is the fabulously uniformed doorman sporting more gold braid than a French admiral. He was born in Macon, he tells you, but has worked the hotels in Atlanta from puberty. He was here in the days of Eugene Talmadge, Richard Russell, and Lester Maddox. He knew Dr. King and has attended the same church as Coretta King.

The doorman just smiles gravely when asked about the days of the marches, the Freedom Riders, and the women who dared to sit in the front seats of buses. He's the most important man at the hotel, really; he gets you in, he gets you out, and he gets you where you've a mind to go, no small feat in Atlanta. Five-dollar tips from the Hard-shoes are buying his retirement home back in Macon. The South was imbued with a primordial sense of belonging once upon a time, and this man is going back to his birthright when he's able.

Atlanta is a churchgoing town. What did the doorman think of the heavy-duty preachifying hereabouts? He laughed. His voice was rich and deep, coming from somewhere down around his heels. He made you feel like part of the real South, as if he was saying, "I know but I won't tell you until you're deep into my family."

What he did say was funny. "My daddy always said, 'Show me four Bab-tists and I'll show you a fifth.' "

Is Atlanta still part of the South? "Well, wherever you go, there you are."

The doorman's voice dignified the bustling aura of Atlanta and his words stayed with you like a Parthian shot. Wherever you go, there you are. Is this existential or fatalistic? Hard to tell in Atlanta, or for that matter anywhere else in the South.

Walking around, seeing and not seeing the huge metroplex supporting millions of people, hundreds of *Fortune* 500 giants and thousands of lesser enterprises, the querulous strains of Emmylou Harris's song "O Atlanta" come to mind and you ask of no one in particular, Where is the real Atlanta? Is it so new that it is resting with the buried zeitgeist of the old Confederacy? Maybe if you once liked the town, you've got the wrong question. It's not Where Atlanta? but Why?

Atlanta's meteoric rise as the capital of the New South began in 1948 amidst the Dixiecrat rebellion. While the South as a whole was busy reviving its Savage Ideal and racial hatreds, Georgia's moderates quietly repealed the ancient shackle of the poll tax first passed in seventeenth-century Jamestown. Abolishing the poll tax voluntarily was a momentous decision in Atlanta; it put the city twenty years ahead of the rest of the South. And despite the lunatic ravings of the Lester Maddoxes, the simple enfranchisement of the black voters created an atmosphere of toleration that Yankee investors could live with. Suddenly all Southern roads started leading to Atlanta. Growth came to the city, steady economic progress built upon moderate politics and abundant cheap labor.

Then serendipity once again blessed the city, and this time in the unlikely guise of a national airline strike. The sleepy regional airport at Atlanta housed the meager headquarters of Southern Airways, the only airline not to take part in the strike of 1966 that crippled air travel in America. If you wanted to fly anywhere in the States that year, you had to take Southern and you had to land in Atlanta. As the flights of the big airlines were canceled and connections became nearly impossible, *Fortune* 500 execs were stacked into Atlanta's hotels. The strike went on for six months and Southern was the only airline operating. Sooner or later just about every executive in America found himself in Atlanta. They began to look at the city and found a veritable glory hole of tax holidays, free utilities, cheap building sites, and unending waves of folks wanting jobs. The execs began making contingency plans for their businesses; here was a great untapped resource that could guarantee the delivery of their goods. Southern Airways made millions off the strike, changed its name to Delta, and stayed in Atlanta. The small regional airport became massive, rivaling JFK and O'Hare. The *Fortune* 500s came in droves, 475 of the top 500 to pan the creeks of this old gold rush town, and they have made Atlanta the hub of a distribution network heretofore unknown in the world.

ATLANTA's good fortunes were not all serendipitous. To understand what happened here between the epochs of Henry Grady and Lester Maddox, it's necessary to answer the question "How?" Far more than Henry Grady's or Martin Luther King's, Atlanta was W. E. B. Du Bois's town. The young Massachusetts-born black man never saw the South until he entered Nashville's famous Fisk University in 1885.

During the summers while he was getting his degree at Fisk, Du Bois was a volunteer teacher in the small, rural black schools of Tennessee where he began to understand why Negroes of the South lived their lives so fatalistically in their own homeland. Though he didn't know it at the time, Du Bois was becoming part of the culture of the South. After getting his doctorate at Harvard, Du Bois would have been welcomed in any academic circle, but he chose to return to the South and to Atlanta University where he was to teach, off and on, through several decades. He found his clear voice of reason during his early years in Atlanta, a voice that the outside world would term radical. With the publication of his master work, *The Souls of Black Folk,* he rallied black activists against Booker T. Washington's accommodation to the whites. Du Bois was always a fighter, not a conciliator or apologist. In 1910 he went to New York to edit *The Crisis* and became the voice of the National Association for the Advancement of Colored People for the next quarter century.

Du Bois returned to Atlanta University in 1934 after becoming deeply disillusioned with the intellectual games being played by the NAACP in New York. He knew that the NAACP had lost touch with what was really going on in the real battleground of the South. Henry Grady's dream had turned into a nightmare. Lynchings were on the rise, the KKK had grown into a multiheaded hydra feeding on the despair of blacks. Intolerance, the old Savage Ideal, had returned with a renewed ardor for blood. Henry Grady's vaunted industrialization had become nothing more than a front to promote white supremacy. The trade unions in Atlanta and other industrial cities of the South had become closed shops denying membership to all skilled black artisans. This perversion was an unforeseen corruption of Grady's pitch to bring Yankee money into the South. The North was investing heavily down here and now was colluding with the Old Order to institutionalize racial hatred. The barbarism Du Bois had known when he first came to the South had changed very little, and he had every reason to be a bitter man. Yet he had grown to love the South. He saw it oddly as the salvation of the black race. He opened his heart when he declared: "The future of the American Negroes is in the South. . . . here is the magnificent climate, here is the fruitful earth under the beauty of the Southern sun; and here is the need of the thinker, the worker, and the dreamer."

In essence William Du Bois was trapped by his love for the South and his dream of simple freedom for blacks. The reality of the age, the Great Depression, would not allow simple answers, and men like Du Bois and Norman Thomas and Eugene Debs were forced almost by default to sign up with the vision of Marxism. By doing so, the thinkers and dreamers became marked and hounded men. They were cast into the pits of J. Edgar Hoover's hell. Hoover hounded Du Bois through the forties and fifties, and even dragged him into court in the 1960s on a vague charge of "practicing Communism." Du Bois was quickly acquitted with apologies from a federal judge. Du Bois found his own separate peace. He resigned his U.S. citizenship, accepted the invitation of the emergent African leader Kwame Nkrumah, and retired to Ghana in 1963.

The world has long believed that W. E. B. Du Bois was an embittered, disillusioned man, but such a perspective ignores the facts. He might have been angry, but he was far from shattered. He left a legacy to Atlanta and the South that would end not so much in victory but with common decency. Du Bois passed the baton of hope to Martin Luther King, Jr., and on the foundation of Du Bois's work King succeeded, though it would require his own martyrdom to do so. Atlanta could have gone the way of Columbia or Orangeburg or even become the Johannesburg of the American South, its citizens defending the parapets of white supremacy to the bitter end. It didn't. There are certainly some severe problems in Atlanta, many of which stem from racism, but to its credit Atlanta spared itself the racial strife that would beset other Southern cities.

Du Bois had been humiliated, abandoned, and mostly forgotten by America. He turned to writing novels as the only way to express his real feelings for the South. Before these fictional works, Du Bois had written what he came to call "The Sorrow Songs." It's difficult to tell whether they are song or poetry, but it's easy to see the influence they had on the deep blues. In his songs, like "The Smoke King," one can hear the melodic, minor-key blue note. William James, George Santayana, and Josiah Royce could only look down from the stars and feel good about their former pupil at Harvard.

ONLY a few people are left in the world who can claim to have known William Edward Burghardt Du Bois: a few old-time civil rights comrades, torch bearers now aging into obscurity, those who loved him and those who ostracized him. Fewer still can recall his last months of exile in Ghana. In his ninety-fifth year, Du Bois was said to have loved the pleasant days of his life there. The people of Ghana admired him and what he stood for. When Du Bois arrived in 1963, Ghana had just achieved its own independence and he found more than just a heady sense of freedom. Something was going on.

A native of Ghana now living in the United States was well acquainted with Du Bois during his last days. Alex Darkwah, now a resident professor of English at Arkansas Tech University, speaks of Du Bois with reverence but sheds some new light on this enigmatic figure.

"In those days things were very good in Ghana," Darkwah recalls. "Our colonial masters, the British, had left money in the World Bank for Ghana's development. The money was substantial, many millions. President Nkrumah was gathering African leaders and world leaders into Accra to begin a movement that could have united all of Africa."

Even at his advanced age, Du Bois was very much a part of Nkrumah's plan for Africa. Darkwah was a teenager at the time and recounts an event that took place in the capital. It was Independence Day and the whole country was in celebration.

"There was a parade and big festival and a state banquet for dignitaries from all over the world. Ralph Bunche of the United Nations was there. So were Richard Nixon and Dr. Martin Luther King, representing the United States. But it was Du Bois who was the most honored man of the proceedings.

"Nkrumah pledged a great deal of money to America and to Dr. King," Darkwah says. "No one knew for sure the exact sum, but it was in the millions. In essence, Kwame Nkrumah was helping to finance the American civil rights movement."

No doubt it was Nkrumah's faith in Du Bois that assured this vital support for King. Du Bois had more or less discovered the brilliant young Atlanta preacher and had made sure he would be in Ghana for the celebration. Even in his dotage and while in self-imposed exile, Du Bois still carried a lot of weight.

In 1963 Dr. King delivered his famous "I Have a Dream" oration in front of hundreds of thousands in Washington and hundreds of millions on TV and radio around the world. On the night before in Accra, W. E. B. Du Bois passed away. King prefaced his speech with the announcement that the greatest civil rights leader in American history had died thousands of miles away from home. What had started way back in 1885 at Fisk College with a black educator's dream had found its strongest and most eloquent voice in this young disciple from Atlanta.

Alex Darkwah, an educator himself, remembers Du Bois as "a giant of a man, strong but gentle and with a kind word for everyone. He especially liked walking the wide boulevards of Accra and stopping to talk to the people or playing with the troops of children who followed after him."

Official photographs of Du Bois make him look to be a distant and troubled man. Darkwah discounts this notion. "The old gentleman was warm, whether being honored at state dinners, receiving the tributes of foreign dignitaries, or gently talking with youngsters. . . . in Ghana we couldn't understand how he could be treated so rudely by his own countrymen. . . . he was a lion of a man, standing upright, with a nimbus of gray in his hair and his distinguished goatee. I'm unsure what the Deity may look like, but Du Bois surely resembled an ancient god."

ATLANTA has plenty of room for monuments. There's one to Henry Grady and more than a few to Martin Luther King. And there are others: Lennox Square (the nation's first successful shopping mall), the John Knox Presbyterian Church, the Peachtree Summit building, the Alliance Theatre, the symphony hall and art museum. All stand as monuments to the architectural genius of Joseph Amisano, whose work in the 1950s and 1960s changed the face of Atlanta. Strange to say, for the baseball town that Atlanta has become, there are no monuments to Georgia's most famous son, Ty Cobb (this omission may be all to the good, given Cobb's xenophobia—he was a KKKer and used to brag about having killed his "nigger"). Even stranger, Atlanta has no proper monument to Henry Aaron, old Number 44, who achieved the unthinkable by hitting more home runs than Babe Ruth. If Hank Aaron had been white, say all baseball purists, Fulton County Stadium would have been renamed Aaron Field.

Baseball may be the pastime in Georgia, but politics is the sport. The state has had ten constitutions since 1777, all of them no doubt designed to ensure the future of its citizens. Yet one obscure law, the Neill Primary Act of 1876, controls the state. The Neill Act in effect chooses all the candidates for Georgia's state and federal constitutional offices, but what it actually has done for more than a century is to entrench a good-old-boy county cabal that has put the whole state of Georgia in a stranglehold. The popular vote is ignored through the simple medium of an arcane electoral college set up on a county-vote quota basis. The big counties get six votes each; the little counties get two votes. Any three of the little counties can negate all the votes in Fulton County. Atlanta and Fulton County have been forced by the Neill Act to become a state within a state, with Atlanta's mayor elevated to the status of a governor and Fulton County's elected officials as staff. Atlanta mostly ignores the state, and the rest of Georgia does its best to pay Atlanta no mind. Even though the Neill Act was abolished by federal court order in 1962, the state's 1945 constitution, which contains the notorious county-unit system, is still in effect.

Georgians have always been capricious about their capital cities; they tended to carry them on their backs as they settled the interior of the state. Savannah was first, then came Augusta and a succession of others, including Louisville in Jefferson County. This little capital only lasted until 1807 but proved to be a volatile one, for it was here that the Yazoo Fraud took place.

The town of Milledgeville north of Macon also served its time as a state capital and with less than honorable results as well. Today the little town is stuck far off the beaten path on U.S. 441 near the Oconee National Forest. It was here in Milledgeville in 1829 that the Georgia legislature passed the law appropriating the lands of the Cherokee Nation. On June 30, 1830, the governor of Georgia signed the bill and simultaneously issued an edict announcing that gold had been discovered on these same Indian lands. What the governor also signed away was Milledgeville's future as the capital, for the gold rush created Atlanta.

The rush into northern Georgia was incredible; thousands of prospectors and land-grabbers swarmed in. Georgia petitioned President Andrew Jackson to pull out the U.S. troops, to let Georgia handle the Indians. And Jackson, who was to fight his whole presidential career against so-called states' rights, in effect gave the Georgians carte blanche to treat the Indians any way they wanted to. Eventually the U.S. Supreme Court ruled the Georgia appropriation law unconstitutional, in violation of solemn treaties between the U.S. government and the Cherokee Nation. Jackson's message to the Court was cold and imperial. The Cherokees had tried to use the white man's system of laws to protect their lands and lives. And they won. But they lost. The Trail of Tears was put in motion here in Milledgeville.

"Purpose" is a difficult abstract noun to get a handle on in the South, where both whites and blacks have blinked at the Southland's Native American victims. In 1825 there were 53,600 Cherokees, Creeks, Choctaws, and Chickasaws living in the South on more than 33 million acres of land. By the time of the great removal in 1838, virtually none of these tribes were left, and all the land had been taken away. The only signs of the Indian and his culture in Georgia are the tribal names given to the rivers and streams, and the place names the whites were pleased to use for their towns, counties, and states.

In 1992 the Georgia legislature amid much media hype pretended to renounce the actions of the Milledgeville legislature of 1830. Headlines reached across the nation proclaiming "Georgia Admits Error That Sent Cherokees on Trail of Tears." It's a fine sentiment and certainly apologies were past due. But the state of Georgia did no such thing. Instead, it pardoned two white missionaries convicted in 1831 for helping the Cherokees and defying the Georgia law. Obviously certain Georgians have guilty consciences and probably they want to confess publicly the sins of their fathers. But the lawyers blocked this simple mea culpa. Were the state of Georgia to admit error, the doors to the golden temple of justice would be thrown wide open to the inevitable lawsuits. Georgia just found a left-handed way of salving its conscience without threatening the pocketbooks of the descendants of the cracker landgrab 150 years ago.

Without the legislative industry to keep it going, Milledgeville has had to settle for the next best thing, the prison business. Even this seems to have gone sour. Maybe the Cherokees did put a curse on the town that condemned them to death or exile, for Milledgeville's own Georgia Women's Correction Institution has been mired in ugly scandal.

Southern prisons in general have earned the reputation as being the worst in the nation. What has happened here in Milledgeville isn't just another scandal—it's a condemnation of the penal system itself and of the brutality with which such systems are run. According to charges filed later, what went on here for years is right out of the sadovoyeuristic nightmare play *Marat/Sade*. Behind the scissor-wire-topped cyclone fences in the barracks, inmates allegedly were raped, sodomized, and tortured. Young girls barely in their teens were coerced into oral sex for a cigarette. Freeworld bulls (civilian cops) and prison bosses were supposedly having sex with women through the bars of the inmates' cells, and it wasn't just the male guards. Of the fourteen people indicted, four were women employees of the prison.

It all started coming to light in 1992 when former prison employees, including a deputy warden, were charged with multiple felonies ranging from aggravated sodomy to rape. One guard was charged with seven counts of sodomy and fourteen of sexual assault. The deputy warden was charged with rape, sodomy, and sexual assault. The number of individual charges was almost irrelevant since the surface of the nightmare had barely been scratched. The investigation spread to the other two Georgia women's prisons.

Just a few blocks away from this women's version of Brueghel's vision of hell come to life nestles the home of another Georgia woman, Flannery O'Connor. Anyone who calls himself a Southerner is well acquainted with Miss O'Connor, and it is just too darkly ironic that her homeplace is barely a misfit's gunshot away from that vicious crazy house calling itself a correctional institution. Flannery O'Connor wrote exclusively about Southern people that some would call freaks. Her characters could easily have inhabited prisons or lunatic asylums. Miss O'Connor was accused of overstatement in her stories on the South, for to people outside the South nothing could be as grotesque.

"My characters aren't grotesque," O'Connor once told a gathering at the Iowa Writers' Workshop. "That's just the way people are in the South."

She wrote about people who had little or no control over their lives, people whose existence was always tinged with a strong sense of absurdity. Miss O'Connor pierced the veil and understood the Janus-faced nature of the Southern psyche. On display in her works were characters who were products of religious guilt gone berserk. Who was Hazel Motes other than the personification of the South's rugged individualism forced to live in a homogenous community that condemned difference or change? Only madness in mythic, Oedipal proportion could be born of such parentage, and in her works O'Connor focused on the critical theme that abnormal response to the abnormal is normal, at least in the South.

ONE other town in Georgia besides Savannah, Augusta, Milledgeville, Louisville, and Atlanta has a capital claim. Macon was once the cotton capital for this part of the Deep South. Photos from the turn of the century show Macon's courthouse square stacked to the spires in cotton bales from the warehouse overflow. The gentleman doorman in Atlanta had spoken of his childhood near Macon when his family worked the cotton fields. He was too young to chop or pick, so he was the water boy, taking tow-sack-wrapped jugs down the rows to his mama and daddy, sister and brothers. He remembered his granddaddy talking about the mule-pulled wagons stretching down the clay road for what seemed like miles, waiting their turn at the cotton gin. But the boll weevil had wiped out Georgia's cotton crops in 1914 and had left such slim pickings, the doorman recalled, that his family exchanged their shotgun shack in the fields for a tenement in Atlanta.

If you're thinking about music to soothe the savage breast, Macon also qualifies as a capital, and in the same league with Memphis,

Nashville, and New Orleans. As we shall see, Memphis got the blues, Nashville got the country, New Orleans got the jazz. Macon got Southern rock. Otis Redding, the soul of Southern rock, grew up in Macon singing in his daddy's Baptist church. With his first single, "Shout Bama Lama," Redding served notice that here was the voice of a new king. Redding's influence on the new vein of Southern rock was just reaching its peak when he died at the age of twenty-six in a plane crash. He had been working on "The Dock of the Bay," which posthumously became the movement's anthem.

Redding's hero, Richard Penniman, was also born in Macon and he, too, began his singing in his local church. By his early teens Penniman sang in minstrel shows all through the South. Later he worked the gay clubs in the big cities, where he played "Princess Lavonne." After Little Richard hit it big with "Tutti-Frutti," "Long Tall Sally," and "Good Golly, Miss Molly," he didn't get a swelled head or a dose of the clap. Instead, he got a bad case of the Southern guilts, dropped out, went to Bible school, and began preaching. Guilt in the South is the same thing as religion, and you can't have one without the other. Little Richard relapsed, though, and made a comeback playing a caricature of his old "jump back in the alley" persona.

The tide generated by Otis Redding's fame created a record label right here in Macon. Capricorn opened the door for the Allman Brothers and soon Macon would be known nationally as the hotbed of Southern rock: the Atlanta Rhythm Section, .38 Special, the Marshall Tucker Band, Lynyrd Skynyrd (named for the group's high school shop teacher), and perhaps the most significant of all, the group simply called The Band.

Southern rock music turned out to be more meaningful than anyone expected. It began to alter some of the imagery that had long controlled the Southern personality. When integration invaded the South, the good-old-boy power structures fell back on a typical demagogic dodge—every city and town in the South set up one or more "Christian" academies for the proper (No Blacks Allowed) education of white boys and girls. The Southern rock scene bore no such apartheid baggage. In the honky-tonks and clubs all through the Southlands, black singers and white musicians, white singers and black musicians were playing to crowds who cursed the federal courts and busing during the day and applauded the bands at night.

Southern rock was sending a message and gaining converts that no amount of civil rights legislation could get across. Color didn't matter. After all, it was soul music.

ATLANTA may be the heart of Georgia today but the state's soul remains in the little drinkwater town called Plains. Folks in this far-flung village of 750 solid cracker souls live the same sylvan existence as their grandparents. You can walk the one main street—past the two-story storefront buildings with the metal awnings, past the worm farm, Scarlet's Cafe, Carter's Antiques—on a Sunday morning in any season and hear the time-blown music being sung in its churches as it was generations ago. The voices are borne from a centuries-old corruption of Gaelic and Welsh and English and German—the sounds of the ancestors of the American South, changed over the years by a hard sun and tobacco juice and pot-distilled corn liquor.

Plains is a Jimmy Carter industry for sure, but it's not a rich town, nowhere near as picturesque as Harper's Ferry. Like so many little Southern towns, Plains is uglied by railroad tracks splitting the town's belly in two. And like other Southern places, Plains has a right and a wrong side of the tracks. Real poverty lives in Plains on the wrong side, with squalid duplexes and trailers and row houses, all black. There are no Habitat for Humanity homes in Plains (those are over in nearby progressive Americus). Plains is a migrant-worker town, mostly Mexican, though some Haitians have been brought in to work the green-bean fields (over the grumbling of the local white farmers). In many ways, if you hadn't seen the road signs, you could be in Hope, Arkansas. Both towns are migrant-worker centers, both are being strangled with poverty, both are the birthplaces of Southern Presidents. Over on the right side of the tracks in Plains, the homes are mostly Harry Truman houses. The tin man has been here, for most of the houses have been re-sided. The white churches—the First Baptist and the Faith Baptist and, oddly for this part of the world, the Lutheran church—are here on the right side, too, along with the town's busiest employer, the Lillian Carter Nursing Center.

Every once in a while a highway work crew of county convicts wearing yellow T-shirts comes to Plains to repair the roads. They're mostly black, their guards are armed, and the whole scene is like a melancholy emblem of the infamous old chain-gang South. Ask the old codger out in front of the worm farm if he's a Carter booster and he'll tell you, "I have to be . . . I live here." Plains's most famous son is the New Age Southern aristocrat. He doesn't mix with his inferiors like his predecessors, the bubbas and captains and demagogues. His ex-Presidency has relieved him of this onerous responsibility. Jimmy Carter simply brings the tablets down from the mountain and lodges them at the Carter Center at One Copenhill, Atlanta, Georgia, 30307, and lets the South and the whole country know what its new purpose is. Carter once shamed the state of Georgia into immunizing its children with one single phrase: "Kids in Biafra are better off than those in Atlanta." Unfortunately, it was true.

Speaking from his philanthropic bunker at the Carter Center, he had time to reflect on his hometown and the South in general. "The South may be losing its identity some," he said. "Television allows the people back up in the hills to see the same thing as people in cities see."

The town of Plains itself? "Well, the highway is wider and there are a few conveniences from when I was a boy, but no real changes."

Carter's people all came from Virginia, he'll tell you. They came down the Great Philly Road, through the gateway of Augusta, and migrated across to the fertile plains of the Fall Line Hills. His grandmother was part of the post–Civil War force that helped rebuild the South.

"The South is a matriarchal society," Carter says. "My mother was able to get more accomplished than my father, and she had more of an influence on me." Until his father died in 1953, all that Carter ever wanted to be was a naval officer. "I never had any political ambitions, I never wanted to be governor, never wanted to be President." Listening to the former President, you begin thinking that maybe what he's done is what his mother wanted him to do with his life.

Those who followed Jimmy Carter's improbable rise all know of his mother, Miss Lillian, the matriarch of the Carter clan, and of the stacks of stories about her. One perspective on Miss Lillian is offered by her grandson Buddy, son of Billy Carter, the most outrageous presidential relative since U. S. Grant's family. Buddy tells of the time when he was a boy here in Plains and the occasion that his grandmother taught him a lasting lesson about love and respect.

Buddy had casually used the word "nigger" in Miss Lillian's presence.

"She beat the devil out of me," Buddy says. "She gave me the whipping of my life."

The proudest long-standing claim of Jimmy Carter is that of being a farmer and a Southerner. The Eastern press used to bear down pretty hard on such humility, but then these detractors didn't have much interest in the verities of the South and even less understanding of the region's existential being. Sometimes it takes a farmer to understand the vagaries of life. And, too, sometimes it takes a Southerner to understand the debilitating effect that someone else's dream can have on what he'd hoped would be a simple, uncomplicated life.

In the 1930s the lands down South were so badly eroded that the Roosevelt administration decided to bring in an effective ground cover. The cotton economy had already been ruined by the Mexican boll weevil, yet now the land was to be saved by intentionally importing an outside element, kudzu, an ornamental Japanese vine known for its profusion. Old codgers in Plains will tell you that the real problems in the South are not race relations or the lack of capital or the corruption of the politicians. These will all be solved eventually.

Jimmy Carter comes back to Plains now and again to look in on his acres and his peanuts. When he does, he ceases to be the great philanthropist and reverts to his bloodlines—he becomes a landowner and a cracker-barrel philosopher. Kudzu is covering him up.

"Kudzu?" Carter questions. "Kudzu? I don't like it. I don't like it one little bit. It's taking over my land and I don't have enough cows to eat it up. You've got to be careful of what foreigners send into the country. A guy once read Shakespeare and copied down a list of all the birds Shakespeare had written about. From this list he imported one hundred of each species into America. That's where the problems with starlings began."

Not a half hour's drive from Plains, just past Americus (where the national press used to hang out when Carter made his curative trips back to his home roots), the Andersonville National Cemetery drapes a pinewood valley in the Fall Line Hills. The press never made much of this infamous old site during Carter's presidential years any more than it does now when Carter comes to Americus to help build Habitat houses for the poor. Andersonville is sequestered from the world today as it was in 1864, and for precisely the same reason: for all its serene ambiance, meticulous care, and federal political correctness, Andersonville is a place of guilt and always will be.

It's easy to see why the prison camp was built here. The rolling hills become rather steep in places, forming box canyons. The Confederates built a pine-log stockade enclosing twenty-seven acres down a ravine utterly cut off from the rest of the world. In the last fifteen months of the war the Confederacy took some 49,500 prisoners, and they were forced to hold them in prisons because of the new Yankee policy that forbade exchange of captured soldiers. Here at Andersonville, thirty-three thousand of those Union prisoners were held in conditions not seen in the South since the first African slaves were penned in barracoons. The Union soldiers succumbed to dehydration, scurvy, gangrene, and starvation. In the end more than thirteen thousand boys in blue would die here in this sloping meadow of west Georgia. It was the South's most impressive victory, if one is into statistics. A total of thirteen thousand enemy dead, with only one Southern casualty, and that after the fact.

C. Vann Woodward and Thomas L. Connelly have both pointed out that the American Dream, the true religion of the country, was that of success, invincibility, and savage innocence. The country had never known any reality other than victory, both as a nation and as individuals. Yet when the South finally fell, the psyche of the losers was no longer American. It became mired in pessimism. "The South's preoccupation was with guilt," stated Professor Woodward in *The Burden of Southern History.* Their God had forsaken them. After the war the only godhead left to the South was in the person of its vanquished hero, Robert Edward Lee. He became the South's martyred savior, crucified on the cross of war and raised to immortality by the South's commitment to myth. Unwittingly, the North joined in the South's strange obsession with mythology. Instead of condemning Lee as the traitor he was, it permitted him a living apotheosis, giving rise to the rebirth of the Southern psyche. The phoenix rose from the ashes but with some heavy baggage, the reaffirmation of the South's preoccupation with its own mythology and its own guilt.

"The South was American a long time before it was Southern,"

Woodward affirms. But with the fall of the Confederacy, the South
ceased being part of the nation. Its soul was now encrusted with
guilt, not because it had lost, but because it had failed to win by the
rules of its God and the American Dream. To soothe its new aborn-
ing psyche, the South had to create new myths—the Lost Cause and
the Better Man theses. Just because we lost doesn't mean you're better than we are; in fact, our cause was just and we're better men because we fought chivalrously.

Romantic bunkum for sure. Andersonville put the lie to the
South's just cause. Following the war, a few Confederate politicians
were jailed briefly, but no Rebel generals (not even those who once
held U.S. commissions) were tried for treason. Bedford Forrest, who
murdered hundreds of black soldiers and their families at Fort Pillow, evaded prosecution. The only person to be tried as a war criminal was Major Henry Wirz, the administrator at Andersonville
prison. Wirz was a Swiss émigré and a medical doctor who after being wounded in 1863 was assigned the bureaucratic post here in
Georgia. At his trial Wirz was not allowed to challenge any of the
conflicting evidence. He was found guilty and sentenced to death by
hanging. Four companies of Union troops boxed the gallows and
called out, "Remember Andersonville!" The hanging itself was
botched and Wirz died of slow strangulation.

Georgia's collective memory still wails at the destruction reaped
by Sherman's march to the sea. Many modern Georgians might wonder why the Yankees were so vindictive here. The prison at Andersonville might supply part of the answer, even though Sherman
decided not to come this way and liberate those thousands of Union
prisoners. Everyone knows about Andersonville, yet there's another
site in the Peachtree State that had more meaning to Sherman's
troops. When the Yankee army came to the little town of Millen,
Georgia, some two hours from Atlanta nowadays, they found a three-
hundred-square-yard log stockade used as a prison for Union soldiers. What the arriving troops found was so sickening that many
simply slumped to the ground and cried. It was a scene to be repeated eighty years later when American GIs first came to the Jewish
death camps in Germany. Outside the stockade at Millen were more
than seven hundred unmarked graves. Inside the prison compound
were some twenty bodies of unburied soldiers. There was no water
in the stockade, no shelter from the weather, no food. The handful

of survivors had the cadaverous look of the living dead that later generations saw at Auschwitz; they were handled tenderly by the furious veterans and sent to hospitals in the North. Surely there can be no doubt why Georgia suffered under Sherman's hands.

Jack Cash intuitively referred to the influence of the Southern physical world as a sort of "cosmic conspiracy against reality in favor of romance." In so doing, Cash defined what the South was (and is), and why it differs from the rest of the nation. The North joined in the conspiracy by failing to humanize the romance. Here at Andersonville was the stark reality of the South's Holy War. Mythology is hard to build on a foundation of atrocity.

PART THREE

THE BUCKLE OF THE BIBLE BELT

"Tell about the South, what's it like there. What do they do there. Why do they live there. Why do they live there at all?"

—WILLIAM FAULKNER, *Absalom, Absalom!*

CHAPTER 6

"Let Us Now Praise Famous Men"

Alabama and Mississippi . . . Redneck Aristocrats, Good Old Boys, and Mean Sumbitches . . . Ralph Ellison . . . The Tuskegee Experiment . . . Morris Dees and the Southern Poverty Law Center . . . The Southern Belle . . . James Agee . . . Elvis

JACK CASH USED HIS "man at the center" yeoman to explain the evolution of aristocracy in the South. It may have taken thirty or forty years of hard work and steady accumulation, but by then this archetype of a successful farmer was viewed by nearly one and all as quality folk. As far as Cash was concerned, the man at the center *was* the South. When he made it, he lorded it some, for that's the American way. Yet he didn't become a belted earl like his European ancestors; he was shrewder than that. He became an aristocrat who could joke and eat and drink with his lessers, a good number of whom were his relatives.

Where did the South go when the man at the center became the man on top? Even though the Civil War had devastated the Southlands, a pattern had already been laid. When Andrew Jackson became President and David Crockett got to Congress, it became acceptable for men of humble beginnings and means to succeed, to face down the milords and challenge the idea of *mon dieu et mon droit*. How much truth is there to the tales of Willie Stark in *All the King's Men* and Big Daddy in *Cat on a Hot Tin Roof*? These are the bigger-than-life stereotypes that dominate the South's Bible Belt. We've watched them weave their way into the cities; we've stood by as they took over the banks, the law offices, the universities; we've let them stand on the steps of the state capitols. They are the South's evolutionary cousins that sprang from the man at the center, and we can call them by name and family and genus:

The Redneck Aristocrat. With him rides the hope of the Neo-South. Much is expected of him when he is born into a family of the genteel poor. The Redneck Aristocrat attends the right Protestant church and is encouraged to keep company with only the right people; he is invited to the social affairs of the local baron as the lesser friend of the baronial spawn.

In his adolescence he was a Methodist or a Baptist lay speaker and was eaten up with the Calvinist dogma of guilt. His attitude toward women is from the Old Testament vision of women as vessels of wrath, a chalice of original sin issuing from Eve.

The Redneck Aristocrat was an ROTC cadet in high school, an honor graduate, salutatorian perhaps but hardly ever valedictorian (a role reserved for the daughter of the local nabob). He attended a private university—Vanderbilt or Duke or even the Ivy League—on a combination of loans and academic or athletic scholarships. One or two of his number even achieved the dizzying heights of a Fulbright or Wilson or Rhodes fellowship.

Military experience was a must and he did his stint in the Korea, Vietnam, or the Gulf Wars. After law school he came home, married into the cadet branch of "A Family" and joined an established law firm with connections in the state government. He became a member of the local country club, the Lions, the Rotary, the American Legion, though he rarely attended the meetings. Wednesday nights find him standing, suit coat off, tie loosened, among the members of the men's Bible-study class down on the town square. Don't look for him on Thursday nights because he'll be with his mistress at the condo he owns in the state capital.

With the influence of his in-laws and the graceful, condescending nod from the local and state Old Guard, he has secured himself a seat in the state legislature where he will do his masters' bidding in perpetuity, all the while paying painfully slow lip service to environmental, social welfare, and political reform issues. His successes pave the way for the adoption of his family into the lists of the South's aristocracy, lists that he is in the process of rewriting.

Nonetheless, the Redneck Aristocrat is a pretender. He still loves hunting dogs, black-eyed peas, cornbread, sour mash whiskey, and his mama. Though he may attend concerts at the state symphony and opera hall, George Jones is who he grew up on and who he still loves 'cause you can't get down and dirty to *Aida.*

The Good Old Boy. The eldest male child born of a family as poor as frogs living in a posthole, the Good Old Boy has forever been known in the South as a horse trader. He's good at everything. He does things with his hands that a lot of men can't. He's got what's known down here as "a little bit of wit, a little bit of grit, and a whole lot of shit." He's funny and he's a trickster, and he'll get his hand in your back pocket faster than his granddaddy, the snake-oil pitchman. He'll beat you at horse, nine-ball, or straight poker. He's got the best coon dogs in the region and knows where to get the best moonshine in four states. He's been around the world once and to two county fairs. His sweet little sister gave him his name as her first word, "Bubber."

The Good Old Boy grew up fighting and whoring and stealing. He survived his thug years and all the girls he knocked up whose daddies would have killed him if he hadn't lied and bullied his way out of it. Some of his kind don't survive and end up doing time picking peas on the state prison farm. The survivor learns a trade the hard way, apprenticed out as a plumber, carpenter, electrician. He may work at the sawmill or learn how to be a long-haul trucker; he may become a true artist with a backhoe or a number-nine cat, uncannily able to trim down to a slick quarter-inch grade on a landfill or housing development. He'll never live in one of those hog mansions that his redneck wife dreams of; he aspires only to a double-wide stuck back among a copse of pine and close to his favorite fishing hole.

He lost his mama to TB and was abandoned by his father before he was thirteen. He worked three poverty-level jobs—paper route, projectionist at the old picture show in town, and rack boy at the pool hall. He fed his six younger brothers and sisters the best he could on baloney, vy-eeny (Vienna) sausages, R.C. Colas, Snickers bars, soda crackers, and popcorn. He got his long-standing girlfriend pregnant and so loved the frictional itch that he married her and lived in an unplumbed shack where the toilet was the backyard. He was a crack pool shooter and hustled quarters on Saturday mornings to buy the week's groceries. He's a cut above his rowdy friends who are known in the region as Southern "go-getters," men who will take their wives to work at Wal-Mart in the morning, stand in line for their unemployment checks, get to the pool hall before noon to shoot nine-ball and drink Bud until it's time to stagger to the pickup and "go get her."

Call him a cracker, peckerwood, hillbilly, shitkicker, or just plain crude—he's cleaned up his act and works regular and hard to get a little bit ahead, mostly because of his good woman. She's the one who made him straighten up, sober up, and get his lazy contrary ass to church, a missionary foot-washing house of redemption with a special pew for his kind in the Amen Corner. He fell in love with his lady and her long, long legs at a girls' fast-pitch softball game. Those long legs in all their voluptuous, achy-breaky glory have kept him at home and put him "right with God," at least most of the time. He can't quite break himself from his poor-white-trash background; he has to go out with the boys every once in a while, getting drunk and raising hell and chasing honky-tonk road whores till he and his other Good Old Boy buddies are living the lyrics of a Hank Williams song one more time. And his wife, his good woman, forgives him, takes him back one last time.

The Good Old Boy believes in the flag, American and Rebel, in God and man's salvation through Jesus. He believes in a heaven with streets paved in gold where he'll meet his long-dead mama someday and she'll be healed. He believes in white supremacy and the Southern way of life. He'll always hate niggers and believe in his heart that they have no soul. He loves his wife, his children, and his dogs. He's a born-again Democrat even though he voted for Nixon, Reagan, and Bush, and ignored Jimmy Carter and Bill Clinton. He's the man that stood at the Bloody Angle at Gettysburg and in the cornfield at Antietam, hollered out, "Lee to the rear!" and charged with Longstreet at Chattanooga and ate parched corn and rats at Vicksburg—he was all the men whose honor was so great that the gods would weep at their sacrifice. Their honor is their life, and so is his. You have no reason to expect it, but you can depend on it. He and they will stand.

The Mean Sumbitch. No redeeming factor involved here. This one is dangerous, in a particularly low, mean, Southern way. The Mean Sumbitch grew up believing that fighting is the way to prove everything—manhood, values, worth, character. He treats women like sewer water. When he was young he slapped his girlfriends around and whipped up on any guy that talked to them. When he married any of his various wives, the poor dumb bitchy things that fell for him went along for a little while with his brutish ways; they were humiliated, beaten, raped, and just to prove his macabre power over women, sodomized. In a real sense he enslaved his women—he married them to keep them away from any real friends, away from any semblance of living. He forbade them to better themselves, wouldn't let them think of further schooling or taking a job just to get a little of their own money, and he watched every penny they spent while he indulged himself in new pickup trucks and bass boats and an arsenal of hunting weapons. His women are pictures of the bereft and lonely, as William Faulkner captured them in the character of Mrs. Armstid in "Spotted Horses." And yet you can see her today in the countless Wal-Mart stores that pimple and boil on the Southern landscape.

The Mean Sumbitch was destined from birth to be a loner. He never has had a real friend, just one or two torpid dolts that he could easily maneuver into his petty larcenies, his nigger knockings, queer bashings, and gang-bangings, all his idea of a good time that the world owed him because of his very nature. All the bad-ass brotherhood to which he belongs hates him even as he despises them. He was whelped onto a misshapened spar of earth from which his kind cannot escape because the only way they can live is through hate and bitterness and blood.

He has killed his man, in 'Nam and on his native soil, with the same kind of precision. He killed in Dallas and Memphis, in Mississippi and Alabama, targets called Freedom Riders and marchers, gunned them down at point-blank range. He sicced the dogs on them or used his boot to stomp them dead after spitting in their faces. You have seen his face, the one caught and preserved in the old magazine photos and newsreels and archives, neatly kept for posterity. He's the one standing beside his trophy, the body of a black man beaten and scoured, still showing a little life and blood in the picture and hung from a rope drawn from the ground. It's called a choke-hanging.

One grows weary of looking for a single streak of goodness in the Mean Sumbitch. Maybe his being is merely a conjunction of his time and our curiosity over questions of value. He is of no worth even as a quirk of nature, whether we be pious or sentimental in our dark guilt over him. "Poor naked wretches, wheresoe'er you are," speaks poet James Agee, "that bide the pelting of this pitiless storm. . . . How shall your houseless heads and unfed sides, your loop'd and window'd raggedness, defend you from seasons such as these?"

And maybe he is lost among the points of a stuck compass of the South. Attempting to understand him is as futile as trying to get inside his head to tame his brutal ways. No rules, no guidelines apply to answer such a dilemma. The fact that he exists in our time makes us know he'd destroy the world if only he had the power. His nights stay fitful and he dreams of still more kills. He kills because . . . because he doesn't know death, doesn't understand what dying is. He is a last stand at a Southern fortress, a final showdown in a citadel of his own making. He shows an open face to the world but holds something inside, a rawness beyond hate.

THE story of the South has benefited from a naturally occurring progression of historical continuity with the sweep of settlement from Virginia through Georgia. This linkage was to be reinforced throughout the remainder of the Southlands because the same sturdy folks who had populated the Old South now laid claim to the new Deep South. These lands, of course, were the Black Belt of Alabama, the lower Mississippi Valley, the blacklands farms of East Texas and non-French Louisiana, as well as parts of Tennessee, Little Dixie in Oklahoma, and the Ozarks of Arkansas and Missouri. It is in this wide, tempestuous region of the Bible Belt where the Jacksonian legacy changed the Janus-head of the South from two faces to three. With the birth of the Mean Sumbitch, the latter-day redneck mentality was whelped.

The great Indian leader Tecumseh had a dream of Confederacy himself. He journeyed from his lands north of the Ohio River in 1811 to the seat of his cousins, the Creeks, at Tuckaubatchee, Alabama, where he preached unity and holy war against the encroaching white flood. The Creeks listened but the Indian defeat at Tippecanoe in Indiana slowed the Southern Indians' response. Tecumseh's dream of an Indian confederacy standing up to the white settlers died with the impatience of his brother, Tenskwatawa, "The Prophet." The Prophet started the war before Tecumseh could get back home from Alabama to coordinate the attacks, and Virginian William Henry Harrison would ride the victory into the White House. After Tippecanoe, part of the Creek Nation in Alabama decided to go to war anyway. Calling themselves Red Sticks, the Creeks followed their leader, a half-breed going by the Christian name of William Weathersford (known as War Eagle).

The Creeks struck at Fort Mims, upriver from Mobile, in 1813; they slaughtered several hundred whites but allowed some two hundred black slaves to escape. The United States was at war with England at the time and had precious few troops to send to Alabama to fight Indians. But Andrew Jackson, then the commander of the Tennessee militia, was more than willing to take on the Spanish-armed, Jesuit-inspired Red Sticks. To avenge Fort Mims, Jackson marched more than two thousand men into Alabama. The Creek warriors defended Horseshoe Bend against Jackson's army to give their women and children a chance to escape across the river. But Jackson's army overwhelmed them, leaving eight hundred Creeks lying dead. Not a single Red Stick warrior was taken prisoner; the wounded were executed on the field. Jackson's men rounded up the Creek women and children and gave them to Jackson's Indian allies as their turncoat payoff.

Jackson, too, rode his Indian victory into the White House. The only artifact that survived the battle of Horseshoe Bend was William Weathersford's Indian sobriquet, War Eagle, which became the nickname of nearby Auburn University's football factory.

Less than twenty miles down from Auburn is the Black Belt town of Tuskegee, made famous by Booker Taliaferro Washington and George Washington Carver. Born a slave in Virginia, Booker T. founded the Tuskegee Normal and Industrial Institute in 1881. Today's blacks and liberal-minded whites think of Washington as an Uncle Tom and of his foundational work as nothing more than a sellout to the Jim Crow laws. Somehow this attitude doesn't fit the times in which Washington was born and forced to live as a black man in a white South. The hope of Washington and his protégé, George Washington Carver, was to raise the pitiable standard of living for the blacks, to get them out of the penal servitude of sharecropping; dignity was denied them both by law and common white custom. Their students could neither read nor write nor cipher; at Tuskegee they were taught that blacks had to be better farmers than the whites and have a stronger moral fiber.

Few white men in the South would lower themselves to teach a black man or even support a black's higher education. Washington sought support in the North, where he found willing teachers and patrons and, more importantly, political support. Theodore Roosevelt and William Howard Taft both invited Washington to their respective White Houses, and later he served as their unofficial adviser on race relations. Washington did the best he could with his fifty-nine years of living in a coercive realm called the South. His brilliant recruit, Carver, turned the humble ground nut into the modern peanut, source of every American kid's staple diet.

Writing in 1903, Professor John Spencer Bassett, then teaching history at Trinity College (soon to become Duke University), said, "After General Lee, Booker T. Washington was the greatest man born in the South in a century." For uttering this sacrilege against the Cult of Lee, Bassett was hounded out of North Carolina and out of the South.

The grounds of Tuskegee Institute are beautiful. The old buildings are covered with ivy and wisteria; the roads are lined with hedges and wild roses. Honeysuckle and white magnolias crowd the air with their scents. Young women in bright summer dresses still promenade the lush green lawns, while the bell in the chapel tower rings the changes.

Such was the setting of Tuskegee that Ralph Waldo Ellison found when he first came there in 1933 to study classical music. He lived his first twenty-two years in the South and it was here, especially in Alabama, that he began to develop his vision and voice. The fact that he ran out of money and left Tuskegee for Harlem in no way severed his attachment to the South and things Southern. The first chapters of *Invisible Man*, one of the most powerful novels of the twentieth century, reflect Ellison's heritage and his dreamlike connection with his grandparents, especially with his grandfather. On his deathbed the old man had said: "After I'm gone I want you to keep up the good fight. I want you to overcome 'em with yesses, undermine 'em with grins, agree 'em to death and destruction, let 'em swoller you till they vomit or bust wide open." The novel reveals the darker side of the black man's search for identity.

"I am not ashamed of my grandparents for having been slaves," Ellison writes. "I am only ashamed of myself for having at one time been ashamed." Here emphatically is the theme of Southern guilt, black and white. The two were so caught up with each other that a volatile synthesis would be inevitable.

Just a year before Ellison came to the Tuskegee Institute, an experiment in human misery was begun in Macon County, Alabama, with its headquarters in the town of Tuskegee. Syphilis was rampant in the nation and particularly in the South. The U.S. Public Health Service struck a deal with Alabama politicos in 1932 to use some four hundred black men in a medical experiment. It turned out that these hundreds of black men would be treated like laboratory rats, just to collect scientific data on syphilis. The Health Service doctors got away with it because these were hard, hard times in the South's Depression, and the doctors dangled the carrot of twenty-five dollars per man and the promise of a free burial. In the poverty-stricken South, decent men and their families, black and white, put greatest store in Christian burial. What at first glance may have seemed a gratuitous offer by the Feds turned out to be the key in recruiting the syphilitic blacks.

Overzealous health professionals came to Macon County and rounded up 412 black men already suffering with syphilis and put them into a controlled experimental program. These blacks were all illiterate and were told that they suffered from "bad blood." It scared them to death because the phrase carried with it the stigma of witchcraft and burnt sulphur. They were given their twenty-five dollars for taking annual physicals, periodic blood tests, and spinal taps. When the men complained of the pain from the spinal taps, they were told that this procedure was "the only cure for bad blood."

The worst had just begun. When penicillin came along in the 1940s, the Tuskegee experiment should have been closed down; the 412 men should have been cured and sent home. The Health Service had accumulated almost fifteen years of medical data, all saying the same thing: a man with syphilis was likely to die, suffering the pains of hell along the way. Yet the experiment was continued; it had developed its own Coriolis effect, like a hurricane. The excuse, unconscionable as it was, stood on the grounds that to cure the men would interfere with data collection. To end the experiment would have put the white-coated doctors out of business.

Some of the original 412 started dying on the doctors, and the doctors' first response was to coerce the bereaved families into permitting autopsies, so even in death the pursuit of data collection continued. A few men in the experiment heard of the miracle drug called penicillin; they tried to obtain treatment from local doctors in clinics. These men were reported to the Feds, tracked down, and told to "get on back home," for they had no business trying to get treated. They were bullied and threatened into horrible deaths.

The experiment that began in 1932 was carried on into the 1950s, the 1960s, and 1970s. Finally, in 1972, a *New York Times* reporter named Jean Heller broke the story. It was such an incredible tale that it drove the Vietnam War headlines off the front pages of the country's newspapers and resounded through the halls of Congress. Senator Birch Bayh, quoted in the *Congressional Record* of July 28, 1972, stated, "These men were permitted to suffer and die even though a cure for the disease was found ten years after the experiment began." Senator William Proxmire called the Tuskegee Study "a moral and ethical nightmare."

In 1973 both the House and Senate investigated the crimes of the U.S. Public Health Service. The most damaging evidence came from a government doctor who was employed by the Alabama Public Health Service during the first two decades of the experiment. Dr. Reginald G. James testified that he believed "the men in the experiment were told not to take the syphilis treatment in exchange for certain benefits." Dr. James pointed out in an interview with journalist Heller: "I was distraught and disturbed whenever one of the patients in the study group appeared. I was advised that the patient was not to be treated. Whenever I insisted on treating such a patient, he never showed up again. They were being advised they shouldn't take treatments or they would be dropped from the study. To receive the benefits the patient had to remain in the study."

The congressional investigations revealed that a cover-up had been going on for forty years. Right up to the end, the U.S. Public Health Service denied any wrongdoing. Dr. John R. Heller, who had participated in and even controlled the experiment, claimed that treatment was "not deliberately denied to any of the men" and that they were "not coerced into the program through offers of benefits." Dr. Heller added that it was his impression that all the study's participants "had received syphilis treatments from private doctors and Tuskegee area clinics."

After all the congressional deploring and ringing of hands, no criminal charges were ever lodged against those carrying out these research crimes. None for manslaughter, wrongful death, or pre-meditated capital murder. A civil suit for $1.8 billion was filed and the U.S. government settled for less than one cent on the dollar. Survivors and the immediate families of the dead received individual payments of $32,550.20.

The U.S. Health Service had practiced unscrupulous and illegal tests—no better than the infamous experiments on Jews in Nazi Germany—in Alabama on black men because they were only "niggers" (people who in the prevailing attitude of the redneck South had no souls). One of the Tuskegee experimenting doctors claimed in a 1993 interview on CBS TV's "60 Minutes" that he had done nothing wrong, that he was not a war criminal, though he reluctantly admitted that what had happened at Tuskegee was "not politically correct."

On the surface Tuskegee has forgotten about the experiment, but the racial memory is still clouded. The town has a VA hospital now, and the Institute has a nursing program in its curriculum. The grounds of the college are as nice today as they were in 1933 when Ralph Ellison was here. Splendid old red-brick buildings testify to the legacy of George Washington Carver, and the new buildings going up reveal that Tuskegee is part of the mainstream of American education, thanks still to the hustling efforts of Booker T. Washington. Tuskegee continues to pay lip service to its agricultural roots, but the college stresses high-tech modernity now. And one has to wonder just how long it will be before the "mainstreaming" will make a difference. Shame, even of the sort felt by Ellison's Invisible Man, remains in short supply when it comes to the way the white South treats its blacks. Yet Tuskegee is still Ralph Ellison's place; one can almost hear his words and his music sifting through the higher frequencies.

COMING into the state capital of Montgomery, the traveler has time to ponder just why the Confederate States of America in 1861 would make this lonesome little town with two hotels to its name its first national capital. Montgomery was on the Upper Federal Road, the Deep South extension of the Great Philly Road, but it had no particular significance when compared to New Orleans, Richmond, or Charleston. Perhaps it was because of the resentment most politi-

cians west of the Alleghenies had against Washington, D.C., for being so remote from the rest of the nation. The state of Virginia issued an invitation to the new Southern Congress to move the capital
to Richmond, the emerging center of military and political activity
(thousands of volunteer soldiers were pouring into Richmond
daily). Montgomery did not suit the tastes of the Confederate congressmen, according to historian William C. Davis in his book *First
Blood;* they found Montgomery "unacceptable and dull," and the
wives of the congressmen were terrorized by the Alabama mosquitoes. Jeff Davis was against the move at first but soon agreed to accept Richmond's invitation.

He traveled to Richmond by railroad and along the way was hailed
by adoring citizens of the new American republic. On his arrival in
Richmond, President Davis was met by the city fathers and presented with a magnificent cabriolet drawn by four white horses; the
carriage was driven by a personal coachman named William A. Jackson, a Virginia slave who turned out to be a Union spy. (During the
course of the war Jackson was able to eavesdrop on Davis and his
cabinet, passing on many military and diplomatic plans. Jackson was
never exposed as a Yankee spy.)

Montgomery today is still a rather dull little town compared to the
more thriving cities of the new Sunbelt South. The only real relic of
the Confederacy is a brass star sunk into the concrete outside the
old state house to denote that the South starts here. It was the spot
where Jeff Davis in his inaugural speech pleaded with the North not
to start a shooting war. One can walk by this memento, stand on it,
take a picture of it, or make a wish on a fallen star. It's Montgomery's
biggest tourist attraction and thousands visit it each year; tour buses
have it on their agenda. Back in 1956 a young Montgomery Baptist
preacher named Martin Luther King, Jr., led a boycott of Montgomery's segregated city buses and thus launched the civil rights
movement here in the first capital of the old Confederacy.

Just across Washington Avenue from the state capitol and Jeff
Davis's fallen star sits the new rising star of the South, the Southern
Poverty Law Center. They call it "The Center" and it is, primarily
because of the efforts of one man, Morris Dees. Back in the truly
abominable Jim Crow days, Southern author G. W. Cable dreamt,
rather naïvely, of the emergence of a Silent South, one where native men and women would stand up for decency and what's

right. Morris Dees's Southern Poverty Law Center redeems Cable's dream.

Morris Dees is a civil man, a native Alabamian who for the past twenty years has defended the rights of the poor, the disenfranchised, and the victims of hate crimes. He went after the United Klans of America the way a slick Montgomery lawyer ought to: he didn't take them to any criminal court but brought them down through civil suits. Dees exposed the UKA in open court for having backed its members' lynching of a young black man; he sued the UKA as a corporation responsible for the actions of its officers and agents. Where the criminal courts couldn't stop the Klan, Dees won a $7 million judgment and forced the Klan to deed its national headquarters and property to the victim's mother. Dees wasn't finished; he took on the West Coast branch of the Klan and hit them for a $12 million-plus judgment. The most remarkable aspect of the Southern Poverty Law Center is that Dees doesn't take a penny. Any and all monies won go directly to the victims or their families. Dees finances his projects through donations (and so far his biggest, though reluctant, contributor has been the Klan and its neo-Nazi allies).

"The Klan in the South is about done," says Morris Dees from his sedate, almost austere law office in the Center. "There are a few Klanners in North Carolina, some in Alabama, but the new direction of intolerance lies with the skinheads and the neo-Nazis. Strangely, their strength is not in the South but in places like Oregon and California. The skinheads tried to rally in Birmingham and the TV cameras had to get a real tight focus because only six heads showed up."

Dees grew up in nearby Mt. Meigs and still lives there. His father was a tolerant man, one of nine children, eight of whom, according to Dees, were "deeply intolerant." Dees graduated from the University of Alabama law school and almost immediately got involved in the civil rights movement. He took part in the Selma-to-Montgomery march in 1965, and his own uncle pulled a gun on him, called him a "nigger lover," and threatened to kill him. He survived threats and snipers and went on to fight the good fight until the civil rights war was won.

"The civil rights movement is over," Dees says. "The NAACP, CORE, and others lost their direction sometime back. Currently they have no direction. The civil rights groups have been wearing blinkers. They are very parochial and won't support women's rights, abortion rights, gay rights."

Dees himself is tall and slender with thinning curly blond hair. He's not a Suit, not a Hardshoe. He wears blue jeans, oxford cotton shirts, and penny loafers. He has a handsome face and a sharp equine nose, but don't make the mistake of believing that Dees is a trendy militant liberal. He is anything but parochial. "I defend the law, not blacks, not whites." He was the first lawyer in America to file a so-called reverse discrimination lawsuit, and he won it.

Dees's passion is his Center's "Teaching Tolerance" program, an educational concept designed to eliminate bigotry and prejudice. It strikes straight to the grassroots of the Savage Ideal and bids to nail the higher echelon as well as the rank-and-file demagogues and supremacists by better educating the children so that one day they won't be so easily duped. As of 1994, more than 41,000 schools and more than 150,000 teachers all over the country are using the Teaching Tolerance program. The scope of the program is so broad that even if the inevitable reactionaries throw the books and videos away, the influence is still contagious. The students and teachers want it— they like it and are learning from it. Dees is probably doing more than any other individual, group, or institution to foster racial tolerance in America. And it's free for the asking.

In Dees's own home county, thirty-five of the seventy-five schools have declined to use Teaching Tolerance. "They say that it would enflame racial tension to teach tolerance," Dees says.

Dees has harnessed a multitalented team that does more than just hope for social change. The Center has broken through the barriers that limited G. W. Cable's dream of a gently healing Silent South. The Center is anything but silent. What else would you expect from an Alabama Sand Hill slicker who says the most fun he's ever had in his professional career was "nailin' Tom Metzger's ass in Oregon." Crypto-Klanner Metzger had told Dees when he first went out to try the suit, "You may be a big shit in Alabama, but you ain't nothing in Oregon." Just before the judge read the verdict, Metzger's son looked over and sneered at lawyer Dees; when the judge found for Dees in the amount of $12.5 million, the son's head shot back and his mouth gaped open like he had just been drilled through the forehead with an assassin's bullet.

Dees is certainly not your stereotypical Southern lawyer, no matter how Southern he is. He feels uncomfortable outside the Deep South, which he believes is a "separate country" from the rest of America. But Dees will travel and he will win. You really don't want him to come to your town if you've got something to hide.

MONTGOMERY is the reputed capital of Southern bellehood. The town has had more Miss Magnolias than Kentucky has colonels. The wives of Jeff Davis and Robert E. Lee, born of Old Line families, were good, dutiful, Christian women; what else, after all, were they allowed to be? But from the antebellum era to the Jazz Age, Southern womanhood went through a number of changes, especially within that class writ in the *Social Register*. Improbable as it may be, Montgomery is the town that gave the world a new class of woman— in the persons of Tallulah Bankhead and Zelda Sayre. These two 'Bama debutantes set the nation on its ear with their outrageous reversal of the Southern maiden's role. They provided intoxicating models for the women of the Southland who were literally fed up with living in the shadow of men and promoting the myth of men's invincibility. The "everyday" women of the South had grown weary of rebuilding a land left scorned and impoverished by their defeated menfolk. Tallulah and Zelda have been embraced by today's Southern woman just as they came to reject Melanie in favor of Miss Scarlet. Zelda and Tallulah showed the popular way, but underneath their ribald declaration of women's independence, the stern mettle of Southern womanhood had an edge that cut deeper.

In the supposedly dissolute Jazz Age, Miss Jesse Daniel Ames became a pioneering champion of interracial social justice in the South. Miss Ames campaigned against the Southern obsession for the random choke-hanging of black men. She founded the Southern Women for the Prevention of Lynching in 1930, and within nine years the organization had forty thousand members. These women were horrified that redneck vigilantes were killing black men in the name of Southern womanhood. Ames's main opposition came from the absurdly titled Woman's National Association for the Preservation of the White Race, which claimed that Miss Ames was "defending criminal Negroes at the expense of innocent white girls." Ames's efforts brought lynching under a measure of control. The belles of the South were finding a new voice despite all the silliness and fluff of the cotillions in Montgomery and Mobile and wherever else the white man's world depended upon crinoline and pantalets.

In the late 1940s politics in the Alabama Black Belt seemed to be taking some progressive steps. James Elisha "Big Jim" Folsom got himself elected governor on a combination populist platform and medicine-show appeal. Big Jim brought in country bands to entertain the folks and lull them into submission, answering all questions with tobacco-juice parables. He set a new standard for the Savage Ideal demagogues of the South by openly criticizing "the Big Mules," the redneck aristocrats. Folsom led the progressive postwar Southern politicians and didn't play the race-baiting card in his campaigns for the simple reason that race really wasn't an issue for the first time since Reconstruction. Folsom championed education, women's rights, one-man-one-vote, better roads, and human dignity. He had come from the Wire Grass region of southeast Alabama, a land of small farms, few blacks, and moderate attitudes. His support came from the country people outside the big cities of Birmingham and Montgomery. The landmark Supreme Court decision of 1954 would not be felt in Alabama politics until 1962. But then it was felt with a vengeance, as the Savage Ideal turned into the theater of the absurd and only one campaign issue came to dominate the entire Southern political stage for the next generation.

Big Jim Folsom didn't have a prayer in his 1962 reelection bid because "the fighting little judge," as the state and national press dubbed George Corley Wallace, "outniggrahed" Folsom and all the Southern demagogues to follow. At his inauguration Wallace proclaimed, "Segregation now! Segregation tomorrow! Segregation forever!" The White Citizens Councils, the rednecks, the crackers, the Klan, the bubbas—none could get enough of this Rebel war whoop. Neither could the press. Wallace was a master at playing to the news boys, and if ever there was a politician created by the press—newspapers, magazines, radio, and the new kid on the media block, TV— it was George Wallace. The press got colorful stories about the little judge: the one about George and his wife, Lurleen, having to live in a chicken house while he was working his way through law school (he later reminisced that no matter where he went, he could never lose the smell of chicken shit); the one about the press charging him with being mentally deficient for receiving a 10 percent GI disability for schizophrenia (he stated proudly that he was the only presidential candidate proven by the government to be 90 percent sane). The press got stacks of Pulitzer Prizes, the demagogues got elected and reelected, and the citizens of the South got another day older and deeper in debt.

Through the integration fights of the 1950s, 1960s, and 1970s, American industry virtually shunned these lands of repression. Wallace served through three decades and Alabama and its people suffered accordingly. Still, a weather change started in the late 1960s with the federal enforcement of voting rights legislation. As blacks were finally allowed to register and vote, the demagogues started changing their tack; they began to court the black vote. Incredibly, they got it. Ironically, it fell to the newly enfranchised black demagogues to teach the Old Order a new lesson. When the blacks trumped the race-baiting card and created a new game, the most unlikely coalition ever to strike Southern politics occurred. Blacks got to be players in this new game and old-line Southern pols like Lester Maddox, George Wallace, Ross Barnett, and even Orval Faubus became fairly competent elected officials. Relieved of the old burden of having to foster racial intolerance, the governors found themselves with more time to put forward reform programs. All of a sudden Yankee industry started pouring in. Here was the birth of the economic miracle called the Sun Belt South.

OLD U.S. Highway 80 runs west out of Montgomery through the town of Selma and over the famous Edmund Pettus Bridge (where Dr. King started his crucible marches on Montgomery). From here the highway carves through the flatland counties of Dallas, Perry, Marengo, and Hale, all the way to the Tombigbee River. Way back when, these Black Belt lands were all given over to cotton; this was the focal point for the settlement of the Deep South and the beginnings of the Cotton Kingdom. Nowadays only the Tombigbee bottoms are rich enough to support the cotton crops. The rest of the land either lies fallow or is taken up with pastures. For a time in the mid-twentieth century, a few wildcatting dreamers searched these alluvial bottoms for oil, but it was all chimera. Today the only vestige of this dream are a few scattered cricket pumps rusted as shut and immovable as the Tin Man in *The Wizard of Oz*.

To a select handful of devotees, these almost forgotten fields are

James Agee country. At the nadir of the Great Depression, Agee and the photographer Walker Evans came South to the fields around the little towns of Moundville, Akron, Eutaw, Demopolis, and Greensboro. The two men visited and lived for a short while with three white sharecropper families in 1936. Out of this experience came the most heartbreaking book ever to be written on the deprivation suffered by the poor whites during the Depression. The photographs taken by Evans stand as monuments to the memory of the obscure men, women, and children who spent their lives on soil owned by the Big Mules.

From a perspective of more than fifty years, *Let Us Now Praise Famous Men* remains a beautiful and angry and fanatic hymn to the poor. For the generation following the Great Depression, James Agee was much more. He was the chronicler of the South, a bereft singer of the poor white's soul, and even today his long, tortured anthem of these dispossessed and forgotten spirits of the South evokes a pain and a heart-hollowing sense of guilt. No one could quite know what Agee was so moved by in his sojourn down here in the godforsaken bottoms of the Tombigbee and Warrior rivers, unless he had once upon a time experienced the existence of living in a shotgun shack with packed earth for a floor and a front yard kept and swept clean of weeds, with flowers growing in a rubber, treadless tire planter (just a few wildflowers gathered from the fields at the dusk of another hard day), a hill of glistening coal by the front door for the pot-bellied stove, the earthen mountain of the storm cellar where the kids played war or king of the hill and maybe sang "My Country 'Tis of Thee" to an invisible audience of crickets and tree frogs and cicadas.

Agee's book is not authentic documentation; it was never intended to be. He gave the farm families depicted in the book fictitious names, almost as if he wanted to spare them the shame of such episodes as going without clothes or shoes, of wasting away in catatonic fever for lack of money to pay a doctor, of one young mother saving all year long to raise a dollar so her kids could enjoy the indescribable delight of one trip to the ice cream store. Because he wanted these families to stand as real but universal symbols of the undeserved suffering of all sharecroppers, Agee took the license of moving places and towns around the landscape of Alabama. He really didn't need to go to such lengths—his words would have offended no one.

The people of Agee's country are the same today. The Big Sandy Swamp is still there and just as murky. Off County Road 21, cotton fields still stretch in every direction. The shotgun shacks are mostly gone because there's no one to live in them on the corporate fields. The old Arnold Place is all burned out and fallen down; Mamie Bates's unpainted, untreated clapboard cabin still stands, with morning glories providing shade for the vacant porch. In the small town of Moundville the old post office is still there, though it's been converted to a senior citizens' center. If you go inside inquiring about families who lived here during the Depression, the kind lady who runs the place will tell you that none of them—the Tingles, the Fieldses, the Burroughses—live here anymore. "They're all moved away or died out." She remembers the Depression and how bad it was. "It was hard on everybody around here." Her voice is soothing, almost healing from the hurt she remembers, and it's as if it comes from some old hymn.

The railway office in Moundville remains, though it only handles an occasional passing freight. The Moundville *Times* comes out weekly and the November 6, 1992, edition proclaimed George Bush the winner over Bill Clinton in Moundville by 16 votes out of the 995 ballots cast. The town's elementary school election gave Clinton the kiddie vote, 99–79, with 22 for Perot. Ray Chandler, columnist for the *Times,* allows as how three little phrases, "I love you," "Thank you," and "I'm sorry," could solve most of the problems in Moundville and the rest of the world.

"It's a way of life for me," writes Chandler. "I've been taught this all of my life by my mama."

The closest big city to Moundville is Tuscaloosa, the home of the University of Alabama and the living mausoleum to Paul "Bear" Bryant. Ten years after his death the businesses of Tuscaloosa are still filled with portraits and full-sized photographs of Bryant. On the actual day of his passing, January 26, 1983, the cars and pickup trucks and eighteen-wheelers, every vehicle bearing an Alabama license plate, pulled over to the shoulders of highways or curbs of streets, turned their headlights on, and observed a moment of silence in memory of their hero.

The road from Bear Bryant's stomping grounds up to the state capital might just as well be renamed Bear Bryant Way, since it was his football program that gave meaning to life in Alabama. Tuscaloosa fed from the legislative troughs of the capital.

Birmingham is really two cities, the gracious old sector that tragically has been allowed to rot and slough off like so much diseased flesh, and the financial district where the new banks and professional buildings rise up in golden splendor. The schizoid nature of the Deep South comes into hapless being in Birmingham. The city is debutante balls in satin and lace, and tatterdemalion hookers. It's bright little children in Montessori schools and dull-eyed waifs hoping for one meal today. It's bankers loaning high and borrowing low, real estate agents scheming their way onto the million-dollar roundtable right next to pimps and pushers selling for cash or fencing stolen stuff or buying food stamps at ten cents on the dollar. It's the country club and Silk Stocking Hill and Champagne versus the shitkicker tonk and lowlife bar selling shots of tokay for a quarter. It's the 'Bama Booster Club and the PTA and Ministerial Alliance versus the blood gangs and skinheads and tent-city faith healers.

What went wrong in Birmingham? How come this semitough town didn't become the Empire City of the South instead of Atlanta? Birmingham was on its way to being the Pittsburgh of the South as a result of massive steel industry expansion during the First and Second World Wars. The city recognized this phenomenon by erecting a statue to its patron saint, Vulcan, the misshapen Norse Roman god of the underworld and of the anvil. The statue on nearby Red Mountain stands guard over the city that poisoned the very air of Alabama, the low and mean hatreds stretching back to the very foundations of the Savage Ideal. What went wrong in Birmingham was the overt racism embraced by a white man's culture unable to adapt or change.

To those who love Birmingham and believe it to be the greatest city in Alabama, the city is a tragic disappointment. It was the one serious chance for any interior city of the Deep South to fulfill Henry Grady's dream of partnership between industrial and agrarian growth. A small but strong element of equality lived in Birmingham back in the 1930s. Labor organizers tried to put together a coalition of black and white workingmen, and Eleanor Roosevelt came to Birmingham to give her blessing to the enterprise. But they were all arrested in a meeting hall for an "illegal assembly of blacks and whites." Such a mixed assembly was against the Jim Crow laws of the state, rigorously enforced by none other than Bull Connor, who would later sic the dogs on lunch-counter demonstrators in this city in the 1960s. Yet the city that gave us Bull Connor also gave us Margaret Walker, author of the groundbreaking novel *Jubilee*, which for the first time in the South challenged the black-faced minstrel image of the Negro-master relationship. Miss Walker forever impugned the Hollywood stereotype of "Yowsa, Marse Robert, you so kind to me," a shuffle-butt conceit epitomized in the works of Thomas Nelson Page, William Gilmore Simms, John Pendleton Kennedy, and, undoubtedly the worst of the lot, William J. Grayson.

"You can go across this entire land, there ain't no place like Burmin'ham," sings Randy Newman in valedictory to this sad old town. They used to call Birmingham "The Magic City," but the only magic dust left is in the hip pockets of those who fled to the new metropolitan community, Anniston. On the surface Anniston is a perfect little city of more than fifty thousand and growing. It started off as a bought-and-sold textile town just like hundreds of others in the Piedmont. And then it picked up chemicals and the all-important Fort McClellan, also known for its chemical expertise (of the germ warfare variety).

Anniston is known locally for the Shakespearean festival it puts on each year. Back before World War II, a Shakespearean play of sorts unfolded here in Calhoun County. The U.S. Army Air Corps established a base here and stationed the 99th Pursuit Squadron on it. This squadron was commanded by Captain Benjamin O. Davis and was officered and manned solely by blacks. It was quite a joke to the Pentagon planners. Captain Davis was the first black man in the twentieth century to graduate from West Point. Others had tried but the thin gray line gave them all the silent treatment, never speaking a single word to the young black men. Somehow Ben Davis endured four long years of this behavior, yet when he graduated he was refused a posting to the air corps. Davis's father was a retired brigadier general who had risen from the ranks and though a black man could pull some strings. The Pentagon was forced to form an all-black fighter squadron because no white unit would accept black pilots. As a final twist, the blacks were made to train in the Jim Crow South. Hitler may not have cared for Jesse Owens, a native Alabaman, at the

Munich Olympics, but *der Führer* liked the 99th even less. Davis and his fellow aces shot down a whole mess of Messerschmitts and were one of the most decorated units in the war.

THE state of Alabama has nothing if not geographic diversity—the Gulf Coast plain and three separate fingers of the Appalachian Highlands (the southernmost projection of the Piedmont Plateau, the Valley and Ridge Province, and the Cumberland Plateau up on the Tennessee border). The high, hilly region of north Alabama is coal country and has been for generations. The whole area at one time was sickled over with the disease of poverty. The little towns of late have taken their cue from the environmentalists and are trying to resuscitate their lands, and as you pass the enormous old slag piles and the deep, dangerous strip pits, you see many that have been filled up and grassed over, while others stand naked looking like a dead man's eyes. The people of this hill country abide by the age-old codes—they live by the feud and with the moonshine. Folks here have no more in common with Jim Folsom's Wire Grass country and the glitzy Gulf Coast than green acorns have with bitterweed.

These are the last hills to be seen for quite a while as one descends toward the mud flats of the Tombigbee and the state of Mississippi. Solemn thoughts occupy the mind as the journey rolls into the corporate cotton fields that surround the town of Tupelo. Ages ago this area was all swampland covered with tupelo forests, the small swamp trees that the Creek Indians used for their lodgings. Make no error, this is Mississippi, the Southern state of mind that carries the greatest hopes and the worst nightmares for the South.

It was here in Tupelo where the long-abiding mother love of Elvis Presley began, for it was his mama, Gladys, who most influenced the life of this American legend. The intensity of the relationship between Southern mothers and their menfolk is roughly comparable to the exploits of Jewish mothers or other Levantine cultures like the Italian and Sicilian *mama mias,* but nowhere does there exist a culture to surpass the scope and status of Southern motherhood. Southern mothers are unshakable in promoting the fate of their brood and just as militant in dealing with anyone who threatens the progress and victory, no matter how marginal, of their progeny. These angels with sharp claws are curiously forgiving of their men's foibles and failures; they bear their disappointment as a proud badge of their care and can even convert failure into success in their mind's eye.

The modest two-room house where Elvis was born and first lived here in Tupelo has been preserved and turned into a museum. All of the artifacts, mementoes, curios, and Elvis memorabilia have been saved over the years and provided by Jeannette McComb, a childhood playmate and lifelong friend of the King's. Elvis is the most popular person ever to come from the South, and that includes Robert E. Lee. It may be tacky to think it, let alone say it out loud, but the image of Lee as the prince of virtue has never died. The personification has merely been transferred to Elvis. There is no more way of explaining Elvis than there is of understanding how Jesus of Nazareth rose from carpentry. After all these years one still has to wonder how it happened. Perhaps it's an embodiment of something everyone, men and women, just had to have, a need satisfied so deeply that reason was eclipsed by faith. In the South the meaning of Elvis becomes even more complex. His rise and enshrinement seem to be inextricably entwined with the ghostly memories of the Lost Cause. And of a poor white kid called a "webfooter" in these bottoms who in his own way conquered the North where the South had failed.

The blazing comet that was Elvis Presley has something to do with the intangible sensation one can still get today by listening to late-night radio call-in shows from Memphis or Pensacola or Dayton or Newark.

The deejay picks up the phone with a crisp "You're on the air." We hear the sobs of a near-hysterical woman. "What is it, lady? What's wrong?"

"It's Elvis . . ."

"Yes, I know. What about Elvis?"

"I just love that poor old dead thing."

AN extraordinary number of special highways grace this jagged land called America, roads that take their travelers into realms of beauty incompatible with the hustle of commerce. There's the Seventeen Mile Drive on coastal California, the trail through the MacIntyre Mountains in upstate New York, the Dells in Wisconsin, the Trail of the Lonesome Pine called the Blue Ridge Parkway in North Carolina. But by far the most exquisite and serene passage for any weary soul anxious about yet more road miles is the Natchez Trace.

The Trace, one of America's most colorful and historic highways, is also about the best way to travel the state of Mississippi. The road was carved out of the wilderness in the early nineteenth century and linked Natchez on the Mississippi River to Nashville, the gateway to the East. The Trace was designed to provide an easier way for the flat and keelboat merchants to get back to their homes in the Midwest on the Ohio River after they had floated their goods down to New Orleans. Ironically, by the time the Natchez Trace was completed, it had become obsolete—the steamboat had taken care of the problem of getting back upstream.

Originally, the old Trace was no wider than a sidewalk, just like its sister highway, the Great Philly Road. Today it is a streamlined two-laner that occasionally flares into four lanes, but it's always a quiet, unrushed passage. The entire Trace, some 450 miles, is immaculately maintained and groomed in contrast to the stark vistas afforded by the interstates. Some folks claim that parts of the Trace are haunted, and as you drive along its tree-lined, bough-shaded route, such a dreaminess comes over you that you almost feel the presence of those who once passed this way . . . Andrew Jackson and his Tennessee Volunteers (including a sixteen-year-old Sam Houston) . . . John Murrell, the most infamous pirate and road agent in the South's history . . . Jefferson Davis, traveling the route between his plantation and the state capital at Jackson . . . William Tecumseh Sherman and his rampaging troops looking for another Mississippi town to burn . . . Joseph Eggleston Johnston, wondering how he could get some relief to Vicksburg . . . Nathan Bedford Forrest, using the old road after the war to find new real estate for his land-development schemes . . . Meriwether Lewis, the great explorer, on his way home to Virginia with a cache of gold and a burden of self-doubt and maybe a suspicion of the awful fate awaiting him at the end of the darkly enchanted road.

Tupelo is right on the Natchez Trace and perhaps that's why the little delta town was founded: it was reachable. Only later did the Tombigbee see the arrival of steam-powered river boats come to transport Tupelo's cotton to Mobile.

From Augusta in Georgia, Conestoga wagons would leave the

Great Philly Road and follow the Upper Federal Road through Georgia and Alabama, bringing tinkers and traders into little market towns like Columbus, Mississippi. Likewise, drummers and horse traders from New Orleans would bring their wares up the Trace and off the main trail down little notch roads to set up shop on creek banks near tiny villages like Philadelphia. The villagers in the nearby hamlets would leave their flat-farm plains to journey the few miles to the cool, shaded grounds of the creek-side trading camp. Over the decades the townspeople built rude clapboard cabins to shelter their families for the summer festival, and by the 1890s the town of Philadelphia had created the most unusual annual gathering site in America, the Neshoba County Fair. The first families of Neshoba County laid out Founders Square in the heart of the fairgrounds; today's cabins, built on the original site of the 1890s, have become more exclusive than Versailles. In the late twentieth century just as in each preceding year, whole families—grandparents, sons, daughters, in-laws, grandchildren, great-grandchildren, and cousins to the nth degree—gather in these spartan cabins that spread concentrically from Founders Square out for blocks and blocks. It's homecoming, it's family reunion, it's relatives stacked triple-bunked to the ceilings on two floors to celebrate a sense of . . . a sense of what? What does this all mean way out here in one of the least populated regions of east central Mississippi? More than fifteen thousand people a day attend the county fair and most of them live on the grounds in cabins and RVs. Not ten thousand people live in the whole of Neshoba County, and that includes the last Choctaw Indian Reservation east of the Mississippi River.

Founders Square is the equivalent of the eighth- and ninth-century Icelandic Althings, themselves traditionally held in high summer. The purpose of these ancient fairs was an annual display of merchants' wares, but more importantly the fairs provided for the assembly of law-sayers whose Romano-Christian roots came from Irish monks bringing the word of God to the heathens of the North Sea. The Neshoba County Fair of the twentieth century became the singular platform for any and all Mississippi politicians, from would-be populist state land agents without a ghost of a chance of being elected, to party-line senators, representatives, governors, and state legislators who had the election in the bag. The giants of Mississippi politics made the pilgrimage to Neshoba County—James Vardaman,

Theodore Bilbo, James Eastland, John Stennis, Ross Barnett. Ronald Reagan came here to stump for votes. So did Michael Dukakis and John Glenn.

Used to be that the organizers of the fair set aside a day for their "black folk." That was the day no white people attended the festivities. One must remember that Mississippi is the state that once forbade a black man and a white man from playing checkers, public or private. Today it's still a white man's fair. Blacks don't take part, mostly because they don't want to. The only blacks you see are the trainers and grooms and hot walkers over at the horse barns where the fair is serious business.

Not everyone who comes to the fair does so out of love. Many come because of family ties, because they have to. One cynic whose wife's sister married a native has been coming to the fair for years, bunking in the family cabin on the corner of the first block off Founders Square. He admits he likes the fair but he thinks they're missing a bet here.

"The Founders Association owns a lot of land just across the road from the fair. What they need to do is put in a theme park that wouldn't be open just ten days in the summer but would be run the year round. They could call it the Three Martyred Civil Rights Workers Theme Park. They could have rides like Mr. Toad's Wild Ride at Disney World, only here the toad would be chased by hooded Klansmen. You could have parachute jumps using Klan sheets all spread out to show the insignia of the Grand Wizard. There could be barbecues over burning crosses and you could use the embers to toast marshmallows. The possibilities are endless . . . something for the kids, something for the adults, and grub for all. . . ."

Black humor has its own hue in the South, even at the Neshoba County Fair. The prime scenes of the fair can be viewed as the families sit down to supper on the porches of their cabins. The fair is held in August, and it's so brutally hot and humid that only someone inured to the pain would even bother to attend the event, so meals on the porch to catch the evening breeze are pretty standard. The provender is piled high, the tables groan with the weight, and the families bow their heads in prayer before digging in. But look at the photos from these evenings and you'll see that the eyes are on the rich blackberry and peach cobblers, banana pudding, and that most obscenely delicious dessert in the South, Mississippi mud pie.

And here is the difference between whites and blacks in Mississippi. The whites' eyes are on the pies and the blacks' eyes are on the prize. And the prize is human dignity. The town of Philadelphia and Neshoba County itself have another heritage, one that is as inescapable as the fatalistic Althing that is the forebear of this fair. *Njal's Saga* and life by the feud was as natural to the medieval Icelanders as it is to the Irish descendants in Mississippi who chose to live by the Savage Ideal. Here in Neshoba County the last battle of the civil rights war was fought in the summer of 1964. Afterwards, the Lost Cause was finally dead, though it would take the martyrdom of three freedom riders, Chaney, Schwerner, and Goodman, to consign it to history.

In 1964 the state of Mississippi was awash with blood. The summer before, Medgar Evers had been murdered and the thousands of protesters who came to Jackson were arrested and held like cattle at the State Fairgrounds. Freedom Summer of 1964 saw yet more thousands of young idealistic volunteers pouring into the state to help register black voters. In a real sense they had come to try to make things fair. The focal point had shifted from the capital at Jackson to crossroads country towns in Neshoba County like Philadelphia.

Others besides Freedom Riders were focusing on Philadelphia, too. They were the prominent and the obscure, sheriff's deputies and local police, farmers, storekeepers, and a few rabble that had been roused. They felt as though they were being pushed off the face of the earth. They had decided to push back. They were the Klan. Word got around that a meeting was being held over in Smith County, in a little clapboard church outside the small town of Raleigh.

Raleigh hasn't changed any more than Jimmy Carter's hometown of Plains. Raleigh doesn't have an ex-President but it does have a man with the same quiet conviction and steady resolve. His name is Bob Evans and he could have been a bubba or a blessed brother of the Great Speckled Bird Church or a grand inquisitor of children's library books on the local school board. But he's not. What he is is a judge, an elected circuit judge. He's a former district attorney and criminal lawyer now in his forties. His family has lived in Smith County for generations and he'll proudly point out the old Methodist church built by his great-grandfather before the Civil War.

"We found out years later that the Klan met covertly in this church, you know," Evans says, "on the night before Chaney and Schwerner and Goodman disappeared."

The story of the murders of the three Philadelphia Freedom Riders has been told many times before, but Judge Evans tells the story in a new light. "One of the cruelest ironies of the murders was that it was an accident," says Evans. "The Klan that had met in my great-granddad's church had not intended to kill Chaney, Schwerner, and Goodman. They had intended to beat them and send them back up North crippled, showing all those Freedom Riders just what would happen to them if they kept coming down here to Mississippi. But the plan backfired. As they were roughing up the young men and pistol-whipping them, a revolver discharged, killing one of them instantly. Here was the accident, and the Klan believed it had no recourse but to kill the other two."

On July 2, 1964, twelve days after the murders, President Lyndon Johnson signed the landmark Civil Rights Act into law. The three Freedom Riders became martyrs and more. They broke the back of the old Savage Ideal and started the sea change that would alter the Southern psyche forever.

Today the chief worries of the barely seven thousand souls who live in Philadelphia are when another fast-food joint besides McDonald's will come in, whether the video store has any new releases, and the chances of getting a cabin closer to Founders Square at the Neshoba County Fair. As one circulates through the big crowds at the fair, one will find kids who never heard of Freedom Summer and adults who've pushed it to the farthest recesses of their memory. But somewhere in these crowds are some of the men who killed those kids back in 1964. They are not recognizable today because they don't have the look they had back then, that swagger and arrogance they showed when they strode into the courthouse and out again as free men.

Sometimes late in the evening at the Neshoba County Fair you can hear muted singing. It's after the children are finally asleep in their bunks and the pulse of the fair has hushed to the calm of grownups sitting up late on the porches. The singing is of hymns but is not church-voiced; it is more of lullaby, family-proved, people feeling good at simply being together, with maybe a little liquor in them that makes them need to start up old songs. They have known the hymnal by heart since childhood and now, unprompted, they sing of out-worn old hopes and fears, of help for the helpless as a darkness deepens, of praise of famous men. From the porches one can almost hear the ghostly voices of those ancient lawgivers chanting their liturgies of transgressions and human failure. The porch voices blend a harmony. Come home, come home, ye who are weary, come home. . . . Listening, you know the fair has a meaning of its own. We come to the fair as pilgrims, wayfaring strangers wanting everything that was still to be true . . . as true as the peace of slumbering children in their bunks at the fair.

CHAPTER 7

WHY WE ALL LIVE AT THE P.O.

Mississippi and Western Tennessee . . . Faulkner and His Heirs . . . The National Tobacco Spitting Contest . . . Eudora Welty . . . Robert Johnson and the Delta Blues . . . Memphis . . . B. B. King and Beale Street

THE STATE OF MISSISSIPPI has had a strange heritage. La Salle claimed it for France in the seventeenth century with no more call than that he had canoed past its western shore. John Law, probably history's most successful swindler, used the territory as part of his early-eighteenth-century con game called the Mississippi Bubble. Less than a century later the state, then part of Georgia's Western Reserve, became the scene of yet another hysterical land grab, the Yazoo Fraud, which you will recall from Chapter 5. During the boom years before the Civil War, cotton and land fortunes changed hands in a matter of hours. In the aftermath of the war, the land and its crops and people were stolen and restolen until no one could tell the difference between carpetbagger and scalawag.

Mississippi remains a Southern anomaly. The state has the best storytellers, finest lawyers, and most colorful characters in the nation. Yet by 1950 its per-capita income was only 51 percent of the national average. In many ways the state still clings to the Jacksonian credo of free enterprise with no federal interference wanted. The epitome of rooted resistance to change was Mississippi's hard-core denial of elemental civil rights in the 1960s when Attorney General Bobby Kennedy became the most hated man in the state since Abraham Lincoln. Even today Bobby's memory won't win any popularity contests down here, but the state is showing signs of social progress with its election of a few able, enlightened governors such as William Winter and Ray Mabus.

Magically, something in the soil, something in the air, has fostered the greatest concentration of literary brilliance in the country's history—William Faulkner, Walker Percy, Tennessee Williams, Eudora Welty, Richard Wright, Shelby Foote, Ellen Douglas, Hodding Carter. A fair question might be: how does this happen in Mississippi and keep on happening? It couldn't be abiogenesis; happenstance wouldn't allow for such multiple births from the void. Perhaps it's a countervalent convergence of destinies, an Emersonian sort of compensation with the profound corruption of the culture being leavened by a fated conscience. James Whitehead, a Mississippian and one of America's better poets, explains the incredible sequence of Mississippi's artists through the generations with the simple declaration "It rubs off." Only in the South could such an ontological observation be so lucid and true.

This mystic "rub-off" affected more than just literary brilliance in Mississippi; it nurtured a natural poetry that gave birth to not one but two new art forms, country music and the blues.

The father of country music was Jimmie Rodgers, who was born in lonesome Meridian, Mississippi, in 1897. Rodgers worked sometimes as a brakeman on the railroads that were finding their way into the remote South; when the jobs played out he worked as a gandy dancer or rode the rails as a hobo, writing songs all the while and indulging his restless spirit. In 1927 Jimmie Rodgers committed to wax the first recorded country song, "The Soldier's Sweetheart," and an old lullaby, "Sleep, Baby, Sleep," where his famous yodel was first heard. Perhaps his most enduring ballad is a sentimental love song with a cutting edge of bitter irony, "Miss the Mississippi and You." Here is the heart of Mississippi's artistry—the senses of bitterness and irony that permeate the catercorner nature of its native-born.

Can the world understand why Mississippi is so bitter? Back in 1863, soon after the fall of Vicksburg, General William Tecumseh Sherman got antsy and decided he'd march from Jackson all the way to Meridian—just to give this nest of Rebels a good whuppin'. Sherman spread his army out on a fifty-mile front, and his troops burned and looted homesteads, hamlets, and towns, reducing the whole area to scorched earth. No Confederate troops worth the mentioning stood in the way. The success of this bloodbath so whetted Sherman's appetite that he repeated the carnage all the way through Georgia and South Carolina to the sea.

Retracing Sherman's invidious episode, the modern traveler can still see the man's touch. Meridian is a pretty lonely spot hiding away in the piney woods of east Mississippi close to the Alabama state line. The town remains as isolated as it was in Sherman's time. Of all the old states of the Confederacy, Mississippi was treated the shabbiest by the vengeful North. Thus General Sherman initiated, as it were, the Northern view of the defeated South as a penal colony in Mississippi. After the war Adelbert Ames (son-in-law of the infamous General Ben F. Butler) served as the federally appointed governor, and he proved to be the most repressive politician during Reconstruction.

IT's easy to get from Meridian to Jackson on the interstate, but if you go that way you'll miss one of the most intriguing, funky little towns in the South—Raleigh, Mississippi. The town perches on the southern edge of the Bienville National Forest; the woods are loaded with wild turkeys and passersby are obliged to stop to let them cross the road—it's common courtesy down here. Raleigh's fleeting fame was based on an extraordinary annual event known locally as "the Spit." But the town's lasting reputation is for one of its own, John Little, the man who pumped, primed, and promoted the National Tobacco Spitting Contest.

The young John Little entered his first Spit in 1955, coming in third. From that moment on, the Spit was the love of John Little's life, the moment of truth, Hemingway's death in the afternoon.

The Spit was originally put together by the Forestry Service but when the Feds reneged on the budget, it was taken over by Little, who literally juiced the event up. The control of that single, gelatinous hocker as it traced its graceful arc heavenward only to splatter into a thousand beads of liquid shrapnel some thirty-odd feet down the launching platform was a bigger high than Alan Shepard's ascent into the ozone.

Little went to Ole Miss and got a degree in pharmacy, following a family tradition. He started working in Jackson but on weekends he devoted himself to promoting this most unique contest. The crowds grew as folks started coming in from all over the South and the nation to Billy John Crumpton's stock pond where the Spit was staged. Raleigh became a must for Mississippi politicians who dared not miss the chance to press the flesh, kiss the babies, and dribble a bit of the amber effluvial down their chins.

"The Spit was serious bidness," John Little says. "Those old boys were truly admired. The last fella to win was from the Gulf and he's still famous down there."

The world-record spit as listed in the *Guinness Book of Records* is thirty-three feet seven inches. Think about it. Thirty-three feet is eleven good-sized paces, a hell of a putt on the golf course, an impossible pole vault, and a respectable triple-jump with a running start. There are no running starts at the Spit. You toe the line, rear back like a cobra, uncoil, and let fly. The crowd numbering in the thousands hoops and hollers and makes heroes out of every Spit category victor. The spirit here, unlike the county fair at Neshoba or the football games at Ole Miss, was a carry-forward from the old village green contests in England, Scotland, Ireland, and Wales. The Spit is all good-natured and respectable, not based on scholarship-trained athleticism or some carny shuck. It was based on the common, God-given ability to propel saliva, something everybody can do.

John Little's calling was not pharmacy. He got the creative bug and enrolled at Millsaps College in the only creative writing course that Miss Eudora Welty ever offered. He went on to get his master's in fine arts in creative writing and then left the South when he accepted a position at the University of North Dakota. Little has taught there for more than twenty-five years, during which time he has published stories, essays, and articles and hosted a radio show that brought the Deep Delta blues to the black hills of Dakota. But Little's heart remains in Mississippi. The Spit is gone but he spends his sabbaticals and vacations in his homeland. He drives home in an antique 1965 Cadillac convertible with a personalized car tag that reads "Poetic." It's not uncommon for someone to follow him off the highway to meet the person who has a "poetic license."

Like a lot of Southerners who've moved away from their homeland, Little suffers from a chronic disease called "home hunger." One time when he was stranded up there in the frozen North, with his Cadillac in the shop, Little got on a Greyhound bus that would bring him back to Raleigh. The bus route from Grand Forks ran to Fargo and through the Twin Cities on into Chicago. Little reminisces that this part of the journey was anesthetizing with hardly any conversation going on. Once the bus was in Chicago, the complexion of the trip changed radically, soulfully, because the people getting on in Chicago were just like Little, home hungry and going South. They were all transplanted Mississippians, Tennesseeans, Arkansawyers. He recalls that the only topic of conversation was food, and the talk got more animated as the bus descended the Mississippi Valley past Cairo, Illinois. The homebound folks discussed the Southern feasts they were going to enjoy when they put their feet beneath the tables of their mamas, their aunts, their grandmas. Turkey and cornbread dressing (not stuffing); oysters on the half-shell or fried or mixed in gumbo; hogshead barbecued or baked or even stewed; cooked sweet potatoes, sliced, put in a skillet with bacon drippings and fried with brown sugar; fresh strawberries smothering just-baked-and-buttered catshead biscuits; chicken and dumplings, the chicken stewed in a pressure cooker until it was falling off the bone; meaty pigs' feet, pickled, breaded or grilled; and every vegetable under God's sky and billowy clouds.

"It never occurred to other passengers that we were all brothers and sisters celebrating our return home," says Little, "just as it didn't dawn on them that I was the only white among them. The need to come home just flat obscured any racial distinction. We were just homesick Southerners and by the time the Greyhound rolled into Memphis, home hunger had taken over."

THE city of Jackson is just a boot-scoot or two over the Strong and Pearl rivers from Raleigh. Folks here seem inordinately proud of their town. An oft-overheard quote goes, "I don't like to be more than three or four hours from Jackson." This attitude allows the restless Jacksonians to travel to Memphis (north Jackson) and New Orleans (south Jackson). Jackson was a sleepy little burg during the Civil War but Sherman torched it anyway. Sherman taught Jackson an early lesson on the sin of pride and burned it so completely that the locals called the city "Chimneyville" for years afterward. Jackson is the state capital and the sole center of the state. Many cities in the United States can qualify for being a "state of mind." San Francisco, the Big Easy, the Big Apple (and maybe Natchitoches in Louisiana). But the city of Jackson doesn't even need to compete with these others, for it is a Southern magical dream come true.

Race-baiting politicians, antediluvian redneck racial mores, preoccupation with illusory what-could-have-beens exist cheek-by-jowl with radical populism, artistic brilliance, and liberal militancy. In short, Jackson is the quintessential Southern dilemma. The city was founded in 1821 soon after Andrew Jackson had coerced the Choctaw Indian Nation into turning over about half of present-day Mississippi for some promises that were never met. As a result of getting all this real estate for nothing, the state legislature decided on a capital to replace the older territorial seats on the Mississippi River. The old capital, Washington, was just outside Natchez; Frederick Law Olmsted visited it on his travels and found it to be about the roughest and meanest town he had seen in the South. And not wanting to name anything "Washington," the state legislature decided on Le Fleurs Bluff here on the Pearl River, with the name changed to honor Old Hickory, the man who had freed up so much of the state for white settlers.

Throughout the nineteenth century, Jackson was overshadowed by its rich sisters, Vicksburg and Natchez, both in population and good sense (representatives from the river cities voted against secession). It wasn't until the 1920s that Jackson became Mississippi's largest city and only true metropolitan area.

In 1963 the crosshairs of the civil rights movement found an unlikely target in the little land-grant Tougaloo College on the northern outskirts of Jackson. That year the NAACP held its national convention on the campus while all hell was breaking loose in the city. Dr. Martin Luther King, Roy Wilkins, and Medgar Evers addressed the convention with high rhetoric but with no real conviction that their cause was about to gain its most important victory. By far the most important figure at the convention turned out to be a young black woman named Anne Moody, a student at Tougaloo. Anne Moody was not by nature an activist; she had grown up in impoverished south Mississippi, had witnessed the white man's brutalities and knew that things were dreadfully wrong. The NAACP in

Jackson had picketed segregated stores like Woolworth's before but had not tried to actually integrate them. Anne Moody would be the first to do so.

Enduring slurs, threats, and a bombardment of paint, mustard, catsup, sugar, and coffee, Moody and two other Tougaloo students broke the whites-only barrier at Woolworth's in downtown Jackson. Many decent white people of Jackson deplored what was about to happen to their city. Moody recorded some of these sentiments in her book, *Coming of Age in Mississippi*. A white woman came up to her as she was being pelted at the lunch counter; the woman was shocked by what was going on and said she'd like to stay and help Moody defy the crowd but that her husband wouldn't let her. No decent Jacksonian wanted the confrontation but they were drowning in the flood of racial emotions now gripping the whole South. The single act of defiance by Anne Moody had given the NAACP courage, and that organization now started picketing Woolworth's under the leadership of Medgar Evers. Mississippi blacks rallied and the city of Jackson became a crucible.

And then on June 12, 1963, Medgar Evers was killed, gunned down at midnight in his driveway. His murderer, Byron de la Beckwith, was not brought to justice until the spring of 1994. Three earlier Mississippi juries had found him not guilty of a crime about which he had boasted for more than thirty years.

Anne Moody had been Medgar Evers's comrade, had spoken with him just hours before he was brutally murdered. Through her courage she had placed herself at the forefront of the movement; without fully realizing it, she had provided the spark in Mississippi that would fire the movement on to a final victory. The next year was 1964, Freedom Summer, and Anne Moody would be there through the horrifying ordeals of Mississippi burnings. Freedom Summer also saw the passage of the landmark Civil Rights Bill that would signal the end of the Black Codes, Jim Crow, the Savage Ideal. It had also been a joyless duration spanning more than six generations, and to the legions of people who had fought so long for these civil liberties, for common decency, the movement had gone on far too long. Sometimes one can only join Thomas Jefferson in fearing for one's country upon the reflection that God is just.

• • •

GIVE or take a few isolated pockets of Klanners posing as weekend survivalists, the redneck veneer of Mississippi has gone away. Still, the ghost of Lucius Quintus Cincinnatus Lamar remains to haunt the state capitol. Right here under the rotunda of these marbled halls, a New South variation on the theme of Belshazzar's Feast is playing. For years a picture hung in the capitol building; it dated from the WPA era of the 1930s and depicted the halcyon days of antebellum Mississippi where life on the plantation was all hoecake, sweet taters, and harmony between master and slave. In the New South some sensitive folks in Jackson demanded the picture's removal as being racially offensive. As with all such things in Mississippi, the issue went to court. The judge made a truly inspired ruling: the capitol could keep the picture and it could still hang on the wall in pride of place; it just couldn't be visible. The judge ordered a black curtain to be installed over the picture—to part this veil requires a court injunction. The court firmly believes it has placated both sides in a ruling that positively floated from the cumulonimbus clouds of the cuckoo South.

The town of Jackson has a lot of fine old homes, but unlike the swaddled picture in the capitol, not one of them is antebellum, courtesy of William Tecumseh Sherman. Perhaps the most notable Jackson home is a two-story Edwardian place serenely enveloped by massive oaks and pines. It's the birthplace and residence until recent years of a rather modest, even humble gentle lady named Eudora Welty. Advancing age has caused Miss Welty to move to a house that requires less upkeep.

Friends come here, people paying their respects to the writer who has glorified American literature and her presence for the past fifty years. The general unspoken rule is that no one shows up uninvited, or at least without calling first, yet Miss Welty greets each visitor as if it's the right face. It's the manner of the South and the graciousness of this fabulous women of the South. She'll take in feature writers looking for interviews, actors, film people, new and old acquaintances from Millsaps, and aspiring new writers just wanting to gaze in hopes that something will rub off.

Miss Welty's old house is a family heirloom now; her father built it at the turn of the century and she's kept it almost exactly as it was. In times past you could have seen her light in the study upstairs where she surrounded herself with shelves and piles of books. Her favorites are the Victorian novels, though she's partial to such twentieth-century writers as Virginia Woolf, William Faulkner, Katherine Anne Porter and Elizabeth Bowen. Her own pet favorite is the little-known Virginia-born author Julien Green. In these latter years Miss Welty has moved her writing studio downstairs to the first floor because the stairs are more demanding than Jacob's ladder.

Just after her first novel, *The Robber Bridegroom*, was published, Miss Welty got a fan letter from an unexpected source. The cryptic note read: "Welty, you're doing all right. Who are you?" The note was signed "William Faulkner." She doesn't choose to talk literature much and certainly doesn't seek compliments, won't take them, because she's from the old Southern school that taught true humility above all. She'd rather talk human things, gossip, who's marrying who and did they have to and who's getting a divorce. She loves to talk food, especially fresh summer vegetables and the prime Smith County watermelons her former students, John Little and Tom Royals, bring her on late summer days.

To her readers the most delightful aspect of Miss Welty's writings is her characters' speech. It's called "having a good ear" and it always has the ring of truth, as in the dotty Rondo family of "Why I Live at the P.O." ("Stella-Rondo? Ooooo! Did that child of yours ever learn to talk? You know, Burdyburdyburdyburdy.") Some literary type once tried to pin Miss Welty down on the secret of her great dialogue, and she replied that she just put people together and let them chatter.

Her eyes are kind, not really as sweet as one would think, but penetrating to the darker frequencies, and never with recrimination. She's not going to jump a body because of his dark side. Yet she knows, almost as if she can identify with her own mean streak. Everybody's got a mean streak, she'll tell you and laugh, and make you laugh. In 1963 Miss Welty reexplored the darkness of man in her short work "Where Is the Voice Coming From?" Somehow she got herself into the head of Medgar Evers's killer and with her succinct monologues created a chilling portrait of Southern hate and despair, the depths of Southern mean sumbitch come to life: "I done what I done for my own pure-D satisfaction . . . we ain't never now never going to be equals and you know why? One of us is dead."

The gnawing question of the South remains. Where is the voice coming from? Maybe it comes from this whole land of betrayal and sacrifice . . . where genius and madness live side by side with loneliness and estrangement. Miss Welty makes no distinction between the dark and the absurd sides of the South. She knows that they both exist, that they live catercorner to each other, just as her character in "Why I Live at the P.O." flees the risible madness and repression of her family to live at the back of the post office where she can "keep her things catercorner to each other the way she likes them." The concatenation of the South makes it happen. The old can never wholly meld with the new . . . until one of them is dead.

Out west of Jackson high up on the Walnut Hills Bluffs sits the most famous town in Mississippi's history, Vicksburg. La Salle noted the impressive site in the seventeenth century (the local Indians attacked the French explorer there until his party paddled across the Mississippi River to the Louisiana side and found the protection of a friendly tribe). The Spanish called the bluffs "Nogales" (for the groves of walnut trees), but Spain wasn't in control long enough for the name to stick. The Right Reverend Samuel Vick, a Methodist evangelical do-gooder, came here in the late eighteenth century to establish a commune of right-thinking Christians. But the rush for land in the Yazoo Fraud muddied Vick's claim and he was dispossessed, though his name was carried on and burged.

Vicksburg became the center of steamboat traffic on the lower Mississippi by the late 1820s; from then through the 1880s not one boat traveled the river without putting in at this commercial hub. The town was also the terminus for the Knights of the River, gamblers with such legendary names as George Devol, King Cole Martin, Posey Jeffers, Canada Bill Jones, Elijah Skaggs, and James Ashley. These nineteenth-century condottieri coming downstream from St. Louis and Louisville would change at Vicksburg to gull the planters and merchants up from New Orleans over a friendly hand of faro. Fortunes, vast and otherwise, changed hands on these cruises, as did titles to thousands of acres or high-yellow mistresses to the hereditary Creole plantation owners.

Some of the steamboats of that era were opulent indeed, with grand staterooms, magnificently chandeliered salons, and restaurants that rivaled Delmonico's in New York. Most of the river craft, however, were bare-boned utilitarian vessels built to carry cotton and wares. Even the fancy boats were loaded from the gunwales to the texas deck in stacked bales of cotton during the season. Gambling did not take place in the salons; there were no dice tables, roulette wheels, or green-baize-covered card tables, Hollywood notwithstanding. The action took place in the barbershop or in the first mate's or captain's quarters. The sharpers paid the crews for the privilege of trimming the passengers and seldom did an honest game take place. Riverboat gambling was never an honorable profession and the gamblers themselves were looked down on; they were a sad and tragic lot, and most came to violent ends or took their own lives in remorse.

The modern Chamber of Commerce of Vicksburg has Disneyfied the old truths and legends of riverboat gambling into an upright, dad-gummed, near-Christian industry. All up and down the Mississippi River, gambling boats (what used to be called "gambling hells") have risen up like so many snags in the river that used to plague the fragile floating palaces of yore. The old-timey knights of the river would almost certainly split their breeches laughing at the way the pendulum has swung in barely a hundred years.

Practically speaking, Vicksburg has been under siege since 1863. The Confederacy didn't plan its war effort in the West all that carefully. New Orleans and Baton Rouge fell at the first harsh word and Memphis followed all too quickly without a shot being fired. Vicksburg became the South's last tangible link to its brothers on the western shore of the Mississippi barely one year after the Civil War started. U. S. Grant moved in the early spring of 1863 to sever that last link. He was in luck, for the Confederate commander at Vicksburg, General John Pemberton, was something of a joke who inspired only laughter among his officers and men. Pemberton was a political appointee, a Pennsylvania Yankee who sided with the South. Though he had been admonished time and again not to get his army trapped inside Fortress Vicksburg, that's exactly what Pemberton did. Grant took full advantage. Though he is romanticized as a hero in Vicksburg, there is no telling what needless hardship and suffering Pemberton brought on the city. Toward the end of the siege the people of the town were literally starving; there wasn't a safe hole anywhere for a rat to hide in.

Great controversy has always surrounded Grant's handling of Pemberton's surrender at Vicksburg. Military strategists, real and armchair, have criticized Grant from 1863 to the present for paroling the Southern army. The thesis of these carpers has been that Grant should have rounded up the some thirty thousand Rebs and packed them off to prison camps up North. But Grant was a shrewd man; he freed the broken, dispirited wretches and let them limp on back home. The sight of these beaten men had Grant's desired effect: the morale of the Deep South plummeted and with the news of Lee's defeat at Gettysburg, recruitment of new soldiers in the Deep South became next to impossible. "Unconditional Surrender" Grant invented a new trick, psychological warfare, that both his detractors and supporters didn't understand.

The Vicksburg battlefield today has sort of been raised to the mythical status of Camelot. Hundreds of acres along the river bluffs are devoted to a beautifully laid out memorial to the combatants of both sides. Millions have been spent by the governments of all the states whose citizen-soldiers fought here. The war just won't end because there are too many tourist bucks riding on the tragic memory. Racial memories, as Joseph Campbell and Northrop Frye have taught us, are what you choose to make of them. The Glorious Revolution of Cromwellian England is an equally famous, and perhaps more significant, civil war. The divine right of kings was forever broken at the Battle of Naseby, which led to the beheading of an English monarch. Yet the English haven't seen the profit in ballyhooing famous fights, be they Roundheads and Cavaliers or Rebs and Yanks. Unlike Vicksburg, Naseby Field is full of sheep, not competing monuments. You can drive through Vicksburg for a couple of hours and not see it all; at Naseby you park on the shoulder of an obscure country road and climb over a fence to see a diminutive stack of stones.

THE monstrous bluffs at Vicksburg are the tail end of the Choctaw Ridge that demarks the delta from the uplands. The delta really begins some forty miles to the northeast of Vicksburg at the comely little town of Yazoo City and continues up the ridge line to the famous Chickasaw Bluffs that hold Memphis back from the Big Muddy. These delta lands have always had rich soil (at one time eons ago the topsoil was said to be more than a hundred feet deep). The citizens of these lands, however, are among the poorest in the nation. Only the families owning an inherited piece of the giant corporate fields reap any benefit from the delta's wealth.

Yazoo City itself is a kind of microcosm of the solid, reputable small towns of the South. It's not overly pretentious, it's hardworking, and it has forced itself into a viable accommodation between the races. It's certainly not a Yazoo Fraud city; it's a pretty little town with a pleasant ambiance, maybe because the people here speak so sweetly, musically even. Yazoo is the home of the most refined Southern drawl extant. And the language is no more luxuriant than the kudzu here. There's enough of the stuff to engulf and cover forever the town and the highways leading to it. The authorities here hardly keep the foot-a-night vine in check. While elsewhere in the South kudzu seems to have taken on the aspect of Public Enemy Number One, the folks of Yazoo City take a more benevolent view and almost accept the smothery vine as a member of the family.

Out north of Yazoo City onto the delta, what appears to be an optical illusion captures the traveler's imagination. It's no mirage. It's a gargantuan crater or glacial imprint distorting the horizon. This vast moraine left over from the Ice Age defines the Mississippi River's lower embayment. At planting time before the cotton is up, the soil is bleached, top-crusted over by a brutal sun; but underneath, the black earth that has been permeated for generations with herbicides and chemical fertilizers is waiting for its boundless cash crop. Cotton. The white fiber has been king here for so long that the soil won't accept any other plant. Millions upon millions of acres from Louisiana to the Upper Mississippi are dedicated to this one-crop mentality. It's not just an agricultural mind-set but a sociological one as well. And in little delta hamlets like Jonestown and Belen the top-heavy relative deprivation of the rural South becomes apparent. The comparison of the Big House and the squalid shanty of the countryside is worse than in the city if for no other reason than the urban rich are forced to share some of their wealth, unlike the cotton kings. Life here was a regressive, revolutionary process. The 1820s reached to the 1930s and beyond, and the plantation was the be-all and end-all of existence for the people who worked its lands.

Plantations come in all sizes, from one to one hundred sections or more. The lands are so much the same that the sense of déjà vu is almost overwhelming. The only thing to break the monotony of the sea of cotton fields is a bleak shotgun shack about every forty acres and the occasional copse of elm or poplar trees marking where the big house of the owner is shaded. Once upon a time, though, a discernible difference existed between plantations that had nothing to do with physical appearance; it concerned the people who were born, grew up, and worked on, and sometimes managed to escape, these feudal estates. They were the creators of a new art-and-life form called "the blues."

The most singular plantation of the delta belonged to Will Dockery. The Dockery Plantation, still intact, dates back to 1895 and is located just outside of Cleveland, Mississippi, on the Sunflower River. Dockery began with a sawmill, bought with a thousand-dollar grubstake from his grandmother. From such a modest beginning Dockery ended up owning forty square miles of timberland and five thousand acres of prime bottomland. What makes the Dockery plantation unique is that Will Dockery didn't try to cheat his black field hands out of their pitiful wages; fifty cents a day wasn't much but the common practice of the era's landowners was to shortchange their illiterate tenants out of even this pittance. Dockery's reputation spread up and down the delta, and he was besieged by wagonloads of black families looking for any kind of square deal.

It was on the Dockery Plantation that the blues began, for it was here that the father of the blues, Robert Johnson, brought the yet suckling music to childhood with his performances in the juke joints that the plantations allowed as entertainments for black workers. Johnson was an extremely talented guitarist who pretended to have an unabashed allegiance to Lucifer and all his temptations. No matter. Johnson used his childhood images of working in the fields and his dark dreams to forge a new American music. He invented the slide technique on the guitar and the "blue note," the flattened or diminished thirds and fifths that became the melodic minor-key tendency so special to the blues sound. Johnson lived almost in legend; nobody remembers him much save for a few of his disciples like McKinley Morganfield, known to the world as Muddy Waters. According to Robert Palmer in his definitive work entitled *Deep Blues*, Johnson died after being slipped "an ice course" in a juke joint. An ice course was poisoned moonshine, and Johnson, goes the legend, died a horrible death by crawling on all fours and barking like a hound of hell.

Strangely, American mercantilism played a major role in the development of the blues. Sears, Roebuck and Montgomery Ward opened up their catalogue businesses in the late nineteenth century with monthly installment payments. This was the only way poor people could manage to buy anything, and the $1.50 guitar became the most popular purchase in the plantation quarters of the blacks. With this breakthrough, the guitar became the major instrument of the blues (the first ever recorded blues artist, Texas Henry Thomas, had used his homemade panpipes because he couldn't afford a guitar before the Sears and Monty Ward days).

In *Deep Blues*, Robert Palmer credits archaeologist Charles Peabody of Harvard College with being the first to put the blues on paper. Peabody had come down to Coahoma County just a few miles north of the Dockery Plantation in 1901 to excavate the ubiquitous Indian mounds along the Mississippi River. He hired black men to do his digging, but rather than focusing on arrowheads and potsherds, Peabody became fascinated with the work songs of his day laborers. Luckily, Peabody had a working knowledge of musical theory and knew he was listening to something completely different. The work songs were variations of field hollers sung by blacks alone at their toil. Called "whooping," the hollers were octave-jump imitations of the natural sounds of the lonely fields, the meadowlark, the blue jay, the mournful dove. These work gangs were keeping alive a tradition of singing that carried back to their heritage in Africa. Peabody wrote down the words and notes of these blues songs and published them in the *Journal of American Folklore* in 1903. Here began the legitimacy of an oral tradition stretching back hundreds of years, the Senegambian contribution to American culture.

Robert Johnson, Texas Henry Thomas, and whooping notwithstanding, the one figure who stands for blues music is Muddy Waters. He popularized the genre and in so doing gave authenticity to the legion of blues singers and musicians who preceded him, the pioneers: W. C. Handy, Alex Lee, Charley Patton, Willie Brown, Son House, Roebuck Staples, Howlin' Wolf, Rubin Lacy, Ma Rainey, Bertha Lee, Bessie Smith, James McCoy, Tommy Johnson. The roll call could go on for days. The names of blues greats are easily available today in the stacks of books, magazines, and especially recordings that date back to the 1920s.

Blues came from the delta and from the plantation life there. Indeed, the music reflected the bittersweet lives of the blacks on the huge slavelike estates. The big difference after the Civil War was that the blacks could at least try to move away from their peonage, and they did so in massive numbers. The migration occurred in waves: Reconstruction, World War I, the Great Depression, World War II. The conduit from the delta was the Illinois Central Railroad from Memphis to Chicago. In the 1930s the adult fare was $11.10, one way. Most of the time no one wanted a return ticket. By the 1970s Chicago had a black population of over 1.5 million people, almost all of whom had fled the South. The South Side of Chicago was known to one and all as "North Mississippi."

Hundreds of blues makers were streaming north by the 1940s; there were jobs and paying crowds and electricity and running water. Men like Muddy Waters and Howlin' Wolf had read copies of the *Defender,* the black newspaper of Chicago sent home by relatives, where they learned of opportunities they could never get in the plantation juke joints. They paid their eleven dollars and a dime and stepped off the train in Union Station and were discovered. They made records and appeared on the radio; they became competitive and they made money. Unlike the field hands who had jobs in the stockyards, Waters and the Wolf could afford to take their acts back to the towns on the delta: Clarksdale, Greenville, Helena, West Memphis. There they played their music on sponsored programs: "It's King Biscuit time with guest star Muddy Waters . . . Sonny Boy Flour presents Howlin' Wolf!" They were playing now to packed crowds all over the delta and selling records in undreamed of numbers. Their music had begun as something wild, something forbidden. It was the first truly outlaw music of America and had been shunned by respectable Caucasian families. But by the end of the 1940s everyone was listening to this music and its first cousin, rock and roll.

Blues great Robert Lockwood, Jr., once told blues chronicler Robert Palmer: "Them white people down there always did like the blues. They just didn't like the people who created the blues."

Traveling across the delta today is not a spiritual experience. The lands are still fertile but virtually empty; the crossroads stores and churches are boarded up, the little towns are deserted and dying, and the juke joints have fallen to the ground. The blacks have almost all moved away. For a time the landowners tried to convince their former tenants in Chicago to move back home. Agents from the Dockery, Stovall, and Wilson plantations went North with pocketfuls of promises, but there were no takers. The black exodus had prompted the full mechanization of the corporate farms.

BESSIE Smith, the Empress of the Blues, died in a car wreck on the delta, in Tunica County on famous old Highway 61. She was on her way from Memphis to a gig in Clarksdale. Bessie would never have stopped in the town of Tunica because there was just nothing there for blacks except poverty and row-crop misery. If she were alive today, she'd have top billing at one of the shiny new casino palaces rising like redeeming spires on the mudflats of the Mississippi. These Neo-South shrines are destined to rival the grandeur of the Taj Mahal, Versailles, and even Xanadu.

Back in the 1930s the hamlet of Tunica was pitiable, a visage of dilapidated, unpainted shacks and boarded-up storefronts across the tracks from the manors of the plantation lords. Tunica was no different in the 1970s and 1980s; it was no different in the early 1990s until the arrival of an apostasy unheard of in this last notch of Bible Belt Mississippi. Then came Splash, having nothing to do with baptisms. Splash was the first casino in this new horse-trading world of the old South.

Mississippi has always been the tail-end state of the Union. For over a hundred years Mississippi has vied with neighboring Arkansas for last and next-to-last place in every category of things good and first or second in things bad. But things are about to change for Mississippi. The income from the casinos locating here is earmarked for the state's education system and the booty will be measured in the hundreds of millions, an unbelievable sum for the poor-as-snakes state of Mississippi. It's not unreasonable to assume that within a generation or even less Mississippi will have the best-funded public schools in the nation. Sooner or later the all-white Christian academies, one of the last bastions of white supremacy left down here, will see the dawn and either rejoin the cash-rich public system or fall so far behind that they'll become the equivalent of the separate-but-equal black schools of the Jim Crow era. Mississippi in the 1990s is reaping a revenue bonanza, but the effects on the state's education system won't be visible for some years, and the state may be jolted out of its quick-fix euphoria. Generally when politicians lobby for lotteries or gaming, it's worked out that the money goes to education, all right, but it doesn't add anything to total expenditures; usually it just replaces tax revenue. In the end, however, one can't blame Mississippi for trying, especially on the delta where prospects were so dim that the alternative was welfare, no employment at all, no schools at all.

So a whole lot of magic has touched down at unlikely Tunica. But sometimes the magic goes away. The river gives and the river takes. If, or rather *when,* the Mississippi floods again as it did in '27, '37, '48, '73, and '93, then a new phenomenon will hit the delta: flood parties. Up here, like the hurricane parties on the Gulf, the thing to do will be to ride out six feet of water in the salons of Splash, Harrah's, Circus Circus, et al., while the good Christians of the Bible Belt belly up to the crap table calling on the good Lord to lend a hand in making six the hard way.

CYNICS and the religious right make disparaging remarks about a state tying itself to gambling, but this ignores the current reality of zero unemployment in Tunica County and in nearby Memphis. The future is virtually boundless with new casinos and hotels and country clubs and theme parks standing in line to get built. The town of Tunica will become the largest city in Mississippi, and the county the richest in the state.

Las Vegas is forsaking the desert for the floodplain, and the epicenter of this new Sodom and Gomorrah is Memphis. This city has always existed as a blur; no one has ever quite figured out the geopolitical reality of Memphis. Does it belong to Tennessee, Mississippi, or maybe even Arkansas? Well, it no longer matters. Memphis has become the Waterhole of the South. After Splash, the Deluge, and Memphis is the ark.

In his delightfully scabrous *American Mercury,* H. L. Mencken once called Tennessee "the buckle of the Bible Belt," and named Memphis the most rural-minded city in the South. These sentiments held for the Menckenian era of the 1920s and 1930s, but had the Baltimore bard been in Memphis before the great yellow fever epidemics of the 1870s, he would have found a rich and diverse European culture. Memphis was the Southern melting pot and had every nationality, practicing religion, and ethnic milieu known to man. All this would be obliterated in less than twenty years following the Civil War. Three times during this era Memphis succumbed to the dreaded "yellow jack," reaching its nadir in 1878 when so many thousands were dying that the death wagons couldn't haul the bodies away fast enough. The population was reduced to a few sickly hundred and Memphis even lost its city charter; rather than help, the state of Tennessee revoked the city's right to exist.

Memphis did exist, lived on, refused to die. If the scarified immigrants from Europe decided to flee and settle elsewhere, the desperate folks laboring on the delta flocked into the nearly deserted city, bringing new life and making Memphis a renewed and uniquely Southern town. Memphis on the river became the wheelhouse of the mid-South. All trains leading north passed through here, just as the rail traffic south laid and changed over in the Bluff City. Memphis was also the terminus for all river traffic north and south. Indeed, river commerce was the reason for Memphis's existence. The town had been founded in 1819 by Andrew Jackson and fellow land speculators, once more taking advantage of the federal government's dispossession of Indian lands. Jackson got scalped himself in his Memphis venture and lost a fortune.

Memphis town. Back when it started, the city fathers had two major problems—the rough, tough river boatmen and the wild bears coming in out of the woods and wandering the streets. Many had difficulty telling them apart. The crews of the flatboats docked at Memphis looking for strong drink, loose women, and brawls. They found it all; the wharves teemed with gambling hells, saloons, and whorehouses (commonly known on the river as "pig boats"). In 1842, with more than five hundred boats crowding the docks, thousands of the crew members stormed into town to protest the gouging wharfage fees (prime source of the city's wealth); they set fire to dozens of buildings and began looting until the city fathers lowered the rates and brought out some whiskey barrels. This was the first industrial strike on the river.

If Memphis was to survive beyond being merely a center for cotton, slaves, and hedonism, it had to introduce at least a semblance of civilization into its makeup. Like many another population core in the South, it got religion. The absence of a strong foreign immigrant culture abandoned the field of choice to the evangelicals, most especially to the hard-shell Baptists who took over as the conscience of the city. Nonetheless, the veneer of morality didn't go down all that deep; in fact, the self-righteousness plowed just enough to give life to demagoguery in the person of Edward Hull "Boss" Crump. Crump was elected mayor of Memphis in 1909, and not even his forced resignation in 1916 could break the clutch of his control. He ruled Memphis with completeness a Mafia don might have envied until his death in 1954. Though little-known to the outside world, Crump became the most powerful demagogue the South had ever produced. He had been forced out of the mayor's office because he had refused to enforce the state's prohibition law (an important source of his power base was selling cheap booze in the barrelhouse saloons of the black section of town called Orange Mound, the largest black ghetto of its time in America). Losing the mayoral title taught Crump his most valuable lesson: demagogues don't rule from the front. Had Crump been a U.S. senator, he would have served eight terms; had he been governor, he would have served twelve terms. The truth is, Boss Crump did all these things because he handpicked every senator, governor, and congressman in Tennessee for nearly half a century.

Old Boss Crump was the genuine article. His overweening probity was certainly two-faced. The Memphis he built and ruled over was so sanitized and steeped in its desired virtues that a person couldn't honk his car horn without getting a ticket. Memphis had sought and gained the reputation as the bluest city in the nation outside of Boston. Blue laws abounded and Memphis banned everything— movies, books, magazines, records, and sacrilege, real and imagined. Crump installed a favorite crony, Lloyd Binford, as the chief censor. Binford took his work seriously and banned the Our Gang film comedies because a black child was shown in the same classroom with white kids. At the same time the city was known throughout the mid-South as the place to go to get anything you wanted, booze or cards or dice or dope. It was all a Southern façade that H. L. Mencken didn't quite understand.

What the blue laws of Memphis couldn't ban, though, was the blues. At the same time Boss Crump had Memphis, Memphis had W. C. Handy; and Handy had Beale Street. Beale was a city unto itself with ethnic strains totally divorced from the rectitude of white Baptist Memphis. The blues migrated from the delta to Beale on its way to Chicago. Handy's band had been paid by Boss Crump in 1909 to help deliver the black vote, but Handy didn't stay paid. He wrote "The Memphis Blues," purportedly the first blues song, which turned out to be a mocking political parody as much as it was an evocation of the new art form:

Mister Crump won't 'low no easy riders here.
Mister Crump won't 'low no easy riders here.
I don't care what Mister Crump don't 'low.
I'm gwine bar'l-house anyhow—
Mister Crump can go an' catch hisself some air!

Handy outlived and outlasted Crump. A statue of Handy stands on Beale Street and a park is named after him. Every year the Handy Award is presented at Beale Street's Orpheum Theatre by the Blues Foundation in recognition of the nation's outstanding blues musician. The Boss has only a boulevard named for him (there was once a Crump Stadium but it's been renamed). And after all these trying years, Handy enjoys the distinction of having written a national anthem, "The St. Louis Blues."

THE significance of radio in the South and the delta in particular has been underestimated by those who study and write about the culture. Radio in Memphis became as civilizing an influence by the 1950s as the old-time religion groupies had been some fifty years earlier. The Memphis stations (WREC, WMC, WHBQ, broadcasting to you "from the banks of the mighty muddy Mississippi") became the call signals of the mid-South. Still, something was missing; Memphis wasn't catering to its huge black population. The blacks in Orange Mound were ignoring the local stations and setting their dials for West Memphis and Helena on the Arkansas side. In 1948, according to the *Encyclopedia of Southern Culture,* a small classical music station in Memphis, WDIA, began to change its broadcasting format. The station hired Nat Williams, a local black high school teacher with a deep, mellifluous voice who drew listeners, white and black, like honey or found money. Williams became the first black deejay in the South to play the wildly popular rhythm and blues. His style almost immediately generated imitators: WSM in Nashville, WLS in

Chicago, WWL in New Orleans and WER, the 500,000-watt outlaw station from Del Rio, Texas (actually transmitting from Villa Acuna, Mexico). Deejay Williams did even more: he recruited the first black women announcers, Wila Monroe and Starr McKinney, who put together society and cultural programs for black women. From the WDIA studios came live radio preachers in their Sunday morning sermons of a different, spirited religious appeal. Within a few months of the station's new format, everyone on the delta from Steel, Missouri, to Clarksdale, Mississippi, suddenly knew the great rhythm-and-blues artists who had been there all the time—Muddy Waters and Howlin' Wolf and John Lee Hooker and Ma Rainey.

Among his many discoveries, Williams brought the young Riley "Blues Boy" King to WDIA in the late 1940s. B. B. King, born on a plantation in the deep delta, got his start in a spiritual quartet. He had his own deejay show on WDIA that featured live performances, and by the 1950s B. B. King was a recording star. Like many a blues and jazz artist, he worked the Chitlin' Circuit doing one-night stands for twenty years before becoming an overnight success in 1968 when the music critics finally began recognizing his monumental talent. King received his just due in 1977 when Yale University honored him with a doctorate in music: the spiritual father of the counterculture, Yale president Kingman Brewster, paid homage to King, the spiritual father of soul.

To the extreme pleasure of his fans and the Memphis city booster community, B. B. King opened up his own club on Beale Street in 1992. For many years before, the city had spent millions in refurbishing the great old street trying to recapture the magic. But Beale was as dead as old Boss Crump until the attraction of King and his fellow blues artists became the magnet to crowds coming in for Memphis festivals.

Beale Street is a natural extension of Orange Mound, a ghetto that began its life as a refuge for the newly freed slaves during Reconstruction. The delta, which ran right up to Orange Mound, had hundreds of plantations before the war and hundreds of thousands of slaves, a literal black rain that nourished the earth. Certainly, the delta wasn't part of the genteel South; no pretenses were ever made to caring for the slaves in any manner, just subsistence enough to keep them alive and working in the fields. This gross inhumanity gave renewed emphasis to the Abolitionist movement, so much so that even over the violent objections of the South the federal government outlawed importing slaves from Africa. Such a prohibition was nothing more than a Band-Aid. The government couldn't stop the forced migration of slaves from the Old South to the delta any more than it could restrain the blockade-running slavers who continued to sneak their human cargoes into the South. Mobile, New Orleans, and Memphis were the slave blocks for these final victims of the Peculiar Institution.

By far the most unusual patron of the slave block in Memphis was Miss Frances Wright, a Scots lady who came to Memphis in 1825 to found a truly unique commune. Miss Wright bought Negro chattels by the hundreds and put them to work on her two-thousand-acre commune plantation just south of the Wolf River on the outskirts of the city. Miss Wright, a high-toned Christian woman, turned the system back upon itself: she paid her "slaves" a salary that she deducted from their purchase price—and when that amount was paid, the slaves were given their freedom. She named her plantation Nashoba, the Indian word for the Wolf River, and it was on the grounds of the plantation that Orange Mound grew up. The profits from Nashoba were considerable, and Frances Wright used them to buy and free yet more slaves. Political turmoil and jealousy doomed the idealistic colony, and in 1828 Wright was forced to sell out. Before she did, she manumitted all the remaining slaves and paid for their passage to Haiti, a free Negro nation. In effect, Miss Wright had conceived, implemented, and tested a truly original idea: leaseback emancipation.

The great fear in the South of losing its multibillion-dollar investment in slaves without recompense is a root cause of the Civil War. Had the Abolitionist movement based in the hard-nosed mercantile center of New England adopted Frances Wright's businesslike Nashoba System instead of fostering martyrs such as John Brown and plotting open, suicidal black rebellion, things could have turned out differently. There would have been no need for the compromises propounded by Henry Clay. William Henry Seward would never have made his "Higher Power" speech in the Senate (an event that crystallized the coming war). And the Civil War might never have reached the fighting stage.

None of this came to pass. Nashoba Colony fell from grace because of the local animosity and fear that white people were cohabiting with blacks. Other communes of the day fared no better. New Harmony and Brook Farm closed their gates. Nineteenth-century intellectuals were no more up to practicality than the communal flower children of the twentieth century. Somehow even with the sell-off of Nashoba, the colony wouldn't quite die. Many a cotton picker and blues picker passed through the acres that were once Miss Wright's colony south of the railroad tracks. These migrants would stay awhile, maybe work down on Beale Street, save up eleven dollars and a dime and go off to Chicago. Frances Wright's legacy is all but forgotten, even though she deserves a few of the accolades that are being passed around freely in Memphis town these days.

JUST a couple of blocks off Beale Street sits the spanking new Martin Luther King Civil Rights Museum built from the desolate remnants of the old Lorraine Motel where King was shot down in 1968. Today the Lorraine is a slick, impressive façade. Inside, one can view most of the history of a movement where people wanted not much more than the right to sit at a public lunch counter or to take any vacant seat on a bus. The same people who once denied these simple aspirations have now spent millions on a monument that has lost any real significance.

The catercorner ways of Mississippi sure make themselves to home in Memphis: there's a $9.9 million testimonial to a martyr side by side with boarded-up projects . . . there's Graceland celebrating a Mississippi webfoot and a park where the statue of Nathan Bedford Forrest celebrates the KKK . . . there's the Pyramid, the last gasp of Egyptian deism, and Boss Crump, the wraithlike lemure of the House of Ramses . . . there's the black mayor who unknowingly has hit upon a Frances Wright parallel of ridding the city of its financial woes by the obvious solution of uniting the white-flight county government with the decaying city . . . there's the funkiest alternative newspaper in the nation turning on readers in the face of hopeless tradition . . . there's Sleep Out Louie's where you can play snooker, have oysters on the half shell for half a sawbuck, and Justine's, the only five-star restaurant in the South, where five bucks won't even get your car parked.

Memphis is a city of anomalies, an imperial Egyptian town in a missionary Baptist pew. Memphis won't allow gambling within its precincts, yet it helps its citizens get down to work in Tunica. It won't elect blacks to the school board, yet has elected a black mayor. It's the friendliest city in the South, yet it has the most exacting closed society. Considering all these characteristics in light of Miss Welty's catercorner world, the best conclusion a body can come up with is that Memphis is the premier city of the South.

CHAPTER 8

THE HIGH-TONED OLD CHRISTIAN WOMAN WEDS THE HORSE TRADER

Eastern Tennessee . . . The Southern Baptist Convention . . . David Lilienthal and the TVA . . . The Scopes Trial . . . Music City, USA . . . Tom T. Hall . . . Brother Will D. Campbell

WHEN THEY SAY "BUCKLE UP" in Tennessee, they mean it, and it has nothing to do with seat belts. It's pure ecclesiastic metaphor, for here is the iron girth of the Bible Belt and the capital of the Southern Baptist Convention. The Southern Baptists got their lofty beginnings in the 1830s when they split from the national Baptists over the issue of property rights (who could hold slaves and who couldn't). Northern Baptists wanted to do away with slavery altogether and the Southern Baptists said, "Over our dead bodies." Here then was a major cause of the coming conflict, a holy war to be fought over property rights.

Why the bitter divisiveness of hard- and soft-shell doctrinaire violence? It all began with Tennessee's version of Jack Cash's "man at the center," the pioneer who chopped civilization from the wilderness and built the foundation for family wealth. After the first wave of pioneers had come down the Great Philadelphia Road and into the marginal interior of the Atlantic Coast South in the 1750s and 1760s, a second wave split off the road in North Carolina in the 1790s to penetrate the Blue Ridge into the valleys and plateaus of east and middle Tennessee.

It was this sturdy stock that settled the fierce, deep interior of the South, and myth would have us believe that before the ax could clear the land, the land had to be cleared of the Indian menace. For the greater good of the emerging nation, the frontiersmen of Tennessee, "the greenest state in the land of the free," banded together into volunteer militia companies to fight the "heathen Redskins," to make the frontier safe for Christian families. The courageous Tennessee Vols left their scattered homesteads in the charge of their devoted womenfolk and though outnumbered and outgunned, the Vols rallied under the inspired leadership of such heroes as Andrew Jackson, David Crockett, and Sam Houston. These "kings of the wild frontier" confounded and converted the godless Indians throughout the frontier South; they liberated Florida from the depraved Spanish; they ran the bloody British down the Mississippi to the Gulf of Mexico; they defied the tyrannical Mexicans at the Alamo. These fighting Volunteers were the symbols of the new America, citizen-soldiers who would abandon all personal hopes to fight for God and country. They followed the preachment of one of their own, David Crockett, who "larnt" them, "Be sure you're right, then go ahead," which words were the pure extrapolation of the American Dream.

Of such myths are legends made and taught in schools. Tennessee, like many a state in the South and elsewhere, indulges itself in these heroic happy truths, but they're just not square with the facts. The Tennessee Volunteers joined together for the express purpose of stealing the possessions and land of the Indians they would kill. When their celebrated Indian campaigns grew difficult, they deserted their hero commanders and laid up in their cabins, living off captured Indian cattle and selling looted furs and captured black slaves for corn liquor. Jackson treated his own men wretchedly, constantly marching them without supplies or winter clothing. His troops threatened mutiny many times, and during the Creek campaign Jackson executed a fourteen-year-old boy for sassing an officer. When the Vols fought the Indians, they did so with benefit of cannon and rifle against bow and arrow. The Tennessee militia always outnumbered the Indians and took no prisoners that couldn't be sold as slaves. The expulsion of Spain from Florida was as easy as it was inevitable (no shots were fired), and Jackson's capture of Pensacola barely covered up his failures in the first Seminole War.

The massacre of the Scots regiments at New Orleans was not Jackson's victory but Jean Lafitte's, and David Crockett's death at the Alamo was not as depicted in the movies or, for that matter, in the history books. According to historian Jeff Long in his book *Duel of Eagles,* Crockett surrendered and thought he had talked his way out of death, until General Santa Anna had Crockett stood up against a wall and shot after the Alamo had fallen. Sam Houston, who had been a teenage soldier during Jackson's Creek campaign, parlayed his Indian fighting into the U.S. Congress, the Tennessee governor's mansion, and eventually into the presidency of the Republic of Texas; in between, Houston was a notorious alcoholic, gambler, philanderer, and failed land speculator. Houston ran up so much debt that he had to flee his native Tennessee for Indian Territory, where he changed squaw wives depending on how many furs he could cheat out of various tribal chiefs. Overall, David Crockett's homily of right reason, delivered out here on the westernmost frontier of America, became the first vibrations of the shock wave that would come to be known as Manifest Destiny.

The Volunteer stock at the beginning of the nineteenth century (the fierce version of Jack Cash's "man at the center") would become the aristocrat, good old boy, and even mean sumbitch of the still-forming redneck South. They started living their roles as cash-poor horse traders, using barter and Indian loot to advance up the social and economic ladder. The lands were too poor to get rich from, good only for turnips or collards or corn. But not for the real South money crop, cotton. So the horse trader used what he could: he raised good horses, distilled good whiskey, used the forests to build wagons, barrels, and axe handles that he sold to new waves of settlers moving farther west. The horses and whiskey could be sold or traded to all comers, and a little wealth was accumulated. The horse trader was never religious by nature; he went sometimes to the Baptist or Methodist, Episcopal or Presbyterian church—to meet a decent woman. After he married her, he kept going to church for two reasons: Sunday-go-to-meeting was his wife's only chance to socialize and it was the place that legitimized his business dealings. The horse trader gave a new meaning to Manifest Destiny, for once the lands of Tennessee were conquered and became a white man's world, the horse trader set out to ring up a profit, his warring days behind him. He could never have reaped the riches he would realize without his good high-toned Christian woman.

The horse trader's courtship of his Christian lady began in earnest as the Baptist churches in the North and South broke apart. The publishing of the banns and the betrothal took place in the bitter, hopeless devastation of the South's defeat in the Civil War; the wedding didn't come off until well into Reconstruction when the Southern Baptist Church became the refuge for millions of shocked and defeated Southerners searching for redemption. Southern historian Thomas L. Connelly has observed that "the postwar Southern generation was unprepared for the reality of defeat. Their pervasive sense of alienation involved a sense of estrangement from God, the American doctrine of success, the mainstream of national life, and even from themselves."

The sole institution left to the South was that of the evangelical church—the last link holding the South together. In the decades following the war, the roll call of evangelical churches saw massive increases. At the turn of the century the South had some six million white Protestant church members, and two-thirds of these were evangelicals; the largest single sect of these were Southern Baptists. The single question of faith plaguing the soul-dead following the Civil War South was "How can I be saved?"

Tennessee didn't go the way of the rest of the South, didn't throw in with the demagogues, whether political or theological. The people of Tennessee for the most part embraced a bona fide, traditional alternative—the Southern Baptist Convention. The wedding of the horse trader and his high-toned old Christian woman was one of convenience and expediency. It owed everything to the shrewdness of the horse trader himself. When H. L. Mencken came to Dayton, Tennessee, to cover the Scopes "monkey trial" in 1925, he disparagingly called Tennessee "the buckle of the Bible Belt." In a sense it was true, is true, because the outreach of the Southern Baptists was enormous, is enormous, throughout the whole South. But Mencken couldn't see through the charade. Tennessee led the South back into the Union and then into the twentieth century; more than likely it will lead the South into the twenty-first.

OUT of Memphis heading east, the land around for some fifty miles retains the look and feel of the Old South with cotton fields and shotgun shacks and a still deeply ingrained black population. This was Rebel country during the Civil War, though the Confederate forts on the Mississippi and Tennessee rivers fell easily, and after Shiloh no Southern army came to these lands again—for the last two years of the war the only Rebel presence in west Tennessee was Bedford Forrest and his "Critter Company." Jackson, Tennessee, is the only town of any size between Memphis and Nashville. The delta plays out here and the land becomes desolate with some scraggy upland cotton, wheat, and hay fields, but mostly it is given over to forests and wildlife refuges.

Jackson was the sometime base for General Forrest on his Comanche-like raids into the Yankee-held countryside. It was from here in Jackson that Forrest launched his infamous attack on Fort Pillow, some fifty miles away on the Mississippi River above Memphis. In April of 1864 Fort Pillow was garrisoned by a few hundred black troops, former slaves who were part of Mr. Lincoln's new 100,000-strong black delta army. Putting blacks in uniform was considered the final insult to the South. Forrest marched to Fort Pillow with no other military purpose than to teach the North the deadliest of object lessons. Ignoring the fort's attempt to surrender, Forrest massacred the helpless black soldiers at Fort Pillow, lynching many and even burning alive some of the black soldiers' women and children. Those few blacks who survived were taken to Jackson and sold back into slavery.

Today Fort Pillow has become a state park, and from the towering Chickasaw bluff nearby visitors get an awesome view of the Mississippi River. Looking down on the river and the fort, one can visualize the attack as the Critter Company closed in on the doomed garrison. Union gunboats and troop-laden paddle wheelers coming from Memphis to rescue the fort turned away out of fear of fighting Nathan Bedford Forrest. The Yankee soldiers didn't share Lincoln's politics; they cared no more for the blacks than did Forrest and sacrificed them to their fate.

About fifty miles east of Jackson begins the Bedford Forrest State Historical Area and Park. It might seem strange to history buffs that the state of Tennessee promotes the name of the archfiend of the Union when the state itself was essentially pro-North. Reputable historians from the North, the South, and as far away as England and

France have gilded the legend of the daring Nathan Bedford Forrest. Even into the 1990s editors have promoted two full-fledged biographies of the general.

It is no doubt appropriate to respect Forrest's talent as a soldier: his motto of "Git thar fustest with the mostest" is one of the most cited maxims of the operational military art, and West Point has used his campaigns as models for classes in tactics and guerrilla warfare. But one can only wonder why the note he scribbled in his semiliterate hand during the attack on Fort Pillow, "My men are a-chillin' 'em," is forgotten, just as is the massacre itself.

Deeper into the heartland of Tennessee, travelers can find another trace of the Forrest legend in the town of Pulaski, where the KKK was founded. In the early 1990s a rally took place on Pulaski's courthouse lawn. The current Grand Wizard of the KKK, Thom Robb, led the celebration and cross burning. The town itself was unhappy about the party—it was bad for business and the town's progressive image. Inside the gorgeous old courthouse are replicas of Lincoln's "Gettysburg Address" and of Robert E. Lee's letter accepting the presidency of Washington University. There's also a copy of the Thirteenth Amendment to the U.S. Constitution. There is no reference anywhere to Nathan Bedford Forrest. You can inquire in the chancery court office about the general, the man who founded the KKK, but the response will be "Never heard of him."

"HAD a high old dream last night. Dreamt I was in hell."

"Rough country?"

This fragment from a traditional Southern folktale unbosoms the pragmatism of the Tennessee horse trader, an approach to life so phlegmatic that it confounds the rest of the world. Tennessee didn't subscribe to the romantic idealism of Virginia or to the crazed arrogance of the rest of the South. Make no mistake, Tennessee is a Southern state. Its notions are Southern, its customs and traditions are Southern, its music and whiskey. One of the truest measures of Southernism is cornbread, and Tennessee's is as authentic as the Mason-Dixon Line. As a whole, the country-smart Tennesseans, especially the horse-trader class, wanted no part of the Civil War. They made what profit they could out of it, but their windfalls would come later.

The Tennessee horse traders rejected the darkness of Bedford Forrest just as they ignored the wasted effort of proclaiming the great Lost Cause. Tennessee knew it had the better men and set about proving it. While Virginia, Georgia, and Louisiana were simpering along in corrupt mediocrity under the demagogic banners of the Byrds, Talmadges, and Longs, Tennessee was quietly forging its economic future. In the first nightmarish tendrils of the Great Depression, Tennessee pulled off the greatest economic miracle since Cheops caused the building of the Great Pyramid. Beginning in 1933 the puny Tennessee River was transformed into the largest public works project in known Christendom.

The Tennessee horse traders—politicians, businessmen, devout church leaders—importuned newly elected Franklin Delano Roosevelt with an innovative idea. The South had long been deprived and was suffering horribly from the Depression. Why not create a single national authority charged with the responsibility of rebuilding an entire region, a region that was larger than England, Scotland, and the Isle of Man combined? It would be a showcase for the New Deal. Elements of the concept had been around for many years but had been rejected by three successive Republican Presidents. Roosevelt approved, and the Tennessee Valley Authority was born.

David E. Lilienthal, the TVA's first director, coined the phrase "grassroots democracy" to herald the great good he fervently believed was being done by the TVA. In the course of its first dozen years, the TVA, which held sway over parts of seven Southern states, constructed sixteen major dams, the reservoirs behind flooding out almost one million acres. Lilienthal's democracy extended only to those who owned the land; these people received federal compensation for their flooded property in the form of new homes, modern amenities, and an upgraded standard of living. The grassroots majority of folks living on these lands—mostly sharecroppers and day laborers—were simply dispossessed.

One of the black marks against the horse trader's craft is its amoral approach to everything. It didn't bother the horse trader that the black man was being excluded from TVA benefits any more than it concerned him that the poor white trash were up the same flooded creeks. They had little choice but to migrate to the burgeoning cities that the TVA was creating; they formed a pool of cheap labor for the benefit of the horse trader's city cousins.

Lilienthal's TVA built sixty-three coal-burning plants (whose emissions were the worst in the nation). The TVA constructed seventeen nuclear power plants, which by the 1980s had been closed down or were going to be by the Nuclear Regulatory Commission. The NRC has issued more than a thousand citations against the TVA for violations—shoddy workmanship, inadequate safety standards, and, if one reads between the lines, downright profiteering. The power brokers behind it all were the wily horse traders of Tennessee and their brethren in the other TVA states. The TVA has been ballyhooed for more than sixty years now for bringing economic development into this vast region, yet the electric rates that consumers here have to pay are consistently higher than those charged by public utilities in adjacent areas not serviced by the TVA.

By far the biggest impact the TVA had on the seven-state region was on its cities. One can travel the whole area and naturally admire the countryside, its forests, rivers, and recreational sites, and still come away a little unsure of what is being seen. A querulous feeling dominates any assessment of what can only be called the TVA sinecure. Why are all these cities here? How did towns with only the barest reason for being explode into metropolitan complexes? Knoxville and Chattanooga in Tennessee; Huntsville and Florence in Alabama; Paducah in Kentucky. These cities didn't mushroom for any reason other than to service the TVA and all its parts. Each is proud of its service diversity, but their satellite industries are inextricably tied to the giant federal presence of producing power. In a heavy manufacturing environment there would be no problem, but precious little manufacturing goes on. Still, electric power is what the TVA is all about, and its capacity to produce that power is enormous. But where's the demand? All the cities in the seven states could burn all their lights twenty-four hours a day every day and not use a fraction of the capacity. And this overcapacity explains why the rates are so high, as the engineers and experts could have told us from TVA's salad days.

The fact that so many people got burnt on the TVA had little impact on the horse traders who brought this big show to town, for they were off promoting other bread-and-circus extravaganzas: the massive Oak Ridge nuclear compound, the ludicrous World's Fair at Knoxville, Opryland, Dollywood, Twitty City, the maze of recording studios in Nashville, the galactic Saturn plant near Nashville, not to forget Senator Howard Baker's favorite pork barrel, the Tenn-Tom Waterway on the Tennessee-Tombigbee rivers. When William Faulkner created the prototype Mississippi slicker, Flem Snopes, he never realized that this prince of horse traders would abandon his native soil for the magic of P. T. Barnum territory in Tennessee. But Flem was cagey enough to see that this neighboring state had traded in the old ragged nightmare of the Lost Cause for a brand-new populist dream, the "every man a king" legerdemain of the Kingfish brought into at least partial reality in Tennessee.

Two brands of fierce aboriginals have existed in the history of Tennessee. Andrew Jackson's pogrom wiped out the Native Americans; the second coming of savagery was in the guise of evangelical Christians whose sharp-tongued intimidation took far more scalps than ever did steel tomahawks. It was this missionary lunatic fringe that led H. L. Mencken to his darkly derisive dismissal of the state as the Bible Belt's buckle.

This unfounded and unfair image has plagued Tennessee most of the twentieth century, and it all started with an essential misunderstanding of the facts surrounding the Scopes trial. From the moment Mencken and his Hearst colleague, Dorothy Kilgallen, began their scathing coverage of John Thomas Scopes's prosecution by the State of Tennessee, ably assisted by expert witness William Jennings Bryan, the nation has always concentrated on the bitter lure of the trial. Mencken, Kilgallen, and others of the Eastern press were actually putting Tennessee and the South on trial for its terminal ignorance. The imagery of Clarence Darrow's heroic defiance of universal intolerance (as depicted in *Inherit the Wind*) has left a keloid scar forever defacing Tennessee and things Southern. Truth told, the Eastern establishment made its judgments without understanding or much caring about what had led to the infamous Scopes trial, or what came afterward.

The fundamentalists had long chafed at the heresy of Darwinian theory. This humanistic creed struck at the very core of their religious dogma that subordinated mankind to the omniscient will of God. These holy vigilantes generated a powerful groundswell in the years following the First World War when they began targeting social evils that threatened their doctrinal answers to life. The groundswell

ultimately led to the Eighteenth Amendment and in 1919 a conservative, Republican-dominated Congress overrode Woodrow Wilson's
veto and passed the Volstead Act that enforced the Prohibition
amendment. Within this repressive climate, the Tennessee legislature allowed itself to be bullied into passing its Butler Bill in 1925—a
law that forbade the teaching of evolution in state schools, and this
despite the fact that Charles Darwin had openly defended the secession of the Confederate states.

And it came to pass that the world's eyes focused on obscure Dayton, Tennessee, a little market town lodged in a valley off the Walden
Ridge on the Cumberland Plateau. Here the civic and business leaders decided to face down the lunatic fringe. Dayton was a fairly prosperous, progressive community, but the Butler Bill looked to them
to be only the first among many soon-to-come handcuffs on future
growth. The American Civil Liberties Union came to Dayton and offered to defend any public school teacher who would defy the law. A
majority of Dayton's citizens had convinced John Scopes to do just
that. Scopes never once taught evolution at the school in Dayton. He
merely announced his intention to do so and was indicted.

A Rhea County jury found Scopes guilty but the astute judge, John
T. Raulston, saw the change in the wind's direction and merely fined
Scopes one hundred dollars. The state supreme court was cannier
than Judge Raulston; it reversed the decision on a technicality in the
sure and certain knowledge that the U.S. Supreme Court would
strike down the Butler Bill as unconstitutional. Scopes was a hero as
was his sister, who later challenged a similar law in Kentucky. But
without the leadership and support of the citizens of Dayton, the
fundamentalists would still be hanging humanist scalps on their
lodge poles. One must remember that there are all kinds of totems
in the South.

Still, the fundamentalists wouldn't give up. In 1933 evangelist Bob
Jones set up his bellicose old-time-religion "college" in nearby Cleveland. Eastern Tennessee seems to have always had a penchant for
such religious radicals; the international headquarters of the
Church of God is parked in Cleveland and there's many a snake handler and holy roller tabernacle up in the surrounding hills. But Bob
Jones was so belligerent that the folks in Cleveland finally ran him
off in 1947. Jones had introduced a dirty horse trader trick into the
doctrine of his church: his students and faculty would boycott any

business in town that didn't play ball with the Jones mob. A typical intimidating ploy would be to proscribe a bookstore if it sold books not to Jones's liking. This technique would latch on to the bowels of the fundamentalist movement like a hookworm in the coming generations of the Moral Majority. After getting the boot in Cleveland, Jones sold the same bill of goods to Greenville, South Carolina, got himself a free two hundred acres, and built the unaccredited Bob Jones University. In the 1970s the Internal Revenue Service suspended the tax-exempt status of the school and not even Ronald Reagan could get it restored, though he moved mountains in trying to save this institution of higher education that once used gun-toting guards to keep agents of the devil from its grounds.

The town of Cleveland could be famous or infamous for another reason, but it's neither. One wonders if any of the tourists who swarm through this route into Gatlinburg and the Great Smokies know that Cleveland was once a concentration camp, that scores of log stockades stood here in the 1830s penning in upwards of fifteen thousand Cherokee Indians like so many cattle. Tribes from Georgia, North Carolina, and Tennessee had been forcibly removed from their homes and massed at Cleveland. Here was the starting point of what the Cherokees were to call "the Trail Where They Cried" and what history now calls "the Trail of Tears." Almost half of these Cherokees would die along the way. Or as a modern-day seminary student in Cleveland, Tennessee, put it, "They might as well have put the Indian babies in a pot and boiled them down to soup stock."

TIME was when all roads in America led to Nashville. Over the years the marquee over the city has proclaimed it to be the Athens of the South, the Protestant Vatican, The Wall Street of the South, and Music City USA. Nashville can still claim a touch of all these attributes but it's really none because it never achieved a multiple choice. Building a replicated Parthenon won't qualify for any part of ancient Greece; nor do the idealistic whimsies of Vanderbilt University's "Fugitive" and "Agrarian" movements represent any true part of a New South philosophy.

The Agrarians and Fugitives were ¡oftentimes one and the same group—young intellectuals and writers who gathered around Professor Donald Davidson. Their number included John Crowe Ransom, Allen Tate, and Robert Penn Warren, poets and novelists who also called themselves "The Fugitives." In 1930 they contributed to the Agrarian manifesto, *I'll Take My Stand*. In essence they wanted to save the South from creeping industrial materialism in favor of traditional Southern values. Their influence was strong for a while but died within the bigger social issues of the Great Depression

The monolithic Southern Baptist Convention complex downtown has long been a center for devolution and splinter politics, considering such weighty matters as the sex of God and whether Jerry Falwell is an apostate or saint; the short-lived hegemony of giant Nashville-based insurance companies can now be dwarfed by any common off-shore banking ruse. And as Roy Clark, the unofficial toastmaster of Country Music USA, said in the middle of the great exodus of country stars to Branson, Missouri: "Will the last one out of Nashville turn off the lights and shut the door?"

Admittedly Nashville had an unusual start in life. The state's first governor residing here was the escaped and finally pardoned John Sevier, putative president of the state of Franklin. Sevier, you will recall, proved to be a fairly unusual person himself: Indian fighter, land speculator, duelist, empire builder, traitor, politician, and plutocrat. He was more: he was the original, genuine Tennessee horse trader who required no panegyrist to immortalize his life.

So what has Nashville become since the heady days of Sevier and Jackson? It's nothing pure but the city is mostly what it's always wanted to be, with an identity that permeates the natives and seduces the Yankees who've moved in over the years. It may seem strange for Nashville to identify itself so defiantly with the Old South inasmuch as the people of middle and eastern Tennessee were so pro-Union during the Civil War. It wasn't so much that they were anti-South; it's just that their down-home grits-and-sidemeat logic told them armed rebellion was water-headed. Tennessee's pro-South perspective starts to make sense when one adds the stone-carved fact that in the aftermath of Reconstruction the occupying Yankee army treated Tennessee worse than it did South Carolina or Virginia. Tennesseans up in these hills have long memories and seemingly won't ever forget the brutality of their occupation by an army and government they had supported. If there were all that many carpetbaggers coming into the South (which fact revisionist historians now deny), their headquarters were in Nashville. Andrew Johnson, a transplanted native from his bonded white slavery in South Carolina and the wartime governor of Tennessee, was President during the mean-spirited occupation of his adopted state, but he was helpless in saving his own people. Had Tennessee gone fully for the South, the war could have lasted for years. Not only that, if the South had held on to the Cumberland and Appalachian ranges, it is feasible that the Confederacy could have achieved a conditional peace. Slavery would have been abolished but the South would have been recompensed, and more importantly, there would have been no wrathful Reconstruction. But the jaded Abolitionists ignored all this and treated loyal Tennessee as Rome did the Carthaginians in the final Punic War. It makes no sense, but then neither did the Civil War.

The Abolitionist North couldn't be satisfied with merely stamping out slavery; it had a seeming determination to imprint the South with the morality of the North (philosophically and economically). Perhaps had the North been somewhat gentler in imposing its will, the South would have changed, but the viciousness of Reconstruction stiffened the South's back and made it look for other answers for its self-imposed guilt. Such an answer came along in the 1920s and 1930s with the unfolding of Donald Davidson's Agrarian Movement. Nashville became the core of an intellectual community based at Vanderbilt under Professor Davidson. His "agrarian" poets, novelists, and thinkers totally rejected the industrialized North, saying that its influence would only disgrace a people tied to the land. Davidson and his followers turned away from Henry Grady's fanciful dream in favor of W. E. B. Du Bois's practical vision. The Agrarians never accomplished much toward their ideal, other than a big splash on the literary scene and academic stage. Their healing philosophy for the defeated and dismayed South came seventy-five years too late—had such a vision been around in the 1840s and 1850s perhaps it would have countered the rise of intolerance, yet even that seems doubtful, for the bloodlines of the Agrarians were tied to the Lost Cause.

Nashville is an unlikely melange of Maybelle Carter's autoharp melodies, Fisk College's Jubilee Singers, redneck politicos, snuff queens and diesel sniffers, Andy Jackson's Hermitage, James K. Polk's Manifest Destiny, Cornelius Vanderbilt's million-dollar bid for Methodist immortality, Indian killers, nigger haters, agrarian poets, guitar and banjo pickers, Greek choruses, and at least forty different recipes for cornbread. Yet Nashville is not just confined to these bluffs along the Cumberland River. If Nashville were merely another city of the New South, it would have faded into anonymity about the time they closed down the old Ryman Theater, signaling the death of the authentic Grand Ole Opry.

"It's Grand Ole Opry time," monotoned the legendary voice of George D. Hay, the solemn old judge. "Let 'er go, boys." The wailing harmonica of DeFord Bailey brought to life the lonesome railroad whistle from far off in the distance and almost became the South's national anthem. The father of the Opry got it rolling in 1925 on radio as a come-on for the National Life and Accident Insurance Company of Nashville. The Opry sold more cheap life insurance policies than any war in the nation's history. In 1927 Hay's radio show followed the NBC Music Appreciation Hour of classical music. Hay took the mike and announced that since they'd been listening to all that grand opera, they were now gonna hear the boney-fidey "Grand Ole Opry." So it began. Hay's Nashville station WSM had started broadcasting with only a thousand watts, but within a few years it was a fifty-thousand-watt clear-channel station blanketing the nation. Under the sponsorship of Prince Albert "Roll Your Own" smoking tobacco, the Grand Ole Opry built up a 176-station network that attracted a weekly audience of ten million listeners, rivaling Jack Benny, Fred Allen, Burns and Allen, the "Hit Parade," and later the fireside chats of President Roosevelt. In 1943 the Grand Ole Opry moved into the famed old Ryman Theater that had begun life as the Gospel Tabernacle in 1892. Purists might have to hold their noses, but here was the most innovative music form since Giovanni Pierluigi Palestrina's *Missa Papae Marcelli* and the classic spin-offs of Bach and Mozart, Brahms, and Beethoven.

"We finally won the Civil War," says Southern poet James Whitehead, "by making the American language Southern, all because of country music and the blues."

Throughout the pioneering era Nashville remained a whites-only convocation, and country music stayed so until Charley Pride and Ray Charles broke the barrier of the Savage Ideal in the 1960s. And this even though country music has all of its roots in the rhythm and blues of black and white Southern music. A melancholy paean floats through the Nashville Sound. The haunting lyrics of Huddie Ledbetter made millions for white singers while "Leadbelly" himself was forbidden to appear on the Grand Ole Opry because of his race, though there was no bigotry when it came to covering his songs for huge profits.

WSM reached down the obscure country roads and along the streets of little towns like French Lick, Indiana; Braggadocio, Missouri; Strawberry Plains, Tennessee; Trashy Lane, Arkansas; Gutherie, Oklahoma; Muleshoe, Texas; Gallipolis, Ohio; Somerset, Pennsylvania; Little Orleans, Maryland; Brattleboro, Vermont; Peterboro, New Hampshire; Deming, New Mexico; Lander, Wyoming; and Weed Patch, California.

Later the new genre would come to be known as "country-western," but it wasn't. It was hillbilly, with all the denigration that slur implies. If you grew up down one of those dusty washboard roads listening to and loving that music and then found yourself in a better uptown life, you felt a twinge maybe of shame at your background— just like young Ralph Ellison, who once was ashamed that his grandparents were slaves. No matter. On Saturdays the whole family would go to town to buy a few staples, walk the streets, and maybe go to the picture show to see all the beloved singing cowboy stars, Gene Autry and Roy Rogers and other, lesser gods who nonetheless sang their way into the heart—Tex Ritter, Jimmy Wakeley, Foy Willing, and the Riders of the Purple Sage, the Sons of the Pioneers, Bob Wills and the Texas Playboys, and everybody's darling, Judy Canova. But the movies appealed only to the eye, not the soul, which stayed at home by the radio. On Saturday nights after the few hours of town fantasy, the mamas and daddies and sisters and brothers came home to the solemn old judge and his cast of thousands: Roy Acuff, Lulabelle and Scottie, Maybelle and A. P. Carter, Bill Monroe, Flatt and Scruggs, Ernest Tubb, Minnie Pearl, Cowboy Copas, Hank Williams, Rod Brasfield, the Browns, Ira and Charlie Lubin, Uncle Dave Macon, Kitty Wells, Patsy Cline, Eddy Arnold, Wilma Lee Cooper, Little Jimmy Dickens, Merle Travis, Doc Watson, Chet Atkins, Lefty Frizzell, Homer and Jethro, Webb Pierce, Jim Reeves . . . and the man who helped start it all way back in 1924 with his "Wreck of the Old 97," Vernon Dalhart.

COUNTRY pickers and singers used to hang out in cold-water walkups in the cheap hotels and boardinghouses around Music Row in Nashville. Nowadays the elite live in hog mansions with gutbucket-shaped swimming pools out in the white-flight suburb of Brentwood. Trips to the studios on Music Row are made in thirty-foot limos. Yet a lot of the stars of today who remain true to their roots like to celebrate their humble beginnings; these old friends get together to reminisce about better times, to sing the time-honored songs, and to have potluck dinner on the ground, with everyone bringing a favorite dish, whether Champagne chicken-liver pâté or turnip greens and pot liquor.

"When I first came to Nashville I was driving a Cadillac I'd made one payment on and I was looking for a parking meter with time left on it," says singer, novelist, storyteller, and poet Tom T. Hall, the man recognized in the industry as the best songwriter since Hank Williams.

Tom T. Hall doesn't live in one of those Brentwood mansions. His home, just off Barry Chapel Road, is a nice spread, a small-scale bluegrass farm where one can see standard Old McDonald animals and a few pet peacocks strolling the grounds.

Tom T. is from the beautifully scenic yet wretchedly poor Green River country of western Kentucky where folks, as Tom says, were "just into survival." The rocky hills of the Green River are the natural home of the Elizabethan mountain music brought to the South by indentured English, Welsh, Scots, and Irish of the seventeenth century. This unique, nasal, contrapuntal music was a way of life for Tom T., and he began singing and playing it when he was thirteen. He started playing with a living legend in country music, Bill Monroe, and the hard-driving, high-harmony music they made came to be called Bluegrass, perhaps the purest form of the new genre called "country." Bill Monroe was the father of bluegrass, though it was the influence of Tom T. Hall that moved the art form from old-timey Saturday-night-social string-band music to the recognizably melodic bluegrass of today.

Hall became recognized as Nashville's natural storyteller pretty much because of his commitment to the old verities crisscrossing the Southlands. He teamed up with the legendary Ralph Stanley to reproduce "Rank Stranger," a banner hill song from Stanley's Virginia coal mining homeland. "Rank Stranger" is as revered as "Wildwood Flower" and "Soldier's Joy," the first tunes every picker learns.

Tom T. stays on the lookout for new material, things peculiar to authentic flavors of the South. Years ago, he toured Australia and discovered the subcontinent's national poet, Henry Lawson. Lawson was the Antipodean answer to America's Walt Whitman and Scotland's Bobby Burns, a poet of the people. Tom T. took one of Lawson's poems about fairies guarding the watery grave of a child and turned it into "Come, Mama, Come," a lament of a grieved mother mourning the loss of her child. "Come, Mama, Come" stands as a tribute to the kindred hearts of the debtors'-prison poor folk that settled Australia and the indentured bond servants who carved out refuges in the hills of the Southlands.

From the affluent estates of Belle Meade close on the Natchez Trace to the nouveau baronies of Nashville cats in Brentwood, the now traditional Southern dilemma of relative deprivation becomes pronounced. The old-line carpetbaggers and scalawags of Belle Meade have learned to tolerate the rich country stars of Brentwood, while the poor white ridge-runners make do in their double-wides and shacks on the wrong side of old Franklin Road. As you enter Tom T.'s gated homestead, you see a big barn off to the left at the base of the ridge and his home atop the rise. Miss Dixie, Tom T.'s wife, is in charge of the house and Tom is master of the barn.

The barn is not a working farm unit; it's Tom T.'s studio office and come-ye-all watering hole for buddies and strangers down on their luck. Tom T. has the habit of adopting street musicians from the country-western rows of Music City USA. The Nashville scene is an eclectic community and many an established star has promoted the careers of talented newcomers (Tom T. started Johnny Rodriguez, just as the Browns—Maxine, Bonnie, and Jim Ed—helped launch the careers of Elvis Presley, Conway Twitty, and Bobby Bare).

The barn is where ideas happen and songs get born. It's also where modern-day cracker-barrel philosophers gather to ruminate about the day. In the past, poets and preachers and ex-Presidents and scholars have congregated here: James Whitehead, Miller Williams, Will D. Campbell, Jimmy Carter, Tom Connelly, Buddy Carter. While they mostly sip on a brew (though everyone in this neck of Tennessee keeps a Mason jar of prized, smooth-sipping mountain dew for their honored guests), what happens is they get drunk on words. The conversation is catholic and no subject is excluded, though sooner or later all spoken prose leads to the South.

Tom T. sees his native South as "a place of tragedy and grandeur."

He believes that the Civil War was a holy war. "The South was driven mad because it thought God had forsaken it." He reasons that maybe the South lost because the Yankees philosophized from deductive intellect while the Southerners relied on intuition.

"The biggest problem in the South," says Tom T., "is that it will not celebrate its best. In a sense, the South eats its young."

Trying to understand the vagaries of class structure in the Southlands, Tom T. explains that the good old boy is a horse trader. "He may have been in prison, may have even killed a man, but he'll give you a fair deal in a trade . . . you can trust his handshake, if he gives it."

And in the final word on the ironies of the South, Tom T. says, "Picking up a snake down here is the same thing as lighting a candle."

The woods around are not very dark or lovely, but there are crazies everywhere, even here in the outskirts of safe Franklin. Sitting in Tom T.'s barn with a small circle of friends, you find that the mood changes as dusk settles. Tom T. will get up, close the blinds, and dim the lights, all with the deft touch of a snake handler. "I don't like to make myself a sitting target in front of a window."

THE ground around Brentwood and Belle Meade at the winter Battle of Franklin is the site of the Confederacy's last offensive in the Civil War. The Army of Tennessee was charged with the defense of everything east of the Mississippi and west of the Appalachians. The men of this army fought like the Spartans at Thermopylae, but the Confederate generals didn't number a single Leonidas. John Bell Hood, the one-armed, one-legged general appointed by Jeff Davis to fill Joseph Johnston's shoes as commander of the Army of Tennessee, lived up to the promise he had shown at West Point (he graduated forty-fourth in a class of forty-five): he got his troops slaughtered in a series of killer frontal attacks. Six Confederate generals and nearly six thousand men were killed here at Franklin in less than five hours. It was the end of the Army of Tennessee and their famous half-moon battle flag.

The old Franklin Road is another of the South's ironies. On one side is the Steeplechase Hotel, a sinecure for the descendants of Tennessee Brits, professional soldiers lured out of England to fight the Confederacy who stayed after the Civil War on lands given to them by a grateful Republic. This legacy lives on in Nashville—Oxonian accents, punting on the Cumberland, and village cricket greens side by side with Southeastern Conference football, bass fishing, and bars. There really are steeplechases held at Belle Meade, flashing hooves on the greensward and riders with necks for sale, with high teas and Amontillado afterward, along with the celebrations of two queens' silver jubilees.

Belle Meade has always cried out for romance; even the name is a concoction of French and Olde English ("lovely meadow"). These gentle lands were the scene of tragedy before the Battle of Franklin. An assignation in the spring of 1863 between the amorous Mrs. Jessie Peters of Springhill and the dashing Confederate general Earl Van Dorn ended in death. Jessie's husband, Dr. George Peters, caught the two lovers in flagrante delicto and laid the general out on a cold slab. Peters, née McKissack, was a ravishing brunette in the mold of Scarlett O'Hara, and poor old Earl Van Dorn got cast in the role of a randy Ashley Wilkes. The incident has assumed the aura of legend, a sordid Victorian love affair raised to the poignant tragedy of Paolo and Francesca.

The sheen of this romantic vision wears thin in the light of an entry in a Confederate staff officer's Civil War diary. In the following year, Jessie Peters's love's labor wasn't entirely lost. On the day before the gruesome battle at Franklin, while her cuckolded doctor husband was skulking in Nashville, Jessie invited stalwart, six-foot-one Nathan Bedford Forrest to tarry awhile at her own version of Tara. Forrest was under orders to press the Yankees all the way to Nashville, but nothing of the sort happened, for General Forrest had disappeared for six hours. The diaries of the era were discreet, to say the least, and no details of the lost hours were forthcoming.

At Franklin on the next day, the last Confederate attack in what Tom T. Hall calls the Holy War took place. The assault was led by the wild Irishman from Arkansas, Patrick Ronayne Cleburne, under the banner of the half moon. The war with all its chances for the South was lost, and when it became apparent that this attack, too, was doomed, General Cleburne lost his reason, mounted his horse, and charged the Union line. After his horse was shot from under him, he charged on foot, waving his cap. His body was discovered the next day riddled with forty-nine bullets.

After the battle John McGavock of Franklin collected the bodies of 1,496 Confederate soldiers and buried them on his Carnton estate. The cemetery today is squarely in the middle of affluent Franklin, peopled by bankers, lawyers, wealth inheritors, the old transplanted English gentry, and country-western picker millionaires. The Carnton Country Club is nearby, and some people find it convenient to cut through the cemetery while jogging or on their way to the links. Teenagers have taken to partying in the cemetery at night, though others come by day to pay homage and place flowers on the graves.

On the other side of Old Franklin Road sits the Travelers Rest Motel, famed for its country music clientele and its reputation for modern-day Nashville assignations. The Travelers Rest was the favorite haunt of stellar Southern historian Tom Connelly, who had a standing reservation at the acclaimed hostelry he used for solitude and meditation. Beginning with *Will Success Spoil Jeff Davis* and carrying through *God and General Longstreet* to *Marble Man* (a realistic view of Robert Lee), Connelly has written of the South, the Civil War, and its aftermath with uncommon insight. There is no Yankee deduction here, just pure Rebel intuition and realism. Connelly explains with the sparkle of honesty and humor how things came to the terrible pass of 1861 and why the South clothed itself in indivisible shame and hatred following the war. A native Tennesseean, Connelly grew up on the Franklin battlefield. As a boy he tramped the fields, hills, and woods hereabouts, occasionally finding souvenirs from the detritus of death—a belt buckle, a rotted canteen, a spent minié ball. Tom Connelly died of lung cancer in 1989.

Franklin had another beauty besides Jessie Peters, and this lady's memory is untarnished. If there were indivisible shame and hatred in the South, there, too, was indivisible love and devotion. This beloved Southern woman was laid to an untimely rest in 1932; her burial was the very last in the Franklin Memorial Cemetery. Her story is told by Buddy Carter, son of Billy and nephew of the former President. Buddy lives in Nashville and works as a landscape architect for the county. He visited the cemetery one day in the autumn and heard a strange, otherworldly noise. Out of curiosity, he walked to the source. Standing next to a gravestone was an elderly gentleman playing "Amazing Grace" on the bagpipe. When the hymn was finished, Buddy struck up a conversation with the man, who told him the story. For sixty years now he'd been coming back to his wife's graveside to play her favorite song. He had moved from Franklin to the Midwest long ago, yet he always returns to honor his wife and their love.

Confederate generals and their doomed men were interred here. Tom Connelly walked the grounds of the cemetery many times memorizing the names. Perhaps Jessie Peters had been buried here, her passion turned to bitter dust. But the love of two youngsters transcends the old despair and the strains of the redemptive anthem could be said to soothe the lingering spirits of those who died in pain as much as those who died in love. Buddy Carter never learned the names of the old gentleman and his wife. But then most of the soldiers who died here were buried in unnamed mass graves, all under the heading of "Southern Soldier, Army of Tennessee, Fell on November 30, 1864."

WAY over on the east side of Nashville, far away from the mandarin pretense of Belle Meade, lives a transplanted Mississippian. He's not of the Snopes clan, and then again he is, in a distant, third-cousin-twice-removed sort of way. His name is Will D. Campbell. Here's a horse trader of a different hue, a man committed to lending a compassionate hand to those who have been beaten down by the mean miseries of life. Far more than any of the ecclesiastic pretenders on the South's religious stage, Brother Will could claim the mantle of spiritual confidant to the Southlands.

Campbell's basic bio is pretty easy. Ordained at age seventeen, service in the South Pacific in World War II, GI Bill graduate of Yale, minister in Louisiana (where he met and married Brenda, his lifelong bride), chaplain at Ole Miss (fired for playing Ping-Pong with a black preacher), mediator for the National Council of Churches (Will and Daisy Bates escorted the black students into Central High School in Little Rock in 1957). Will was in Montgomery, Birmingham, Jackson, Oxford, Philadelphia, Orangeburg, Atlanta, Memphis, everywhere there was a crisis in the civil rights crusade—his own private holy war. He is the unofficial chaplain of Nashville's Music Row; the confessor of Presidents; a proselytizer of the nation's CEOs and liberal churches; the hospicer of prisoners on Death Row and of the dying country music icon, Roger Miller; and minister to black sharecroppers and Klanners and unreconstructed drunks and dopers. He has counted as his friends Walker Percy, Robert Penn Warren, David Halberstam, Tom Connelly, Jules Feiffer, Stokely Carmichael, and Martin Luther King, Jr. He's written ten books and damned the pharisees in their temples. He's howled at the moon, pulled on the jug, and saved babies from oblivion. He's the pick of the litter from the consummation of the horse trader and high-toned old Christian woman's marriage. You can trust his handshake; he'll make you a good deal.

To get to Will's place, a twenty-one-acre hilly hermitage, one takes the Hermitage exit that takes you to Andrew Jackson's home and now tourist attraction, and drives out Mount Juliet Road for ten miles or so, and "if you come," says Will, "you'll have big house privileges." Will will likely be down the pasture in his little cabin reading a book by one of his writer friends or maybe working on one of his own. The cabin is primitive and comfortable, heated by an old wood stove, and all catercornered with books and mementoes of his many callings. Sitting here in this deliberately austere cabin, you get the feeling that Will Campbell is determined to keep the link to his forebears alive.

Out of dirt-poor, fierce Amite County, Mississippi, on the Louisiana border, the Campbells were testimonials to the South's good people; there were no baronial halls or "big house" privileges here. His great-grandfather was a deserter in the Civil War, a fact that Will is both ashamed and proud of. His grandfather couldn't read or write but his native good sense and common decency had figured out the reasoning of the world when intellectuals couldn't, and he taught Will that you don't slur people because of their color or look down on them because they're poor.

Brother Will is a humanist in a Baptist South that now condemns the very concept as apostasy. Some of the faithful think that Will ministers with a split personality, part Francis of Assisi and part Girolamo Savonarola. Will doesn't talk to the birds but he does preach with the same emotional, humorous, cuss-word-larded, theatrical passion as did his Dominican predecessor back in fifteenth-century Florence. Just as fiery Brother Savonarola was threatened with interdict by Pope Alexander VI, Brother Campbell has had his ordination threatened by the Southern Baptists. The civil authorities of Florence betrayed their reforming cleric—Savonarola was arrested, tried, hanged, and burned. The reactionary zealots of the South have long wished the same fate for Brother Will (in the 1960s the Mississippi Klan put a shoot-on-sight target on Campbell), but his congregation defies the Southlands.

Brother Will gets called to preach at Ivy League chapels, Manhattan sanctuaries, and libertarian tabernacles, yet the only kind of structured church he can abide is the country tavern called Gasses over the hill near Mount Juliet. It's a honky-tonk where everyone knows everybody's name. Gasses looks rough outside and in, but it's a family place featuring country breakfasts (grits, blindfolded eggs, ham, sausage, bacon, biscuits, and fried taters), country dinners at noon, and suppers of chicken-fried steak, mashed potatoes, milk gravy, black-eyed peas, fried green tomatoes and cornbread. When the sun goes down there's dancing and drinking and denouement. The bandstand becomes the pulpit when Will is called to preach. The patrons of Gasses don't really come for the food—they come for the nutrition of old-time religion where Will teaches them that they're all sorry bastards but God loves them each and every one.

Will discounts the organized religions and megatechnic sprawl of the Southern Baptist bastions in downtown Nashville. While the "messengers" of the Southern Baptist Convention use "secret" formulas to expose who's going to hell, Will Campbell agonizes over the realities of abortion and capital punishment. And while the Southern Baptists extol godhead over relative humanity, Brother Will works to expunge slurs such as "cracker," "redneck," and "poor white trash," which he says are just as demeaning as "nigger" and "coon."

No one can quite get a line on Will Campbell. He can be as crafty as a Southern fox, as courageous as any mad dog Rebel soldier who ever stood his ground in the face of the Yankee horde, and you might as well not ever try to make him stand at attention. He scoffs at man's absurd institutions, shames the devil and tickles his funny bone. You're never five minutes in Will Campbell's presence before he's got you laughing. He's a pretty fair country picker and singer, and he's fond of just breaking into a snatch of Roger Miller's "Dang Me" or using a phrase from one of Ray Stevens's crazy ditties to announce to the world his mood for today: "Are you nekkid!"

It has never entered Will Campbell's mind that he is not a loyal Southerner dedicated to the South despite its failings. In an interview with journalist Marshall Frady, Will once prophesied that "the South still has a better chance of working out its problems than the more urbanized rest of the country, simply because more of us know one another's names."

In a way, one can understand why Brother Will has been deemed an outlaw in his own church. He's created a new working trinity for his ministry, a brew of B. F. Skinner's behaviorism, John the Baptist's pantheism, and Albert Camus's existentialism, not your run-of-the-mill theology. Will's pastorage cabin back at his Mount Juliet home is a reflection of his Mississippi transcendentalism that just won't tolerate pretentious piety. You can see pain in his face, through the scratchy lenses of his horn-rimmed bifocals to his water-piercing eyes. The eyes look like they just can't endure it anymore. But they will. These eyes tell you something, perhaps a lesson you won't want to learn. No pain, no suffering, no tragedy has any significance unless you can make meaning out of it.

On second thought, maybe Brother Will does talk to the birds. Behind his modest home is a hand-laid brick veranda festooned with birdhouses and tables and memorials to his symbolic life. There's an old brick from a black church bombed by the KKK in McComb, Mississippi, and a corroded, antique bell salvaged from the steeple of an abandoned church.

Will guides his guests through the intricacies and simplicity of his memories. To him there is a natural consensus built into this patio, the whole long, sad, proud history of his homeland. He'll walk down the yard to his pickup, reach in and honk the horn. After the opening strains of "Dixie" have faded into the trees and the birds have finished their nervous fluttering, Will points to the patio and devilishly intones:

"The South starts right here."

CHAPTER 9

OUTLANDERS

*Kentucky and West Virginia . . . Tobacco Auctions and Bourbon
Whiskey . . . Louisville and Lexington . . . Woody Stephens and Churchill
Downs . . . Mother Jones . . . Appalachia . . . Snake Handling and Glossolalia*

DO YOU HAVE A map of the Great Smoky Mountains—in your mind?
If you've flown over them you've seen match-flame rays of sun or
moon whiplashing among dew-smoldering peaks and vales that
seem to lift up to the very moon. If you were a great speckled bird,
you'd have to drift on the thinnest of air currents over fifty peaks and
valleys; you'd float over an easy narrow plateau that steps up to yet
another fifty peaks—all this before you found the Cherokee Forest,
the heart of the Great Smokies. From sweet little Gatlinburg alone
you'd need to arch through and over some fifty more man-named
heaps before you got over the Nantahala—a tame, insipid little
range compared to what you've just come through—and reached
the Joyce Kilmer Memorial.

Simple to say yet easy to forget, the men and women who settled
New World America had no maps, and as a consequence had no
idea beyond the horizon of their eyes of what they were getting into.
Had maps been available, surely most of the adventurous folks
would have stayed home. The rough trails followed by the early settlers into Tennessee and Kentucky had been made by Indians and
followed by a rugged, enterprising breed of man, such as those
sketched by John Mack Faragher, biographer of Daniel Boone.

Faragher writes of a certain John Findley who packed trading goods through these mountains, ravines, and passes into the hidden Indian villages beyond. Rum, blankets, looking glasses, and steel hatchets for furs, ponies, silver, and gold. Findley and his kind were the godfathers of the Tennessee horse traders; they were also walking Mercators, the closest things to maps pioneer America had.

The first waves of settlers in Kentucky swept over the Appalachians to escape the Revolutionary War. They were an odd mixture of loyalists and rebels who simply didn't want to fight one another on the coastal plains because they had no commitment to, no sympathy for, no gain perceived in throwing in with the ruling class. These pioneers pushed out into Kentucky not out of restless spirit or the simple lure of the other side of the mountain (it would take modern myth to create such explanations for the character of the prototype Outlander). The romantic spirit of Natty Bumppo notwithstanding, the real lure of crossing the mountains into Kentucky was gain—property that could be taken from the Indians and furs that could be sold for cash money to the traders back east of the mountains. Any restlessness that these settlers may have felt came from the sad fact that they had no antecedents in America. Like Natty and Dan'l Boone, they went west to grow their own family trees.

The quest of these rootless outcasts from Pennsylvania, Virginia, and North Carolina made them into Outlanders. The hunger for an identity of their own became an intractable and composed idée fixe, an "Outlander" psyche indelibly stamped on their character. Here in the hills and mountains, the spirit of rugged individualism evolved into its natural state. It became Southern, to be sure, but different from the patrician Tidewater and the Savage Ideal of the Deep South. The Outlander had grown his own proud roots and was beholden to no man or class. "What I got might not be much, but it belongs to me and mine." This code became the composed part of the Outlander's intractable personality.

Kentucky had no truck with the Civil War; it declared neutrality. There certainly were thousands of Kentuckians who fought in the war on both sides, but the state didn't secede. When a Confederate army marched into Kentucky in 1862, expecting Bluegrass volunteers to rally around the Bonnie Blue flag, Kentucky was virtually mute. Neither did the Kentuckians pledge their long rifles to the

Yankees in great numbers. Like their forebears who fled the Revolutionary War, they just didn't want to hook up to a cause not of their choosing. But not even neutrality was good enough for the victorious Union.

Just as in Tennessee, Reconstruction in Kentucky was actually harsher than it was in Virginia. Once again the Abolitionists would drive a nominal state of the South into the folds of the Lost Causers. Kentucky's new-breed individualism didn't end. Many sought out new lands in the Ozarks of Missouri and Arkansas, where they rebuilt their Outlander society. For those who stayed, the Outlander creed lived on. As late as one hundred years after the war, Kentucky had 110,000 farms of less than 140 acres. It was the place where Jefferson's dream of independent self-sufficient yeoman farms had come true. Daniel Boone's original "Trace to Kentakee" of 1777 comprised what is now part of Virginia, West Virginia, Kentucky, Ohio, Tennessee, and North Carolina, with bits even of Maryland and Pennsylvania. Safe back on the eastern side of the Appalachians, the Tidewater gentry and the grandees could keep their Cavalier grandeur—these new Southerners would take the wilderness "meadowlands" and make new legends of their own.

SOMETIMES the concoctions bubbling up from home-brewed rugged individualism put a considerable strain on standard definitions of fair play. Kentuckians feuded over the concept of toll roads versus free roads from the time there were any roads at all in the state. Not unusual, one might think, but in Kentucky toll roads were privately owned. To get from Maysfield to Lexington, a traveler might have had to use fifty different toll roads, and at a penny each the tariff mounted up in the cash-poor state. By 1897 the feud turned violent, and the toll-or-free-road issue became the crux of the gubernatorial election of 1900.

The Democrat, William Goebel, wanted toll roads; the Republican, William Taylor, didn't. Taylor was elected but Goebel demanded a recount, and the Kentucky legislature, Jacksonian Whigs to a man, declared Goebel the winner. His success was short-lived; an irate free-roader shot Goebel down, and it took until 1912 before a state highway commission was even formed and until 1914 before the legislature authorized free roads in any part of the state. In Kentucky a man's home might or might not have been his castle, but his plank road was "by God" inviolate.

In retrospect the Hatfield-McCoy–like conflict over personal property is symptomatic of the Outlander personality. In the same era, other peculiarities of the Commonwealth of Kentucky came to the fore. Between 1904 and 1909 the Black Patch War was fought over the price of tobacco, with tobacco magnate James B. Duke the instigator. Duke's American Tobacco Company combine had by now a full monopoly over the nation's tobacco crop with control over not only the retail price of plug and cigarettes, but the price paid for the raw tobacco. The wrath of the rebellious small farmers was sufficient to burn down Duke's warehouses and to torch the barns and fields of any fellow Kentuckians who sold at the monopoly-controlled price. Suddenly personal property became less than sacrosanct. The state motto, "United We Stand, Divided We Fall," can be read the other way around just as easily. It fell to Teddy Roosevelt to bust the tobacco trust, and for a change there was a benefit for the common clay. Tobacco auctions came to replace monopoly gouging and coercion.

The Black Patch War was violent and deadly; some folks were even burned to death, but when it was all over, this Outlander revolt led directly to the birth of an institution in the South, the mellifluous-voiced tobacco auctioneer. It was a totem that vied with the country fiddler and the Stars and Bars. Few Americans alive before World War II can forget the Dobbs-hatted auctioneer intoning the rival bids of tobacco companies large and small for the choicest burley leaf, culminating with the declaration, "Sold American!"

Hand-in-hand with Kentucky tobacco (a much darker leaf than that grown in Virginia and North Carolina) goes the straight bourbon whiskey of the Bluegrass State. From the start, this whiskey was meant to be a substantially different form, taste, and color of distilled "busthead" than that produced in neighboring Tennessee. The Outlanders of Kentucky never consciously tried to be rivals of other Southern states. It's just that they intended to do things their own way—to create their own original in everything. No matter what Lem Motlow, founder of the Jack Daniel's Distillery, might think, Kentucky bourbon became and remains the tipple of choice in the South. From the fortunes made off tobacco and whiskey, the pride of Kentucky became affordable—thoroughbred horse racing. Even in this, a real contrast in horses, owners, and traditions grew between the two seats of power in Kentucky: Louisville (a midwestern commercial city) and Lexington (an intuitively Southern town).

Louisville retained much of the Old South flavor, though it tied itself to midwestern commerce, while Lexington embraced Outlander individualism and created its own style of aristocracy. The simplest way of contrasting the difference between the two cities is by comparing etymologies: Louisville ("Looeyville") is gallicized snobbery. Virginia scion George Rogers Clark named the town for the French king Louis XVI, though there's hardly anything French about modern Louisville. Lexington was named as a memorial to the farmers who stood and fired the shot heard 'round the world. Louisville is just another rich river port with enough old money to buy and promote a racetrack and one famous race. Lexington is the home of the most famous breeding farms in the nation and the sarcophagus of Adolph Rupp, the man who truly invented college basketball.

Downtown Lexington has become a study in image making, with a touch of Charleston and Columbia. It's charming, quaint, and, when they're not playing ball at Rupp Arena, dead. The Great Compromiser, who in no way championed egalitarian causes, would surely be pleased with the face of his old town today, for no compromises have distorted Lexington's patrician façade. Henry Clay spent his legislative life propping up the institution of slavery; his kinsman, Cassius Marcellus Clay, was a famed Abolitionist who once freed seven hundred slaves in a single day. Cassius Clay also founded the Republican Party, two years before the great Whig Henry Clay died (the Republicans absorbed what was left of the tattered Whig Party). When Cassius Clay died in 1903, lightning struck the statue of Henry Clay here in Lexington, throwing the exalted head thirty feet in the air. Old old-timers in Lexington used to muse that this was the closest old Henry ever got to heaven. The name of Henry Clay is all but forgotten today, while the memory of Cassius Clay was reborn in the 1960s through the unlikely medium of Muhammad Ali, who won his Olympic gold medal, and the heavyweight championship of the world, under the name his mother and father gave him.

The trunk road through Lexington is U.S. 60. East of the city this highway is called the Winchester Pike, and it leads the traveler past

Ashland and Transylvania College, the oldest institution of higher learning west of the Appalachians. There were only a baker's dozen of colleges in America at the time and Transylvania, founded in 1780, was just one of four established during the Revolutionary War. Jefferson Davis attended the college here before being admitted to West Point, yet its highest accolade came from Thomas Jefferson, for whom Transylvania was the college of choice throughout the South. "You can send your sons to Harvard," Jefferson remarked, "but they'll come back strangers." The fact that Lexingtonians founded a college way back then rather explains the contrast in mind-sets between Lexington and Louisville. Lexington had its mind set on civilized life, schools, churches, and law and order; Louisville was a growing depot for expeditions against the Indians, and it remained a depot for commerce.

Out past Rupp Arena leading west, Highway 60 is called Versailles Road. On this highway in the spring of every year one can find the most admirable concentration of quality thoroughbred horseflesh in the world at the Keeneland yearling sale. Just as the dogwoods come into bloom, Lexington becomes the gathering place of oil sheiks, princes, business tycoons, Japanese industrialists, and simple millionaires. Over the years they have spent hundreds of millions for the untried, unproven offspring of famous racehorses like Secretariat, Seattle Slew, Citation, Whirlaway, Man of War, Affirmed, and Alydar.

"Betting on these horses' 'gets' is the biggest crapshoot in the world," says the dean of America's horse trainers, the estimable Woody Stephens. "They spend millions on horses that might never pay for their feed."

Woody Stephens is a tall, angular, ageless patrician. When he was feeling poorly in the early 1990s there was some talk he'd retire, but he's taking care of himself and the old Woody spark is back in his eye, the spring in his step. He's back on the circuit with some fresh stock, and Lord knows horse racing needs him. No man in the industry is more respected: he won the first race ever run here at newly built Keeneland with Wise Dart in 1936; he beat Calumet's Whirlaway with his dark horse, Our Boots, in the Kentucky Derby of 1941. Woodrow Stephens has won every American race of any importance, including the Preakness, the Kentucky Derby, and the Belmont five times in a row. Even though he'll say privately, "There's nothing I haven't won that sets me on fire," don't bet against Woody Stephens winning the Triple Crown.

Woody is a native-born Kentucky Outlander and a racing traditionalist who has never bet more than a twenty-dollar win and twenty-dollar place on any horse. He disdains the exotic gimmick bets—exactas, trifectas, pick-sixes—that have taken over racetrack betting. "Hell, I can't even pick a daily double," he laughs with his habitual, sweet Kentucky drawl.

Woody Stephens is an intensely generous, hospitable, gentle man. Regardless of the track, no matter where or when, he always has the time to pause and talk serious horse talk with interviewers and two-dollar bettors.

Interest in thoroughbred racing has spawned an enormous industry and it all began in 1783 in Harrodsburg, where the first racetrack in the South was laid out. Within the environs of Lexington, on a radius of no more than ten miles from the city center, there are more than fifty breeding farms carrying on the tradition started by the antebellum racehorse named Lexington. Between 1861 and 1875, Lexington sired 238 stakes winners, a breeding feat never approached by any of the great sires of the twentieth century. All the world knows Churchill Downs, but the thoroughbred fact of the matter is that the big money tracks are on the East and West Coasts. The South, though, is still the lifeblood of the industry, and the heart of it all is here in Lexington on the Versailles Road.

Nowadays these gently rolling hills are the home of the most famous breeding farm ever, Calumet, and of the most exquisite, High Episcopal racetrack in America, Keeneland. With dark grandstands and towers of granite, Keeneland more naturally resembles a monastery than a racetrack. The grounds are marked by pebbled plazas and walkways; parking for the patrons is not on asphalt but on a lawn beneath the shade of stately old oaks; the horses are saddled beside numbered trees instead of in a urine-bathed, feces-bespattered paddock. Coming here, one surmises, is supposed to be a religious experience. There are no crudely dressed, money-grubbing railbirds, no tip sheets, no touts. Keeneland is a festival for the nobility of Lexington. Folks show up in Kentucky-chic suits, sun dresses, broad-brimmed hats, jewelry, furs, shined shoes. Where Churchill Downs accommodates more than a hundred thousand on Derby Day, packing the mob in like the crowds in St. Peter's Square on

Easter, Keeneland has trouble handling 25,000 on its best day. Keeneland really isn't into entertainment, certainly not for the horse racing fan. There is no track announcer, no call to the post, no call of the race. The only evidence that a race is under way is the anemic little swoon from the crowd as the horses come out of the chute. "*Whee* . . ." Cheering is almost out of place. People don't come here for the races, and they don't really come here to be seen. They come here to occupy their pew. Churchill Downs is the Vulgate church and Keeneland is the College of Cardinals.

The stately elegance of Calumet Farm adjacent to Keeneland is the very picture, the immaculate, pristine image of a Kentucky bluegrass horse farm. You'd expect to see Elizabeth Taylor cantering the grounds on National Velvet or Mickey Rooney grooming the black stallion. Calumet's deep blue-green fields are lined with white wooden fences just as Hollywood has always depicted them. Its barns are roofed in tile, its stables painted white, the stall doors a soothing shade of green, its bridle path swept and manicured. Here in November of 1990, Alydar, one of the greatest racehorses ever to carry the Calumet silks, died under suspicious circumstances.

Calumet's immense success over the years was based on raising and racing its own horses and then collecting huge stud fees for the services of its retired champions. Like so many success stories, Calumet's was based on the ability of one man, Warren Wright. His Calumet Baking Powder Company had prospered so well that he was able to establish himself in the sport of kings on an exquisite eight-hundred-acre farm within shouting distance of Adolph Rupp's basketball empire. With the demise of Mr. Wright, the fortunes of Calumet went into a decline until by 1990 the farm was $120 million in debt and had to be taken over by new ownership.

One of Calumet's great champions and sires was Alydar, who gave the racing world some of its most thrilling moments in 1978 when he dueled stride for stride with Affirmed and barely lost in all three of the Triple Crown races. Since that year Alydar's offspring have won many high-stakes races and millions in purses. Then one day something happened to Alydar. He was found in his stall with his right hind leg shattered so badly that he had to be put to sleep. The racing industry was thrown into turmoil later with rumors and accusations that Alydar might have been attacked by a "sandman" who was going around the country killing thoroughbreds and show horses in a sequence of insurance frauds. Headlines hit the sports pages and front pages connecting the sandman with brutal attacks on horses so owners could collect big insurance claims. Stories surfaced that the sandman had been caught, had turned state's evidence, and was put in a Witness Protection Program. Calumet denied any involvement in Alydar's death, and no evidence surfaced to the contrary.

If Alydar was so brutally attacked, it was an act of desperation amounting to an Outlander hubris, for Kentucky more than any other state has been responsible for the rise of the Sport of Kings. Since its inception horse racing has fought for public credibility because of the criminal element that invariably attaches itself to gambling. North America has more than a hundred racetracks, plus countless stables and breeding farms. They've all been in trouble since the tax shelters were taken away in the 1980s. The door was left open for the sport's decline, making it not the sport of kings but of sleazy kingpins.

Woody Stephens was deeply saddened when he heard that Alydar had died the way he did. "I just can't believe that anyone in this industry would stoop so low." Other trainers and owners echoed the same sentiment around the country, and they know a dark cloud will forever hang over Alydar. It's a big industry, however, and they know, too, that for every honorable horseman like Woody Stephens there is a loathsome creature like the sandman.

A few thoroughbreds, special ones like Alydar, know when they are the best and know when they are winning. Some racetrack folks in Kentucky will tell you that Alydar thought he had won when he dueled to the wire with Affirmed in all the Triple Crown races of 1978. "That horse sure thought he had it," say hot walker and groom alike. "He might not have won the purse, but he won your heart."

"If you've never been crazy about thoroughbreds it's because you've never been around where they are much and don't know any better," wrote Sherwood Anderson in "I Want to Know Why," a definitive story on Kentucky horse racing. In the tale a young boy whose love for horses is unbounded becomes disillusioned by a trainer who takes prideful credit for the heart of a courageous horse. The young boy is so bewildered that all he can do is cry out in anguish, "I want to know why." In the tragic incident of Alydar's death, there is only one response from all who are crazy about thoroughbreds. They want to know why.

. . .

THE Outlander mentality didn't evolve simply or rapidly into the attendant patrician pride of horse colonels and whiskey barons; it required generations and a variety of raw material. Sometimes Outlanders are just folks with a wandering psyche that has nothing to do with the fitful peregrinations of Daniel Boone. Then again, maybe it has everything to do with that fitfulness. Modern Kentuckians do love their state and want everyone in every other part of the South to know it. It's not that Kentuckians are worried about how the Yankees see their state—it's that they care how *the South* looks upon Kentucky and in this the old-time Southern manifestations bubble to the surface. Kentucky people are as proud of their virtues as they are of their faults, and they make visitors feel at home with both sides of their Outlander version of the Savage Ideal. The prevailing need to be Southern is evident most any place in Outland Kentucky.

Washington: onetime territorial center and meadowland hometown to men who would become legends. Albert Sidney Johnson, the general whom Jeff Davis called the Confederacy's finest, hailed from Washington. Johnson returned to the South after a daring escape from California through the Southwest deserts to take command of the Army of Tennessee; he led the renowned "Army of the Heartland" and fell at Shiloh, bleeding to death from a wound he refused to tend. Another Washington native was Frank James (né Howard). Young Frank migrated with his folks to Missouri, where the Howards put down outlaw Outlander roots. Brother Jesse would be born up in Clay County, Missouri, where the James Gang would start forming with the Younger brothers, who incidentally were cousins of Frank and Jesse and the only ones in the gang that Jesse could ever trust. But perhaps the most notorious Washington product was Judge Roy Bean, who left Kentucky to grubstake himself by robbing the Butterfield Stage before somehow becoming the only law west of the Pecos in Texas's Big Bend country.

Maysville: site of the Daniel Boone Tavern and the intrepid explorer's last home before he took flight from his creditors.

Carr Creek: the capital of Outlander poverty. Legend has it that Carr Creek was once so poor that its hill clans were reduced to only one slice of bacon to last out the winter. In 1928 Carr Creek won the state basketball tournament. The team had only five players and the folks around chipped in their pennies and nickels to buy their team of deadeye shooters some uniforms and jockstraps. It turns out that the ability to estimate range by eye is known as Kentucky windage for reasons other than just rifle sighting. These rawboned country boys took on the city slickers of Louisville, Lexington, and Frankfurt and beat the pants off them. Kentucky was not always known as the rabid basketball state that its reputation rests on today; it was the little scruffy places like Carr Creek—ones that started beating up on the city teams—that built the grassroots passion and stirred the legend of Kentucky basketball.

Renfro Valley: just south of Lexington in Madison County, the place that in the 1920s and 1930s actually preceded the "Grand Ole Opry" with its famous radio "Barn Dance." All the country music stars came to Renfro Valley, many getting their start to fame here, and the "Barn Dance" was featured on NBC Radio for three decades.

Blackey: deep in the coal hills of Kentucky, the dark soul of Appalachian poverty. Blackey was home to Loretta and Moonie Lynn and the setting for *Coal Miner's Daughter*. Caudle's General Store, a landmark in Blackey, is no different today than it was during the Depression, and the baloney, Moonie Lynn's favorite snack, still makes a body horny.

Berea: in the foothills of Appalachia, a poor but pig-iron proud county seat with more concern for its people than for the letter or spirit of Jacksonian law. Way back in 1855 some good souls put up Berea College for the children of the poor coal miners. The tradition of helping rather than beggaring thy neighbor lives on at Berea.

Van Lear: bent double in grief by the mining disasters in the 1930s but holding on to the Outland traditions of Elizabeth Madox Roberts. Stories here in Van Lear are told in the before-TV language of the hills, and there's never a hint of self-pity, only the gentle self-deprecating of a people sunk to the hocks in poverty. "We're so poor here the only thing we've got to be proud of is our humility."

LIFE is still hard for those who people the lands of eastern Kentucky. Many of their children have left to find new lives. Some, like the Howards, tracked into the Ozarks to rebuild in similar surroundings, but most migrated to the familiar urban respite of Lexington and that town's suburbs.

Two such wandering offsprings of the Outlands are Bruce Asbury and Tom Atkinson, natives of Paris, Kentucky, and emblems of their state's irrepressible spirit. One shoots from the hip, the other shoots from the lip. Asbury is a television personality and Atkinson is the law west of the Licking River. They're boyhood and lifelong friends with a wandering spirit that makes them prototype "city slickers"—at least of the Billy Crystal variety. Together they've retraced Boone's trail through the Cumberland Gap, crossed the Mississippi on the path of De Soto, scaled Pike's Peak, and camped on Captain Bonneville's salt flats. Asbury and Atkinson have hunkered down in a blizzard in the Donner Pass, ridden the twenty-mule-train Borax wagons in Death Valley, chased stray dogies on the Chisholm Trail, and whipped their horses through the hell of the Jornado del Morte. Somehow you have to believe they've done all these things; they're free spirits and just a tad crazy, but really what Asbury and Atkinson are, they're Kentucky's best ambassadors.

If there is a New South, one forging a new identity that repudiates the old neuroses, then it is lodged in the personality of baby boomers such as Asbury and Atkinson. Neither man could have focused his life on changing the complexion of his world had it not been for parents who'd been galvanized by the chaos of the Depression and World War II into a realization that the Southern world called out for restructuring. Asbury's Confederate great-grandfather had his horse shot from under him at the Battle of Pikeville in eastern Kentucky. At least one Asbury has fought in every American war since the Revolution. The family not only claims kinship with Indian leader Tecumseh, it also keeps up an old Daniel Boone cabin on the family farm in Nicholas. Asbury's grandfather invented his own reaper and baler, though he never gave a thought to getting patents. Asbury's father's silks were on the winner of the 1953 Kentucky Derby.

Tom Atkinson's family were Outlander pioneers come West to grow their own family trees. They helped settle the hard lands of east Kentucky and brought a strength of purpose and resolve to Elizabeth Madox Roberts's meadowlands. Atkinson's father, Fred Temple, was the longtime mayor of Paris; his mother was an artist.

Both Asbury and Atkinson went to Paris High School. Asbury

went off to the University of Cincinnati to major in dramatics, and football standout Atkinson went on scholarship to Morehead State. After college Atkinson coached high school football before beginning a law-enforcement career as a federal agent, a Revenuer, though now he's turned his talents to being a federal parole officer for his former moonshiner, dope-runner quarry up the back hollers of the mountains. Asbury became a popular regional TV personality working at all points of the compass, entertaining children and adults alike.

While they have a hip, cosmopolitan air about them, both Asbury and Atkinson are beyond doubt Southerners. They carry their Southernness lightly; it's not a burden to them. They have no conceit, exhibit no hypocrisy, nor are they ashamed of being Southern. Asbury talks about a unique stone fence in his hometown. It stretches from Paris to Lexington. The land here is rocky, and over the years before the Civil War the stones from clearing the land were put in place.

"That fence has never been torn down," says Asbury, "even though it was built by slaves. Well, it's a damn good fence, and good labor is good labor. Besides, the fence is more of a memorial to leave it standing than to tear it down."

Asbury has a great following on TV. He intersperses his programming with satiric monologues in the manner of Jonathan Winters and appeals to children as if he's a combination of Rocky and Bullwinkle. He no longer has a Southern accent on screen; a test of Southern vigor is the stamina shown by the drawl in the face of the powerful tendency toward homogenization in the android-speak TV industry. Off-camera, he speaks the language of his people—not slow but measured, with a composed hill twang of honesty.

The way they speak is the way they are. Kentucky has the reputation of being as much midwestern as Southern, but Asbury says that "anywhere you go in Kentucky they still play Dixie . . . except maybe Louisville."

Unlike Asbury, Tom Atkinson hasn't worked much outside of Kentucky, yet he, too, shows his Southernness in subtle ways. His speech is recognizably Kentuckian, but not ponderously so. His conversation is richly anecdotal, recalling the many episodes of his law-enforcement career, but there is no mimicry in his voice. As a federal parole officer based in Lexington, Atkinson has to keep up with any number of transgressors (folks he maybe arrested when he was an ATF agent). Most of his "clientele" are convicted dope and moonshine runners. He spends a lot of his time up in the hills of eastern Kentucky close onto the West Virginia border. It's frontier outland, rough and primitive country where people still live by the feud and the old code of the hills.

The way of life up here has always been bare. Fighting the wolf and the copperheads breeds a hardened, often mean, psyche. "There's a dignity here, too," says Atkinson, "one that up the logging roads and back hollers says they're doing what they've chosen to do, and if you don't like it, then don't come around here . . . they'd just as soon be left alone anyway."

Atkinson knows most of the people and their clans, many of them by first name. He drives through the hills without any fear; he feels he knows his people. He tells the story of the time when he was a Revenuer: "I went up to an old man's place who'd done some time for making 'shine. No one was in the house so I walked on back into the deep woods. I found a still and some sheds. There hunkered the old man working on his copper tubing—his grandson was feeding the fire. When I walked up, the boy pulled a gun on me. His grandpap reached over and boxed his ears and said, 'No need for a gun . . . the man's just doing his job.' "

MANY parts, far too many parts, of the South have been battlegrounds over the decades since the sixteenth century—Spanish and French and Dutch and Swedes and Palatine Germans and Mexicans and the English all fought each other and all fought the Indians. Americans, when they became so, fought Europeans and Indians and themselves. About the only ones not fighting were the women. Especially in the Southlands, the fact most often overlooked by chronicler, historian, and sociologist is that after each conflict the women tried to rebuild from the physical and emotional wreckage strewn by their menfolk. After the Civil War Southerners created a new enemy to fight, the newly enfranchised black citizens whom they attacked with arms, ropes, hatred, and the most egregious set of laws imaginable.

Well, not quite. *Plessy* v. *Ferguson* was pretty bad since it permitted the Jim Crow laws to abuse millions of blacks, but the social conscience of the whiteman South was equally capable of abusing its own. The South has always had an incurable contempt for labor unions; perhaps it's the word "union" that upsets the leaders and followers of the old Confederacy. The bosses of the industrialized North had no more use for the rights of labor than their counterparts below the Mason-Dixon Line. Still, the North was forced to face reality if for no other reason than that labor union members voted against politicians who voted against the unions. Down South nothing of the sort happened, for the simple reason that very few Southerners joined unions. Southern men only get together for warring, whoring, hell-raising, hunting, and footballing.

With Southern women it was different. The women's suffrage movement, the engine of American history that propelled the growth of human rights and just plain human decency, offered the one nexus in the South where progressive thought could find collective expression. Nowhere was this felt more than in the growth of the labor unions.

The great exemplar linking women and labor was Mary Harris "Mother" Jones. A County Cork Irish girl born in 1830, Mary Harris moved to America and married a union man, George Jones. She lost her husband and four children to the Great Yellow Fever Plague in Memphis in 1867 and lost all of her possessions to the great Chicago Fire of 1871. Dressed in black, she fought for the children impressed in the textile mills. She fought for the steelworkers of her husband's Iron Molders Union; for the copper miners of the American and Canadian West; for the women working in the sweatshops of the garment industry in New York; for the women working sixteen-hour days in the breweries of the Midwest. But above all, Mary Harris Jones devoted her one-hundred-year-life to the cause of her beloved coal miners.

Throughout her life, coal miners, whether organized or not, petitioned Mother Jones by telegram, saying, "Come quick, we need you." Toward the end of her life, when she was being hailed as a great humanitarian by scholars and statesmen, Mother Jones would respond, "Get it right. I'm not a humanitarian . . . I'm a hell-raiser."

When southern Illinois miners were murdered by strikebreakers at Virde in 1898, Mother Jones was there. When the Cabin and Paint Creek, West Virginia, coal miners were slaughtered by Baldwin-Felts strikebreakers in 1912, Mother Jones was there. When the Matewan,

West Virginia, miners were massacred by the state militia in 1920, Mother Jones was there. When two thousand federal troops and a squadron of U.S. Army bombers lashed at the West Virginia miners at the Battle of Blair Mountain in 1921, Mother Jones was there. More importantly, Mary Harris Jones was in the mining communities throughout Appalachia during the aftermath of the so-called natural disasters, mine cave-ins and explosions that killed thousands and destroyed families.

Mother Jones fought for everyone but herself. In her eighties she was caught up in the Logan County, West Virginia, fight between the mine owners and the miners and thrown into a makeshift prison by the state militia. It was wintertime and her cell was a one-room, unheated shack with damp straw on the floor for a bed. The militia was afraid to release her, afraid she'd raise more hell and rouse more rabble. But Henry D. Hatfield, governor of West Virginia and a descendant of the old outlaw clan, exerted some Outlander spunk himself. He had been listening to Mother Jones and figured she was making good sense. Hatfield went to the prison, freed Mother Jones, and escorted her to Charleston, where he put her up in the capital's finest hotel and had her taken care of by his personal physician. Governor Hatfield was a child of these coal mountains and knew that the miners were being treated horrendously by the profit-sucking owners. He'd heard her speak at a rally where she castigated the owners: "God almighty, come with me and see the wrecks of women, of babies, then ask yourself, 'How can I sleep at night, how can your wife sleep at night?' "

Mother Jones is almost forgotten today. You can go into the union halls of the UMW all over Appalachia but you won't see any photographs or paintings memorializing the "Angel of the Miners." The prized photo in these halls is of John L. Lewis. Just weeks before her death in 1930 Mother Jones donated a thousand dollars to a campaign to oust the bristle-browed union president because she believed he was selling out his members. Yet the memory of Mary Harris Jones is being kept alive by historians such as Philip S. Foner, professor emeritus of history at Lincoln University. Foner devoted much of his career to the great lady of the labor movement, and his comprehensive biography of her, *Mother Jones Speaks*, is a treasure of her century-long struggle for women and labor. Professor Foner has written, "The truth is that Mother Jones was a fighter for the working class everywhere."

Mother Jones said that no nation would ever go beyond the development of its women. "Lift up the women, make them intellectual. Thus will great sons be born, and men find true comrades in their wives." She also said, "Pray for the dead but fight like hell for the living." At her own request, Mother Jones was buried at the Mount Olive cemetery in southern Illinois next to the victims of the 1898 "Virden Massacre." The inscription on the monument to the murdered miners reads: "WE COUNT IT DEATH TO FALTER, NOT TO DIE."

DESPITE the best efforts of Mother Jones and the short-lived enlightenment of Governor Hatfield, the coal miners were beaten down. The coal wars had been fought over an increase in wages that would have amounted to a nickel a week in the miners' pockets. But the free-enterprise system of the era vested rights with owners alone. The lives of the defeated miners were wretched; worse, were hopeless. Mother Jones was right: families were being destroyed for no better reason than profit. From this despair, the miners sought succor wherever they could find it.

They shall speak with new tongues; they shall take up serpents; and if they drink any deadly thing, it shall not hurt them; they shall lay hands on the sick, and they shall recover. Thus the written imperative from St. Mark passed down through the generations via the miracle of illuminated manuscript, the Gutenberg press, and the Linotype machine. St. Mark little realized what would be done with his words. Literal translations of these injunctions to worship can be traced back to the deserts of Libya, Egypt, and the Holy Land during the times of Caligula, Claudius, and Nero. Zealots flailed themselves with thorns to prove their unworthiness, bricked themselves into waterless, alkaline caves in the wilderness to prove their holiness, and rejoiced in the skin diseases of the unclean as signs of divine inspiration. They weren't a cheerful lot, and for that matter neither were St. Mark's words—but all who heeded were true believers.

Long after the passing of the Old World zealots, the verses of St. Mark found an unlikely home in the poverty-bound mountains of Appalachia, the ranges of which became the center of ophidian worship in the New World. According to sociologist Nathan L. Gerrard in his study of West Virginia, the practice of taking up serpents as part of a church service was started around 1900 by an itinerant preacher named George Went Hensley. Hensley's evangelical circuit included Tennessee, Kentucky, West Virginia, and Virginia, and his proselytes spread the word throughout the remainder of the South. In today's Southlands more than a thousand of these serpent tabernacles coexist with your basic high-toned Protestant churches. They may call themselves the Church of All Nations, Church of Jesus, or the Church of the Holy Ghost—they're all independent sects not tied to one another, and they all believe in a literal interpretation of the King James version of the Bible. They do everlastingly believe in anointing, speaking in tongues, slaying in spirit, drinking poison, convulsive dancing, and testifying.

The sorrowful coal-mining villages of Appalachia were the breeding grounds for the snake-handling congregations. The hidden world of these mountains hasn't changed all that much from the time of Reconstruction. For close to a hundred years these folks have found no comfort in the churches of organized religion of the Baptists, the Methodists, or even the holy rollers of the Great Speckled Bird. The near-destitute mining families were looked down upon, and these people knew in their hearts that the established churches were ashamed of them. So they began turning to the teachings of Brother Hensley, who had brought the literal tablets of evangelical truth into these mountains. The truth of the word was there for all to read, Mark 16:17, 18—Search no further, fear not for your soul, God is the glory.

Serpent churches sprang up like little hill forts in the towns of Jolo, Scrabble Creek, Logan, Oak Hill, Prosperity, Dixie, Jolly Bridge, and Camp Creek. Modernity has slowly crept into these hills, yet one can find any of these little churches and be welcomed. No shame, conceit, or hypocrisy taints the face of the congregations.

Even if you grew up within this bizarre sense of rapture, attendance at a service is beset with fear and trembling. As you come through the door you are embraced and kissed on the lips by the men and the women, for, though these people have their own taboos, same-sex kissing isn't one of them. The service begins, though there is no leader, no preacher. Music starts up from guitars, tambourines, and an accordion. People stomp and clap and begin to dance and to sing an old hill song, all punctuated with hallelujahs and glories be to God, shouting in victory and speaking in tongues (that incomprehensible other-world code talk with God to keep the devil from understanding). The singing in high bluegrass harmony is piped out in pure and sweet language that goes back to the Anglo-Saxon . . . *and baet leoht lyht on oystrum* . . . for here the people are singing of the light shining in the darkness. And when the speaking in tongues starts up it is a buzzing noise, fast at first and too urgent but measured, precise as dactylic hexameters or what seem to be dactylic hexameters, but they are not words, just strained breath, and if you understood you would be some kind of god.

You marvel and shiver as the dancing becomes convulsive with rag-doll-like circling and flailing of arms as if controlled by some demented puppeteer. Men and women fall writhing on the floor in unknowable rapture. And the testifying begins. It becomes somnambulistic jerkings and gyratings as words explode from contorted mouths. The prayers begin. Some strangers you have known as aunts and uncles and cousins, before you set forth in the world to defile yourself, embrace you. Some stand with arms akimbo; others raise their hands high in supplication; still others kneel, pressing their hands viciously to their foreheads to shade their eyes from the unholiness of the world you are a part of. You feel fear sweating from their purity. "God made the world out of one blood . . . the Holy Ghost is calling . . . hain't it Jesus calling, hyurring my prurr . . . lead me, Lord, lead me the way I want to go . . . I feel the quickening power . . ."

And you know this is an outland place, an out-world. You begin to agitate from the sheer energy here and feel almost pulled back into the strange ritual, eyeless in Gaza. And then they open up those wooden boxes up there on the altar, the double-lidded ammunition boxes, cartons of fear from the depths of hell and the bestial eyes of Beelzebub, the Lord of Flies. You have told yourself that this time you will not look, for you have seen people bitten—you have seen blood splattering on the floor—and many have died from the snakes and from the drinking of poison. But your eyes stray, are compelled to see. Delicate copperheads, sleek diamondbacks and timber rattlers, and you see the reptilian eyes bright and fixed. No fakir tricks here, the snakes haven't been addled with opium smoke or had their fangs pulled. You are compelled to watch as the women and men take up the snakes and dance with them, caress them, and you take up the reverie of your own youth when you went on snake hunts with your cousins and buddies, and you open your eyes again to see the faces of your childhood here in this hall, dowdy women with pur-blind gazes, comely willing young girls, handsome and hungry young men, and lank, gaunt hillmen beat down by these coal hills, wheezing out their black-lung prayers, all dancing with snakes in the earth, all with the desire that God will choose them to be bitten so to prove their worthiness.

The faces of these churches so peculiar to the Southlands have changed since the 1970s. In the 1990s they have become glossier and cool, with steel and electric guitars and drum sets and preachers. There has been no lessening of their numbers; they're expanding into the flatlands and building citified churches. With this sophisti-cation they seemed to have lost something, maybe their way. They still dance and make a joyful noise and practice the taking up of ser-pents. Modern sociologists call it hedonism and maybe it is. More likely it is complicated beyond such academic certainties. Perhaps it is a safety valve, a search for identity, perhaps a search for the myth that will make them whole. Southern poet Miller Williams, himself the son of a Methodist minister, perhaps put it better than any soci-ologist when he wrote about coming down out of the hills of cer-tainty into uncertainty: "Failing is an act of love because like sin it is the commonality within."

Living conditions in Appalachia are not as bad now as thirty years ago. Mostly gone are the old frame and native stone cabins, replaced here and there by modest houses, prefabs, and the ever-present dou-ble-wide. Poverty is still there; one simply has to go farther back up into the hills to find it. Traveling over this headland, one comes to an awareness that Appalachia has its own certainty beyond the poet's words. It is true that the folks of these hills have had the need for a connection to the ancient Old Testament culture; it is also true that they find ways to bring simple joy into their lives. They have their churches, their cars, and TV, and there are a few better jobs to be had than in the bad old days. But those simple joys somehow re-main; the truth of it flows through these hills with the same certainty as their native river, the New, which has been there since the glacial melt and is the oldest river in this hemisphere. Composer Aaron Copland translated this original energy in his *Appalachian Spring*, and the same people who find God in taking up serpents see native beauty in the singing of the old ballads "Barbara Allen" and "In the Pines" and "Go Tell Aunt Rhody."

Out on the mountain lives an old couple in their nineties; they've lived in the same dog-run house for seventy years and they sit on the porch and look off into the mist of the blue mountains. If you go slow and raise no dust they'll welcome you in, for Southern hospitality is as fair here as in the lowlands. She'll sing you a song called "The Water Is Wide," all about a brokenhearted maiden, and he'll tell you how things have been here in these hills for almost a century. "We never knew we was poor," he says. "We figured that was the way it was made. It took people like you coming by here to learn us how poor we was."

Two major routes allowed the settlement of the Southern outlands. The first and least important was the national road begun in the 1780s by the founding American government. It wasn't a road in the modern sense, just a trail impeded by stumps and boulders that barely allowed single wagons through, though the road did connect the mountains of West Virginia with Washington City. By far the most important route was the great Ohio River itself. By raft, barge, flat and keelboat, hundreds of thousands settled on both the north and south shores of the river first called "Ouabache" by the Iroquois. From this point on in American history the nation's rivers would become more than impediments; they served as massive conduits for trade and settlement. Pioneers taking the river used it again and again to move on a few miles farther in their search for better land and newer fortune. The Ohio River itself has very little delta, and the settlers had to march inland to carve farmsteads out of the wilderness. A constant resettlement took place on both shores, and this mixing of North and South created an amended Outlander singularity, a shared heritage of individualism in spirit and kinship that exists to this day.

This Outlander singularity was exemplified by an Ohio dreamer named Harman Blennerhassett in the 1790s. Blennerhassett and his young wife came down the Ohio and set up a plantation on a river island not far from West Virginia and Kentucky. Their place was the most splendid in three states. Blennerhassett's young wife intro-

duced inoculation against smallpox to the frontier families, saving
scores of children from the dread ubiquitous killer. Such humanitarian acts hardly existed on the American frontier and were to lead to
a bad end in the case of the Blennerhassetts. In 1804, after having
gunned down Alexander Hamilton, Aaron Burr stopped at Blennerhassett's island and enlisted him in a scheme to carve out a south-
western empire in Louisiana, Texas, and Mexico. Burr's plan was to
raise a rebellion in French New Orleans, to control the commerce
on the Ohio and Mississippi Rivers, and from this base to strike into
the silver mines of Mexico. Blennerhassett yielded to Burr's dream
and to his powers of persuasion; both men journeyed down the Mississippi to New Orleans. Their rebellion was under way when they
were captured in Natchez. They were tried for treason, but Burr, the
archconspirator, got off on a technicality. Blennerhassett was put in
prison and while he was there, his island was pillaged by the fathers
of the children whom his wife had saved. Aaron Burr sailed to Europe, where he hobnobbed with royalty before returning to a successful law practice in New York City; he even married a rich widow
(one who claimed to have slept with George Washington and
Napoleon). Poor, deluded Harman Blennerhassett tried to make a
go of plantation farming in Louisiana but succumbed to the moneylenders and died in poverty. His anguished wife had to return to her
family on the Isle of Jersey.

Over on the north shore lie the low southern hills of Ohio. It's a
gentler land with an absence of the harsh realities of life by the feud,
yet family is the anchor of these people's lives just as on the south
shore. Boys in Kentucky and West Virginia play King of the Mountain; children in southern Ohio while away late autumn afternoons
playing Go Sheepy Go. On the edge of the Appalachian Plateau that
covers the eastern half of Ohio lives a poet and singer who was born
knowing the tactile kinship between the north and south shores of
the Ohio, indeed between North and South. He's a storyteller in the
mold of Henry Lawson. His name is Damon Thompson, and his short
stories and lyrics evoke the bittersweet yearnings of adolescence.

Thompson taught at Marshall University in Huntington, West Virginia, for many years. In one year he had three Kentucky Hatfields
and two West Virginia McCoys in his class. The Hatfields were dark-
complected and the McCoys fair-skinned. "Both families were at-
tractive, intelligent, and well-bred," Thompson says. He and his wife,

Jeannie, often visited the Hatfield family cemetery near Matewan. They had to walk through briars and climb over a barbed-wire fence to see the graves of the archetypes of the American vendetta.

"The popular myth is that the feud had its beginnings as a star-crossed love affair between a McCoy girl and a Hatfield boy. Maybe, but more likely it was over property rights. Nonetheless, I like to sing the ballad of Roseanne McCoy whenever I'm in Matewan."

The dialect of Thompson's home country at Beaver, Ohio, situated in a gap between the two segments of the Wayne National Forest, is distinctly Southern hills: "Hain't everthang still? 'M glad it's summer, hain't you? I'm gonna quit goin' down by the bridge if them big girls don't stop comin' down there and seein' how nosey they can be . . ."

Thompson says they never thought of themselves as Northern or Southern here in Beaver. "We were always hillbillies up here. We never had an affinity for the Midwest. I suppose our allegiance was with our brothers across the river."

ALTHOUGH the Ohio River has always been politically neutral, the people of the north shore feel the need to be Southern, and the common thread, as disreputable as it is, between these people and those of the Old South is their xenophobia toward the blacks. It must be remembered that the KKK was stronger in Indiana than in any state of the South. Since antebellum days, there have been two ways of explaining this xenophobia: the whites who held this hatred were so poor that the blacks were the only ones they could look down on; or the old saw come true—white folks in the North loved the black race but hated the individual, while white folks in the South hated the black race but loved the individual. However outlandish these notions might have seemed, they spun the common thread. Nowhere was this more pronounced than on the mutual banks of the Ohio River.

The tale of America's great rivers is momentous. Each has a claim on the sweep of our history that is frightening in simplicity and time. The Ohio was the first river of the American West. The whole of the Midwest cataracts into twin basins as two old Indian rivers, the Mechesebe and the Ouabache, surge down to meet each other at the confluence of America. Ouabache in lore was the Indian name for "beautiful"; Mechesebe meant "Great Waters." A long-standing myth, tinged with modern reality, assigns the headwaters of the great Mississippi to a tranquil little lake up in Minnesota, but the Ohio could make a better claim as the source, for it lays an original waterway network all the way to the Great Lakes while it drains the Appalachian Plateau, the Northern Plains, and a major part of the midwestern corn belt.

La Salle accidentally discovered the Ohio River in the late seventeenth century, and from that day on the great Indian nations could only hold their breath. In rapid succession would come the fierce Indian conquerors: Mad Anthony Wayne, William Henry Harrison, George Rogers Clark—and in turn Pontiac and Tecumseh and Black Hawk would fall to the long knives and cannon of the white man's civilization. The Ohio is broad and fast and carries great momentum from its mountainous headwaters. Once the boats left Pittsburgh and started floating the Ohio, it took only a generation to seal the doom of the red men east of the Mississippi and north of the Ohio. Where once a few thousand Indians lived in the forests and plains, millions of whites would come to till the fields and build their factories.

The power of the Ohio terrified La Salle, who left it at the whitewater rapids just below Louisville. The rapids continued to be a serious hazard to navigation for the next two centuries. In 1811 the first steamboat in Western waters, Nicholas Roosevelt's *New Orleans,* was stymied by the same rapids and by one of the most extraordinary natural catastrophes in American history, the eruption of the New Madrid fault. The earthquake was of such magnitude that it caused the Mississippi River to flow upstream into the Ohio. Roosevelt's *New Orleans* rode through the quake and made it all the way to New Orleans, heralding in a new age of transportation, settlement, and commerce.

Louisville cashed in on this new river traffic and in fact became the terminus not only for the commerce on the rivers but for the great steamboat races originating in New Orleans. The big-money steamboat lines owed their success or failure to the times posted between New Orleans and Louisville, not New Orleans and St. Louis (which was in the steamboat era merely a depot for furs and corn). Louisville offered a more prestigious form of corn—blended Kentucky bourbon. In the 1830s and 1840s Louisville assumed the mien of a major city because of its docks and its whiskey barrels. Louisville likes to think that its city anthem is Stephen Foster's "My Old Kentucky Home," but George Jones's "Drowning in a Whiskey River" might be closer to the truth.

Louisville did drown once. Living on a floodplain is always dangerous no matter what precautions are taken. The Lower Mississippi was devastated by the Great Flood of 1927 and suffered badly in the flood ten years later. But Louisville was inundated in 1937, virtually washed away, and after the water receded the streets collapsed, breaking the gas lines and causing the city to be consumed in flames. Despite a disaster that would have made most cities give up, Louisville bounced back with grit, and with uncommon prescience. The city never had much of an Outlander mentality until its redneck back was up against the wall. Before the 1937 flood, Louisville had tried to ape the midwestern gloss of Chicago, St. Louis, Cincinnati, and Cleveland. But out of tragedy, Louisville gathered on its innate Southern strengths and horse-traded its way into a new prosperity and image.

Louisville always had a certain sports pedigree. In 1875 the first Kentucky Derby was run here and the victor, Aristides, got the winner's share of the $2,850 purse. Hypesters since then have taken the bluegrass image of Kentucky colonels and mint juleps and parlayed it into one of the top three sporting mega-events of the world. Yet the city's sports heritage started with baseball and in the same era as the first Kentucky Derby. In a real sense Louisville became the home of baseball, outdistancing the clubs in New York, Boston, Baltimore, and Chicago. Although it lost its major-league franchise before the turn of the century, Louisville is still in the show. The city is the center of baseball equipment manufacturing—bats, gloves, paraphernalia, and chewing tobacco.

Memories are short in Louisville. The Outlander strength and resolve is now scoffed at and denigrated. Maybe the town needs a metaphorical flood to test its newly acquired glitzy character. No one cares to remember the 1937 flood, save for a few folks in their seventies and older who rebuilt on higher ground.

THE Mississippi, called Big Muddy, and the wide Missouri, also known as Big Muddy, have hogged the riparian folklore of America. The Mississippi had its famous "wholesale" cutthroat pirates, John Murrell and Jean Lafitte. The Missouri is infamous for its Robber Baron fur traders led by René Auguste Chouteau and John Jacob Astor. The Ohio, though, has had more than its share of hard men, half-alligator and half-human. Mike Fink, the prototype for Mark Twain's "Child of Calamity," was the creation of the wonderful exaggerations of master storytellers. He was a crack shot, could drink any ten men under the table, had a harem in every port, and could eat the rear end out of a bear while it was running. Like all the other pirates on the rivers, Fink preyed on the new commerce floating down to New Orleans before the steamboat took control. Lesser legends grew up on both shores of the Ohio: the Harpe Brothers, Big and Little, who terrified the Green River country of Kentucky, gaining entry to homesteads by singing hymns and then slaying all in the household; and Wilson's Liquor Vault and House of Entertainment, a bawdy house in a cave that lured flatboat crews to their deaths with the promise of strong drink and bad women.

The Ohio is no placid farmer's river (Davis Grubb portrays the savagery and beauty of both the river and its people in his powerful novel *Night of the Hunter*). Boulders jut from the Ohio's banks and stone walls rise above its swirling current. Its own azure waters have changed to commercial gray over the industrial centuries, and the Ohio is now as toxic as any of its sister rivers that drain the great basins of America.

As the river passes the coasts of Kentucky, Indiana, and Illinois, it gains in strength from its tributaries, the Tennessee, the Cumberland, and the Wabash, until it finally collides with the Mississippi at the confluence of America. Below Cairo on the southernmost tip of Illinois, the Ohio refuses to merge with the Mississippi. For a hundred miles or more the two great rivers sweep southward in studied belligerence, neither willing to give in. You understand that each river has its own static electrical charge and that it takes miles and miles to neutralize the impact. But such standard explanations fail to give comfort. The Ohio is a Northern river and just to be cantankerous, the Southern Mississippi will have nothing to do with it.

Standing here at this convergence, you get the feeling that you're floating on the irony line. You see the two rivers fighting at Cairo and you can see the Civil War all over again, and what is irony in the South but the conflict between North and South? You wonder if the two will ever merge. You know only one thing: that after a hundred miles the Ohio and the Mississippi rivers give up the old causes, the old clichés, the old everything—to become a new river.

CHAPTER 10

THE LATTER-DAY PHOENICIANS

Arkansas and Missouri . . . Uncle Witt Stephens and the Merchant Princes . . . Little Rock . . . Clinton . . . Augustus Hill Garland . . . The Capo of Hot Springs . . . Branson and the Ozarks . . . Cole Younger's Descendants

"AT LAST THE GREAT captain died." So goes the epitaph in a children's book on Hernando de Soto just before his men stuffed his ravaged body into a hollow log and slid the makeshift catafalque into the swirling current of the Mississippi River. De Soto had led his retinue in a trek across most of what is now known as the American South in a rueful search for plunder and the legendary cities of gold. What de Soto's conquistadors mostly found was death, but they brought the scourge of death to the native tribes before they found it themselves.

De Soto's "conquering" army had landed in the South in 1539, way down in Florida on Tampa Bay. It was the same year that Henry VIII was tricked by the Holbein painting of Anne of Cleves into signing a marriage contract with that stout German matron. That marriage was never consummated, and neither was de Soto's passion for treasure. In the same year that Coronado was wandering the American West and Francisco de Orellana was descending the Amazon, de Soto was running smack into a flooding Mississippi River and rafting across it into the jungles of Arkansas. It would be seventy-six years before the landing at Jamestown and seven score more until La Salle would canoe down the Big Muddy.

The conflict between the Mississippi and Ohio rivers rages into the Lower Mississippi Valley and into the general region just below Memphis where de Soto is said to have crossed the Big Muddy. This mysterious crossing gives rise to what is probably the most torturous question in American historical folklore: just where did the great captain cross the river? Whole legions of amateur and professional scholars have devoted learned conferences, sabbaticals, and esoteric dissertations to this perplexing and meaningless question. The only period reference available is the diary of a Portuguese ne'er-do-well named Elvas who accompanied de Soto. The greatest worth of Elvas's diary, despite its being cited by every scholar in Christendom, is the insight it gives into the laconic acceptance of the violence the Spanish visited upon the Indians (captured Indians were routinely burned at the stake, beheaded, and mutilated). The diary contains no historical meat, no proof or evidence of anything other than barbaric cruelty.

More than two hundred years elapsed before other white men would cross the Mississippi into the jungles of Arkansas. Those coming over from Mississippi, Tennessee, and Kentucky were the culls, the outcasts, the fellows who had ended up on the short end of the horse traders' deals. Even the slaves they brought along were rejects, as evidenced in the true story of a Memphis slave auction: a field hand with the name of George Washington was put on the block, but the auctioneer refused to sell him, saying, "I know he's the father of his nation, but he's also got the pox . . . take him over to the Arkansas side where folks ain't so particular." An early explorer of the Arkansas Territory got lost and wandered around in the wild for a couple of weeks, and when he was finally found, he declared, "Arkansas is not one of the places that Jesus Christ died for."

Anything and anyone west of the Mississippi River became marked with a different psyche. Out here in this godforsaken land a man was on his own and had to be savage to survive. Arkansas became American because of the Louisiana Purchase, but its lands were so obscure and wild that for years it couldn't even be surveyed. The stone near Marvell, Arkansas, used as the base point for the 1815 survey of the entire Louisiana Territory, was lost for 126 years before it was rediscovered in 1921. The Catholic entrepreneurs Marquette and Joliet camped out near the mouth of the Arkansas River in 1673, but probably the first civilized man to set up a permanent camp in the territory was Henri De Tonti, the "Iron Hand" of La Salle. Tonti proved to be resourceful, intelligent, and loyal; he was instrumental in La Salle's discoveries. Tonti's Arkansas Post was a few miles up the Arkansas River and from here French *coureurs de bois* haphazardly explored the region while trapping for furs. Yet up to the year of its statehood in 1836, semicivilized Arkansas was essentially restricted to the alluvial plains of the Arkansas River running from the Mississippi River past the foothills of the Ozarks into the Indian Territory that would become Oklahoma.

No one is sure how Arkansas got its name, though a reasonable guess is that it's a French transliteration of a Quapaw Indian word probably meaning "enemy." Tonti did name the most significant mountain range in the region, giving the Ozarks the name of his outpost, Aux Arcs. The state was so primitive that Frederick Law Olmsted dared not travel through it, though he visited every other part of the Cotton Kingdom in the 1850s. Edward King, the next great travel writer to the South, was equally horrified at the violence of Arkansas in the 1870s. Indeed, the three primary pastimes of the first settlers were racing mules, drinking rotgut whiskey, and killing their neighbors.

Aside from the random knifings, shootings, armed robberies, and lynchings that frightened King, this New York writer commented in his book *The Great South* on the almost complete lack of financial investment in the state. He noted that Arkansas was in debt but he didn't explain the origin. Had he followed up, he could have easily found the reason for Arkansas's miserable economic condition. It all started with statehood and a $5 million bond issue that was floated by the founding horse traders in the 1830s. These mountebanks running the political show in Little Rock induced the New York bond market to finance the new state, and as soon as the money arrived it found its way into the pockets of the chosen few. The state of Arkansas then reneged on the debt and the New York financial bosses blackballed the state for more than a hundred years—ironically until the time of the Great Depression, when a new class of horse trader would emerge in Arkansas with such phenomenal success that it can only be seen as the second coming of the Phoenicians.

The immediate effect of the bond swindle was to limit Arkansas to one source of wealth, cotton. Tying itself to this one-crop mentality put the state securely in the arms of the Deep South despite the fact that Arkansas had nothing in common with the Old South either politically or culturally other than its deep-seeded preoccupation with the Savage Ideal. When the Civil War came, the plantation owners and slaveholders voted their pocketbooks and Arkansas went to war. After the Civil War the whole of the fertile flatland from the bootheel of Missouri to the sugarcane fields of Louisiana was transformed into a vast sea of cotton. The defeat of the South should have brought on land reforms, but it didn't. The smaller homestead farms all but disappeared, gobbled up by the giant plantations. The proud Dockery Plantation occupied huge tracts on both sides of the Mississippi River; the Robert E. Lee Wilson estate in northeast Arkansas was a duchy the size of Luxembourg. The plantation families sent their ducal heirs to Eastern finishing schools and Ivy League universities, owned blocks of property in Memphis, and vacation homes in Europe and the Caribbean. Reconstruction Arkansas was no different from its antebellum predecessor because cotton remained the only source of wealth and political power.

Meanwhile back in the fields, poor white trash and even poorer blacks chopped and picked cotton, lived in clapboard shotgun shacks, and subsisted on fatback and field peas. It was a peonage as dark as the Middle Ages and it was called sharecropping. This involuntary servitude persisted through Reconstruction, the Gilded Age, and into the first decades of the twentieth century. Between the Civil War and World War I, through all political administrations and reform movements, including the Populists, nothing was done to break the chain of serfdom on the delta. When on rare occasions a few brave souls tried to do something about it, they were met with brute force. What happened in the little plantation town of Elaine, Arkansas, in 1919 is such an example.

Following World War I some young black men who had served in France tried to improve their wretched conditions in Phillips County, Arkansas. They formed a union, the Household Union of America, and presented to the plantation owners the then-outrageous demand of fifty cents a day cash money for their labor. In 1919 indentured blacks on the plantations got no money at all for their work. To keep them going, they were periodically given a sack of flour and cornmeal, a bag of pinto beans, and a bucket of lard. They received for special treats the leavings from the hog killings—the feet, the brains, the liver and kidneys, the skin, and the intestines. Sometimes in good crop years when there was no flood or drought, the children got a sack of hardrock candy for Christmas.

The demand of cash money for labor was unthinkable to the white planters and they pronounced the union a "Communist conspiracy." A bloodbath ensued. A few whites thought to intimidate the young soldiers by shooting at their church in the dead of night; when the blacks shot back, the cry of open rebellion spread quickly throughout the delta. White vigilantes from four states rushed to Elaine to shoot black Commies. The carnage continued for a week, and hundreds, perhaps thousands, of black people were slain. Finally the white plantation owners themselves put an end to the massacre, not out of any humanitarian concern but because it was harvest time and the cotton was rotting in the fields. Arkansas governor Charles Brough sent in troops, and when order was restored the blacks were put back to work. The end result of the uprising was that 122 black men were sent to prison on charges ranging from insurrection to murder—not one white man was accused or brought to trial. There would be no unions, no cash money for labor, this year or for years to come.

The Reconstruction had signaled an exodus of blacks from the delta, and now the Elaine Massacre caused a second mass exodus. For those that remained, some attempts were made by well-meaning people to help the poor blacks and whites. Norman Thomas, the great socialist, came to a little flatland church in Lepanto, Arkansas, trying to organize a farmers' union, but plantation owners marched into the church, cursed and threatened the workers, and ran Thomas out of town. The Dyess Colony near the Wilson Plantation in Arkansas and Providence Commune in Mississippi were established to lend a helping hand to bereft sharecroppers in the face of constant threats from the local power structure. Commonwealth College in south Arkansas was built to educate and train union organizers for the South. In the end all these efforts proved futile. They spoke to the existence of a faint Silent South but little benefit ever came of them. The planters had created a class structure that caused few of the plantation hierarchy any guilt, and if the occasional grandee felt a twinge of pity or of hurt for what was being done, he felt impotent to make a change. The Savage Ideal was still too strong, too deeply rooted to die.

· · ·

THE poverty and misery of Reconstruction and the Great Depression can still be seen on the delta. About two or three corporate fields over from Elaine sits the once-proud little town of Marianna, Arkansas. Back in the boom days of cotton in the 1940s and 1950s Marianna was graced with tree-lined streets, fresh-painted houses, flowering gardens, thriving stores. All the country folk came into town on Saturday to promenade Main Street, to buy or to be seen, to go to the picture show, the women delighting in the new fashions at the Sterlings or the Kress stores, the men dawdling in the pool halls.

Today Marianna is close on to being the single most depressing sight in the whole South. Most of the stores in the town are boarded up, burnt out, or knocked down. The trees have rotted and the flower gardens are long fallow. The high school no longer has a marching band; the school district can't afford the instruments, and the football team plays and the cheerleaders cheer in homemade uniforms. The town is derelict and civic pride is a sardonic memory. The rich drained off every penny from the land without so much as a by-your-leave and never put anything back. The picture of Marianna today is a microcosm of life on the delta.

The tremulous voice of the Silent South can be heard above the racket of the picking machines, combines, and cotton gins and crop-dusters here in Lee County. Dr. Beverly Divers-White, a native Arkansawyer, educator, and black woman, took over as superintendent of schools for the county in 1989. Within three years she achieved the unachievable. She took a down-and-completely-out public school system in the poorest county of a state known as the worst educationally in the nation and made it into a center of excellence.

From the very first day that Dr. White came to Marianna, she set about changing the order of things in the closed society of Lee County. She defied the entrenched landowners and got the county to pass its first millage increase since World War II. She instituted a probation officer and Big Brother program to keep her students out of juvenile court. She implemented a holiday and weekend outings package that allows her students to escape the drudgery of Marianna (a town that doesn't even have a McDonald's for a hangout). She started a drug program to keep the dealers out of the schools. She began a condom and sex education program over the objections of both black and white parents (this in a state leading the nation in teenage pregnancies and venereal diseases). She established several youth apprenticeship programs in a county that runs a consistent 17 percent unemployment rate. She changed the high school course requirements, stressing math and science and English to prepare her students for college. She introduced the study of Russian, Japanese, French, and Spanish to broaden the outlook of her students. She went after every grant available to change the very scope of public education in Lee County.

The end result of Dr. White's reforms adds up to her most spectacular achievement: more than 60 percent of her students not only finish high school but go on to college. It's all the more remarkable when contrasted with the fact that only 25 percent of Arkansas's high school graduates attend college.

Like so many places in the South, Lee County operates a dual education system. Only about 20 percent of the white children attend the public schools; the rest go to the so-called Christian academies, the last vestiges of the Jim Crow South. "One young white girl enrolled in my ninth-grade class," Dr. White says. "Just as soon as she did, her parents were cut off completely from the genteel white community. They were snubbed at church and ostracized from every other social gathering. The poor couple was forced to take their child out of public school and put her back into one of the academies."

Dr. White can only sigh with exasperation over this all-too-recurrent incident. "The irony," she says, "is that the level of education in the academies isn't nearly as good as in the county schools. The question isn't quality of education—the issue is still integration."

Beverly Divers-White grew up in Little Rock and was a little girl when the school crisis hit in 1957. "Orval Faubus drove my parents and many like us out," she says. "My parents wanted better for us than the same old bigoted mentality." Yet she was one of those Southerners who chose to come back home, and in her case to work in education. She became a strong, positive force for improved education under Governor Bill Clinton's reform programs; her reputation grew to such a point that she was handpicked by Hillary Rodham Clinton to take on the toughest job in Arkansas—the Lee County schools.

Although Dr. White has seen her projects make some difference in the lives of Lee County's young people, she is the first to advise that conditions have moved only from near despair to nearly hopeless. And if you ask her when the conditions might become hopeful, she can only reply ruefully, "Not in my lifetime."

Marianna dwindles apace. Moving through it, one can see vestiges of what used to be regarded as pleasant or even pretty—the grand old planter homes now crumbling, the rather stately old high school now condemned and closed. One finds it passing strange to even think of anything on the delta in terms of beauty. Yet here one beholds brilliant empurpled sunsets over windrowed plains that resemble the seas of the moon. To the children of the delta, the fields run on forever like the hereditary gardens of Pharaoh, and the vision of one lone oak standing stark and naked on the perimeters of the section line is an abstract delta art all to itself.

As documented by W. J. Cash (and in the songs of Johnny Cash), while the black families of the delta were always treated with contempt, the poor whites who numbered nearly as many as the blacks were treated like pawns in the perennial rich man's game of playing one race off the other to keep power for themselves. Very few escaped this one-hand game. But up at the very top of Arkansas's delta, two sisters born of the Depression live on in the town of Blytheville and their stories shed light on the lives of poor whites. Both Ruby Jo Bisher and Ella Faye Chitwood came down from the Ozarks with their family in the late 1930s. A mama, a daddy, six daughters, and three sons fled the abject poverty of the hills to subsist as day laborers on the cotton plantations of the flatlands.

"We lived a little while at Dyess Colony," says Ruby Bisher. "Just to get something to eat because we were about starved. The bank had foreclosed on my daddy's place up in Stone County, and we moved from one plantation to the next working as field hands, as sharecroppers, as renters. My mama saved up nine hundred dollars to pay off the debt on our old place in the hills. She could never get the farm back and she was not obliged to pay off the old note, but she did anyway . . . because she wasn't about to be beholden to anyone."

Mrs. Bisher tells the story of how her mother stood up to a

landowner who wanted to take the kids out of school to pick cotton all fall. "Mama told that man that he'd have to throw them off the land before she'd deprive her kids of the only chance they'd ever get."

With all those growing kids being strong hands, the family was always able to get work and to improve itself, eventually moving to town where some opportunities existed. They had survived the banker in Stone County and the peonage of sharecropping to create a whole life for themselves, no matter that their mama never tired of telling whoever would listen that the family all had had a better time on the farm.

Ruby Bisher's sister Ella Faye Chitwood remembers being a little girl when her family moved from the Dyess Colony to a shotgun shack on an old gravel road called Shady Lane but known as Trashy Lane by those who had to live there.

"We moved in bitter winter and didn't even have wood for the stove. I went with my daddy over to an old black preacher's house. Daddy wanted to borrow a saw to cut some wood, and I remember them on the porch talking, saying, 'White man, working man, come to borry a saw.' They loaned daddy a saw and the preacher's wife gave us a plate of biscuits and fried salt meat to take back home. They were real Christian folks and we wouldn't have made it through that first winter without them."

Both sisters live in comfortable retirement and across the street from each other; they spend most of their time with their grandchildren. Their fondest memories are not of the delta but of their old home in the hills. They recall a time back in the 1930s when they got to see the famous movie cowboy Tom Mix and his wonder horse in Red Stripe, an Ozark town no longer on the map. Both sisters agree that if it hadn't been for a picture show now and then, "We wouldn't even have known we were in the United States of America . . . and if it hadn't have been for the radio, we'd have gone crazy, but Jimmie Rodgers and the Carter Family and the Chuck Wagon Gang did everything they could to help us keep our sanity."

As the exodus from the delta intensified during the Depression and again following World War II, the cheap labor pool habitually squeezed by the plantation owners shrank to almost nothing. The planters were faced with the choice of either paying a living wage or stumping up a huge capital investment to buy machinery. The owners did neither; they found the easy way out by selling their land to the corporate East. It had taken nearly a hundred years since the Civil War, but the Cotton Kingdom finally cashed in its chips. When it was all over, fewer people were living on the delta than before the Civil War.

When the plantation owners pulled out, the state of Arkansas was left without a source of wealth. Then something unlooked for began to happen in what derisively used to be called "the land of opportunity." One must remember that Arkansas still lay under the New York interdict for the century-old bond fraud, but that denial of capital created an environment for a really clever man not only to break the bank but to take over and then own the bank. The world knows the names of the barons of American industry, Morgan and Rockefeller and company. The world at large has never heard more than a whisper of a man named Wilton R. Stephens and would hardly believe that this poor boy from Prattsville, Arkansas, was able to buy and sell the old-time Robber Barons with the same magical bond-scheme subterfuge so favored by the Wall Street elite.

"Uncle Witt" Stephens, as he liked to be known, started by selling belt buckles to soldiers at Fort Sill, Oklahoma, at the start of the Depression. He took this seed money in an era when cash was almost impossible to come by and got into treasury and municipal bonds, first investing and then floating. At the height of the Depression Stephens was earning $5,000 a week as the Neo-Bond Daddy of the South. He had a strong hand in building the eighth wonder of the world, Judge Hofheinz's Astrodome, and financed New Orleans's Superdome on his own. He built skyscrapers in major cities around the world, and with his little brother Jackson, he owned utilities, interstate banking complexes, retirement cities, brokerage houses, shipping lines, gold and diamond mines, and parts of countries. Uncle Witt has elected governors, senators, congressmen, and begrudgingly had the last word in bringing the forty-second President to the Oval Office (even though, as usual, he had backed both candidates).

Stephens did suffer a number of foster sons who rose to incredible success. The names of Walton, Tyson, Hunt, Dillard, and Smith were unknown until Arkansas chic became à la mode. Sam Walton, before he died America's richest man east of Bill Gates, was fired from his job as a clerk at a Ben Franklin five-and-dime; Don Tyson, heir presumptive to Walton's title because he controls the international poultry industry, began by selling chickens out of the back of his daddy's truck; J. B. Hunt, trucking and banking magnate, began by dressing chickens on his kitchen table; Bill Dillard, number-one department store owner in the nation, started with a jot-'em-down store that had $1.62 in sales one day in the late Depression; Fred Smith, originator and owner of Federal Express, garnered a C-minus on his management course paper outlining the overnight delivery concept.

No one seems to be able to explain how this massively powerful cabal of independent back-country hucksters got established in Arkansas, a state known mainly for its lockstep march into oblivion. One explanation involves the rub-off theory like the literary mastery of Mississippi, but this smacks of voodoo or of some kind of mystic runes. Leading economists are at a loss to explain the rise and dominance of Walton, Tyson, *et alia*. When all the stock exchange analysts have exhausted their fund of clichés, the only answer left is an obscure economic theory, a Southern economic theory if you will, since it's the only region in the world where it apparently works. It's called random walk and it's mathematically provable, though no one believes it and in no place but the South has it been so intuitively embraced.

Simply put, random walk tells us that nothing we do today has anything to do with what happened yesterday and will have nothing to do with the events of tomorrow. It's Southern existential deviation taken beyond its twilight zone limits. The spiritual archetypes of Arkansas's latter-day Phoenicians had been the trading masters of the Mediterranean. Anyone who's been to Sunday school knows the story of the Canaanites who, for their sins, were dispossessed of their lands in Palestine in the Third Millennium B.C. and exiled to what is now Lebanon. From their twin commercial centers of Sidon and Tyre the ancestral Phoenicians put together a trading hegemony that lasted a thousand years; they settled Greece, Carthage, and Sicily, and gave the Western world its alphabet before finally succumbing to the phalanxes of Alexander the Great. On the surface, it may seem farfetched but the Arkansas Cartel is nothing more than expelled Canaanites, their offense dating back to that old bond fraud of the 1830s. The jungles of Arkansas were settled by dispossessed people, and while it took the Phoenicians almost two thou-

sand years to rise from obscurity, these latter-day Phoenicians as-
cended their golden thrones in barely more than a century. While
Wall Street wasn't looking, Witt Stephens's children—Walton and
Tyson and Hunt and Dillard and Smith—along with a host of lesser
and still arising merchant princes, have created their own empires.
Here deep in the Bible Belt their anthem can be none other than
"Just a Random Walk with Thee."

Witt Stephens had started out in Arkansas like many an outcast
horse trader. He was a silver-tongued salesman with the innate ability to slip a poniard through his patron's ribs even as they were shaking hands. While other captains of industry could claim the same
ability, Stephens's true gift was his organizational genius, which
served him almost to the end of his life. Uncle Witt's initial fortune
had come from the infant natural gas industry. By the 1960s he had
convinced most everyone that gas was the only way to heat and cool
their homes, light their streets and backyards, and barbecue their
spareribs. Toward the end of his life, however, Stephens's ego would
suffer the unkindest cut of all, and from his own. He had groomed
young protégés to control the vast Stephens holdings. But these disciples would slip the famous Stephens knife into their benefactor's
back. Through Arkansas-Louisiana Gas Company, Stephens's flagship, they cooked up what some said was the most venal sweetheart
deal of the century—and right under their own Uncle Witt's nose.
Gas reserves owned by the public utility were sold for a pittance and
repurchased for hundreds of millions. When the news of the deed finally leaked out, the public was outraged, but the state's Public Service Commission (whose members are appointed by the governor)
washed its hands of the débâcle with the pronouncement that the
deal was done and legal enough for government work. Truth be
known, the purchase and repurchase agreements were so complex
they would make the Whitewater scandal look like the balance sheet
of a corner candy shop. The participants casually cached hundreds
of millions and got even more: America's team, the Dallas Cowboys,
was bought with part of the profits; control of the state Republican
Party came with the money; a shot at state political power was financed with part of the takings; and the sure chance of building future empires of their own will come from the compound interest
accruing from the booty.

Witt Stephens, the patriarch of the new Phoenicians, died a bitter man. He had created Orval Faubus and controlled most of the politicians in Arkansas. He made himself the czar of the world's largest pool of natural gas reserves, the Anadarco Basin. For decades he had brought in nothing but naturals, had blued and tattooed just about everyone who had opposed his ways. In the final analysis he lost. It wasn't so much the money that bothered him—it was the game. He had been sharped by his own clones.

BACK in the 1950s when Arkansas's Phoenicians were just getting set up, master jazz pianist Dave Brubeck had a hit called "Little Rock Getaway." The town was never a place you tried to get away to, but from, and the most famous escape was accomplished by Bill Clinton himself. Certainly Little Rock became the base camp for the assault on the high-table political summit, but the Clinton brain trust and the myriad hangers-on to the Arkansas sheik have packed their tents and moved to D.C. Little Rock was never Bill Clinton's town anyway, even though it got to be the bromidic nerve center of the 1992 campaign (for which the only amusing sidelight involved gonzo relic Hunter Thompson, who both made an ass of himself in local restaurants and got his ass arrested trying to break into the Clinton headquarters, proving once again that rednecks and gonzo don't mix). In times past, journalism in Little Rock had a higher calling and meaning, most notably in the 1950s when editor Harry Ashmore and editorialist Jerry Neil raised the *Arkansas Gazette* to national prominence with a courageous stand against Orval Faubus.

A stellar journalist carrying on the good work of Ashmore and Neil is Ernest Dumas. Now a professor of journalism at the University of Central Arkansas, Dumas began his newspaper career in the 1960s, covering Orval Faubus, the segregationist governor who served from 1954 to 1966. Dumas knew all the figures in Faubus's machine, understood the self-serving rhetoric and the patterns of deceit. In his twilight years Faubus sought to sweeten his image as a "compassionate and misunderstood statesman" who somehow guided Arkansas through a minefield of explosive racial tension and economic ruin. The conservative press in Arkansas has gone along and added to the whitewash, and even some in-state political scientists are writing that Faubus was, after all, an effective governor. Dumas discounts all this and says that Faubus was always a master manipulator and opportunist. Dumas speaks of his worst Faubus memory, and surprisingly, it isn't of the Central High School crisis.

"In 1965," Dumas relates, "some civil rights groups came to the state capitol to integrate the cafeteria down in the basement of the building. Faubus had tried to get around integrating the state-owned and operated cafeteria by declaring it a private club. The protest started out with a loud rumbling noise, and those of us who were there as reporters rushed down to see what was going on. We saw state cops beating up on the protesters, throwing them around and using clubs. It turns out that one of those being beaten was a reporter not wearing a suit, so the cops thought he was just a white sympathizer and fair game, and they beat him up, too." The sympathizer was a young journalist for the *Pine Bluff Commercial* named Bob Lancaster. He was in his early twenties and just beginning his career. Governor Faubus went on statewide television that night and leveled a vicious personal attack upon Lancaster, accusing him of being a lowlife who beat his child and abandoned his wife. It was clear that Faubus was using one of his favorite old tricks of diverting attention away from the real issue. "The verbal attack on Lancaster was disgraceful," says Dumas. "And of all the chicanery associated with Faubus, it is still my worst memory of him."

Little Rock didn't play much of a role in the Civil War. The town was captured early and the Confederate solons set up shop in the lonesome little hamlet of Washington in southwest Arkansas. In the end Little Rock did get to keep *Robert E. Lee,* the paddle wheeler, not the general. The graceful old river steamer beat the *Natchez* in the legendary steamboat race of 1870, but ended its days on the Little Rock wharf as a shabby paint locker. The *Robert E. Lee* couldn't get away.

TODAY an interstate highway runs down from Little Rock to Hope, Arkansas, but the first road was winding, weariful, and shadowed by unhappy legends into the twentieth century. Folks living in the hills north of Hope used to believe that the surrounding lands were damned, cursed by a legacy of outrageous ambitions and broken dreams. In the early years the tiny settlement called Hope was connected to the umbilical of nearby prosperous Washington, but after the Civil War no beneficences were awarded to makeshift Confederate state capitals, and the later railroad ignored Washington and went through Hope (even though Jim Bowie had invented his knife at a Washington blacksmith shop and no less a personage than Sam Houston lived in the Reb state capital. David Crockett passed thru here on his way to die in Tejas). No one ever came to Hope itself in search of a fortune, though the town has become a little famous and even a little recognizable largely due to the efforts of the forty-second President's fellow Arkansawyers, Harry and Linda Bloodworth-Thomason, whose *Man from Hope* film at the 1992 Democratic Convention made much of the convenient symbolism of the town's name.

Hope has always been like that: convenient. Strange indeed but a great number of famous people have come to Hope, passed through it, and left their touch, big or small, before going on to fame and glory or infamy in the glamorous outside world that's always left Hope alone.

"People have been using this nothing town as a jumpoff place ever since it was just a high spot near the Red River floodplain," says a wise old timberman in the senior citizens' domino parlor in Hope. Nobody pays attention to domino parlor stragglers, but maybe the old codger is onto something. West of Hope lie the beckoning blackland farms of Texas; to the south loom vast timberlands and oil-boom lowlands; just north slumbers a crater of diamonds that once enticed the world's financial titans to these dirt-poor environs.

If you linger in the domino parlor, chances are someone will teach you the lesson of all the fuss over little Hope since the '92 campaign. "We're not talking Ecclesiastes," says a little banty of a man who claims he was once a professor. " 'Ali Hafed was beggared and starving while the diamonds of Golconda were lying in his own garden sands.' My friend, that is the story of this sorry state."

The professor knows most of the untold story of the diamond kings of Arkansas. In 1906 an illiterate farmer named John Wesley Huddleston was out in his field scattering rock salt for his hogs when he noticed two shiny stones winking in the dirt. Huddleston took the stones to a local banker but it was Samuel Reyburn, a Little Rock banker, who bought the stones and Huddleston's hog farm for the princely sum of $36,000; banker Reyburn would truly make a silk purse out of a sow's ear. The stones were authenticated by the nation's leading authority on precious stones, Dr. George F. Kunz, who came down to Arkansas by train and mule wagon. Dr. Kunz even found a diamond on his own at the Murfreesboro hog-and-diamond farm about twenty miles north of Hope.

By 1907 a diamond rush was on in Pike County, Arkansas, that would rival the Kimberly rush of the 1870s in South Africa. The whole countryside from Texarkana to Murfreesboro was overrun with a rowdy, moiling throng of would-be diamond kings. An Arkansas town, New Kimberly, sprang up and became a three-mile-long nightmare of frantic men jostling and fighting for a ten-square-foot space to dig their mines. The only hotel in town turned away ten thousand fortune seekers, but one interested visitor was welcomed with open arms. He was Sir Ernest Oppenheimer, the principal officer of the De Beers Consolidated Diamond Mines of Johannesburg in South Africa, spiritual successor to Cecil Rhodes, and the head of the world's oldest established cartel. Newspapers throughout the Southwest carried pictures of Sir Ernest inspecting the diamond field, and everyone expected Arkansas to become rich as soon as De Beers began mining.

De Beers never started a mining operation in Arkansas and no successful attempt at commercial mining has ever taken place here. Banker Reyburn went to New York, flashed his sack of big diamonds around, and raised $3 million to start his own operations. Two years later Reyburn sadly announced to his stockholders that the Arkansas mine had been deemed "impracticable for profitable mining." At this point a grand conspiracy was hatched, the conspirators this time being the international diamond cartel in concert with J. P. Morgan himself. A message was sent throughout the world: the fabulously real diamond strike in Arkansas was passed off as a hoax; the diamonds, if they existed at all, were so inferior as to be worthless. This despite the fact that banker Reyburn still swaggered through the swank salons of Manhattan with a pouch of gemstones valued at $15 million. Reyburn has to qualify as the first of Arkansas's latter-day Phoenicians. He became a full partner in the Morgan–De Beers conspiracy to corner the world's diamond market, and at the same time he fleeced Wall Street just as his forebears had in the 1830s.

There's still a diamond mine in Arkansas, and it's about the size of a baseball field. It's a state park now where vacationers pay a small fee and grub in the dirt for diamonds, occasionally finding one worth a few thousand dollars (as late as the summer of 1994 a prospector unearthed a marble-sized diamond purportedly worth more than $50,000). Governor Winthrop Rockefeller bought the site for Arkansas in 1972 from the heirs of Glenn Martin of Martin-Marietta aircraft fame; Martin had bought it from auto magnate Henry Ford. Even in the 1990s there's still lusty interest in the Arkansas mine. The giant multinational mining corporation Anaconda—no stranger itself to geo-Realpolitik—has drilled exploratory shafts, and other mining companies are showing more and more interest. None realize the extent of the century-old conspiracy. Back during World War II President Franklin Roosevelt ordered this mine to be put into full operation to produce desperately needed industrial diamonds, but former De Beers geologists, working for the Bureau of Mines, convinced the War Department that it would be counterproductive to open the Arkansas mine (these same geologists returned to the employ of De Beers following the war).

Our salty little professor in Hope's domino parlor puts it best and most realistically: "The corporate bigwigs know you don't often come across a neglected resource with an eleven-figure potential. The state will finally give in and allow the ransacking of its little piece of Ali Hafed's marvelous garden."

The Crater of Diamonds is certainly not a marvelous garden, though it is a handsome, well-cared-for park where people enjoy indulging in pipe dreams. The park's benefactor, Governor Win Rockefeller, was a frequent visitor; in fact, he launched his successful gubernatorial campaign against Orval Faubus in nearby Hope in 1966. Arkansawyers believed Rockefeller to be a pipe dreamer himself when he settled in the state in the 1950s to become a gentleman farmer atop rustic Petit Jean Mountain.

"Well, old Win drank his quart or two of vodka a day and smoked his five packs of Picayunes," say the hangers-on at the domino parlor, "but he was a right fair governor . . . best thing that ever happened to this state."

Despite his carousing playboy image, Rockefeller did turn out to be a good farmer, a fair politician, and as governor of this backward state a champion of good, though often lost, causes. He was unable to effect meaningful legislation in a state run by the cronyism of the Faubus machine, but Rockefeller did succeed in gaining great popularity with the people and he turned around the "simple-shit" image that had forever plagued Arkansas. Where Faubus had brought the in-

tegration crisis to a violent boil in 1957, soon to be governor Rockefeller stood on the steps of the state capitol with civil rights leaders in
1965 and sang "We Shall Overcome." He did more. No industry what-
soever had located in Arkansas since the coming of Faubus, but that
began to change drastically with Rockefeller's national influence. He
did away with a repressive loyalty oath for public school teachers; he
began to break the stranglehold the good old boys had on state government. He sent in platoons of state troopers to chop up and destroy the gaming tables and slots of the illegal casinos in Hot Springs
that had thrived for decades under a corrupt partnership between
governors and the godfathership of crime lord Owen Madden, whom
we shall meet below. In his last official act as governor in 1970 Rockefeller abolished capital punishment in the state. When he died of em-
physema in 1973 the yellow-dog Democrat people of Arkansas paid
high tribute to their Yankee governor; they turned out schools for the
funeral and closed down all the state offices. The closest expression
of sentiment to this in Arkansas was the death of Robert E. Lee.

Not often in history has a state so mired in political despair been
able to redeem itself as promptly as Arkansas did with Win Rockefeller and his successors.

"Winthrop Rockefeller was in many ways the state's best governor,"
longtime political analyst Ernest Dumas says. "He always stood for
something and that was the common good. He wanted to do the
right thing."

As a young man back in the 1930s, Faubus traveled the road to
Hope. He had grown up in the Ozarks, had served in World War I,
and was a bright, promising young man. His father, Sam Faubus,
had tried to instill in young Orval a sense of purpose and idealism
and had even named him "Eugene" after the great American socialist Eugene Debs. Orval came down from the hills and through Hope
on his way to Mena, where he enrolled in Commonwealth College,
the socialist commune whose purpose was to train labor organizers.
Later, out of political expediency, Faubus would recant his association with Commonwealth, though it is perhaps too melancholy an
indulgence to think of what might have been if young Orval had followed his father Sam's leanings and gone on to work for instead of
against the workers of his long-suffering state.

At home in Conway, Arkansas, "Ol' Orv" enjoyed an avuncular
popularity as he advanced into his dotage, revising his image steady

as he went. Still caught occasionally misrepresenting the facts, Faubus simply shrugged and fell back with a straight face on one of his trusty saws: "Just because I said it doesn't make it so." Faubus died early in the winter of 1994.

THE whole world knows of the man from Hope, Bill Clinton, yet as incomprehensible as it may sound, Hope could have been the home place of *two* U.S. Presidents, both long shots to be sure but both with impressive pedigrees. Augustus Hill Garland of Hope, Arkansas, was a young lawyer when the Civil War broke out, and he served the Confederate cause throughout that conflict. After the war Garland was caught in the vise of Abolitionist witch hunts that forbade ex-Confederates from holding federal office and even from practicing law before any federal court. Garland broke the barrier and gave the South its first victory since Appomattox with his landmark case argued before the Supreme Court in 1866, which pulled the teeth of Abolitionist rancor toward the South: after Garland's plea before the Court, the lawyers of the Reconstruction South were permitted to practice law in federal courts for the first time and were free to seek federal office. Remarkable indeed that this constitutional defense of the South should have been made by an unknown from the wilds of Arkansas instead of by some polished lawyer from the grand families of Virginia or South Carolina.

Garland became the first post-Reconstruction governor of Arkansas and after two terms was elected to the U.S. Senate in 1876; he became the most respected senator since before the war. Halfway through his second term in the Senate, Garland was appointed Attorney General in Grover Cleveland's administration. Had it not been for the stigma of being a Southerner in this age of political mediocrity, Garland was certainly qualified to be and could have been the first Democratic President since the antebellum period. After his Cabinet days in the era when the Robber Barons took almost total control of the body politic of America, offering neither faith nor hope nor charity, Augustus Hill Garland returned to Arkansas where he was never heard from much again. His historical reward from his fellow Arkansawyers was to be the namesake of Garland County (which would prove to be the most corrupt county in the South and the nation).

William Jefferson Blythe IV was born in Hope, but Bill Clinton moved to Hot Springs, Garland County, Arkansas when he was five years old. The town of Hot Springs had always seemed destined to become a sink of corruption. Theodore Roosevelt declared the city a national park on the basis of the curative hot sulphur springs that give the town its name. The cure being taken was for the king's pox—the social disease, syphilis. America was no different from Europe in this regard, and just as well-heeled gents like Lord Randolph Churchill (Winston's daddy) would journey to Spa in Germany, the rich of New York and Boston and Chicago headed to Hot Springs hoping to get well. Of course hot water won't cure a dose, but the quacks running the bathhouses weren't about to hand out that information.

The truly beautiful little city of Hot Springs, built in the sheltering lees of twin mountain ranges and surrounded by gentle lakes, claims to have been discovered by none other than the conquistador Hernando de Soto. The story goes that the native Quapaw Indians invited the great captain and his weary men for a communal bath with such restorative results that the Spaniards raced their horses along the current bathhouse row for the amusement of the crowd. Hot Springs became the most famous unknown little town in America, a haven for the rich, notable, and notorious. Stephen Crane holed up in one of the bathhouse hotels and revised the galleys of *The Red Badge of Courage* there. The Brooklyn Robins (before they became the Dodgers) held spring training there. Babe Ruth and the Yankees trained there, too. Thomas Wolfe came to Hot Springs with his mother for the baths. Herbert Hoover, while still a mining engineer, came for the baths and gold prospecting (he found gold but reported back to his company that the deposit was impracticable for mining). This spa has hosted financiers, politicians, Presidents, movie and opera stars, powerful generals, oil billionaires, and some of the finest brothels this side of the Place Pigalle. Everyone loved Hot Springs, in spite of, or perhaps because of, the fact that it was anything but clean. Over the decades the pastimes of the rich patrons who visited here were catered to, and if they involved a certain amount of immorality, then Hot Springs didn't blanch. Its moral wellsprings weren't ever totally polluted; they were just discolored. The town's virtue may have suffered a few minor amputations, but the corruption wasn't fatal.

The real conquistador of Hot Springs didn't arrive in the Spa City until well into the twentieth century. He was no Spaniard but he brought disease and plague with him just as de Soto had. His name was Owen "Owney" Madden and he was the very first godfather of New York's criminal underworld. Before Albert Anastasia and Lucky Luciano and the Sicilian mafiosi, Madden ruled New York's underworld from his lair in the famous Cotton Club. His fall from grace in New York and exile to Hot Springs is, even given the extraordinary corruption of the times, an amazing story. The law couldn't get Madden for racketeering, murder, or an array of other crimes, so the Feds trapped him on income-tax evasion and Madden went to Sing Sing.

"When he got out, he was met at the prison gate by a committee of Italian opera lovers who brought their violin cases with them. Owney was told that the Mafia was now running New York and that if he stepped into the city, he'd be taking a bath in the East River wearing concrete galoshes. And so to avoid a mob war, Owney was given some vigorish—the whole town of Hot Springs, Arkansas."

The man talking about Owen Madden so intimately today was once Madden's henchman, enforcer, and friend. He was at the forefront during Madden's reign in this pristine little Southern town. And while the story may sound like a Runyonesque version of Rocko and Bugsy, it's all too true. The storyteller has lived all his life in Hot Springs; he's been an elected official, a legitimate businessman, and is still a prominent citizen. Why a man with so many dark chapters in his life would agree to talk this openly is almost as brazen as the story of Hot Springs itself. One has to keep in mind that this man was an outlaw with no compunctions, yet he doesn't mince his words or try to put himself in a better light, though he's not so foolish as to divulge his name. It's as if the act of telling the truth satisfied some sort of secret amusement of his own.

"From the very start Owney owned this whole town," the storyteller declares. "We ran the mayor's office, the City Council, the police chief, the courts, all the way down to the garbage collectors. The most powerful man in town was the judge, and we owned him too. He was Owney's main front man and ran things, the casinos, the cathouses, the protection racket, the grease to buy the politicians."

Nevertheless, Hot Springs was a cultured, cosmopolitan city sunk in the middle of the Bible Belt. Hot Springs was a decadent, safe town that attracted more than just the rich—it became the favorite watering hole of gangsters and mob bosses. Al Capone and Frank Costello loved the town, and came here often to take the baths, play golf, and sport with the gorgeous hookers who thrived in the clubs up and down Central Avenue.

"There was no crime in our city," the story goes on. "Owney wouldn't tolerate gunplay or robbery. The off-duty cops were the valets and security at the casinos and clubs. The Chicago mob tried more than once to muscle in, and when they did we just shut the town down, a week or two or a month, until they gave up and left. People of this state believed all those years that Hot Springs was run by the Chicago mob, but it just wasn't true. We were the only ones running this town."

According to almost anyone you talked to in Hot Springs, Madden was a generous man who took care of his people and his friends. The storyteller used to delight in pointing to pictures on his nightclub office wall, pictures of horses in the winner's circle at Oaklawn Park here in town. "We fixed that one and that one," he says, "for friends here and in Kentucky and New York . . . Owney always helped his friends out." Madden had eclectic friendships: actor George Raft was his bodyguard at the Cotton Club and went on with Owney's influence to stardom in Hollywood; Owney was Joseph Kennedy's business partner in the Canadian whiskey combine during Prohibition; he and Fulgencio Batista were buddies (Owney liked Batista's style because he rose from sergeant-major to the presidency of Cuba). Madden was a devoted family man. "The only time he ever went back to New York was when he sneaked in to attend his mother's funeral."

One thing certain about Madden, though. You didn't want to get on his wrong side. "Owney gave jobs to every member of his family. He trusted and sometimes he got double-crossed. Two of his young nephews plotted against him and he had to have them killed. He told me the next day that it really bothered him having to do it. He said, 'I had trouble getting to sleep last night over that. It took me more than an hour.' "

Despite its sun-and-fun image, beautiful Hot Springs National Park was a cynical town. Everyone suspected the depth of the corruption, that the whole town was on the take. The only way the spa could stay so wide open was to bribe the state officials. "We bribed the legislature and all the governors, every single one of them up to Rockefeller. Francis Cherry was the greediest. He must have known he wasn't going to get reelected and he squeezed us pretty hard—sometimes fifty thousand at a time." Years later, Faubus would claim that any money he may have received from Madden was simply a "campaign contribution."

So what was it like for a future President of the United States to grow up in a town like Hot Springs? With most every vice easily attainable, it certainly wasn't the normal upbringing. A particular amoral freedom suffused the environment for Hot Springs' youth, a sort of sophisticated air that wasn't available anywhere else in the South except New Orleans. The kids had more than ample opportunity to become jaded, but the exposure perhaps uniquely prepared them in a way that other young people weren't. Kids from Hot Springs had an innocent cynicism about them that too many have interpreted as cockiness or being "slick."

The sea of print produced by the pack press in covering the rise of Bill Clinton holds that he is a fresh breath of air, that he's too slick, that he's liberal, progressive, conservative, that he couldn't make middle management in business, that he's the most intellectual President since Thomas Jefferson, that he walks in his own shadow, that he casts no shadow at all. The journalists are all right and they're all wrong. One would think that there ought to be more to the pack press story than that. If only these hard-put seers had a different perspective, or any perspective at all, they'd understand that the gift he acquired early on in his home place, that aura of innocent cynicism, lifted him and set him apart, so much so that he could go among the throngs, the washed and the unwashed, and make them all feel that they owed him.

Preposterous as it seems, Bill Clinton's gift comes from Owen Madden, who if nothing more created the ambiance that nurtured Clinton. But the chain stretches back even further, to the other man from Hope, Augustus Garland. The two Arkansawyers' lives parallel each other too closely to ignore. Both suffered the loss of their fathers when barely in their infancy; both were raised and strongly influenced by their mothers; both were classically schooled, were superb lawyers, governors of their home state, and national political figures (in a lighter vein, both were enamored of little ol' Hot Springs—for when he returned from D.C., Garland was a habitué of Bathhouse Row).

The nation's political pundits by now have taken their best shots at Bill Clinton, but none of them have seriously shown they understand the man's Southern psyche. The standard-brands approach has been a vituperative comparison between Clinton and his Southern predecessor Jimmy Carter. The pundits might have a case if the two men had anything in common. Jimmy Carter is a silver-spooned patrician of the Deep South; Clinton is the son of a nurse and a used-car salesman in Outlander Arkansas, a state that never had anything in common with the Deep South anyway. The real comparison, if one is necessary between Southern Presidents, should be between Clinton and his Virginia predecessor Woodrow Wilson. Unconsciously or not, Wilson proved to be an advocate of the Savage Ideal, that profound distaste for change, and strangely, almost ironically, so is Bill Clinton. Despite being elected by a coalition of liberals, old-line populists, disenchanted moderates, and hard-line yellow-dog Democrats (most of whom are from the North and that separate nation called California), Clinton simply cannot justify his inner being with any concept other than the Savage Ideal; and therein lies Clinton's inner conflict—the fight between the verities of the Old Testament, espoused by Wilson and Clinton, and the desire for free will, as evidenced by the drive of both men to change everything from the ground up.

Yet another shortcoming of the political seers is their misreading of what's been going on in Arkansas for thirty years and more. The random-walk economic theory that works so uncannily in explaining the rise of the world-class Arkansas businessmen is equally applicable to Neo-South presidents (what else is a politician but a salable commodity?). Bill Clinton is not only the random-walk President, he's the CEO of the latter-day Phoenicians. The Arkansas Mafia billionaires are all free agents beholden to no one, but Clinton has somehow convinced them that they owe him, enough to help put him in the White House.

THERE was a time before the advent of the latter-day Phoenicians and Bill Clinton when the citizens of Arkansas were ashamed to admit that the state was their home. It wasn't that they were ashamed of themselves; they were embarrassed over the state's image. Everyone outside of Arkansas laughed at and derided the state. A pathetic but fairly common example was Tommy "Bear Mountain" Freeman of Hot Springs, a welterweight boxing champion of the world during the Depression. After he won the title Freeman told sportswriters that he was from Erie, Pennsylvania, even though he'd never been close to the place. A raft of other Arkansawyers who made it to the big time of the outside world declined to claim the state as their home; they believed such an admission would diminish them. Of all the Southern states, Arkansas was the guiltiest in teaching self-abnegation, in commanding its children "not to get above their raising." Success was not a virtue but a betrayal of humble roots. The national derision of Arkansas didn't emanate from the delta land poverty and peonage. Rather it had as its source the Ozarks and the deliberately unprogressive culture of that backward escarpment.

The best road into the Ozarks starts in Hot Springs; it's Arkansas Highway 7 North, one of the top ten scenic drives in the world. It's twisty-turny and steep and runs over and around mountains, rivers, creeks, and lakes that yield more fighting fish than the mountain streams cascading down from Pamplona. Highway 7 is usually crowded with Winnebagos, Apollos, Airstreams, and logging trucks. All but the loggers are heading for the safe part of the Ozarks in Missouri at Branson, the Neo-Music City of the nation. For eons these were uncluttered hills. The Ozarks just barely spill over the state line into Missouri and as late as the 1980s, travelers could breeze right through Branson and on to Rockaway Beach. Today Branson has become the most unabashed traffic gridlock this side of Manhattan during a five-alarm fire.

The scene in Branson isn't new; it's both a transplant from Nashville and a rekindled version of country music saint Red Foley's "Ozark Jubilee" from nearby Springfield. And it's far more: it's the New Arena America stuck like a clot in Redneck Wonderland, with Vegas and Nashville mixed in with Disney. The Ozarks never had a gold rush if you don't count the James Gang putting the bum's rush on stagecoaches, trains, and Yankee banks. The Howards and Youngers (Jesse, Frank, Cole, and the boys) left an indelible print all over the Ozarks—a tradition of highwaymanry, the time-honored challenge of "stand and deliver," along with the perverse pride of having ridden with Bloody Bill Anderson and William Clarke Quantrill. Today's highwaymen have eschewed .45 Colts and Bowie knives in favor of cover charges, watered drinks, twenty-dollar double-eagle buffets, and washed-up nasal songbirds of the ilk of Roy Clark, Loretta Lynn, Andy Williams, and the Osmond family.

The Ozarks have always been a crossroads of ironic parallel. Promontory bluffs dotted along Highway 7 look out on a panorama of tens of thousands of acres of pine and maple, sycamore, hickory, and scrub cedar. The road is like a great grapevine scar winding through nature, and in season the redbuds and dogwoods and fields of wild azaleas that have been there since time began gave false promise to the early settlers of a rich and fecund life that they never found. The pioneers of the early 1800s were the wild spirits of Appalachia who couldn't stand seeping civilization. The Savage Ideal found its most acute being in these hills. "Resistance to change has always been the chief regional characteristic of the Ozark people," wrote Vance Randolph, foremost folklorist of the Ozark Mountains and author of more than twenty books on the subject. Dr. Randolph traipsed the hills and ridges for decades collecting tales and beliefs from these intensely private and superstitious people. One of his most amazing revelations concerned a Pentecostal preacher who had seen a strange scar on an eggshell. The preacher saw it as a godly prophecy: "Jesus Christ was going to visit the United States, run for President on the Democratic ticket, and stump the whole state of Arkansas!"

Deep in the Arkansas Ozarks, divorced in spirit from the persiflage of Branson, the little town of Harrison perches on a hidden ridge and rigidly holds on to its stern Old Testament sense of irony. Two signs posted in the town once identified the austere nature of these mountain people. Until recently one of the signs warned "coloreds" not to let the sun set with them still in town. The other sign, which stands on the courthouse lawn, is a memory of kindred souls who once left the town in hope and died in fear. The plaque commemorates some 140 people from these hills who were slain at the infamous Mountain Meadows Massacre in Utah in 1857. The wagon train of Ozark families was attacked by Mormons dressed as Indians and a war party of Paiutes whom the Mormons had bribed with a promise of booty. A much persecuted sect, the Mormons had fled the Midwest to establish a homeland in the desert, and what little motivation that could be found for the massacre must lie with their desire to persecute their tormenters. The wagon train was besieged for three days and had to surrender after running out of water. The Mormons executed the men, took captive the children too young to remember the carnage, but had no stomach for killing the older children and the women. They turned this task over to the Paiutes, who raped, murdered, and cannibalized the innocents.

The people of the Ozarks live by their savage ideals, by the feud, by the biblical injunction of an eye for an eye. But there was never any revenge to be had for Mountain Meadows. Two decades after the massacre, a few of the captive children were returned to Arkansas, and one Mormon, John D. Lee, was tried and executed by a Mormon firing squad at the very site of the massacre. Lee went to his grave hollering that he was nothing but a scapegoat for Brigham Young.

Even with the fields of wild azaleas, columbine, flowering dogwoods, and redbuds, the Ozarks are a poor country, suitable for holding the world together but not much more. That's why the wagon train carried away 140 people in 1857—to find better land, land that could support a family beyond simple subsistence. Yet the Ozarks have always attracted and retained a particular kind of person who built his cabin and fences of stone and tended kitchen gardens and kept a milk cow for the children and plowed the slate rock fields behind a mule or even a yoke of oxen. The Ozark man expected nothing from others, wanted nothing but the binding of family and his own counsel. These mountains gave birth to superstition and, strangely, to common sense. There were no medical doctors here, only yarb (herb) doctors and goose-bone prophets. Healing from wound or disease came from nature's herbs taken as an infusion or applied to the flesh as a poultice. The yarb doctor was a respected woman (some said witch, but always with awe in their voice), for they had seen her cure a sickly child of the croup by breathing into the infant's mouth. They had seen her cure warts and sores, boils and "risens." The hills needed no medicine doctor. Like their forebears from Europe and the mountains on the East Coast of America, the people of the Ozarks took the auspices through a goose-bone prophet, a seer who read the future in the entrails of sacrificial animals and from the bones left behind. The people lived in little villages that used to be called Red Stripe and Buckhorn; they

hunted the great bear in the Oil Trough Bottoms for food and hung
the bear bacon from the rafters of their cabins; they made their soap
from the rendered fat in their ash hoppers; their children learned to
swim in the crystal waters of Sylamore Creek and hunted for the
buried treasure of the James Gang or the Younger Brothers in the
myriad caves that course like distended veins and arteries throughout the ancient mountain range. And the spiritual center of all this
was a little Ozark town called Mountain View.

It's an old frame and native-stone town; all the buildings come
from the surrounding land. Once a year as many as a hundred thousand outsiders crowd into Mountain View's folk festival to hear the
fiddle, banjo, and mandolin picking and to see the buck dancing.
Afterwards the crowd ebbs back to the town's five or six thousand citizens. Every day of the year hundreds come to the folk center where
the old way of life is on display; they also come to see nearby Blan-
chard Springs, some of the most imposing, graceful caverns in the
world. Still, the social, political, economic, and emotional heart of
the town has always been the courthouse. Inside the courthouse in
1919 a spectacular murder trial took place attracting national attention. The prosecutor was seeking the death penalty for a beautiful
young woman accused of killing her lover, a handsome, fast-talking
pitchman known as "Carney." As the jury was about to deliver a certain guilty verdict, Carney, or at least someone who was a dead
ringer, strolled into the courtroom saying he'd been off on a job and
demanded the release of the innocent woman. Here in Stone
County, the very marrow of the Ozarks, affairs of the heart are considered admissible evidence. She was set free.

Many another trial has taken place in this storied old courthouse.
Murder, holdups, cattle rustling, moonshining, barn burning. One
murder, though, taking place in the depths of the Depression right
there on the courthouse steps with dozens of eyewitnesses, was never
brought to trial. William Younger, known as "Shorter Bill," and a direct descendant of the Younger clan, lay dead, but the sheriff didn't
set off after the killer. The sheriff went to the Younger clan out at the
little hamlet called Buckhorn.

"The sheriff came to our house and told me that they'd let my
other brother, Buster, off his conviction of cattle rustling if we
Youngers wouldn't do anything about the killing of Bill. I went to
Paw and said, 'What must we do?' and he said, 'Let it go.' "

The voice speaking this Ozark saga is that of Hattie Amelia Younger, known in all the hills as Dutch. She's a woman who has lived most of the years of the twentieth century, and she is speaking from the Younger enclave at Buckhorn, called St. James on today's map. Hattie Younger stands in the Methodist Church graveyard where many of her family are laid to rest. To her right is the marker for Shorter Bill, died June 9, 1936, the very day her youngest child was born. Her grandfather had died in the Civil War at the age of twenty-two, holding the commission of major—a nearby monument commemorates his memory. Her grandmother lived to be more than a hundred; her father was a Younger and her mother was a Cherokee woman, gifted with the power of healing. Hattie Amelia was one of eight children, four brothers and four sisters. She gave birth to twelve children of her own, nine of whom survived infancy.

"The Youngers were not always good," she says, "and sometimes they could act mean and get in bad ways, but my brother Bill couldn't stand to see people being beat down and treated low. One time in the raw days of the Depression when everybody was about starving there was this woman in Mountain View that was slurring the people and telling them they were lazy and worthless. She was in charge of the relief that was sent to the county and when the people come in out of the hills to get their share of lard and beans and flour, she refused it to them. There was a big crowd in town gathered around the courthouse and she just shirked them. My brother Bill went into the courthouse and got that woman and carried her upstairs and out on the balcony. The people commenced to say, 'Throw her over! Throw her over!' And he lifted her up and held her out over the railing and she was scared to death and begging him not to let her go. Bill made her promise to share out the food and she did. They opened up the crates right there on the grounds of the courthouse. There was a lot of little babies there, my babies, too, and at least we didn't go hungry."

Bill Younger, grand nephew of Cole Younger, had been killed by his partner in a moonshining operation. The partner was a county official and kin to the woman that had refused the food. "Bill dunned the man in his courthouse office," says Hattie Younger. "It was in front of the man's friends and he got angry, shouting that he would kill Bill. He pulled a pistol and chased Bill out of the courthouse and shot him in the back. One of Bill Younger's friends, Paul

Foster, ran to him there on the courthouse steps and Bill asked him to pull off his boots. Paul did that and then cradled Bill's head in his arms till he died."

Back when Hattie Younger's paw told her to "let it go," he hadn't meant to let it die. About a year after her brother died, his killer was walking the streets of Fort Smith, Arkansas, when he was shot and killed, but not from the back. "I'm not saying who killed him," minds Hattie Younger. "But up in these hills, revenge is a better meal cold."

CHAPTER 11

LITTLE DIXIE

Oklahoma and Texas . . . The Trail of Tears . . . Dee Brown . . . Dallas . . . Pappy
Joiner and the Spindletop Field . . . Joe Don Looney

IF BRANSON, MISSOURI, IS the cultural boundary to the north of the
Ozarks, then Fort Smith, Arkansas, is the western edge. From the beginning Fort Smith was the borderline between the South and the
West. It was the first of a chain of forts stretching from the Arkansas
to the Wisconsin territories built in the early nineteenth century to
demark Indian Territory from white folks' land. The country to the
west of Fort Smith would become known as the Badlands, a refuge
for outlaws, renegades, and cutthroats, all accurately depicted in
Isaac Parker's *Hell on the Border* and Charles Portis's *True Grit*. Fort
Smith became the only center of law and justice east of Roy Bean's
"Vinegaroon." And the judge of Fort Smith was "Hanging Judge
Parker."

Though Portis got a deserved classic from his work of fiction,
Judge Parker got a bad rap in history. In his twenty-one years on the
Fort Smith bench, Parker sentenced 165 men to death by hanging
but it took him more than 10,000 trials to do it—only seventy-nine
were actually executed in all these years. Parker was willing to promote the myth of his wrathful Old Testament image because he was
the only civilizing force in a territory infested with killers, goons,
and outlaws of every stripe. What he was actually doing was making
his hellish border safe for the horse trader, the high-toned old

Christian woman, and the latter-day Phoenicians yet to come. The man who really cashed in on the myth was George Maledon, who became known as the "Prince of Hangmen." After his years of service as chief executioner for Judge Parker, Maledon went on the Wild West circuit, touring with such notables as Frank James and Cole Younger, who would have been hanged if they'd come before Parker's court. Judge Parker had always prided himself on doing "equal and exact justice," but the type of criminals he had to deal with colored his generally benign attitude and made him seem a monster. One such outlaw was Cherokee Bill, a notorious thief and murderer. When Cherokee Bill was led onto the gallows by Maledon, Judge Parker asked him if he had any last words, and Bill replied: "Get it over with, Judge. I want to be in hell in time for dinner."

The old gallows still stand in Fort Smith as a tourist attraction, yet another monument to Arena America where public hangings always played to full audiences. Modern Fort Smith has the widest main street in the nation; Garrison Avenue was constructed to accommodate the giant herds of longhorns coming up from Texas. Fort Smith is still a cowtown with more cowboys and cowgirls than Calgary at Stampede time. Despite the Western motif, every man, woman, and dog in Fort Smith believes himself, herself, or itself to be Southern. The dogs even bark with a Southern drawl on this outpost of the Wild West.

No one much thinks about it, but the Trail of Tears ended in Arkansas. In 1817 President James Monroe traded land with some four thousand Cherokees living in Tennessee, Alabama, and Georgia for equivalent acres in the Arkansas Territory, which at that time included the Badlands of Oklahoma. And so it began—twenty years of guile, theft, murder, and profit—until General Winfield Scott rounded up the last of the Cherokees and marched them thousands of miles to these badlands. Monroe understood in 1817 what Andrew Jackson came to realize in 1829, that America's economic future depended upon expansion into the West. The only stopping block to this inevitable march toward capitalist nirvana were the native tribes who were themselves no serious military threat. The tribes were, however, a definite obstacle to unrestricted settling, and certainly the "civilized" folks Up East would have looked upon the removal with shock and moral outrage. So the issue became one of morals only, and the tale of morality is one of great confusion and wheels within wheels.

The Cherokees of the Tennessee River Valley into Georgia were bitterly divided about giving up their ancestral lands. Most histories make no real distinction between the rival groups. The paramount chief of the Cherokees, John Ross, opposed relocation almost to the end, preferring to challenge the federal government in its own courts. Ross never intended to fight; he was trying to conform to the white man's ways. Ross's opposition within the Cherokee Nation came from two chiefs, Stand Watie and Major Ridge; their appeasement group sought to get what they could while they could, so they sold their land to Andrew Jackson. Chief Ross won in the courts but Jackson ignored the judgments. What is not generally known is that there were two separate waves of relocation. The first, in 1837, was led by Chiefs Ridge and Watie. They and their followers traveled first-class by flatboat and river steamer via the Tennessee, Mississippi, and Arkansas rivers past Fort Smith to Fort Gibson. All in all it was a pleasant twenty-three-day trip, plenty of food and no real problems. The only fatality, according to the attending physician, a Dr. Lillybridge, was one man who died of a long-standing case of syphilis. The doctor also noted in his diary that the Cherokees were "mostly drunk all the way."

The second wave of some eight thousand Cherokees—and the one that everyone knows as the Trail of Tears—came a year later. These were the followers of John Ross and were opposed to relocation under any circumstance. They had been abandoned by Ross, who, like Watie and Ridge, had taken payment for his land and had gone to Oklahoma by boat. Ross's people had no boats, little food, and were attacked by savage white men all along the circuitous routes. Their cattle and possessions were stolen, many of their women raped. Of the eight thousand who started on the trail, a total of four thousand died along the way. This was a bitter trail.

Yet the true story behind the Trail of Tears isn't to be found in 1817 or in 1837–38. The pivotal year was 1832, and in that year a strange odyssey was coming to its end on these Oklahoma plains. The questors were Auguste Pierre Chouteau, Jr. (whose grandfather founded the city of St. Louis and started the world's largest fur trade); Henry Ellsworth (past president of Aetna Life Insurance Company, newly appointed federal Indian commissioner, and representative of the Eastern financial bloc); Washington Irving (the father of American belles lettres); and an assorted retinue of fops, dandies, noblemen, and hangers-on lending an incognito cloak to an almost inconceivable intrigue.

They had all traveled down from St. Louis, where they had met with General William Clark, the famous explorer and then-governor of all the lands known as the Louisiana Purchase. Here on the plains, this curious entourage had come to meet, of all people, Sam Houston, former congressman from and governor of Tennessee (and disgraced drunkard of the first branch water), who had been hunkered down in the Badlands since 1829. But this party of movers and shakers was not here on an idle tour of the prairies.

Ostensibly, Houston was here on a binge of heroic proportions; Chouteau was looking for an untapped source of furs; and Ellsworth, who had never seen an Indian in his life, was scouting for land that would implement Andrew Jackson's reprehensible removal of the tribes. What was going on was much more. Houston, a Jackson protégé and longtime friend, was here as the President's point man for America's expansion into the Southwest. Chouteau had brought along a plentiful supply of firewater to addle the Osage and get them to cede their claim to the plains. Ellsworth, the well-connected scion of the Eastern establishment that Jackson sorely needed for re-election, was scouting out the prime lands of the Missouri and Arkansas territories for the purpose of land speculation. Put them all together and they spell dream of empire.

This expedition into the uncharted wilds of the Louisiana Purchase represented nascent Manifest Destiny stacked on top of a 150-year-old plot to build an empire that was to have stretched from the Mississippi River to the silver mines of Potosi, Mexico. The original scheme had come from Louis XIV and his point man, La Salle; the next to pick it up was Andrew Jackson's old friend and fellow plotter Aaron Burr; and finally, sitting President Jackson determined to try it one more time.

This time the scheme worked, mostly. The virtually worthless Badlands were officially designated as the relocation site for the civilized tribes. Ellsworth took his findings and reports back East, and land speculation yielded huge profits to those in the know. Jackson got the support of the East Coast money men for his second term, and Sam Houston went straight to Texas as Jackson's agent provocateur to foment rebellion. Within four years Texas became an independent republic with Houston as president. Within twelve more years, the United States had emasculated Mexico and filled in the continental borders of America as we know them today. And the last ramification of the scheme would include the acquisition of lands south of the Missouri Compromise line, ensuring the expansion of slave states. If any revisionist historian were ever to question the shrewdness, the craftiness of Andrew Jackson, this prairie odyssey should quell the thought.

After the odyssey was concluded, the remaining travelers quit the Badlands and went their separate ways to fame and fortune. Chouteau used his excellent connections to escape numerous charges of running liquor and guns to the Indians. As an extra emolument for services rendered, Ellsworth was named U.S. Commissioner for Patents by President Jackson. And what of the hangers-on? A young Swiss count, Philippe Pourtales, whose purpose on this journey to the plains seems to have been the seduction of as many Osage maidens as he could gather to him, got his fill and returned home, ending his career as an ambassador for Prussia. Having spent so many of his early years abroad, Washington Irving used this trip to reestablish his American voice with *A Tour on the Prairies* and *The Adventures of Captain Bonneville, USA.*

Fort Gibson today is as rustic and ingenuous a national park as is to be found in America. Its stockaded walls and interior grounds are fully and accurately renovated and look exactly the same as they did in 1832 (except for Sam Houston's store of Chouteau's whiskey barrels). A plaque on the parade grounds commemorates the history of the fort, including the fact that young Lieutenant Jefferson Davis served a tour here; the plaque doesn't mention the fact that Davis married General Zachary Taylor's daughter, thereby escaping the drudgery of future frontier postings. Across the street from the fort rests an unassuming little cemetery where many of the chiefs of the Five Civilized Tribes are buried.

Fort Gibson isn't swarming with visitors, though there is a steady trickle. One frequent visitor is Dee Brown, author of *Bury My Heart at Wounded Knee,* the book that did more to raise the awareness of the American conscience toward Native Americans than any other single event or effort of man in the last one hundred years. The book is unquestionably one of the ten most important books of the twentieth century, yet the mind-set of the federal government hasn't changed since Sheridan wasted all the tribes of the plains and told the world that "the only good Indian is a dead Indian." *Bury My Heart at Wounded Knee* is a federally banned book. The book is excluded from the historical site and Indian reservation gift shop at Wounded Knee, the official line being that this universally acclaimed work "doesn't project the proper image."

Standing in the cemetery across from Fort Gibson, Dee Brown shrugs and says of his book, "I didn't make anything up. I didn't have to. The whole story was there in the official government archives."

Dee Brown is a gentleman and a gentle man. Now in his eighties, he is the author of more than two dozen books, fiction and nonfiction, and has published countless articles in various national journals. He grew up in the oil-boom town of Stephens, Arkansas, where he met his first Indians, roughnecks coming in from the Oklahoma oil fields. Brown's young widowed mother moved her family to Little Rock so that Dee and his sister could go to better schools. It was there while hanging around the old Southern Association ballpark that he met probably the most influential person in his life.

"There was this pitcher named Moses Yellowhorse and he set us all on fire . . . he was a full-blooded Indian who'd pitched some in the Major Leagues . . . he had a pure Indian face that must have intimidated opposing batters when he put on his scowl and fired one of his fastballs over the plate. . . . ." Brown tells that Yellowhorse was kind to all the knothole kids of Little Rock, teaching them how to throw various pitches and tossing them baseballs that they could use as free passes into the game.

"I became Moses's friend and his deeds taught me that American Indians could be kind and generous and good-humored." From that time Dee Brown scorned the old tales of frontier Indian savagery. "When I went to the Western movies on Saturday afternoons, I cheered the warriors who were always cast as villains."

The Indian burying ground across from old Fort Gibson is situated on a gentle ridge, and from it one can see the sweep of the plains and the river winding off yonder. Nearby is pasture land with a few head of cattle grazing. They say that in 1838, when the last Cherokees were being rounded up by the army, the cows and dogs in the Indian villages began a woeful lowing and howling that seemed to presage the coming disaster. The only memorial to the

Cherokee are the ageless winds of the plains. No sense of irony lingers, not even melancholy. The tale of morality hereabouts can only be heard in the constant winds.

FROM this Cherokee Strip spreading from Fort Gibson over to Tahle-quah and the Cherokee Hills and back along the Arkansas River basin, the region known as Little Dixie launches itself. Its white set-tlers were Southern refugees trying to find a better life after the Civil War and people looking for free land in the Sooner rush before the government-owned land was legally open for settlement at the turn of the century. The land itself was no good except for a thin strip of Oklahoma's proud "green country" close on to the Arkansas border. Much of Sooner Little Dixie was Dust Bowl country during the Great Depression. Beat-up old pickup trucks bounce along the state's new roads and broken pieces of Route 66, the grand old high-way to the West. The spartan trucks belong to the Indians who gather by twos and threes at bait shops and convenience stores dot-ted around Lake Eufaula, a spidery sea that extends all the way to McAlester. Tom Joad spent some time in the prison here before join-ing the other Joads on their white trail of tears to the bitter vineyards of California.

Oklahomans don't want to talk about the "grapes of wrath" (Stein-beck's novel was banned by the state during the Depression). Nei-ther are they willing to rehash the plight of the Indians, but the true Indians that are left are ready to talk. Over near Yanush and the Choctaw capital, one can hear tribal elders sitting around with the help of eighty-eight-cent half pints of vodka earnestly discussing their past, present, and future: "How'd you like to chew on turpen-tine rags and try to bend pig iron all your life . . . they took the land, they threw us down in this washboard of a salt flat, and when we asked them for a few measly acres of scrub hill land over in Arkansas, they just laughed. What kind of goddamned planet is this, anyway?"

Bounded on the west by the Brazos River Valley, Little Dixie courses across the Red River into blackland East Texas. Moses Austin made it possible for the first American settlers to claim the tillable land between the Brazos and the Colorado rivers. Austin was the consummate horse trader looking for a deal. In his chiseling career he had been a dry-goods salesman in Philadelphia, a mine operator in Virginia, a judge in Louisiana, and a bankrupt loan shark in Missouri. Just before Mexican independence, Austin talked the Spanish authorities into granting huge tracts of land for three hundred American families who set up antebellum plantations, bringing their slaves with them in defiance of Spanish and then Mexican law—these were the so-called first families of Texas, every bit as arrogant as Tidewater Cavaliers and South Carolina grandees.

Little Dixie runs all the way to the Gulf, and this region is truly the last notch on the Bible Belt. Texas. The empire that Louis of France, Aaron Burr, Sam Houston, and Andrew Jackson conspired to capture is not, after all, the homogeneous domain they wanted it to be. It's a country with several little states of mind. When Sherman saw it, he declared that if he owned it, he would rent it out and live in hell. Sherman was an Ohio Yankee overly fond of hellish epigrams, though there is some truth behind his vision of Texas, even in these lands imbued with the unwieldy hubris of the Southern psyche— Texican Little Dixie. Make no mistake about it, Texas east of the Brazos is a paid-up player of the South even though its legendary rose is from New York. The first of the yellow roses had appeared in the early 1880s in the backyard of a New York lawyer; no one wanted to buy the odd-colored flower so the lawyer gave cuttings to settlers headed West; the rose flourished and became known as "the yellow rose of Texas." It's as Southern as five-alarm squirrel chili and lonesome doves calling across the prairie and the Texas regiments that fought under Bedford Forrest and the boys that died at the Rapido River and the thirteen stars of the Rebel battle flag and yellow roses putting out the gentlest of scents on a cool summer's evening and tall, hollyhock-stemmed girls as fetching and sensuous as any belles of Natchez or Montgomery or Charleston. It's got as many members of the KKK, hateful demagogues, mean sumbitches, good old boys, and redneck aristocrats as any other state of mind in the South, and Texas is five times as big to boot.

Like a discomfited Buddha, Dallas sits on its broad rump contemplating its identity. The capital of Little Dixie south of the Red River, Dallas once thought it was destined to be the capital of the New South. But three big things happened to Dallas: the tragic events of November 1963 reduced the city to the status of a cursed Thebes; then the oil recession of the seventies and eighties visited Dallas as did the plagues that afflicted that capital of ancient Greece; and finally, almost by default, Atlanta took over as the capital of the New South, just as Athens succeeded Thebes.

Dallas has never quite figured out what it is or what it's supposed to be. The city has reconsecrated itself too many times for anyone to have much faith in its heritage. The city's founder has been alternately a commodore named Dallas, a congressman named Dallas, a U.S. Vice President named Dallas, almost anyone named Dallas except the man who first settled on these mudflats of the Trinity River—Joseph Dallas, a pioneer from Arkansas.

Whatever Dallas is today, it is the creation of Haroldson Lafayette Hunt, perhaps the most influential satrap of the twentieth century. Hunt could lay claim to being a charter member of Arkansas's latter-day Phoenicians, for it was in the oil country around the boomtown of Smackover, Arkansas, in the 1920s that he got his start. He got his first taste of big oil money there before he migrated to the East Texas fields with all the other wildcatters. Hunt was already something of a legend in Arkansas with his high-stakes poker playing and his horse-trader land deals. But it was not H. L. Hunt who made the big strike—that honor went to C. M. "Pappy" Joiner, a Choctaw Indian from Ardmore, Oklahoma.

Pappy Joiner was the epitome of the oil-field wildcatter. From the time Spindletop gushed in shortly after the turn of the century, new-sprung oil towns became like Alladin's palace. Prices were outlandish; shares in leases became barter for bed and board; local farmers reaped more profit from the sale of a single acre than in twenty years of backbreaking labor; half an hour with a cabaret girl cost as much as a year's crop once yielded. With money flowing freely, swindling and thievery rushed in. The Bible Belt was indeed part of the Texas frontier, but when a strike of oil did bring a boomtown, the spirit of temperance sneaked behind private doors, and a livelier religion called black gold rolled over the sprawling new settlements of honky-tonks and saloons with as many fancy women and panderers as there were wildcatters. Over in East Texas's own black gold triangle of Tyler, Temple, and Longview, Pappy Joiner brought in the biggest oil gusher in all of Texas, a literal ocean. The history books say that Joiner sold out his interest in the strike for $8 million to H. L. Hunt. Truth told, Joiner went the way of most wildcatters—he was swindled out of his interest in the strike.

Joiner's grandniece, Mrs. Frances Sammons, tells the story: "H. L.
Hunt and his cronies got Uncle C. M. drunk and in a poker game
that he thought was friendly. He was always a generous man, free
with his money, and would do almost anything for a friend. But they
cheated him and got him to sign his lease rights away." Mrs. Sammons tells how later Hunt was shamed into paying Joiner what
sounded at the time like a fortune, the $8 million, but as it turned
out that wasn't even a penny on the million. "That's why the Hunts
are rich and our family doesn't have a dime."

Joiner used his few millions chasing more Texas-tea rainbows and
ended his days broke. Hunt went on to become the richest oilman
in American history, creating Dallas and Houston and myriad oil
towns in between. In the late 1930s Hunt flew his airplane full of
gold to Saudi Arabia, bought up Ibn Saud's oil, and brought back to
Texas and America the Petroleum Way of Life. The world was on the
verge of a revolution—henceforth life on this planet was going to
run on oil.

Texas oilmen understood that World War II wasn't going to be
fought as others in the past; it was to be a machine war absolutely dependent on oil. The Nazi blitz of Europe used up 12 million barrels
of oil; the German invasion of Russia cost 24 million barrels; altogether the Axis burned up more than 255 million barrels in the war
before the Normandy invasion. The United States and the Allies
would need much more, and Texas not only gave it to them but built
a pipeline system to get it to where it was needed most. It was called
the Big Inch. It was a marvel of American technology, a great
pipeline twenty-four inches in diameter laid all the way from East
Texas to the New Jersey coastal refineries. In that huge tunnel, at any
given time four million barrels of oil flowed constantly. If the Axis
powers had had such a resource, they could have prolonged the war
another five decades. The Big Inch was constructed in wartime under the Petroleum Industry War Council, under the leadership of
Interior Secretary Harold LeClair Ickes, and at a cost of more than
$1 billion (more than $15 billion today . . . considerably more than
the Superconducting Supercollider, the Dream of Waxahachie,
Texas). The entire oil industry had a hand in it, from H. L. Hunt to
survey gangs and dynamite shooters to graders, muckers, welders,
crane operators, to pick-and-shovel men. It should have taken five
years to build; it was completed in less than one. In a very real sense,

the death blow against Hitler's Germany was struck in the oil fields of Texas.

It was with the building of the Big Inch that the petroleum industry learned just what strength and influence it had on the American way of life. It found out about itself, learned that it could come to control the entire country, learned its that oilmen would have the final say-so in the country's affairs for generations to come. And Dallas was the capital of it all.... because that's where H. L. Hunt decided it would be.

For forty years after World War II Dallas was the homing center of the oil industry and of opportunity for the young people from the surrounding poor states. Today, the oil recessions of the seventies and eighties have created a barren landscape of skyscrapers begging for tenants (all major cities of the South dependent on oil have become the same). Another impact of the oil recession has been the tightening up of the class structure. The only millionaires left are North Dallas old money, and the young urban professionals are finding it harder and harder to plan their vacations to Vail, junkets to Cancun, and box seats at the NFL games. Dallas has always loved its bigger-than-life personalities, the H. L. Hunt–styled oil barons and the playboy spawn. What Dallas is reduced to now is a tiny tycoon, H. Ross Perot, notorious for his mixed metaphors, and a transplanted Arkansawyer, Jerry Jones, who owns America's team, the Cowboys. Like Atlanta, Dallas has its share of young executive studs who frequent the upscale clubs in trendy West End (not many long Texas strides from the spot where John Kennedy was shot dead).

Once upon a time Dallas had real cowboys with ten-gallon hats, but that was more than half a century ago, and the image of J. R. Ewing was so dead wrong that it wasn't even an inside joke in Dallas; the only ones who believed were people in Des Moines or Peoria or maybe the town of Weatherford, Texas, where Larry Hagman had roots. Since the coming of the oil barons, Dallas has been a cosmopolitan town and rather cold, not friendly at all.

Back in the days when Texas was hard on horses and women, the Texas Railroad Commission was established to keep the railroad companies from owning the better part of the state. When the big gushers started coming in, the commission was the only bona fide organization to regulate the oil industry and keep corruption to a minimum. The early commission accomplished two things: it kicked

John D. Rockefeller out of the state, and it established a minuscule royalty on each barrel of oil to be paid to the public schools. That pittance a barrel turned out to be a king's ransom and brought an enormous amount of money to Texas's wretchedly poor schools, college and secondary. In the long run it gave Texas the most impressive schoolboy sports program in the nation. Texas has always had a mania for sports, especially football, and in an odd way this Texican fixation on sport paved the way for early and smooth integration in the state. A Texan always put winning first and be damned to the color of the athlete—an almost total reversal of the Savage Ideal and the white man's world in the South.

One of the more reputable and least parochial voices on the Southern sports scene is Kevin Sherrington, feature writer for the *Dallas Morning News.* He's an essayist by nature, not given to puff pieces. He picks unconventional or little-known subjects to write about and gives real insight into the cliché-riddled world of sports. Starting with Moses Yellowhorse, the South has been the home of the finest outlaw athletes the country's ever seen. Some were well-known and some not, but they all had one thing in common—they were legitimate Southern crazies, and football especially brought out the weird in them. Perhaps the weirdest of all was a Texas boy named Joe Don Looney. He was almost the perfect athlete, aficionados of Texas football say. He could run a ten-flat hundred with pads on, throw the ball eighty yards, and kick it out of the stadium. He tried to play college ball at Oklahoma for legendary coach Bud Wilkinson but Joe Don just couldn't put up with Wilkinson's rigid discipline and mind control. Everyone believed he could have been All-American three years running had he been able to tame down his wild, free spirit. In the pros, it was much the same and they couldn't tame him either. Yet Looney was one of the first media stars of the 1960s, and only his outlaw ways shortened a nevertheless meteoric career.

"Joe Don Looney was an Adonis," says Kevin Sherrington, "but with some tragic features. He was a kid at heart and refused to think of football as anything but a game. He put fun back in the sport and the fans loved him for it. The coaches, both college and pro, just weren't imaginative or fun enough for Joe Don. They'd put him in a game to punt and if he thought he could make it, he'd take off running. Coaches in college and later in the pros benched him as a disciplinary move. In a sense life itself benched Joe Don Looney, benched the unquenchable spirit in him." Kevin Sherrington was the only sportswriter in America who took the trouble to travel down toward the Big Bend and the little town of Alpine to attend the funeral of Joe Don Looney. Alpine had taken the wayward boy in and folks around say Joe Don had been doing fine of late.

Looney grew up in Fort Worth and graduated from Paschal High School, whose teams were rich in Texas schoolboy football tradition. Fort Worth nurtured Joe Don and in the end he came to be everything the town was itself. It was wild and rowdy and quick-tempered and sometimes arrogant. Fort Worth was only thirty miles from flashy Dallas but in temperament it was as far away as the buffalo and Comanches that once possessed these plains. Dallas was big money and mirrored skyscrapers and academically correct SMU. Fort Worth was true cowboys and stockyards and gritty TCU. The town owed its existence to rawboned drovers pushing their herds into this once and future cowtown. It was the town of Ammon Carter, who thought he was bigger'n Dallas but could never outbuild or outbrag or outdo his archrival, H. L. Hunt. Fort Worth also came to be Quannah Parker's town. This last chief of the Comanches outlasted the frontier, got himself civilized, and became the richest Native American in the land. And it was at the famous old Worth Hotel in town that Quannah proved just how fierce and unbeatable his Comanche blood was. One time he checked into the Worth Hotel and blew out the fire in the newfangled gas stove in his room before going to bed. Somehow he survived the deadly fumes through the night—he was just too tough to kill.

From this background and this mettle sprang a big, strapping, good-looking kid named Joe Don Looney who did everything in his life to live up to his crazy moniker. He was the first of the colorful bad boys of sports created by TV in the early sixties. The cameras and the commentators couldn't get enough of his on-field capers and off-field frolics. During pregame workouts at Oklahoma Joe Don would put down a small blanket and punt the ball eighty yards precisely onto that blanket. He would flip coins in the huddle to see which way he was going to run his next touchdown. But he was too wild for college ball, couldn't get along with teammates or coaches, and it was probably TV exposure that extended his career into the pro ranks. Crowds were wild for him and the media loved him the same way they would later come to love Joe Namath and Muhammad Ali. In all Joe Don played for five NFL teams and set no records except for arousing the ire of coaches or hotshot quarterbacks he had no stomach for.

"To understand Joe Don you had to know about his relationship with his father," says Kevin Sherrington. "His dad was a star receiver for the old Philadelphia Eagles and maybe that's the real Joe Don Looney story. He idolized his father and no doubt feared him and always tried to please him. It's the old story, the Jock-Dad syndrome, and Joe Don was trapped in it all his life."

People in Fort Worth today who were close to Joe Don will tell you that he was not the stereotype that he might have appeared, all brawn, no brains, a brute who'd have to be tamed down. He was a very intelligent young man with a strange sensitive streak. After his NFL days he served in Vietnam for a year and when he came back he was changed from his old wild ways; he had had the 'Nam drug experience and got to see guys blown apart. He wasn't yet twenty-five, he had tried to teach his world how to prance and fly, but now everyone was wearing a Halloween mask. He took off for India, found his guru, studied and meditated. There were pictures of him sometimes in the sports pages, Joe Don Looney on a prayer mat, Joe Don Looney riding an elephant or teaching Indian kids how to kick a football.

And then he came back home and dropped away from the scene that had once craved him. Friends heard from him now and then. He was down in south Texas somewhere and taking it easy, at peace with himself. He indulged in one of his old pleasures, a motorcycle he called his crotch-rocket. He took it out for a little spin; the weather was just turning cool in south Texas. It was September 1988.

Joe Don Looney was buried in the pretty little town of Alpine, Texas, on September 27, 1988. He was just thirteen days away from his forty-sixth birthday. A few of his old Fort Worth classmates showed up for the funeral, along with his favorite coach, Leroy Montgomery, who had brought Joe Don along at Cameron Junior College up in Lawton, Oklahoma. Also present were some family, one sportswriter, and Joe Don's good friend, Alex Hawkins, who'd been an NFL teammate.

Hawkins spoke briefly during the funeral service, saying, "I never could figure out who was stranger, him or me . . . maybe in the whole scheme of things we're all strange."

When the news hit the sports world that Joe Don Looney had died in a motorcycle crash, those who remembered him as "that Southern crazy" probably felt a gripping pause that comes over a body in the whole scheme of things. The Joe Dons have always been hard to figure out down here. You were glad he had finally got in touch with his spiritual side, and you never had to wonder why you liked him so much. He was the maverick older brother you worshiped as a kid, the outlaw uncle that everybody needs, the defiant Quannah Parker and the defunct Buffalo Bill. He was as raucous as a jaybird and as crazy as a road lizard, and you just had to have him.

"The fact that he died in a motorcycle spinout added to his legend," says Sherrington, "though it was a freakish accident and Joe Don wasn't drinking. Those that remembered him probably thought it was just crazy Joe Don again, taking big chances like he always did. This time he wasn't. He was into the community spirit and was even helping out with coaching the local teams. He had made his separate peace."

MOSES Austin's first three hundred families of Texas might not all have been Southerners but the next waves certainly were. They came from the Deep and Outlander South and were almost universally the derelicts of emerging America. They came for land that could be had in the thousands of acres (ordinary homesteads in the rest of the country were limited to eighty acres). By the 1830s these immigrants were arriving at the rate of one thousand a month. By the time of the Republic, 1836, the Anglo population of Texas exceeded thirty thousand—and by the time Texas was admitted as a state, 1845, it had almost 150,000 people.

It was Sam Houston who lured these people into Texas, Sam Houston and Andrew Jackson. Not Jim Bowie or William Barrett Travis or Mirabeau Buonaparte Lamar. The conspiracy that Houston and Jackson had hatched back in 1832 was coming to full flight. Sam Houston always believed that his totem was the eagle, not the raven—and the eagle of Texas was about to take over the eagle of Mexico. On his way to Washington, D.C., Houston had met with Jim

Bowie and persuaded him to go to San Antonio de Bexar and start fomenting a rebellion against the Mexicans. Houston journeyed to Washington to collect some money and last-minute instructions from Andrew Jackson. Houston's own brand of manifest destiny, the godchild of Andrew Jackson, was attracting throngs of settlers all the while. It would take the blood debt of Bowie, Travis, and David Crockett at the Alamo to establish Houston as the bona fide hero and father of Texas.

By historical consensus, conspiracies are supposed to be relatively simple affairs—the more people that are involved, the more complicated the affair becomes. In the case of Texas, the more people that were involved, the smoother things worked out. When Houston avenged the Alamo martyrs by defeating and capturing the jaded Santa Anna at San Jacinto in 1836, the conspiracy hatched by Jackson, Houston, et al. to steal Texas was complete. Houston and the strange amalgam of Texas patriots had pulled a coup as momentous and bold as the American or French Revolution. With Texas now a new republic, the Eastern establishment poured money into its development. And the greater portion of the capital flowing into Texas went to the purchase of slaves. In 1835 a total of only seven hundred slaves existed in Texas; by the start of the Civil War the state held nearly a quarter of a million. The Deep Old South had found a new home all along the rich deltas of the Brazos, the Colorado, the Trinity, and the Sabine River valleys. Little wonder then that these farmlands all the way to the coast were called Little Dixie.

Texas didn't become civilized merely because the Mexican government was expelled and a republic was erected. Texas was ruled by guns and guts and the Bible. "What is a Christian but a shark well governed," wrote Herman Melville at the height of America's nineteenth-century expansion. And most of that expansion emanated from the South outward. What had happened first in the Deep South with the influx of almost savage settlers and the resultant civilizing of same by half-wild journeyman preachers began now to evolve in the plentiful lands of Texas as thousands rushed in to claim free land. It was a wide sea of land sharks and the taming force was that selfsame corps of preachers that soon began to find itself at the center of every dusty little settlement. The Bible Belt cinched so tightly around Anglo Texas, the new bright Dixie, that by statehood the Lone Star State was John the Baptist's brightest beacon. Church colleges and Bible colleges sprouted like the mesquite and juniper brush that choked the long, horizonless prairies.

Yet Texicans were almost a breed apart. Once they got there, they became Texans first, not Alabamians, Georgians, or Kentuckians. They took on a pride in their new beginnings and began almost immediately to show a hardheaded loyalty. They were lusty and greedy and obstinately individualistic; they were God-fearing and two-faced and swallowed up with original sin and guilt. So perhaps the Texans, all being from the Old South, were the truest Southerners of all. If the Deep South was pitted with hard-shell churches, Texas became pocked with them, like the seas of the moon. Dallas itself, not Nashville, was the home of the biggest Baptist church in the world. And Waco, some eighty miles from Dallas on down Little Dixie, could boast of a whole modern city of hard-shells and soft-shells and foot-washers and missionary tithers.

The town of Waco has taken on a peculiar significance that no one could have predicted, and it came out of guilt and, oddly, the need to be neighborly. David Koresh, a Charles Manson act-alike and self-styled messiah, ran a religious commune out east of Waco no differently than any number of jerk-leg preachers ran churches in the town or county. Maybe no one in town liked Koresh but no one really cared what he was doing and no one persecuted him or his followers. It was standard-brand redneck hospitality. There were outstanding warrants against Koresh but the local sheriff wasn't worried—the warrants were for guns and everyone in Texas has more guns than most Central American revolutionaries.

"It never had to happen," believe many Waco locals. "It's a real shame because what happened . . . the storming of the Alamo again . . . said something about Waco that just wasn't true. If all the outsiders had let the local authorities take care of it, there would not have been any shooting and those women and children would still be alive."

Texas understands guilt, and as much as any place in the state Waco realizes the sins of its founding fathers. Waco is deep Baptist Belt on the Brazos, with blackland cotton plantations and antebellum splendor since the origin of the republic. The city was once the epitome of the white man's world in all the South—a vibrant brand of discrimination that extended over three races, black and Hispanic and Indian. The Huecos Indians once held these rich lands but were wiped out, and now the only thing left of them is their name, Waco. By 1993, when the Koresh immolation struck the town, the image of Waco's neighborliness disappeared with the sooty black smoke.

Waco once had as much claim to becoming the capital of the new Texas republic as any other town in the state. Houston was a malarial swamp, Washington on the Brazos reminded too many people of the insipid Stephen F. Austin, San Antonio was too close to Mexico for comfort, Nacogdoches was too close to Louisiana and America, and Goliad had too many bad memories (it was at Goliad that James Walker Fannin's army, intended as the relief column for the Alamo, was captured by Santa Anna and executed like dogs in a ditch). At least Waco had a Texas Ranger fort, which was far more than Austin had when it was selected as the new capital. The choice of the capital city was typical of the Texas psyche—not based on proximity to the population or on commercial viability, and not even on ancestral lands. Austin was selected out of pure political expediency.

Mirabeau Buonaparte Lamar succeeded Sam Houston as the second president of the Republic of Texas and sought to isolate the Raven in his scandal-ridden, diseased, and corrupt base of Houston town. In 1838 President-elect Lamar and a party of his cronies jaunted up from the Brazos Bottoms on a buffalo-slaughtering junket and discovered the pretty vistas along the Colorado River. Lamar decided to make this his new capital, he said, because of its "lightness of air, free of fevers." The town was originally called Waterloo but was changed to Austin to take advantage of the venerated Texas name. Austin town was a laughingstock to Lamar's foe, Sam Houston. Indians attacked it during the day and roamed the streets at night looking for hair; the state legislators arrived in town under armed guard. Refusing to be shut out, Houston came to Austin and established himself in a hovel across the street from Lamar's newly built stately mansion. The main street of Austin, Congress Avenue, divided the followers of Houston and Lamar, but when the lawmakers convened in the capital building, the scene became a living facsimile of a Thomas Nast cartoon: duels got fought on the chamber floors, senators drew down on one another, and Bowie knives were more evident than law books. Former comrades-in-arms turned bitter rivals, Lamar and Houston never dueled but faced each other down each day as they cursed and hackled from hovel to mansion.

These were colorful, wild, and critical days to the future of Texas. In the end, crude rude Sam Houston (given to blowing his nose without benefit of a handkerchief) outlasted the elegant, effete Mirabeau Lamar (given to penning romantic verse without benefit of education or taste).

Austin today is out of place in Texas. It's cosmopolitan, sophisticated, has the richest university in the country outside of Harvard, is surrounded by unisex massage parlors specializing in executive relief, and has a university library that would have humbled Alexandria in the days of Thucydides. Depending on the vagaries of Baptist temperance, Austin's got nude beaches out on Lake Travis. The university also has one of the finest history departments in the world, and should any of its students visit these artificial beaches they might bring a copy of Thucydides, perhaps his account of the Amazons. Or they might read the diary of William Barrett Travis, the namesake of this lake, and his curious entry, *"Chingaba una mujer que es cincuenta y seis en mi vida,"* which says that old "Buck" Travis had just scored with the fifty-sixth woman of his lifetime. This macho crowing might appear sleazy to the casual reader but not to the students of the University of Texas. These children of the 1990s have a genuine regard for their history; they just aren't lost in the legends. They know Travis had syphilis and that he was taking mercurous chloride, the cure recommended by the quacks of the 1830s. The students know, too, that Travis was literally crazy as a road lizard when he commanded at the Alamo. The whole point is that they love him anyway. So goes the soul of Texas.

The state of Texas has had a lot of international attention over the years but none more than during its brief span as a republic. The John C. Calhoun South wanted it, the James K. Polk Union wanted it, Spain idly dreamed of getting it back. More importantly, Great Britain and France both wanted Texas, mostly because the one of them thought about it and the other was determined it shouldn't happen. An episode over a hog kept Texas from becoming a French colony. There came to Austin a certain Count Saligny, chargé d'affaires to the Republic of Texas from France. Saligny, a dandy and a snob, abhorred the Texas wilderness and was horrified by the savage Indians. He built himself a splendidly vulgar château, a provincial wonder with imported French doors and glassware. At that time France was about to lend Texas some $7 million in an attempt to woo it away from thoughts of statehood. The Pig Episode began when a shoat belonging to an innkeeper broke into the count's stable and ate a good fill of corn. Saligny ordered his manservant to execute the pig. When the innkeeper heard of his pig's demise, he held his Irish temper until Saligny and his servant came to eat at the tavern one night, whereupon the innkeeper gave the servant a good thrashing and tossed the nobleman out into the muddy street. The Count packed up and left, and Texas lost its $7 million.

Texas managed to survive without the Gallic influence. It was about the poorest state this side of Appalachia until the "goddamn black goo" started pouring at Spindletop. After that the Savage Ideal began to mollify. In 1940 the University of Texas had ten thousand students, a graduating class of twelve hundred, and it invited the originator of the Savage Ideal concept to deliver the commencement address. Homer P. Rainey, president of the university, was so enthralled with *The Mind of the South* that he asked W. J. Cash to come to Austin and discuss his revolutionary theses that might set the South on a path toward progress. Sadly, Texas was the last image of the United States that Cash was ever to see. In a matter of days Jack Cash committed suicide in Mexico City.

IF Henry Grady's idealistic plan for a renascence in the South had failed miserably in the decades following the Civil War, a true "New South" did actually evolve, and in the most improbable of places, Texas. Rising from the withered Grange movement, populism, the strongest hope for uniting the workers of both races in a common cause, was born in the 1870s on the blackland farms of east Texas. At first it was called the Farmers Alliance and it was the brainchild of Dr. Charles W. Macune. Macune devised a system to create a network of warehouses where farmers could deposit crops, receive up to 80 percent of the market value, and repay these advances when the crops were sold. Macune's plan was to take the small farmer out of the clutches of the banks and the commodities exchanges. His system was so simple that no one had ever thought of it before, and though Dr. Macune never lived to see his plan implemented, it would lead eventually to FDR's New Deal some sixty years later. Macune's Farmers Alliance was the birth of populism. The idea of populism, if it resonates at all in today's world, recalls the names of

William Jennings Bryan and Robert La Follette; perhaps the fallout of populism helped to create the great socialist fighters Eugene Debs and Norman Thomas. All these social reformers were midwestern and history gives them the primary credit for the movement, leaving Macune a barely noticeable footnote for a bold venture that for a time would unite whites and blacks, Southerners and Yankees in a common cause.

Populism's essential feature was that it would take control of the currency away from the banks and the moneylenders, and it had an extensive impact on American politics, North and South. By the 1890s populism controlled most of the South's Democratic Party—it elected four governors and controlled eight state legislatures. It had its own strong voice, its own press with hundreds of local newspapers from Texas westward and across the entire Midwest. Yet populism ultimately became far too militantly liberal for conservative Northerners, and with the death of its national orator, Leonidas Polk, the movement faded as quickly as it had arisen, except in the South where demagogues under the guise of poor-white populism were taking over the power (Pitchfork Ben Tillman in South Carolina, Tom Watson in Georgia, James Kimble Vardaman in Mississippi, and Jeff Davis in Arkansas).

Little Dixie, as it descended the Red River Valley of Texas and swung toward the bayous of Louisiana, became the last defense of slavery, the Confederacy and Southern populism. During the last two years of the Civil War more than 200,000 slaves were marched into the blackland farm region of East Texas by their owners from the Deep South who were doing their best to keep the slaves from being freed by the conquering Yankee army. These slaves were not being sold or traded; they were being put into a safe refuge, the idea being the protection of assets and capital. This enormous pool of cheap labor virtually ensured that sharecropping would become the favored economic model for Little Dixie.

After the fall of Vicksburg in 1863, the only continuing source of cotton in the South was up the Red River in East Texas. The textile lobby in Washington was desperate for cotton, and Congressman Thaddeus Stevens, perhaps the most vocal Abolitionist in Congress, put pressure on President Lincoln and his treasury secretary, Salmon P. Chase, to get the white gold of the Red River. With Lincoln's full blessing, Chase devised a plan that would get the cotton to the New England mills. His plan was called the "Licensed Cotton Trader Program" and it permitted federal agents to go up the Red River and buy cotton from the enemy. The enemy was more than willing to sell it. The official Confederate line from the politicians in Richmond was that the South would stop growing cotton altogether and have no commercial contact with the enemy. The cotton growers' response to their wartime leaders was to plant more cotton in 1863 than the whole South had in 1860.

Despite Jeff Davis's pathetic stricture to "grow corn, not cotton," every last acre in the Red River Valley was under cotton cultivation. Armed with licenses being sold by Chase's treasury agents for $50,000 apiece, whole regiments of cotton traders invaded Louisiana. Historian James M. McPherson notes in his book *Battle Cry of Freedom* that the licensed traders began to "bribe Union soldiers to look the other way when cotton was going through the lines." Cotton fever broke out all down the Mississippi Valley and all up the Red River. Anywhere cotton was being picked and baled, the agents met willing brokers. These Union agents carried saddlebags and chests full of gold and greenbacks to pay for the cotton. Grant and Sherman were appalled as they watched the morale of their officers and men deteriorate. Grant appealed to Washington, saying that the practices of the traders were directly aiding the Southern war effort. Secretary Chase replied, "The traders must be allowed to buy what and where they can, bonding themselves not to make any deal that would give aid and comfort to the enemy." At the same time Chase's treasury agents averred that it was no part of their business "to investigate the morals of transactions connected with any bale of cotton." Loyalist cotton looked the same as secessionist cotton, and the cotton flowed in enormous quantities. Abraham Lincoln himself estimated that "at least 900,000 bales of cotton found their way North." And that did not take into account that twice that many bales were going South through Little Dixie and into Mexico. The corruption of the Union army was matched by the corruption of the Confederate officers.

While the private soldiers on both sides fought with great valor, their officers were making millions in contraband cotton. This pursuit of profit prolonged the war for at least a year, during which time hundreds of thousands died or were maimed. The North had betrayed the North and the South had betrayed the South.

Up North cotton was going for the outrageous sum of more than a dollar a pound, and everybody knew that contraband cotton was getting over the Mexican border and being sold to British and French buyers for fifty cents a pound, paid in gold. This profit was being divvied up among a cabal of Southern planters, politicians, speculators, and army officers. At best the strapped Confederacy was receiving a couple of pennies a pound of the proceeds. The rest was being deposited in numbered bank accounts in Europe and New York. The central figure in this contraband controversy was General Edmund Kirby Smith, commander of Confederate armies in Louisiana, Arkansas, and Texas. Smith is celebrated even today as one of the Confederacy's greatest heroes; his soldiers fought desperately without shoes or rations, and often the only guns they had were the ones they took off dead Yankee soldiers. Beyond doubt Kirby Smith's reputation as a hard-fighting general is deserved, though the motivation behind his fight-to-the-death orders has always been questionable. While Southern arms were thumping the invading Yankees in the Red River campaign of 1864, Smith was shipping cotton to Mexico. At one time Smith claimed he had burned 150,000 bales to keep the Union from getting it. That much cotton at the time was worth $100 million, and aside from the physical impossibility of burning that many bales, there was no way the cabalists would let that much money go up in smoke. Smith denied complicity to his dying day but retired in guarded splendor.

After the war the lands of Little Dixie were ravaged and its people left destitute. The Northern armies confiscated every bale of cotton left over, and worse, the price of cotton fell to pennies a pound. It was still the only economy people could turn to, only now it was to labor as sharecroppers under the repressive hand of peonage. No relief, no reform, no hope came to this stark land—serfs don't vote under populism. Louisiana would have to wait until the second decade of the twentieth century before Dr. Macune's movement was reborn in the unlikely form of Huey P. Long.

Huey Pierce Long, Jr., became the prototype populist dictator of Louisiana with his election as governor in 1928. Seemingly the Kingfish was guided by the sophomoric precepts of William Henley's "Invictus." The Long clan was from the devastated lands of Little Dixie in northern Louisiana, and Huey's ways appealed to the poor whites and blacks. He got them together as never before by pointing to the old Creole order that had let the state north of the Red River go to pieces, almost lapse into jungle. Journalist A. J. Liebling said of the time: "The regime that ran Louisiana right on from the Purchase discouraged the idea that a man had the right to live decently. It was new stuff when Huey put it out, 'Share the wealth; every man a king.' " Liebling wrote for New York newspapers and *The New Yorker* over five decades and is revered in the journalistic world as the quintessential professional. He was a New York Jewish intellectual, the scourge of the Southern demagogue, and yet he wrote with a dedicated sense of simpatico about the South, particularly Louisiana and the Long clan.

In his definitive book, *The Earl of Louisiana*, Liebling explains how Huey Long came to power: "Huey got all the poor people over on one side. And there were a lot more of them. He made the poor redneck and the poor Frenchman and the poor Negro see that what they had in common was more important for voting purposes than the differences." The time was ripe for a rebellion of the poor people, and Long put together a coalition of poor whites, Cajuns, coonasses, stumpwormers, bougalees, Catholics, and Protestants—an amazing collation of redneck poor from Little Dixie and redneck French from below the Red River. In so doing, Long became not only the master of Lousiana and the Southern mind-set, but also the captain of its soul. Writing about the same epoch, Liebling's contemporary, W. J. Cash, would expand on this rebirth of populism in *The Mind of the South:* "Huey Long did represent a long step in the development of the Southern demagogue, a definite passage toward increasing attention to and emphasis upon the economic and social case of the common man. And his appearance, his swift rise, and the worshipful enthusiasm of the crowd for him, all stand as evidence that there was a groundswell in Dixie in these years."

The assassination of Huey Long didn't end the Longs' control in Louisiana. The Kingfish had installed his own political machine in the state, and his famous "deduct system" continued to finance the machine even without Huey. The "deduct" was unique in the history of American political corruption (which is biting off a huge claim). It was a payroll deduction from the salaries of Louisiana's state employees that went straight to the Long machine. Apparently com-

pletely legal, the system generated millions—and confused the paper trail on kickbacks, bribes, and other forms of illicit income that
the FBI and IRS were always trying to trip Huey and his cronies up
on. On the night of the Kingfish's death, a Long confidant flew to
New York, picked up the deduct box, and brought it home to
Brother Earl. Earl Long used the money to keep the machine alive
and get himself elected.

With the deduct box as his Grail, Earl Kemp Long launched a
reign of political power and corruption that would span parts of
seven decades. Earl himself served, off and mostly on, from 1936 to
1960, and on the day of his death had just been elected to the U.S.
Congress. The best of Earl Long was that he was a populist liberal
who championed racial equality at a time when the South was a powder keg ready to explode. "Uncle Earl" stood up to the Klan, to the
White Citizens Councils, the racists and extremists whom he called
"grass eaters." He refused to back the Dixiecrats, remaining loyal to
the man he respected, Harry Truman. He fought for voter registration for blacks and supported the civil rights movement as it was beginning. In his own state legislature he had to yell out: "There's no
longer slavery! To keep fine, honorable gray-headed men and
women off the registration rolls, some of whom have been voting as
much as sixty or sixty-five years—I plead with you in all candor. I'm a
candidate for governor. If it hurts me, it'll just have to hurt."

It did hurt Earl. This was the governor's race of 1959 in Louisiana,
and Earl lost it on the issue of race. He was beaten by Jimmy Davis, a
psalm-singing hillbilly who wrote "You Are My Sunshine, My Only
Sunshine." Davis's motto was "I Never Done Nobody No Harm."
When he sold out to the racists to get elected, he not only "done
harm," he put the lights out in Louisiana. A. J. Liebling wrote after
the campaign that Earl Long was "The only true liberal in the
South."

Earl Long was not only a flamboyant politician but was, in his own
words, "the last of the Red Hot Poppas." He was famous for his whoring sprees, whether it was bouncing bountiful beauties on each knee
at the Kentucky Derby, flying a whole planeload of female entertain-
ers in from Atlanta, frequenting the cathouses on Bourbon Street,
or running wild with the twenty-three-year-old stripper Blaze Starr.
Old-timers in the French Quarter still talk of Uncle Earl's nocturnal

escapades. In their book *Earl K. Long,* biographers Michael Kurtz and Morgan Peoples recount an episode in 1959 when Earl was visiting one of the Quarter's "houses." Upon hearing a loud scream from a female inside the house, Earl's bodyguard knocked on the door to ask if his governor was okay; Earl came to the door and hollered, "You stupid ass! I told you to come get me if *I* screamed, not if *she* screamed!"

Perhaps Earl Long's greatest saving grace was that he was a funny man; he did such outrageous things that you just couldn't help liking him. Uncle Earl was renowned for his bizarre shopping sprees. He bought not by retail or wholesale but by the freight truck—seventy-two pairs of cowboy boots, three hundred pairs of shoes, forty-four crates of cantaloupes, corncob pipes by the box, sides of bacon, cases of liquor, stacks of army-navy surplus wool blankets. Perhaps the best story of his sprees comes from A. J. Liebling:

One time Earl stopped the day's business at the state capitol and gathered up ten state policemen and a dozen politicians to go buy potatoes that were on sale at forty-nine cents a ten-pound sack. He loaded the politicians into his official Cadillac like cordwood and with all sirens blowing. Inside the store, the governor bought one hundred pounds of potatoes and told a state senator to carry them out to the car; he bought three hundred dollars' worth of alarm clocks on sale and instructed some upcountry representatives to carry them; he bought eighty-seven dozen goldfish in individual plastic bags of water, and two cases of sweet wine, and told his new superintendent of state police to load up. "By the time they came out it looked like a safari, with all the politicians as native bearers." The load was so big the trunk lid wouldn't close, so Earl had a judge go back into the store, buy some rope, and climb under the car to get the rope around as best he could. Down on his knees, the judge said, "I wonder what the governors of the forty-nine other states are doing right this minute!" Uncle Earl was sitting in his air-conditioned Cadillac eating watermelon with salt.

"Louisianians often tell this story and they never fail to laugh at it," says Liebling. "It could be the subject of a Daumier lithograph, and they have a Daumier sense of humor."

The major Longs, Huey and Earl, based their claims to electoral fame and love on what they did for Louisiana's roads, schools, and pensions. Certainly state roads were built where none had been before; schools were constructed and upgraded and teachers' salaries enhanced; and generous old-age pensions were put into effect well before FDR's modest Social Security System. But the graft and theft and corruption associated with the Longs' programs were endemic and over the years drained billions from the state treasury—and the people of Louisiana footed all the bills. Where Huey and Earl and the other Longites showed their arrogance was not preventing the state from marrying the petroleum industry. Starting with the oil booms all over Louisiana, the state became little more than a Middle East kingdom with rich princes and sheiks and a state full of poor people. Oil people bought politicians like lottery tickets and the jackpot was paid out by the state that had already sold its soul. The petrochemical industry has managed to spoil every river and stream in the state. The state's motto, "Sportsman's Paradise," is a joke black with oil.

The legacy of the Longs can be seen in Louisiana today. The state isn't virtually bankrupt, it's broke. The old state roads that Huey and Earl took so much pride in are busted up and used mainly for detours. Just about every city and town in Louisiana depends on the interstate highways to get around. Louisiana's schools are falling pathetically behind their sister states (as late as 1989 science textbooks were not up to date enough to mention man's landing on the moon). The colleges are losing enrollment and teachers because the state can't meet payrolls and maintain academic standards.

What had started as a populist revolt in Little Dixie with a promise of reform to "share the wealth" had ended no better in the twentieth century than it had in the nineteenth. Louisiana's one-crop mentality had simply traded oil for cotton with the same attendant corruption.

The dream of a "Little Dixie" might have occupied the minds of new settlers in the nineteenth century, but the reality of it ends as one crosses the Red River: the landscape changes from pine woods to canebrakes, sloughs, and bayous; the culture begins to mutate and take on a different character. One doesn't travel very far down this land once named for Louis XIV before realizing that the dressings of the Bible Belt are slipping away—that hard-shell north Louisiana has no more in common with Catholic south Louisiana than mint has with turpentine. Just back over the Red River sits the Bible Belt church, a castle keep of the Savage Ideal. It is still the Kingfish's domain, and his legacy with its demagogic brotherhood tries to stump along, though a trust stays there, too, the salving voice of Will Campbell, who sounds a lonely hope that "all men are sorry bastards but God loves them anyway."

ART FOUR

THE GRAECIA MAXIMA

The Mediterranean, Caribbean and Gulf of Mexico form a homogeneous, though interrupted, sea.

—A. J. LIEBLING, *The Earl of Louisiana*

CHAPTER 12

THE SALTWATER WAY

*The Gulf Coast . . . Brownsville . . . The Alamo . . . The Rapido River
Affair . . . Zydeco . . . New Orleans . . . The Kingfish*

WHILE THERE IS A literal irony boundary marking the metaphysical
opposites of North and South at the Mason-Dixon Line, there is a lit-
toral irony line dividing, ever so subtly, the South of Dixie from the
Mediterranean South—what could be called the Salt Line South.
The Mediterraneans who inhabited the shores of A. J. Liebling's interrupted sea "scurried across the gap between the Azores and
Puerto Rico," as Liebling put it, "like a woman crossing a drafty hall
in a sheer nightgown to get to a warm bed with a man in it." Being
sensible people, Liebling thought to add, they never went far inland.
The disenfranchised of Europe, the serfs and peasants, poured into
the interior of North America from the Atlantic Coast and settled
the great land mass. The Mediterranean peoples were content with
their lives on the saltwater of their forebears, and therein lay the difference between the psyches of "fresh" and "saltwater" Dixie.

America's Mediterranean, its own Graecia Maxima, stretches from
Brownsville, Texas, to Miami, Florida. Its history is one of Spanish
neglect and incompetence and French dreams of empire on the
cheap. The St. Die map of 1507 portrayed the land from Mexico to
Florida as a small cup of a bay, smaller than the land mass of Isabella
Insula (known today as Cuba). The St. Die cartographers naïvely believed Columbus's assertion that he had discovered the true Indies,

so they called the new world "America" for the Florentine Italian
Amerigo Vespucci, a contemporary of the Admiral of the Ocean Sea
who knew full well that Columbus was in error. In the first half of the
sixteenth century the Spaniards cruised the length and breadth of
the Gulf of Mexico, and like the proverbial Spanish ducesa's nightgown, they touched everything and covered nothing. Cabeza de
Vaca, Panfilo de Narvaez, Juan Ponce de Leon, Hernandez de Cor-
doba, Pedro Menendez de Aviles. Romantic names to be sure but
about all they bequeathed were multiple atrocities, a few crumbling
architectural masterworks, and grist for the mills of latter-day historians. By 1550 French privateers were using the Gulf Coast as havens
for piracy on Spanish treasure ships. The French attempted to establish colonies on the Atlantic Coast of Florida and the Carolinas but
were put to the sword by the Spanish. After destroying the French,
Spain concentrated on silver and gold mines in Mexico and ignored
the Gulf Coast. It would be more than a hundred years before any attempt at settling this Graecia Maxima, and when the colonies began
to spring up they were almost exclusively French.

Aside from the fact that France and Spain were constantly at war
in Europe, the Spanish enmity for the French in the New World
stemmed from Spain's fear that the French would incite rebellion
among the Negro slaves Spain held in thrall. Though the French
had no history of slavery they learned fast; the Gulf became the gateway for slaves into the interior of the South, with the French learning to act as the middlemen. From the beginning, precious little
slavery existed within the Salt Line. Despite its Levantine nature, the
Sultry South, as first referred to by historian Francis Parkman,
adopted the Spanish model of slavery out of economic necessity.
There were no nuggets of silver and gold to be picked up off the
ground in the Deep South any more than there were in Jamestown.
Commercial viability rested with massive plantation farms and slave
labor. Ralph Waldo Emerson, America's first great philosopher and
the spiritual father of the Abolitionist movement, once hypothesized
that "wherever snow falls there is usually civil freedom, but where
the banana grows man is usually sensual and cruel." Emersonian
metaphysics couldn't find it in its heart to say a good word about the
slaveholding South (even though Emerson based his beliefs upon
slaveholding Greek and Roman worlds). The difference between the
Levantine way of life and the Calvinist Puritan ethic of the north Eu-

ropeans was and is as different as Sol Invictus and the shoes of the fisherman. If Emerson had ever ventured into the South he would have discovered the true variations of the Southern psyche: those living above the Salt Line strive for a grip on life; those within the Line strive for a grip on joy, even if they have to sing in their chains.

THE southernmost extremity of the Graecia Maxima actually begins some thirty miles up the Rio Grande at Brownsville, Texas. One almost has to blink one's eyes to keep from believing that Brownsville is on the Italian Riviera somewhere near Genoa where the lemon trees bear fruit as big as the grapefruits of south Texas. Like their Italian counterparts, the folks in Brownsville have always been adaptable. While part of Confederate Texas, the town was loyal Rebel; when the Yankees landed, the small Confederate force ran two days before the Yanks got within gunshot range (Confederate General H. P. Bee lost his command but he didn't lose any men). When the Union army marched into Brownsville, the populace cheered (they liked parades). In true Levantine manner, business proceeded as usual—before the Yanks it was contraband cotton over the border to Matamoros, and after the Yanks took over, it was contraband cotton without the bother of the Mexican middleman, for the South sold the cotton straight to Salmon P. Chase's agents.

The people of Brownsville have a long, somewhat unsettling tradition of living with worthless currencies (a tradition that continues today as the town's merchants collect upwards of a billion pesos a week from their customers on the Rio Bravo side). One incident back in 1864 illustrates Brownsville's equivocal relationship with bad paper. Contraband cotton had been selling for gold or silver, greenbacks, pound sterling, or Napoléons d'or—all 100 percent spendable. But the Confederate cotton agents had trouble keeping up with the cotton. One agent in Matamoros sold cotton through a Mexican factor who paid in cash money. Another Confederate agent sold the same cotton to the Yankees, Brits, and French and made delivery. As a consequence, the Mexican didn't get his paid-for cotton. Irate, he crossed the border and hijacked seven crates of newly printed Confederate currency with a face value of $16 million, threatening to keep the money unless he received his cotton. Unbelievably, the Brownsville Confederates caved in and gave the man his cotton. At the time a Confederate dollar was worth about two pennies.

Today Brownsville is a sprawling, prosperous town reaping the benefit of the *Maquilladoras* just across the river. These are American-owned factories set up in Mexico, where they avoid U.S. pollution laws and higher labor costs. Brownsville is a contented town and with its history, why not? The town can even lay claim to once being the capital of Texas, at least Yankee Texas, during the last six months of the Civil War. It's also rumored that more dope passes through here than is shipped down the Orinoco River in Venezuela.

When General Bee eschewed a pointless fight at Brownsville, he hightailed it through the desolate lands just inland from the Gulf Coast. Bee reasoned that a region that took fifty acres to keep one cow alive would be sufficiently daunting to scare off an invading Yankee army. Bee was right and the Yankees turned back. The entire diamond-shaped tip from San Antonio over across the Trans-Pecos was free-range cattle country both before and during the Civil War. And if some enterprising Confederate officers made fortunes out of contraband cotton, the boys in Texas did their own selves proud by running contraband cattle up to Sedalia for Yankee greenbacks. From 1866 to 1888 more than five million beeves were trail-herded into Sedalia alone, creating the first of the Texas millionaires. Cattle costing three dollars to five dollars each sold for ten times that at the Northern railheads.

J. Frank Dobie's myth of the Texas cowboy was born of this age and carried over into dime-novel and film lore. An iconoclast and Texas free spirit, Dobie wrote of frontier Texas and captured the dream of the Wild West in his many books, notably *The Texas Rangers* and *Coronado's Children*. The cowboys of Texas were a rare breed, a mixture of Mexican *vaquero*, Anglo misfit, and black freedman. They were hard-riding, hard-driving men working for "a dollar a day and found," but there was never any racial trouble among them. In this early Texas the color of skin made no difference. It was truly the era of the magnificent Texas longhorn, until a drought in the summer of 1886 and the following bitter winter destroyed millions of cows. The plains and arroyos, the creeks and draws were literally choked with rotting carcasses. The cattle boom days were over; so many cattle companies went bankrupt that Texas had its own version of the Great Depression.

The lands here are still daunting. Untrammeled Canadian winds scream down the high plains into Texas and down to the Gulf; the forceful winds now beat up siroccos that vanquish the prairie, and only at night do they abate, becoming mere northers that chill the bones. The people living here experience a despair not unlike those who live through the summer sirocco blowing across the Libyan desert and into Sicily, Italy, and southern France, where the suicide rates quadruple with the enervating winds. In the blowing one can almost hear the doleful voice of balladeer Jimmie Rodgers intoning, "T for Texas . . . " Rich Texas, but rich at a price. Billions of gallons of oil lie in buried tanks up and down these coastal plains. And, too, a considerable percentage of the nation's nuclear wastes is sunk into the coastal acreage. It was not only the winds that blew south—freight car after freight car funneled down the rails to these coastal dumps . . . an ill wind of a different sort to plague the Texas psyche.

The feeling of bigness is here, a giant land made larger still by its sheer emptiness. The fabled King Ranch rides to the western horizon and beyond, an unfenced holding so large its boundaries have never been completely surveyed. Maybe the Kings' acquisitiveness was inspired by the patriarchal figure of Jim Bowie, who amassed title to 750,000 acres of land outside of San Antonio de Bexar. Of course Bowie got his land by subterfuge and bilking his teenage Mexican wife's relatives.

The quality of distance is an existential absurdity to these salt-line Texans. Folks down here think nothing of driving 150 miles to go to a movie or a new restaurant or a bootscoot (what country dancers call their two-step). There are whole counties in this neck of the prairie that don't offer the simple amenity of gasoline for your car. It's crazy but distance does that to the mind in Texas. Out here all roads lead to "San Antone." Back in 1836 there weren't any roads to San Antonio but there was plenty of sand to cross and still 183 men found their way to a broken down old mission called the Alamo.

For no apparent military reason these 183 men hunkered down inside the mission while Santa Anna's army marched up and surrounded them. For twelve days William B. Travis tried to negotiate a surrender; then on the night of March 5, 1836, Travis drew a line in the sand with his sword and asked all who would fight to the death to cross over to him. All but one of the men crossed over (and he would slip the wall around midnight and be the only man to survive). The next morning before dawn the Mexicans attacked. Travis died, perhaps the first of the garrison to do so. Jim Bowie died, as did both Travis's and Bowie's slaves. A total of 176 men were killed. At the end of the assault on the Alamo, the Mexican troops ran amok, repeatedly bayoneting and mutilating the dead. Suddenly a pocket of six survivors was discovered and the wild-eyed Mexican soldiers, drunk on blood, rushed to get a piece of these Anglos. In his account of the battle, *Duel of Eagles,* Texas author Jeff Long explains what happened: "A gracious, aging general named Manuel Fernandez Castrillon happened to be present. General Castrillon approached the terrified rebels, placed his hand upon his breast, and declared, 'Here is a hand and a heart to protect you . . . you shall be saved.' "

Legend tells that Davy Crockett stood like an embattled Hector smiting the Mexicans hip and thigh until finally he was overcome by numbers and perished a hero's death. Good Texas historians know this to be untrue. Crockett was one of the six saved by Castrillon. Seemingly the former U.S. congressman and dreamer of Texas empire had grinned down another bear. But Castrillon didn't have the last word, and Santa Anna was determined to put down the Anglo rebellion with inquisitional terror. According to Castrillon's diary, as brought to light in Jeff Long's illuminating book, the following conversation took place:

> "Santa Anna, the august," Castrillon pronounced. "I deliver up to you six brave prisoners of war."
> "Who has given you orders to take prisoners?" Santa Anna demanded. "I do not want to see those men living. Shoot them."

Over 150 years later, the Alamo has become a premier tourist call. With its picturesque downtown canal, charming sidewalk cafés, and out-of-the-way auberges, San Antonio has become a favorite trysting place for young lovers. This old Spanish town oddly serves as something of a bedroom community for Houston some two hundred miles away. The Spanish influence remains, though German immigrants swamped the town in the 1840s—one of the main downtown drags was named "Wilhelmstrasse" until 1918 when sentiment against the Kaiser caused it to be changed to King William Street. The famous Menger Hotel is still there (Robert E. Lee once rode

Traveler into the hotel lobby just for the hell of it). Teddy Roosevelt organized his Rough Riders in San Antonio. Both Lee and Roosevelt's troops savored the Menger family homemade brew; San Antonio is still the home of the last two Texas beers, Lone Star and Pearl.

Up at nearby New Braunsfels, a sizable German settlement lives on. Until just a few years back the newspaper in this Teutonic town was printed in English and German. New Braunsfels features German architecture and culture along with the finest middle Europe cuisine this side of München land.

Dictator-for-life Santa Anna never returned to the Alamo. After Sam Houston captured him at San Jacinto, Santa Anna preposterously was given his freedom by the Raven. The butcher of the patriots at the Alamo and of Fannin's four hundred at Goliad was allowed to return to Mexico, where he was in and out of power according to Mexican whims for the next two decades. President James K. Polk brought Santa Anna to Washington, where he was feted and fawned over as though he were the king of Romania; the dictator was financed and sent back to Mexico as America's puppet and stooge, and he continued to play out the tragedy of military repression that plagued Mexico for decades.

It's no cliché to say that Texans still remember the Alamo and continue to be bitter over the betrayal of their honored dead. Texan and editor Charles Neighbors can speak to the point of Texas's betrayals and bitterness. Neighbors is from San Antonio and a graduate of Texas A&M. He speaks for generations of Texans as he recounts a tragic second saga associated with the Alamo. It concerns the Alamo Division, the 36th, of the Texas National Guard that fought in Italy in World War II.

"The only difference between the battle of the Alamo and the fighting in Italy was that the Germans didn't play the cutthroat song, the 'Deguello,' like Santa Anna did," Neighbors reflects. "No, the Texans in Italy were sent to their deaths by the incompetent hand of General Mark Clark."

Many of the 36th Division's junior officers were graduates of the A&M Cadet Corps. "When I was in college I learned that the governor of Texas presented the division with a Lone Star flag emblazoned with Travis's legendary defiance of Santa Anna, 'We shall never surrender or retreat.' Part of the sad tradition of the corps is that most of the Alamo Division never got a chance to do either one. They took casualties by the thousands on the beaches at Salerno and the following mountain campaign. And then the 36th that had proved itself to be an elite fighting unit, losing 50 percent of its men in four months of combat, came to the Rapido River." Within forty-eight hours in late January 1944, nearly four thousand Texans were killed on the banks of the Rapido River in southern Italy. General Clark was trying to establish his beachhead at Anzio, and the 36th Division was to push across the river and occupy the Germans around Monte Cassino; the plan was to break the deadlock in the mountains and push on to Rome. Except that two of the three regiments of the 36th Division were annihilated. The bitterness of the fighting on the banks of the tiny river was surpassed only by the bitterness of the few survivors who knew their comrades had died needlessly. British troops a few miles north of this site were to have crossed the river in a coordinated attack, but they turned back under the heavy German barrage; General Clark, frustrated and pinned on the beaches at Anzio, kept reaffirming his order to the 36th to cross the river.

Infantry companies 180 strong at the beginning of the attack ended the two-day battle with fifteen men still alive. One of the survivors of the 143rd Regiment, Orin Kelsey, now living in retirement in Manning, Louisiana, was one of the last fifteen survivors who swam back across the icy waters of the Rapido. Kelsey remembers the scene:

"There were bodies on the banks on both sides of the river. And bodies floating in the water. And dead men snagged on the broken cables of the bridges the engineers had tried to build. The water had turned red from all the blood."

The Germans were amazed at the pointlessness of the attack. They were also horrified at the losses the Texans had suffered. A German officer came down to the Rapido under a white flag and granted the Americans a truce so they could come across in rubber boats to get their dead and wounded.

Two months later some twenty-five young officers of the 141st and 143rd Regiments gathered secretly in a cattle barn in Italy and drafted a resolution calling the attempted crossing of the Rapido "one of the most colossal blunders of the Second World War" and vowing to see that the officials responsible were brought to justice.

On the second anniversary of the Rapido massacre, the division veterans held a reunion in Brownwood, Texas, and passed a resolution calling for a congressional investigation into the conduct of Mark Clark. Texas members of Congress forced the issue and the House Committee on Military Affairs convened to hear the complaints. The committee listened on the morning of March 18, 1946, and then recessed for lunch. It never reconvened.

The army stuck by its four-star general despite the evidence and Clark went on to command in the Korean War for fifteen months, until the U.S. Army finally realized that he was incompetent and allowed him to retire. The Texas State Legislature met and in angry speeches Texans declared that Clark should be sent to the Alamo in chains, stood up against the old mission's wall, and shot by a firing squad of the survivors.

Charles Neighbors attended Texas A&M in the 1950s, some ten years after the war. As a cadet he studied all the military campaigns of World War II. The Italian campaign, he attests, was a military fiasco from start to finish and was marked by blunders and military incompetence. "They may not admit it at West Point," Neighbors says, "but on our A&M campus, General Clark was as infamous as Santa Anna at the Alamo."

A gaunt and lonely statue of bronze stands wearily on a point in Matagorda Bay on an eternal vigil over a desolate coast. It is a memorial to the ineffable folly of the Salt Line's oldest dead Frenchman—René-Robert Cavelier, sieur de La Salle, the man who discovered the Ohio River and first traversed the Mississippi all the way to its estuary on the Gulf. The statue here is mute testimony to an unrealized dream for the New World.

Matagorda Bay is almost as desolate today as it was in 1685 when La Salle came to this sultry coast to attempt a colony. Just three years earlier La Salle had canoed down the Big Muddy and claimed the entire Mississippi Basin for his most Christian majesty, Louis XIV (whom Mark Twain dubbed "His Putridness"). Now La Salle returned to the New World with four tall ships and a company of soldiers, artisans, and settlers, including thirty teenage girls swept from the streets of Paris with the rueful promise of becoming the "little mothers of New France." To say that La Salle's objective was to plant a colony here would be stretching a truth; his purpose was to establish a colony, no doubt, but not here. Other motives were at work on this seventeenth-century Texas coast.

Mexican gold and silver gave rise to the dream of empire that would tempt Aaron Burr, Andrew Jackson, Sam Houston, and the pirate Murrell. And the dream began here. Louis XIV wanted the Spanish treasures, and though most histories don't accord it so, La Salle's "Texas colony" could easily have had the ulterior purpose of establishing a base for assaults upon New Spain's mineral wealth. Standard history tries to explain away La Salle's lost Texas colony as a tragic result of navigational blundering. The colony was ostensibly intended for the mouth of the Mississippi; instead, La Salle overshot the river by four hundred miles. Here is the historical conundrum: could La Salle have mistaken Matagorda Bay, guarded by reefs and with buffalo on the shore, for the multiple-mouthed estuary of the Mississippi? La Salle had explored the Mississippi extensively, and while he might not have known its longitude, he was thoroughly familiar with its appearance. Further, part of La Salle's deal with King Louis was that La Salle would go back up the Mississippi Valley where he could raise an army of fifty thousand Indians he had already converted for the express purpose of invading Mexico. The idea was so bizarre that only a mystical Frenchman could dream it. The scheme wasn't impossible (one must remember that Cortez had conquered Mexico with fewer than three hundred men). La Salle's 1685 expedition, then, was merely the first wave in France's grand design to possess the silver of Potosí and the gold of Montezuma.

The Matagorda Bay Colony was so remote that it was a thousand miles to the nearest Spaniard. La Salle's ships carried provisions for two years, cannons for the defense of the colony, artisans to build a fortress, one hundred professional soldiers, and scores of Frenchmen to people a colony. Most importantly, the expedition had La Salle himself, a mystic and a dreamer but a shaker and a mover with a commanding presence for European and Indian alike. It was a precise and brilliant plan but with no room for error. Everything had to work perfectly to pull the grand scheme off.

Almost tragicomically, the plan started falling apart even before the fleet left Rouen. The fleet commander wouldn't listen to La Salle, wouldn't accept his authority, and the two bickered all the way to the Caribbean. At Ste. Dominique La Salle fell deathly ill and his soldiers and settlers went ashore for a month's debauch. One of the ships wandered off course and was captured by a Spanish man-of-war. When they finally arrived at Matagorda Bay, the provision ship loaded with cannons, tools, and most of the food struck a reef and sank. This same ship was to be La Salle's vessel of communication with the Mississippi River and the army of Indians he needed to raise. The fleet commander watched contemptuously as the supply ship sank and then took the two remaining ships and sailed away, abandoning La Salle.

Still bedridden, La Salle was unable to control the colonists and had to watch as his brother, the Jesuit Abbé Cavelier, openly conspired against him. A full two-thirds of his soldiers had contracted venereal disease at Ste. Dominique and now lay dying on the mudflats of the bay. The colony began to dwindle from lack of food and clean water and proper clothing. A priest was gored by a buffalo; another man was trapped in the jaws of a giant alligator and dragged off into the swamp while the horrified colonists stood by and watched. The colonists were at the mercy of the ferocious Karankawas, a cannibal tribe that raided the makeshift fort day and night.

Francis Parkman, arguably this country's greatest historian, made a thorough study of La Salle's life and his doomed Texas colony. In his biography Parkman paints a wretched picture of La Salle's last days: Two years to the day after the landing, La Salle set off with the last few able men of the colony. Despite earlier failures, they were going to try to walk all the way up the wild country to Canada. They wandered around the East Texas jungle for weeks until, half-crazy with hunger, La Salle's men, including his brother, turned on him. Robert Cavelier, known as La Salle, died in the Texas wilderness on March 19, 1687. He was forty-four. He was murdered by gunfire from ambush, his body dumped into a ravine and left for the carrion fowl.

Six months after the murder of La Salle, a Spanish search party found the site of the ruined colony. The palisade and interior structure of the fort had been knocked down and burned; the Indians had attacked the weak fort and wiped it out. The last members of La Salle's colony had been butchered and thrown into the creek to be eaten by alligators. The Spanish did find three white children living contentedly with adoptive Indian parents in a nearby village. According to the Spanish diary, the Indians wept to see the children being taken away.

The Indian villages have long vanished from the Texas coast and so have the alligators. There used to be good shrimping and fishing out from Matagorda Bay, but offshore pollution took care of that and the little ports along the coast have fallen on hard times. Nearby, the fetching little resort of Port Lavaca has just enough commerce and tourism to keep it alive. Now and then a carload of students stops off on their way to the fun beaches at Padre Island. Matagorda Bay has no white sand, no beaches at all, just the mudbanks that plagued La Salle's people. The state of Texas did erect an outsized statue to the memory of La Salle but it seems more of a historical curiosity than any commemoration. It's a handsome facsimile of the great explorer that captures his tortured demeanor, though it seems out of place to honor the man for his most abject failure. The wind always seems to blow viciously on this lonely cape, a warning perhaps that everything hereabouts is haunted or cursed.

THE Texas coastline has never really had a satisfactory niche in history. The Spanish conquistadors ignored it, the Mexican republic ignored it, the Texas Republic ignored it, and the French should have ignored it. The coast was so barren and offered such little reward that only a pirate could grow to love it. That pirate's name was Jean Lafitte. The only place on the Texas coast that can claim proper title to being a thriving port was Galveston, and for all practical purposes this town was founded (in 1816) by Jean Lafitte.

Galveston is actually an island and Lafitte fortified it, ran up the Venezuelan flag (his flag of convenience at the moment), and created a fortress here as a new center for his entrepreneurial piracy. Despite having won the Battle of New Orleans and having received a presidential pardon for past indiscretions on the high seas, Jean Lafitte was forced out of his Barataria island base south of New Orleans and needed a new lair. He took advantage of the conflict between royal Spain and its Mexican colony and established himself here as the "bos." He named the island "Campeachy" and, according to biographer Lyle Saxon, established it as a commune. About a thousand pirates operated out of the stronghold on a fleet of privateers. Lafitte was not above making a buck on the land. Slavery had been outlawed since 1808 (one could buy and sell only those slaves already in the country), but Lafitte ran contraband blacks in from Cuba and sold them for a dollar a pound in Galveston. Among the buyers were Jim Bowie and his two brothers. The Bowies would herd the slaves to Louisiana, where they would turn themselves in to the local magistrate; the punishment for slave running was confiscation of the slaves, who were immediately sold on the auction block. Because of the reward for turning in slave runners (themselves), the Bowies could afford to make the highest bid at the auctions, getting half the price back. Then by buying the same slaves in Louisiana, they received legal title and could take them to New Orleans and resell them for an average of a thousand dollars apiece. The 1808 law was unenforceable. The Spanish had had antislavery laws for more than a century and still allowed slaves to be held in Cuban pens for the U.S. market. The Louisiana magistrate—a sort of role model for his twentieth-century brethren—was a paid-off party to the Bowie charade, and the legal title used by the Bowies to sell the slaves in New Orleans was no more than a judicial game. The lesson must be that laws based on relative moralities always yield healthy profits.

Campeachy waxed fat until the summer of 1818, when a tropical hurricane of massive proportions swept through the Texas coast and washed the settlement away, including Lafitte's stronghold and all the ships in the harbor. Lafitte tried to rebuild and kept his island going for about a year, but as biographer Saxon writes, "doubloons were no longer as plentiful as biscuits." No one knows exactly what happened to him, but in 1821 Lafitte sailed out of Galveston and vanished into what could have been obscurity were it not for Lord Byron, whose poem "The Corsair" thrilled poetry lovers and treasure hunters on two continents: "He left a corsair's name to other times, / Linked with one virtue and a thousand crimes."

Galveston is to Houston what Piraeus is to Athens, the natural God-made port. Yet the big dreams of Houston city's eponymous forebear got translated into a ship canal on primitive old Buffalo Bayou. It was an unnecessary canal unless Houston wanted to become the greatest Christmas tree light show in the world, for that's what it got, mile after mile of amber illumination on Refinery Row lining the canal all the way to the sea. Drive this Henry Adams *son et lumière* dynamo bereft of its Virgin and see the evanescent fires on the canal, the eruptions of red and yellow light from the volcanic stacks of the cracking plants and the eerie blue-glow flame from the chemical soup of the canal itself. Then one realizes what Houston wanted to become; the oil trough of planet earth. When Adams first saw the dynamo at the Paris Exposition about a century ago, he was both awed and terrified—awed at the possibilities and terrified at the portent to man's fate. In Houston today it is not yet clear whether mankind has been fully enslaved by the dynamo, but this city is certainly Henry Adams's nightmare made real. Houston is the tragic city of the South.

Houston and Galveston are on the Saltwater Way but their claim to this heritage is all but obscured now by the habitual oil spills and red tides that afflict the once-beautiful coastline. Yet the Salt Line is a mile-deep pure vein at Port Arthur and the Sabine River Pass. It was here that the South achieved its most imposing insignificant victory of the entire war. A fleet of two dozen Union ships with an invading army of five thousand tough veterans was scattered to the four winds by Lieutenant Dick Dowling and his forty-five drunken Irishmen known as the "Jeff Davis Volunteers." Four Yankee ships were hulled, beached, or scuttled, four hundred prisoners taken, tons of supplies and guns captured, and General Nathaniel Banks made to look eight kinds of a fool in about a thirty-minute fight. It all happened right at the Sabine Pass and not one of those Southern Irishmen was so much as scratched. They did it with six popgun cannons that had no business firing at ships anyway. When it was over and the whiskey ran out, the Confederates went on home to plow their fields. About a hundred years later, Port Arthur's own Janis Joplin, a descendant of these hard-fighting, harder-drinking micks, sang paeans of praise to the spirit of these saltwater crazies.

The Acadian angle of the Saltwater Way actually begins in Houston, out in the black French Fifth Ward where the "Bon Ton Roulet" is played all the way out into the country and the call *"Zydeco ce soir, chez moi!"* is heard most every weekend. It's a very poor ward whose people are descendants of the French-speaking mulattoes and free blacks that escaped the Haitian revolution of 1803. The Acadian angle continues from Salt Bayou in Jefferson County, Texas, along the coast to Barataria Bay in Jefferson Parish, Louisiana.

The heritage of Louisiana's Cajuns dates to 1763, when England took over Canada and evicted French families from Nova Scotia, putting them down in the humid wilds of south Louisiana. These "Acadians" were made famous in Longfellow's poem "Evangeline," though Longfellow took poetic license by having the French families go through a hellish trip by raft down the Mississippi. In truth, about five thousand Canadian French made a sea voyage to the Gulf Coast.

Enter here bona fide Cajun Country, the land of Evangeline. Except for the interstate highway and the intercoastal waterway, one may as well not even try to follow road signs in Acadiana. These are Louisiana state highways and the folks that built them and put up those signs are Cajuns, who had a relaxed attitude toward direction and distance and time. It's an attitude of truly Mediterranean character that has soaked into the mind-set of these lands. The best way of experiencing the Saltwater Way is to travel with no particular destination in mind, to let the Way wash over you in much the same fashion that Zorba taught the Englishman to dance. The next best is to fall in with a Louisiana talker, and in the instance of this Saltwater Way sojourn the talker is a member of the lost brotherhood of Southern-born living in self-imposed exile outside the South.

His name is Ardner Cheshire, a Louisiana native now practicing law in Arizona. If he had a mind to, he could still be a professor of English or a practicing engineer (he has graduate degrees in both fields, plus his doctorate of jurisprudence). Periodically Cheshire, like all Southerners, has to come home to get his booster shot of things Southern and to learn how to dance again. Cheshire might get you lost but he has an inner peace about the direction he's taking you in.

"Down here the signposts are a little touch frivolous," he says. "Look there." He points to a sign saying that Mermenteau is fifteen miles away. Ten minutes later the distance is narrowed to eleven miles, but in ten more minutes the sign says twelve miles to go.

The color of the land is light brown like the syrup from the sugarcane filling the fields. Just as their Franciscan brothers in Neapolitan Italy invented the pretzel to make a little cash money, the priesthood in Louisiana brought in the cane from the Caribbean and taught their flock how to have a cash crop. And while the Jamestown settlers tried to sell sassafras as a cure for everything from headaches to syphilis, "The Acadians," Cheshire says, "took the sassafras leaves, dried and powdered them, and made the finest seasoning in the world . . . filé is what you come home for." Food is also a religious experience down here, which is why one would take such an odyssey in this sunken, undefined, impossibly alluring land.

"The holy trinity of the South," remarks Cheshire, "may be bad women, bad booze, and the law . . . but the trinity of taste of Acadiana is celery, onion, and garlic."

The best times in Louisiana are when they're putting on their festivals, you learn from this Louisianan, and that's at least every day in some part of the Way. Cajun and Creole food comes out of the bayous and swamps and the people set up booths and cook the real soul food on the spot—sweet potato biscuits, fried catfish and peppery cornbread, alligator nuggets, crawfish bread, po'boys, jambalaya, muffalettas, soft-shell crab in busters, a dozen types of gumbo, boudin, bourbon-flavored bread pudding, Sazerac cocktails.

"Where it's happening is where you are," Cheshire says. "The capital of Acadiana changes . . . it could be Lake Charles, Abbeville, Lafayette, St. Martinville, New Iberia, Jenerette, Breaux Bridge, Thibodaux, or Mamou."

The Cheshire-guided trek winds its way toward Mamou in Evangeline Parish to see some dancing at the famous Fred's Imperial Lounge. It's not a nightspot, it's a day spot, and not exactly a honky-tonk. Fred's opens at 7:00 A.M. and closes promptly at 3:00 P.M. There's no hard liquor or wine, only beer, and no food (you have to bring your own po'boy and peel-your-own crawfish, or muffaletta).

"Country-and-western fans worship at the shrine of Roy Acuff in Nashville," says Cheshire. "Rock-and-roll fanatics pour into Graceland or the Fillmore West, and the rhythm-and-blues folks show up at B. B. King's in Memphis. Well, the shrine of Cajun music, the direct lineal descendant of seventeenth- and eighteenth-century French folk music transplanted from Europe and Canada, is right here at Fred's in Mamou."

Someone is singing of "Ay Vonn Jell Leen" and the dancing is a two-step Cajun waltz performed out on the dance floor by young and old alike. Beautiful young Cajun couples and distingué graybeards and their normally somber wives move with a syrupy sensuousness unknown to the formalism of Vienna and Johann Strauss.

The music at Fred's is broadcast live to the faithful throughout Acadiana. The farther east from Mamou you travel, the less influence that French waltz has. The music and dancing become a blend of Cajun and Caribbean and rhythm and blues. The fiddle, accordion, and triangle remain in the band but the closer you get to New Orleans, the instruments are joined by the vest-frottoir (a tin washboard played with an old-fashioned church key), steel and lead guitar, and piano. The dancing builds on the two-step to become a West Indies Calinda, very wild, very close dancing—the kind that makes traditional French grandmas very angry with their shameless granddaughters. It's called zydeco and it's a Creole sound.

A. J. Liebling wrote that Hellenism spread to the shores of the Caribbean and Gulf but stopped short of both the Atlantic edge of Europe and the New World. "Culture on both shores of the North Atlantic is therefore a paraphrase," decries Liebling. "It's as though the Choctaw had learned English from the Cherokee." Acadiana never much cottoned onto the English language, any more than it did to English common law or English food.

"The basic political subdivision is the parish, not the county," says lawyer Ardner Cheshire. "And law is more or less based on the Code Napoléon rather than the superficiality of a state constitution. Neither should visitors down here assume that Acadiana is French. It's not. Nor is any reasonable facsimile of the modern French language spoken here. Put a Parisian in Thibodaux and he would communicate a lot better with his Cajun cousins in English than in French."

"NEW Orleans resembles Genoa or Marseilles, or Beirut or the Egyptian Alexandria . . . like Havana and Port-au-Prince, New Orleans is within the orbit of a Hellenistic world that never touched the North Atlantic." So wrote A. J. Liebling, the great honorary citoyen of Louisiana. People have been trying to own and understand New Orleans since La Salle sailed by and missed it in 1685. Yet this modern Byzantine city has defied possession and comprehension for going on half a millennium. It's now called the Crescent City, which is pretty obscure, though perhaps it's a recognition of the old Constantinople occupied by the Turk infidel and renamed "Istanbul." All kinds of thalassic cultures swell the Crescent City—not many Turks, but there is belly dancing on Decatur Street, and Algiers is just across the river.

What would have happened if La Salle had found the estuary of the Mississippi in 1685? The answer is that most of the settlers would have died from the fevers just as did the subsequent colonies. Yet the presence of La Salle on the Mississippi River would have made a difference, if only because he got along so well with the Indians, and his strong spirit almost certainly would have made the colony succeed. Instead, lesser Frenchmen came here.

New Orleans was founded in 1718 by the youngest of the Le Moyne brothers, Jean Baptiste, sieur de Bienville, who with his older brother Pierre, sieur d'Iberville, had first settled the area in 1699 at old Biloxi on the east side of Lake Pontchartrain. The Biloxi colony was not fruitful, and after establishing a small colony at Mobile in 1710, Bienville chose the site for New Orleans and named it for the Prince Regent, the Duke of Orleans. The Le Moynes were petty aristocrats from Canada searching for a fate that would elevate them to the true aristocracy in France. According to the diaries of the early colonists, Bienville was a petty tyrant doing nothing to help the beleaguered settlers (he taxed unmercifully, even to taking such little food as they could produce). Brother Pierre, however, was the genuine article, a Frenchman who had no use at all for cursed Albion. In a twenty-year career of fighting the English, Pierre le Moyne led more than ten expeditions against the English in Canada, the American colonies, and what is now the Virgin Islands, yet it was his last crusade that was the most ambitious of them all. In 1706 Iberville assembled a fleet of warships and transports along with a fighting army. His destination was the entire Eastern Seaboard and his goal was the sacking and pillaging of Philadelphia, Baltimore, New York, and Boston. If he were successful, the French would own North America. Alas, Iberville and all his sailors and soldiers perished from the yellow fever as they were trying to sail out of the Caribbean.

The implications of total French victory in North America are pretty intriguing and not really all that farfetched (after all, the English threw the French out of Canada in 1763). In 1706 the War of Austrian Succession was in full swing on the continent of Europe, and England was totally committed there; it was in fact this war that moved England so far up the ladder of Realpolitik of that age. Had Iberville succeeded in his goals, England would have had no chance of sending reinforcements to its colonies. France couldn't send troops either, but it could rely on the massive army of its Indian allies, with whom the French had always had good relations since the days of Cartier. Imagine a French America: no Indian tribes to decimate and relocate; no waves of European immigrants (they would have only South America and Africa left to them); no Revolutionary War; and absolutely no slavery. Fanciful thinking indeed, but the end result would have been an expansion of the Hellenistic world beyond anyone's belief.

Instead, all that America got out of Iberville's dream was New Orleans and two streets in the French Quarter named for the Le Moyne brothers. Yet by the beginning of the nineteenth century New Orleans was recognized as the most important port in America (Jefferson knew it and that is the reason he bought it from the French, getting the huge unmapped territories west of the Mississippi thrown into the bargain). The town began to take on the tone of Naples; it had been French, Spanish, French again, now American, with the British coming along in 1815 to try to pick it off. Just southeast of town are the boggy plains of Chalmette, where Major General Andrew Jackson is said to have beaten the bloody British a few days after the War of 1812 ended. Jackson indeed was the general-in-chief but Jean Lafitte was the real hero behind the cotton bales on Chalmette Plantation, for it was Lafitte's warehouses that supplied the American army with powder, ball, flint, cannon, and shot. And just for good measure, several hundred of Lafitte's pirates joined in to get a lick at Albion.

Realistically, 1815 was the last battle ever fought over New Orleans (if one doesn't count pimp fights and whore brawls). One pointless battle was enough for the Saltwater Way psyche of the Orleanaise. When the Yankee fleet and army showed up in 1862, the Rebel troops took to their heels. The town's gamblers dressed themselves up in brown corduroy uniforms with gold epaulets and plumage and surrendered New Orleans to General Ben F. Butler in fine Cavalier style. Nary a shot was fired (the gamblers immediately went to work for Butler running the cathouses and faro parlors).

Modernity has made some heavy inroads into the old culture of New Orleans—the Superdome, Shell Plaza, the old Jax Brewery made into a new mall, riverboat casinos right in the Quarter. Somehow the tourists think of the French Quarter as a separate and distinct part of the city. While the opinions of tourists are important (tourism is the only thing keeping New Orleans alive since the death rattle of the oil industry), this notion is wrong. The French Quarter is the most significant part of New Orleans. The street in the Quarter that most everyone wants to get to is Bourbon, the anemic replica of old-time Storyville. The folks from out of town come here to get drunk, laid, and go a little wild. Bourbon Street, of course, is a shuck, always has been since the Place aux Armes was renamed Jackson Square.

As of 1994 New Orleans is the most dangerous city in the nation. It has the highest incidence of violent crime and the highest incidence of police brutality. Yet coming to New Orleans over the Pontchartrain Causeway, you are awed again by the Mediterranean aspect of the town, as though you are sailing to Byzantium—it seems to lift itself above the horizon, burnished and suspended in its empurpled, chemical cloudbank under a sweltering Southern sun.

The city exists in daily peril because of the Mississippi River that runs several feet higher than the land New Orleans is built on. If the levee breaks, as it often has, the Crescent City will go underwater and return to the fishes and the cypress swamps. New Orleans is a town that knows it is doomed and seems to accept the fact, adding to the fatalism and concurrent madness of its people, and perhaps this explains in part the city's universal appeal. New Orleans was long the nation's greatest port, New York notwithstanding, and has always taken in the world's mulligan stew and slumgullion of cultures. It exults in its renewing mix of mestizos and Lithuanians and Vietnamese and Yugoslavians. Stay awhile in New Orleans and you will convince yourself that it is uncannily like New York City—Greenwich Village yielding to Washington Square and Soho to Little Italy and Chinatown just as New Orleans's French Quarter becomes separate villages with discernible personalities all their own: Chartres Street tries to stay French but just five minutes over on Decatur the taste of life is distinctively Greek, Turkish, and Italian. If Bourbon Street is pure Southern decadence, then Canal Street is where the soul of New Orleans puts itself on view twenty-four hours a day.

Canal is the busiest street in New Orleans, for the common folk of the city congregate here in something akin to biological thrall. The "locals" are drawn here almost as though on the chance that something will happen to them. Few cities have achieved the mythic proportions that New Orleans encompasses. Except for two widely disparate works, G. W. Cable's *The Grandissimes* and Tennessee Williams's *A Streetcar Named Desire*, New Orleans has never had a great book, no masterwork—until the coming of John Kennedy

Toole's *A Confederacy of Dunces,* a hilarious melodrama that plays upon the mirth and madness of modern New Orleans. Its antihero is a neurotic mama's boy who speaks to the social ills not just of the city but of the South at large. With a focus directly on Canal Street, Toole snares New Orleans's eccentric deadbeats and crackpots; he jousts with gamblers, prostitutes, exhibitionists, anti-Christs, alcoholics, sodomites, drug addicts, fetishists, onanists, pornographers, frauds, jades, litterbugs—all along Canal Street and into the nether world of the French Quarter.

John Kennedy Toole committed suicide in 1969. The literary world owes a heavy debt to Louisiana author Walker Percy, who was prevailed upon by Toole's mother to help get the novel published. Critics and scholars have hailed it as a masterpiece of wit and tone and universality. The title is drawn from Jonathan Swift, who once wrote, "When a true genius appears in the world, you may know him by this sign, that the dunces are all in confederacy against him." Walker Percy never met John Kennedy Toole, though the book he helped get published won a Pulitzer and was uniformly praised as wholly original, a classic creation of character that would last through the ages along with Gulliver and Don Quixote.

Percy and Toole are both gone now from New Orleans but the myth is still very much alive along Canal. If you look close you'll see Ignatius J. Reilly, the novel's hero, waddling along, maybe stopping to jot down in his Big Chief tablet another indictment of our century.

Tourists don't sashay down Canal Street. The only reason they go on it at all is to catch the electric trolley out to the Garden District. Besides the free ferry over from the Quarter to old Algiers, this trolley ride is the best bargain in New Orleans. It costs a buck one-way and it runs from Canal all the way out to resplendent Audubon Park, past pretty Tulane University and along rows of antebellum houses whose architecture ranges from classical Greek to gaudy gingerbread. The same people one sees at night on Bourbon will be here in the daylight soaking up an Old South culture put here 150 years ago by absentee plantation owners. The occupying Yankees preserved these landmarks and used them as headquarters for their contraband cotton deals and other New Orleans rake-offs. So one can still see the rewards of greed here, Yankee and Rebel. But just a block or two off the Garden District boulevard begins the sprawl of

New Orleans poverty. If Charleston, South Carolina, has its modest, though blatant relative deprivation, New Orleans practices it on a grand scale. The surrounding honeycomb of barrios flows with the river right back to the heart of the city.

Coming back to town, the trolley passes near the site of the old Roosevelt Hotel, where once upon a time the best swing bands played, including Bob Crosby's Bobcats and Phil Harris's Dixieland band (Harris became Jack Benny's bandleader on radio). Louis Armstrong, of course, was in New Orleans then, too, but he was restricted to dives in the Quarter. Dreamy dreams in New Orleans would have put Harris and Armstrong together on stage with a duet of their classics, "That's What I Like About the South" and "What a Wonderful World."

The Roosevelt Hotel was often an unofficial capital of the state. Huey Long kept a suite here year-round, and it was in the Roosevelt Hotel that the Kingfish pulled off his dirtiest deal. Recently declassified FBI files reveal that Huey Long was fully in cahoots with crime boss Frank Costello. The two had first met at Costello's home in New York in 1933, and Costello was Long's frequent guest later at the Roosevelt Hotel. When Fiorello La Guardia began closing down Costello's action in New York, Long invited his new friend to move his operations to New Orleans. Long provided city and state protection for pinball and slot machines, bookie joints, gambling casinos, the numbers racket, and prostitution. After the Kingfish's assassination, the arrangement was continued by brother Earl Long. In a 1936 meeting in Hot Springs, Arkansas, Earl sealed a new agreement with Costello and his new partner, Meyer Lansky, the financial genius of the national crime syndicate.

It is common currency in Louisiana that Huey and Earl were not close brothers, not even friendly; in fact, Earl was jealous of his brother and knew that as long as Huey was in power, Earl would at best be a second banana. There has never been a satisfactory theory explaining why Huey Long was assassinated. Somehow, an unknown and seemingly innocuous doctor, Carl Weiss, slipped through the protective cordon and shot the Kingfish before being killed seconds later in an absolute hail of bodyguard gunfire.

One of those bodyguards—a professional, not a state cop—was James Brocato (soon to be known in New Orleans as "Diamond Jimmy Moran"). Brocato wasn't dismissed for his failure to protect the Kingfish; he was in fact promoted by Earl Long to become the Long machine's liaison with the Costello family in New Orleans. The FBI kept the documentation of Huey and Earl Long's connection with Costello, Lansky, and the mob (including the information about Brocato) classified and under wraps for more than fifty years. What is certain is that the Kingfish died and that the circumstances were and are mysterious. What is also certain is that Earl personally quashed an attempt by the Louisiana state legislature to investigate his brother's death. What is reasonable is that an angry brother would have fired or even banished the failed bodyguard of his dead brother; surely he would never have promoted him into such a linchpin position. What is unknown is what additional files are lodged in the classified archives of the FBI.

The coalition that supported the Longs through parts of four decades could accept the fact that their shady heroes had gone to bed with New Orleans harlots. They could accept that Huey and Earl took gobs of money from the oil cartels they cursed and damned in public. Scandals and corruption are part of the fatalism of the Saltwater Way. Yet these same worldly Longites can never believe that their populist heroes had gone to bed with the vermin of the Mafia. Walker Percy once described Baton Rouge as a model of cultural cooperation: politicians looting the state with Protestant industry and Catholic gaiety. In striving for joy, the Longs lost sight of their chains, and Louisianans were left to sing "Every Man a King" as a dirge.

Although New Orleans is more than a hundred nautical miles from the Gulf, it is a port for oceangoing vessels because the Mississippi River runs several hundred feet deep all the way upriver to Baton Rouge. For about thirty miles above New Orleans the river parishes form a rather unique cultural strip that is sometimes called the German Coast. This area got started when a group of German colonists at the original settlement at Biloxi moved to the river's swampland. The German colonists were dying of diseases and starvation; they would have perished like many in the original French colonies except for the efforts of one man, Charles Frederick D'Arensbourg, a former officer in the Swedish army under King Charles XII. D'Arensbourg went to Bienville in the 1720s and pleaded for the right to start a settlement up the river from the disease-ridden coast. Bienville gets credit for founding New Orleans, but it was the leadership of D'Arensbourg that led to whatever success there was in those first colonial years.

The Germans had a bad time of it. Their numbers almost dwindled to nothing through starvation, the fevers, floods of the river, and hurricanes that raked the coast. Survive somehow the settlers did, and through D'Arensbourg's leadership they even began to find a measure of prosperity. These industrious Germans cleared large tracts of land and carved a niche of civilization out of the swamps. Even though they were Lutheran, they got along with the French Catholic government in New Orleans; several times they brought food relief to the city in times of emergency and hardship. In all, D'Arensbourg governed the German Coast for fifty years—until the Spanish arrested him for supporting a German settlers' rebellion against the oppressive Spanish rule. Charles Frederick D'Arensbourg spent the last eight years of his life in a Spanish prison in New Orleans.

Through the nineteenth and into the twentieth century, the descendants of D'Arensbourg's colonists retained their Old World ways, though they spoke French now as much as German and thought of themselves as Creole. The German Coast still exists, though it, too, lives behind the mask of modernity that dents and scrapes Louisiana the same way it does most of the New South. Efforts have been made in recent years to preserve the old culture; joint German and Acadian groups are sponsoring genealogical research, and several archaeological digs along the river have been going on since the early 1990s.

Roberta Rainwater of LaPlace, right on the Mississippi, takes more than an avid interest in the German Coast. She has written a weekly column for the *New Orleans Times-Picayune* called "Upriver Memoirs," and she focuses on colorful but mostly overlooked facets of the German Coast culture. She has dug out of the archives old accounts and pictures and has interviewed direct descendants of the first settlers, one of whom is Mabel D'Arensbourg Breaux, the great-great-great-granddaughter of Charles D'Arensbourg. Mabel Breaux still lives on the German Coast in the little river town of Reserve, near the site of one of the original villages.

"King Louis XV of France presented the title of Chevalier of St. Louis to Charles D'Arensbourg," she says. "The story was handed down from one generation to the next. Charles D'Arensbourg also was presented a sword and a baton with a solid gold apple on its top. The apple, I'm afraid, got melted down to make a belt buckle for a cousin."

Mabel Breaux also tells the story of her father, Horace D'Arensbourg, and how he used to teach her and the other children little French songs and stories. "He was a sweet and gentle father who never left the parish and he lived to be 101 years old."

Roberta Rainwater herself can speak of the German Coast's people and culture. Members of her family live in the area, and she came back home with her husband, John, to be closer to these roots. Much of the publicity of the river corridor between Baton Rouge and New Orleans is entirely negative because of the national focus on the so-called Cancer Corridor of the giant petrochemical industry. The EPA, Greenpeace, and other environmental groups have focused on these *Fortune* 500 companies for their past practices of polluting and contaminating the corridor.

"It wasn't until the 1930s that agriculture here began to be replaced with manufacture," she says, "and not until the sixties that heavy industry came in to buy up the beautiful plantations and destroy too many plantation homes. One home destroyed by a chemical company is one too many."

The local people are as bitter about the destruction of some of the old culture as they are about the toxic wastes in the river. "There's going on to three hundred years of heritage here," Roberta Rainwater says, "and the big companies are trying to counter that with what they call 'corporate culture.' That's what they call it. But the people here will not sell out. The German Coast is Familyville and the people won't give that up. They have long memories and they don't forget. The corporations won't spoil this area; the people just have too much good sense."

The corporate culture on the Mississippi is barely thirty years old, whereas there's more than 270 years of rich tradition that is the bedrock of life here on the German Coast. "That tradition is so much a part of life here," says Roberta, "that our history is not a dead thing. It lives. It lives in the fine old homes, some of which are still lived in, often by the original family owners. It lives in Providence Baptist Church, founded by free blacks after the Civil War. It lives in St. Charles Borromeo Church—known locally as the Red Church for its red roof. It's one of the first churches founded on the river coast. It lives in the foods, in the sausage still made from recipes adapted from European ones. It lives in the faces of river coast natives in St. Charles, St. John the Baptist, and St. James parishes. They're friendly people who like to know your genealogy before they ask anything else about you."

Despite the corporate culture that has laid claim to the Mississippi River, Roberta Rainwater has an abiding respect for what the old river has been. "When I see the river, that fierce, swift-running fountain barely contained within the levees, I think of the fierce independence that lurks beneath the surface of every person born and bred on the river coast. And I celebrate those qualities."

While some of the big companies have had very questionable practices in the past, even openly violating new regulations or using banned materials, Roberta says that others are respectful and are trying to work with the community. She is not at all sure that the "corporate culture" idea will work, but she can speak for the various communities along the river in saying that none of the *Fortune* 500s should feel they can operate any longer with full impunity.

Louisiana has probably got a longer way to go than many other Southern states, culturally and economically. The Rainwaters own and run a small art gallery in LaPlace where they try to promote good but unrecognized Louisiana artists. They have classes and gatherings for artists and writers. "The fact is," says Roberta, "artists and creative people feel they have to leave here to survive. This is in glaring contrast to the way the state of Mississippi treats its 'creatives.' There, exquisite art can be found around every corner, as well as with the people who want art in their homes and offices. Here we have to try to teach people that art is not the enemy. Here, people who are originals are led to understand that they are allowed to live only in hiding. It's strange because Louisiana breeds eccentrics like mosquitoes. The artistic eccentrics must all have left for Mississippi, while the political eccentrics get elected governor."

Roberta Rainwater thinks of her home state as luscious and strange, and perhaps mixed in this image is the pull of the old Levantine culture in the face of change that both threatens and tempts. In this saltwater world, Louisiana has always been pretty much a man's province. "The women of this and other areas of Louisiana were captured and tamed so long ago," says Roberta, "that it's only now that a few courageous ones are escaping their psychological bonds to speak out for change."

It's not just change in women's equality that has been long in coming to Louisiana, though the jobs came in windfalls starting with the petrochemical boom of thirty years ago. From above the state capital at Baton Rouge to below New Orleans, the huge *Fortune* 500 companies have dug in, seemingly for the duration of this century and the next. Jobs mean families and communities and cultural bonding, and it isn't difficult to see the profit motive at work in the big companies' notion of "corporate culture," whatever in the world that could imply. It is a fact that in the *Fortune* 500 firms there is a beguiling practice known as the "golden glove," a basic understanding that the higher you rise in the ranks of the company, the stronger the grip the company has upon you. Or as Hal Geneen used to say of his senior execs when he ran ITT, "I've got 'em by their limos." The nation knows this stretch of the Mississippi River as the infamous Cancer Corridor, and no matter how much the public relations officers of the companies point out statistics showing that cancer is no more likely here than on any other river or industrial belt of the country, the image and some hard facts remain: the toxic wastes and the contamination of the air are at the crisis stage. People want to keep the factories and their jobs and homes, but something akin to psychological numbness definitely has set in along the Mississippi River. The common people have just about given up hope that there will ever be a change or, for that matter, that anybody in the rest of the nation really gives a damn.

CHAPTER 13

THE SUNBELT SOUTH

*The Redneck Riviera . . . Mobile Bay . . . The Mother Teresa of Cervantes
Street . . . Pensacola and Tallahassee . . . The Everglades . . . Henry Flagler and the
Gold Coast . . . The Keys*

ALL THE WORLD KNOWS that the South, every particle of it, gets more
than its share of the sun. To some people such a benefit calls to mind
sunbaked clay soil crusted white in fields built of a one-crop mentality and succeeding waves of black and white folks fleeing to the
frigid North in search of jobs. To others the Sunbelt calls up the vision of the post–World War II movement of marginal industries
from the North to the South, exploiting the last one-crop fixation of
Southerners, cheap labor to run the mills and shoe factories. The
prevailing metaphor came not from Henry Grady but from Tennessee Williams and Erskine Caldwell, whose characters got fired for
trying to organize a labor union and writing a poem on the lid of a
shoe box.

The reality of the Sunbelt, the ultimate consummation devoutly to
be wished, was the Glengarry Glen Ross syndrome that transformed
league upon league of waterless sand and bottomless marsh into
dreams of paradise and a place in the sun. Such dreams touched the
lives of every segment of the freezing North, the rich and the industrious middle class stockpiling their savings to live in the warm salty
air. Even the poor, the Ratso Rizzos and Joe Bucks, came to plant the
flag of midnight on the pure white sands.

It's fitting that the modern Sunbelt South begins just east of New Orleans at Bay St. Louis, for this is the first and last tendril of John Law's scheme. It was along here that John Law's Mississippi Bubble of the 1720s was to have founded a New World paradise, though Law himself never set foot on Mississippi soil and would see his scheme destroy the French economy. The Mississippi Gulf Coast is where the rich live, with the Big House in every direction you look. This miniature Sunbelt coast was the precursor of Florida. It didn't attract Northern migrants because its lands had already been picked off by the antebellum grandee class. The Gulf-front property has always been dear, and to own an estate here was a mark of success higher than if your family had once lived in the shadows of the plantations on the Teche. Many of the stately homes date back to the pre–Civil War boom of the 1840s when the cotton barons of the lower South built pleasure domes to accommodate their Prince Regent dreams of cotillions and Chinese gardens, summering here away from the killing heat and oppressive humidity and debilitating fevers. It was fashionable in those days to trace one's genealogy to the early settlements that Iberville brought down here, but those family trees won't bark much, since those early folk mostly perished. Today the best historians of the Mississippi Gulf Coast are the carpenters who rebuild or remodel these great old stately homes; the carpenters know the houses back to antebellum days, who built them or inherited them, what landed baron shot which rake for seducing a daughter or lonely young wife and which hurricane blew it all away.

If you're not third- or fourth-generation rich, the thing to do if you're Louisiana- or Mississippi-born is to get on up North and make your fortune out of bonds or pork bellies so's you can come back and strut with a hog mansion, cement pond, Louis Seize furniture, and medieval blown-glass windows. But just because the area is wealthy, one can't assume that it is staid. From Bay St. Louis past Gulfport to Biloxi, what used to be a silk-stocking strand has now become Casino Alley. At one time it was a well-to-do but rather sleepy expanse of pretty beaches and picturesque fishing ports, all with the obligatory grand estates perched here and there where the higher gentry of New Orleans and Jackson, Memphis and Chicago lived beach front to beach front with retired judges, senators, and vice lords—a sort of Canal Street cultural potpourri for the rich and infamous. Nowadays the coastal highways are packed like California freeways with casino crazies. They come from New Orleans and Mobile and Pensacola and Jackson; they fly in from Dallas, Atlanta, Charleston, and Miami.

"There's a kind of a claustrophobic sense of hill fort estate here," says a retired venture-capital banker living in Bay St. Louis. "They're like Old World barons, dukes, petty and high kings, living in some guarded fear and more arrogance. There's not much sense of community among them, just high ridges to separate them. As such, the nabobs don't mind the casinos and the low rollers coming in."

The Gulf Coast is crazy Levantine country and will stay that way for as long as there are hurricane parties. When the U.S. Weather Service puts out a serious advisory, sane people retreat into the hinterlands, but a special reckless breed stays. They don't rush to put up storm shutters; they rush to the liquor store to buy up Champagne and cognac and the ingredients for the incredible Sazerac and hurricane cocktails they'll drink to toast the arrival of the big blow. Sometimes it's exhilarating, like watching the Wallendas work without a net, and sometimes it's fatal. In 1969 the hurricane of the century, Camille, killed hundreds coastwide, and at Pass Christian dozens died at a single hurricane party. According to the few survivors, the crowd was singing and drinking and making merry when Camille hit, and the same survivors say you could hear the voices go from songs to screams. Yet even these deaths don't stop the hurricane tradition; when Andrew hit, they were lifting their cups high along this coast in a peculiar, fever-pitched kind of defiance, a Levantine fatalism bordering on what the great Irish poet W. B. Yeats called a "lonely impulse of delight."

ONCE upon a time the coastlands of condos, marinas, malls, and private beaches that begin at Gautier (pronounced "Go Shay"), Mississippi, and extend to Pensacola, Florida, were known as the Redneck Riviera. It was a time and place celebrated in the legend and lore of those who have lived to see it disappear, and many a good old boy has mourned its passing. The most vibrant days of the Riviera stretched from the 1940s through the 1960s, until the coming of the monied leisure class. During those twenty-five years the true trinity of the South—bad booze, bad women, and the law—held sway here with a life force beyond the ken of the Bible Belt. It was without doubt a man's world. Every young boy born of the baby-boom era who came of age in this gritty half world learned his lessons early or didn't learn them at all. If he was lucky he had an outlaw uncle who taught the lessons he'd take with him through his life. "The beer tasted better and so did the women," said his uncle, who had won the Silver Star and Purple Heart only to come home, get in some trouble just raising hell, and serve a little time at Parchman or Angola or Folsom. "The honky-tonks had better bands and the fights were more worthwhile," his uncle allowed. The men—truckers, longshoremen, mechanics, hot-tar roofers, shrimpers—were the people that lived the country songs. They didn't need Zorba, they already knew how to dance. "And the good times were a lot closer to good."

What happened down here on the poorer stretch of the Gulf was a kind of spiritual relative deprivation. The soul feels trapped or smothered and it seeks freedom in either sweetness or wildness. When one sees a redneck getting drunk and cutting loose on the world, one understands it is his soul trying to fight free. In the tonks and blade joints they sang their ludicrous grief and lachrymous sincerity in bitter paeans to cheating, cold, cold hearts. Theirs was a chimerical hold upon the reality of their geographic culture so tenuous that a transitory natural disaster could wipe it out. Devastating hurricanes in the sixties and seventies, coupled with the developers' rush to turn the Gulf into a sand-and-sun paradise, removed almost all traces of the Redneck Riviera, as though the myth of Atlantis were visited upon the Gulf Coast. In all it lasted little less than the vaunted Deep South culture of which it was a demeaned cousin. Still, its legend continues to draw the curious who search for lost potshards and middens scattered now and then in the gloss of hotels and marinas and condos stuck all along these capes.

The little town of Gautier, Mississippi, lives on as a small emblem of the old Redneck Riviera. Gautier isn't at all as prettied up as its historically elite neighbors, Bay St. Louis and Biloxi. Where they have antebellum homes, palm trees, rich old hotels, new condos, and a garden club malaise, Gautier has plain houses and nice streets running to seedy. Talk with old-timers reveals that Go Shay hangs on to the Redneck Riviera heritage. "There's no pecking order here like you see over at Biloxi or Gulfport or even up at Natchez." Used to be some wild times in the dives hereabouts but "now they got recreation halls . . . safe but mighty dull."

No remnants of Indian civilization remain on the Mississippi coast, other than the derivative name, Pascagoula. An enormous amount of barge traffic, both river and inland waterway, passes through this growing port town, but from here to Mobile Bay the coast is virtually deserted, with nothing but bayous, causeways, inland bays, and saltwater swamps. It's an unlooked- for gap in the hedonism of the Sunbelt. This is back country with a French character or a different political hue. The Acadians (Cajuns) were French refugees placed down in the swampy lands in and around New Orleans; when this land became more valuable, they were pushed off of it and persecuted by the Catholic aristocracy; they did manage to build a world of their own west of New Orleans and their influence swept as far away as the Gulf Coast of Lake Charles. But Alabama has its French flavor, though the 'Bama French are Napoleonic, tricolor fighting men who bled at Jena, Austerlitz, Wagram, and Eylau. They fought to the end at Waterloo, just like General Cambronne says, and then migrated to the old dream of the New World.

These Napoleonic French brought with them another difference—the stiff-necked bigotry of defeat. Here in the Alabama of the 1820s came the refugees of the great European Lost Cause, the defeat of the masses at the hands of the royal houses. They, too, became a part of the Redneck Riviera into the twentieth century, and one has only to drive a few back roads to find their progeny in little ports and towns like Gasque, Bon Secour, Bayou La Batry, Daphne, Mon Louis, Josephine, and Rabun. So here to the American South came the seeds of the French *fleurs de mal* that would sprout with the defeat of the South.

Bienville, founder of New Orleans, touched down at Mobile Bay in 1702; he came back to found the town of Mobile in 1710. For a while the town was the capital of French Louisiana, though it would peter out after New Orleans became the major port of the Gulf. New Orleans gets all the glitz but Mobile was always a better, more natural port. It never rose to much prominence because it lacked the Northern connections that the Mississippi River provided. The closest to greatness Mobile could ever get was during the Civil War when as the last surviving Confederate port the city prospered. U. S. Grant believed Mobile to be the key to the early defeat of the Confederacy; after his victory at Vicksburg he wanted to turn Sherman loose to capture the fortress of Mobile from the land side. But Northern politicians and textile magnates wanted the cotton of Louisiana and Texas, and Grant's Mobile plan was turned down.

It was right here on Mobile Bay in the summer of 1864 that the immortal David Glasgow Farragut, first full admiral in the history of the U.S. Navy, uttered his famous injunction, "Damn the torpedoes! Full speed ahead!" Farragut captured Mobile, and for his feat of derring-do the Congress voted him a prize of $50,000. Despite such a telling memorial, the city of Mobile had its own naval hero, Commander Raphael Semmes, the most successful high-sea raider in the history of naval warfare. Like Robert E. Lee, Semmes was a career officer with few promotions who chose to keep the Southern faith. From his flagship, the C.S.S. *Alabama* (whose home port was Mobile), Semmes captured the astounding total of 392 Union vessels with a worth of more than $20 million. After the *Alabama* was finally sunk, Semmes led sailors in infantry battles; he was the only officer on either side to hold commissions in both the army and the navy—Semmes was both a brigadier general and a rear admiral.

So formidable was Semmes in his slashing attacks upon the Union navy and upon Yankee commerce that he remained a marked man after the war. He was the only officer in the South imprisoned and held for treason; the charges against him held no water and Semmes was released after several months in a federal prison. A law student before the war, Semmes had been admitted to the bar and was something of a crack lawyer. He used that background to help escape the clutches of the vindictive Yankee authorities that trumped up a piracy charge against him. After his release he even managed to get himself elected to a judgeship in Mobile, but the carpetbaggers wouldn't let up on him and simply had his election annulled. Semmes lived out his life in Mobile as a marine lawyer but never received the proper acclaim as one of the most famous and successful sea captains in American history.

Mobile today is anything but the boomtown it was just before the Civil War. Back then the state of Alabama knew nothing but boom times. Both the settlement of the state and the growth of Mobile as a big port didn't really begin until the 1820s. Certainly the flush times were brought on by the tremendously rich cotton lands of Alabama's

Black Belt, and the culture that evolved conformed dramatically with W. J. Cash's "man at the center" concept. With the growth of cotton wealth, Mobile had a viable purpose as a port and began to build an appropriately ostentatious cultural façade around its stately mansions, girls' finishing schools, military academies, and cotillion halls. Alabama, however, would always have a squirrel-hunting gentry in its background and a heritage of outlaws such as James Copeland, a legendary Alabama figure who looted in the Deep South in the same era that pirate John Murrell was the scourge of the Mississippi River Valley.

Copeland made his name as a pig thief, barn burner, counterfeiter, pirate, and slave stealer. He was caught, put on trial, convicted, and hanged for murder in 1857. Had he lived a couple more years he no doubt would have fallen into a slave treasure. The last ship trying to bring slaves into America came into Mobile Bay in 1859 and sailed up the Mobile River before the gunboats got after it. This last slave ship was called the *Clothilde* and its crew quickly scuttled it to avoid being captured. Some thirty slaves were on board and they suddenly found themselves in a sinking vessel. They swam and waded ashore and huddled together. When no one came to claim them they simply began to make themselves at home. Eventually they built a small village that they called "Africatown." Slavers dared not claim them and the local folk steered clear of their village. So in a bizarre way the folks of Africatown got lucky: they escaped outlaws and slave stealers and even avoided the Confederacy after the Civil War began. This town existed as a black community for decades, enjoying self-rule as the white world around them paid no mind. The last lineal descendant from the last slave ship lived until 1992. Born in Africatown, Clara Eva Bell Allen Jones, daughter of one of the *Clothilde* slaves, died at the age of ninety-seven and was returned to the cemetery of the Africatown settlers. Ms. Allen was possessed of a remarkable memory, almost total recall, and spoke of Africatown lovingly; life for those descendants of the last slave ship was good there, they were left alone, and her only regret was having to leave after she was a grown woman.

In the year of its capture by Farragut, Mobile boasted a population of nearly 200,000, but it would take almost a hundred years for the city to reach such a level of prosperity again. Mobile had to wait for World War II for its second boom, this time in shipbuilding, not cotton, and since then the city has dwindled. The biggest hope for the port's revival was the Tennessee-Tombigbee Waterway, but that fell far below expectations. No significant commerce has appeared on this Corps of Engineers pipe dream, so instead of growth Mobile shows a steady decline. Withal, Mobile is a lovely old Southern place graced still with Old South natural charm, or as one sixth-generation citizen put it, "Mobile wants to be mobile but about all it can do is cover up the shoddy and wait for another boom."

The enduring joy of Mobile is the city's claim to being the oldest celebrant of Fat Tuesday in America, for Mobile was, after all, settled before New Orleans. The town puts on a Mardi Gras festival each year that many believe is more colorful and less commercialized than the one in New Orleans. The entry of the oldest krewe is "The Order of Myths," always the last float in the parade; the perennial topic of the float is "Folly chasing Death around a broken Greek column while beating him about the head and shoulders with a golden pig bladder."

BOTH shores of Mobile Bay used to be alive with the frolics of the Redneck Riviera, and the vestiges of the Graecia Maxima ran on to Pensacola, a Southern cloud-cuckoo town if ever one existed. In some ways one could have called Pensacola the capital of the Redneck Riviera, but that was back in the old days before Pensacola got so useful to modern times. Then again, Pensacola has always been a useful town: the Spanish had it as the capital of their last toehold on North America; the British used it during the Revolutionary War and the War of 1812; the French tried a colony here but decided they really didn't need it; and Andrew Jackson used it to hang British magistrates and intimidate the Spanish, the Seminoles, and runaway slaves.

Pensacola's thirteen-mile-long bay was once known as Apalachee, named for the first of the Indian tribes hereabouts to succumb to the Spanish, and perhaps that is why some old-time lore holds that this coast, too, might have been cursed, as evidenced even by the names of the rivers—the Styx and the Perdido—that feed into the Gulf. Above Pensacola, the Apalachicola River became the scene in 1816 of one of the most amazing though little-known slave uprisings in American history. Runaway slaves sought haven in the forest and

swampy terrain along the Apalachicola River; they built themselves
something of a stronghold here and called it Negro Fort. Most of the
runaways had escaped from plantations in Georgia, and in their
numbers they steeled nerve enough to stand for their independence. They took on all comers, the Spanish and the headhunter
Seminoles who came after them as slave catchers. Their stronghold
stood, but soon they would have to face the combined arms of the
American army. In July 1816, the Americans came with troops and
gunboats to lay siege to Negro Fort. The battle raged for several days
until a misaimed cannonball struck the fort's powder supply. The explosion decimated the fort and slaughtered all but three of the 334
black renegades inside. One of the survivors was the fort's leader, a
man known only as Garçon. He was hanged by the Americans.

Several bands of Seminole Indians had assisted in the siege of Negro Fort (they were working for a bounty of fifty dollars a head), and
after the slaughter from the explosion, the Americans paid off their
Indian allies in captured muskets, rifles, carbines, and pistols. This
payoff would work out to be a bad decision, for the guns were used
later by the same Seminoles to fight American armies to a standstill
in the Seminole Wars. Never again would there be runaway slaves on
the scale of Negro Fort; when Andrew Jackson opened up Alabama
and Florida, tens of thousands of white settlers rushed in and there
simply were no havens left for runaways. Some freedmen found
their way down the Apalachicola or across the Florida panhandle to
put down communities like Niggertown Knoll and Niggertown
Marsh in the rural highlands (it would take the local authorities until the 1990s to change these embarrassing place names).

The town of Pensacola is perhaps the last lingering vestige of the
Jacksonian South. An old colonial ambiance is still here—all that titled corruption and elegance and licentiousness. Pensacola remains
Andy Jackson country with a mix of some gentility, a bit of low-down
arrogance that resists change, and a peppery spirit, all making it one
of the more interesting towns in the South. Jackson was the first territorial governor of Florida and Pensacola was his headquarters, yet
the town hasn't ever thought of building an industry around him,
not even a puny theme park. It's an unassuming little city that hasn't
fallen for the gimmicks that attract hordes of tourists to the rest of
Florida. Pensacola always seemed to be satisfied with what it is, a big
bad Baptist town, Spanish influence or no. Neither does it mind be-

ing thought of as an out-of-place, old-fashioned Bible Belt town in the Sunbelt South.

The life fiber of Pensacola is Cervantes Street. It is a thread stitching through this old Spanish town and has the colors of the social and cultural spectrum that extends all the way through the city, from the upwardly mobile condos on Escambia Bay to the redneck immobility of west Pensacola. East Cervantes is the higher class and its colors are the cool blues and earth tones so loved by the young professionals; a little bridge crosses Bayou Texar where the really rich live. Class smudges begin to appear at Palafox, the north-and-south commercial corridor of the city coinciding with Cervantes in age and importance. Here the busy traffic sweeps by a Jewish synagogue, the obligatory Confederate statue, and the huge First Baptist Church that tells you what Pensacola's soul is all about.

Cervantes climbs into an array of eighteenth- and nineteenth-century mansions refurbished to within an inch of their lives. The class smudges don't last long until one begins to notice the distinct lines of the town's rainbow psyche, the purples and greens and golds and all the old badges of deferred dreams that belonged to the black communities snug up against the white historic North Hill District. This black community was always called Tan Yard, and at Tan Yard begins the decline from the North Hill District, all comprising the dual personality of Pensacola's relative deprivation. Liquor stores, dope drops, crack houses, and cheap tenements occupy the homes that once were built to hold the blacks who climbed North Hill to work in the whites' houses and raise their children. Nowadays the colors that bleed into the thread of Cervantes Street are the despairing grays and rusty browns and flat blacks. Here and there a sequestered little AME church faces off with a juke joint; mamas and aunts coming out of the churches bawl out at the youngsters who have sought the company of drunkards and pushers, everybody standing out in the open. In Tan Yard they come outside—outside the churches, outside the clustered projects, outside the welfare shacks that hold them. At first you puzzle why they must be outside and then you come to know that there must be a need to be seen, known, and identified. Grandmothers raise the children of the slums and teach them not ever to be afraid but to be alert and to duck down if anyone makes a sudden move. The drug dealers are on the street corners and the newly arrived Jamaican Posse appears sud-

denly, like phantom sailors from out there over the bay; the Posse
looks sleek and self-important and it stands casually chattering out a
street litany. It is a new twist on an old Southern pattern of bullies or
Boy Scouts or jocks on the corner in their letter sweaters, the new
mean sumbitches.

And there's more to Cervantes. There's Brownsville. For years
Brownsville was the place where the action got kindled and blazed,
where the deals went down, the prostitutes slouched, the feuds
started, the blood reprisals erupted. Today Brownsville is under reform. Crisp, polite navy blue and white are trying to drive out the
scarlet of the whores.

The person who knows Cervantes Street most intimately is one
who has lived on it for many years doing the work of a Mother Teresa
without benefit of nun's habit. Her name is Jo Anderson, though all
over Pensacola and indeed this part of the South she is known simply as "Mama Jo." Mama Jo and her preacher husband, Buddy Anderson, are doing more than simply running a mission for the
inner-city ministries of Pensacola. Everyone on Cervantes is familiar
with a term called "The Life." It refers to that nebulous, dangerous
subaltern world that has become emblematic of urban America.
What Mama Jo and Buddy Anderson do is try to bring as many as
they can out of "The Life."

The Andersons had firsthand knowledge of The Life from a pimp
called Tony and his domain. Tony had girls and boys in drag working
as hard as plantation slaves; they cluttered the street corners night
and day to bring in their quotas. "We rented a place and turned it
into a coffeehouse so the girls and boys could have a place to come
in and rest," says Mama Jo. "We got to know them all and helped a
few get out of 'The Life.' We even got several students from the Bible
college in town interested in helping; they were crazy about the idea
because that's what they're looking for, a spiritual gangbusters' high.
But Tony the pimp was persuasive himself. He had such charisma
that he enticed one of the Bible college girls into working as a
hooker for him."

Things got so bad in Pensacola that the city went after Tony. Eventually he got busted and so did his doctor patron. "The only prostitutes who walk the street now are the few scattered ones on
Cervantes," says Mama Jo. "We have known two who got their throats

slit . . . one survived and one didn't. The one who survived goes in and out of that profession and our lives. Right now she's out."

If you find yourself alone and hungry with no place to lay your head in the mean streets of this picturesque little city on the Gulf, you'll likely come to know Mama Jo and Brother Buddy. They run a place called the House of Liberty just off Cervantes. It's a big old rambling martin box with a solarium, large dining room, and meditation center where at any one time twenty or thirty people live as family. They're former business execs, lawyers, truckers, carpenters, drug addicts, alcoholics. The Andersons take no money from the city or state, apply for no grants, have few if any strings. The House operates fully on donations (the house itself was a gift from a well-to-do individual that Mama Jo and Buddy helped come back alive).

The House of Liberty is always a cannery hall of activity. On any given day the kitchen will be filled with the rich aroma of red beans, rice, and ham hocks cooking in huge pots; Buddy is in his study counseling a troubled young couple, mostly letting them talk; Mama Jo is trying to help someone get a job or some young couple a house. "People come to us sad and lonely," Mama Jo says. "In the House we dread the seasons, Christmas and Thanksgiving. They experience such loneliness over the families they've left behind and the bonds that have been broken." The Andersons have been at this business for thirty years, since they gave up high-salaried jobs back in the 1960s. "There's big money in caring for the homeless now," Mama Jo says. "It's trendy and profitable and people are getting in on it. The 'organizers' have plush offices and drive around in a Mercedes and a BMW. It's happening right here in Pensacola."

The Andersons don't consider themselves do-gooders or even very pious church people. "I was born in the Ouachita Mountains near the old Commonwealth College," says Mama Jo, "and a book I read in college changed my life. It wasn't the Bible but James Agee's *Let Us Now Praise Famous Men*. Those were my people and I knew I had to live my life for them."

Her maiden name was Anella Jo Harris and she was profoundly influenced by her father, a strong-willed working man who was the spirit of Agee's Alabama sharecroppers. Her tastes are consistently Southern and run from classical music to country, to movies like *Tender Mercies*, and to such writers as Faulkner, Agee, and Thomas

Wolfe. She never doubts that she's a Southerner, a lover of all things South.

"The South got its unique character from losing everything," she says. "It lost its reputation and all the things that it could take pride in and losing cast it down in the depths of anger and bitterness and hate and envy. In the very depths of its loss was an elusive trophy that is hard to recognize as a prize. Having lost all that the world holds dear, the South still has the opportunity to find something that can only be found among the bitterness and anger and pain.

"I don't know what to call it unless I call it love. You can't define that. You can only hope to be understood. It's only after you lose everything that you are able to concentrate on loving. Not so much being loved as loving. Loving can seem a state of mental illness and that is why so many Southerners seem slap-damn crazy. Having been stripped of all else, they were able to try to love. The people in other regions of America had too much else to cover and protect them. The South has always been more naked than any of them. Where there is more loss and more nakedness, God hovers. He has hovered over the South and the South has had the chance to gain its life because it lost it. All the literature and the great stories and the unforgettable people and the culture that is more lasting came out of the struggle with their hovering God."

In her youth Anella Jo Harris Anderson aspired to the love of art and life, but now she has found meaning hidden in the pellucid reality of Cervantes Street, the mythic and naked South. Without cois or habit, her badge of authority is not based on ritual. It comes from her Deep South instinct.

THE odd traveler can never quite tell what's going to happen next in this slap-damn crazy world of the Gulf, but a Southerner on a long pilgrimage knows by birthright that logic and history mean little in the face of the instinct so prized by Southerners. That instinct has not always—or even very often—been in the service of virtue; this coast has been the home of some of the best hell-raising times in all the South's history, a heritage of the ancient stiff-necked bigotry brought to these shores by the French, later honed razor-sharp by the defeat in the Civil War. All that was put aside for one episode that took place here in May 1978 on Escambia Bay when Southern instinct made for the stuff of heroism.

En route from New Orleans, a National Airlines flight was coming in for a landing at Pensacola Airport. The time was 9:21 P.M. and the jetliner was carrying fifty-three passengers and seven crew members. Visibility was four miles under an overcast sky. The pilot had made this run many times before and though there was ground fog, nothing seemed out of the ordinary. The Boeing 727 touched down on what the cockpit crew thought was the runway. A split second later came the horrifying realization that the plane wasn't on the runway but two miles out in the bay. It began to sink in thirteen feet of water. The passengers thought the craft had simply made a hard landing and it was only a few seconds later, when water started pouring into the cabin, that they realized they had hit down in the bay. Now suddenly the cabin was in full panic. The rear and over-wing emergency doors were already going underwater, leaving the only exits at the front of the plane. The stewardesses and crew began passing out life jackets and urging the passengers not to rush. All would have to jump into the void of the dark waters below.

And an amazing thing happened. One moment, the people had only the choice of sinking with the plane or plunging into the water—and the next moment they found themselves being pulled free. Brawny arms covered with scars and tattoos lifted the hysterical men and women and children out of the murk and onto the decks of two shrimp boats. It was a one-in-a-million chance. At the same time the jetliner was coming in, some enterprising good old boys were running a little dope up the bay, sneaking through the DEA's standing blockade to hidden bayous. The shrimpers had heard the plane coming down right over them and had seen the crash. They heard the screams as the passengers jumped into the water. The shrimpers were caught in an awkward dilemma—save their dope cargo or save the people. In this instance the good old boys turned redneck aristocrats. They quickly dumped their bales of marijuana into the water and sped to the crash site. They had no rescue equipment, no rafts, no life jackets for themselves. Yet they jumped in and saved all they could.

After about a half hour some civilian, commercial, and Coast Guard craft converged on the scene. Two helicopters circled overhead and provided spotlights for the search. The real rescue work had already been done. The good old boys didn't want any credit for their efforts that night, and they didn't get any either. Perhaps it was just as well, for it saved having to answer questions about "shrimping" in the dead of night. Miraculously, a total of fifty-seven of the sixty persons on the airplane survived the crash; three drowned inside the plane.

For days and weeks after the plane crash, some funny-looking herbs washed up all along Escambia Bay. One could walk along the shore and pick them up by the armload, a doper's heaven. The DEA has the reputation for collaring the small fry while letting the kingpins skate. These Pensacola dope runners were small fry, the same as their Copperhead Road cousins way up in the hills. But in this case, no arrests or even inquiries were ever made. A lot of passengers on the downed plane will remember that night all their lives and will keep these Redneck Riviera heroes in their hearts forever.

THINK Sunbelt and you think Florida. Were it not for its name, the beaches at Fort Walton, Florida, would rival those at Marrakesh in the lore of sun and sand around the world. Fort Walton's beaches are like the white fur on a baby seal. It is here that the opulence of the Sunbelt truly begins. Certainly the Sunbelt embraces the Florida peninsula all along its nine-thousand-odd miles of sandy beaches. Because of the preponderance of transplanted Yankees now living in Florida, thinking Sunbelt is not necessarily synonymous with thinking South. There are some who believe the only two things south of Tallahassee that qualify as truly Southern are the Everglades and the Florida Keys. This popular attitude would have us believe that there are only nuances of things Southern the deeper you travel into the Florida peninsula, like listening to Dixie being played ten miles away with no amplifiers, just a desultory breeze to waft the spirit of the Lost Cause to the true believers. But Dixie remains the metaphorical anthem down here, the one the radio stations still use as the sign-off music (even though it might be played with a calypso beat).

The Panhandle town of Tallahassee is one of the fastest-growing cities in the South and it is a land of true believers. It's Protestant, it's redneck, it's educated, it's pretty, and it has all the remnants of the Lost Cause. Florida was easily the least affected part of the Confederacy during the Civil War, yet one minor action just before the surrender has clothed Florida's Lost Causers in the Rebel battle flag forever. Toward the end of the war, the Union tried to capture Tallahassee. A ragtag force of old men and young boys from the local military school not only stood at the battle of Natural Bridge but drove the Yankees away. At first yawn it doesn't seem that Tallahassee has a lot of room for Sir Walter Scott romance; Waverly somehow doesn't fit the conscience of a town that as recently as 1994 turned out thousands marching through the city center to protest their rights to pack their shooting irons, and the Brady Bill be damned. The state of Florida has earned the reputation as the burn capital of the South and nation because it has so eagerly executed Death Row inmates. Florida's reputation was so strong that it worked in a macabre way to bring the death-wish scourge of serial killer Ted Bundy down upon Tallahassee itself. The town, then, certainly qualifies as a true Southern town if for no other reason than its double-gaited nature—pistol-toting bubbas alongside the Southern romance of defiance and defeat. Too, there's a surprising connection between Old Tallahassee and the Mediterranean, for it is in this capital of Florida that the remains of Achille Murat, son of Joachim, King of Naples and nephew of Napoleon, is laid to rest beneath the swaying palms. So, unlooked for, there is a French connection (though it's mainly used as a theme for Junior League balls).

What Florida does is to tie the South to the tropics, to the Saltwater Way itself, to in a sense metamorphose the old American Dream of progress through Manifest Destiny into the new narcolepsy of sun and sand and retirement. It's a new kind of destiny but just as compelling as the old. Florida pointed the direction for yet another variation of Manifest Destiny, a crackbrained scheme whose intent was for America to control all the lands and islands contiguous to the Gulf of Mexico. This bastard version of Destiny began in the 1840s and was called the Golden Circle. It was a forlorn hope to increase the slave-holding states of the Southland and was the toy of one George Fitzhugh, putative philosopher of slavery as a benevolent institution. Fitzhugh was a fanatic who set up crypto chambers of commerce to promote the takeover of Central America and the Caribbean Islands and impose slavery on every man, woman, and child. He was not without his credentials; he was well-educated, and worked for the Attorney General of the United States, the Confederate congress during the war, and, of all things, the Freedmen's Bureau after the war. Strangely, Fitzhugh's racial diatribes are still included in anthologies of American literature, and though he died as bankrupt as his concepts, he would have a profound influence on the ideas underlining the Vanderbilt Agrarians of the twentieth century.

Of course the Civil War destroyed slavery, but the Golden Circle was never quite unmade; it simply got translated into American imperialism. Although Fitzhugh never saw Florida, his dream of empire would soon be visited upon this wild, new garden of Eden. Up to that time anyone who thought of Florida looked upon it as a vast swamp, but it was really a river of grass, the greatest natural reserve of fresh water and wetlands ever to be seen in America. This sawgrass sea began at Lake Okeechobee and extended through the Big Cypress and into the Everglades covering millions of acres. But for one man this great natural resource might still be with us.

In 1883 John D. Rockefeller's chief partner in the Standard Oil Company, Henry Morrison Flagler, came to the east coast of Florida with bags of money and his own version of the Golden Circle. He came not for a season or a year but forever; he would create in the lands of Florida a civilization unknown since the days of Babylon.

If Pensacola and Tallahassee were the last vestiges of the Jacksonian South, the little port of Jacksonville was hardly alive when Henry Flagler arrived on his famous scouting expedition. In fact, Jacksonville and Florida itself as we know them in the twentieth century would not have existed if Flagler could have found a flush toilet anywhere in the vicinity. He was so chagrined at the poor accommodations that he determined to do something about it. Where others had turned away from the barren sands and inland swamps as an impossible realm to conquer, Flagler looked and dreamed of a winter playground for the rich of the East Coast. Within thirty years he would virtually own Florida all the way to the Keys.

At the turn of the century Jacksonville was still a sleepy little port with old-fashioned beach houses and screened-in porches. Writer Stephen Crane convalesced here after his ordeal at sea when the ship the *Commodore* was sabotaged on its way to Cuba in the Spanish-American War; Crane survived with three other men in an open boat and from the experience he wrote one of the great masterpieces of American literature. He spent his days recuperating at the Hotel de Dream, a cut-rate house of joy, and it was here that he fell in love with Cora Taylor, the bordello's madam. Because of his stature as a writer (and the quixotic nature of his life), the hotel could have been enshrined like Hemingway's haunts in Key West, but unfortunately the Hotel de Dream burned down just seven years after Crane's tragic death in 1900 from tuberculosis.

Even though it's the gateway to Henry Flagler's fabulous American Riviera, Jacksonville took a long time in growing. To get into Florida before the boom years, one had to travel back roads and take one's chances with the "stand-and-deliver" constabulary that preyed on Northern tourists. Author Melissa Fay Greene's *Praying for Sheetrock* details the crooked Georgia cops and sheriffs of McIntosh County on the Georgia-Florida borders; these thugs with badges fleeced travelers out of millions of dollars over the years until they were shut down by Georgia's governor Lester Maddox. Nowadays the back roads are gone and the biggest holdup is that it's more difficult to get over to the coolest spot in the whole of the South, Okefenokee Swamp and the beloved old Suwannee River.

Jacksonville is part of Flagler's dreamed-of Riviera, and the most beautiful part is Fernandina Beach, with its immaculate surf and sand and rich resort villages full of retired or active-duty military families. The world's largest submarine base is located here at Jacksonville. One of the more popular pastimes among the locals, aside from scalping tickets for the new NFL team in town, is going down to the beach to watch the giant nuclear subs lubber into their pens. The sub commanders to a man will tell you that Jacksonville was about the worst possible choice for a sub base and that it's hard as hell—and dangerous—maneuvering the narrows along the coast.

Florida's double-barreled psyche sets itself here in Jacksonville— the cosmopolitan, rich city itself (the largest in Florida) surrounded by snake-handling, holy-rolling redneck Bible Belters. If it be true what they say about Dixie—that the South don't go into uppity, above-its-raisin' Florida—then Jacksonville must be part of Georgia.

SOUTH of the panhandle, the population on the east coast of Florida centers on towns all of whose names seem to end with the word "Beach," "Shores," "Bay," "Park," or "By-the-Sea." The panorama stretches from Stephen Crane's Hotel de Dream to E. A. Robinson's Richard Cory at Palm Beach. In between, one finds every personality and none, from the down-and-out to the clean-favored and imperially slim. Henry Flagler built his railroads here, running from Daytona to Palm Beach to Miami. In the fine tradition of federal land grants for track laid, Flagler got every other section of land as a bequest from a grateful Uncle Sam. Along the way he built luxury hotels and marinas, indulged in huge land speculation, acquired steamship lines, and dredged the Miami harbor for his own use.

Flagler's Miami was meant for the rich and they began to come in waves from Cape Cod, Newport, Narragansett, from West Chester, from East Hampton, Bridgehampton, Southampton, and even Lionel Hampton. If Miami denies even being Southern, somehow it is still the most vibrant city of the Southlands. Miami continues to struggle for an identity because it is trapped somewhere between A. J. Liebling's uninterrupted sea and George Fitzhugh's Golden Circle. Despite its social ills and thousandfold inequities, it is a city that tries to be happy, must be happy, and is. The tempo of the city carries a curious admixture. Once it swung to a Cugat beat, then waltzed to a moon over Miami, all changing to the beat of the rhythm of the night. Somewhere still in Miami they're wallowing in the melancholy of old dogs and children and watermelon wine.

At the same time Henry Flagler was terra-forming the coastline of Florida, he was laying out the whole interior with a matrix of canals and lakes and clear-cut land. The first canals were dug in the 1880s, starting the evisceration of the Everglades. For centuries the Everglades provided a buffer zone against the ravages of nature. This giant sawgrass sea could hold the rain, keep back flooding, and prevent drought. In less than one century of drainage canals, military bomb and artillery ranges, farming, and hordes of people rushing in, the Everglades have become polluted and are drying out, with spontaneous forest fires a perennial danger. Even hurricanes now have a dramatic environmental effect. Hurricane Andrew cut a twenty-mile-wide gash through the national park, putting more pressure on an ecosystem already threatening to become a wasteland void of fish and fowl and vegetation. The Everglades are fast becoming like the cattle-ranch plains of Texas.

From Ocala to Arcadia, inland Florida is the greenest land east of the Imperial Valley. The highways are lined with stretching miles of citrus groves and were always as much an attraction as the sandy beaches. You don't get the succulent odor of orange blossoms here anymore, just the bull rush of the smudge pots. For decades the center of orange and grapefruit production was in the middle of the peninsula, but now urbanization has begun to push the groves south into the Devil's Garden and the Everglades.

Florida today is more concerned with saving face than with saving the peninsula. The state's citrus commission has a history of hiring happy faces to promote its public image, but it changed its tack by taking on an environmental hitman, Rush Limbaugh, as its orange-juice hypester. Limbaugh's method is to appeal to the virulent attitudes and dim suspicions of the Far Right, but what Limbaugh's wide audience of the 1990s isn't privy to is that he was once a so-called knee-jerk liberal who for years hosted a so-so radio talk show. Admired now as an archconservative, Limbaugh simply jumped onto the side of the angels, and what he has become is simply a very successful Southern good old boy horse trader, for he always held the right credentials. He hails from Cape Girardeau, Missouri, a Southern gateway town on the Mississippi River, and his roots have simply worked their way to the surface. Though his outreach now is vast, Southerners understand Limbaugh best and perhaps can even forgive him, and forgive his horse trader's handshake. The Florida Citrus Commission, however, had second thoughts about Rush's image; it has forgone his services as spokesperson and it is unlikely that old Rush will be showing up in those driveling commercials.

Henry Flagler's thirty years of ruthless land speculation came to its inevitable, even logical climax with the Golden Gate Swindle of the 1960s, when his cunning and grim kindred spirits (known to this age as real estate developers) set in motion a scam not seen in America since John Law's Mississippi Bubble. The Gulf American Corporation bought over two hundred square miles of swamp and started selling tens of thousands of estates on the installment plan to gullible retirees all over the nation. The development was to be called Golden Gate, a new city to be carved from the wilderness and designed to replace Miami and Havana and even Rio. Gulf American dredged miles of canals through the swamplands to make the land habitable for an envisioned new city of millions. In less than ten years the canals were carrying freshwater to the sea and the wetlands' life was decimated. The droughts and forest fires made the huge area uninhabitable. Today Golden Gate Estates is a ghost town and the lands stretching through Alligator Alley are now desert, greatly affecting the Everglades. What had started out for want of a toilet ended up as a dry bog. The millions of people intended for Golden Gates did come after all, even though the scheme came a cropper. Instead, the millions flushed into the boondocks of Orlando with the coming of Disney World.

GOING down the long coastline, one is strangely haunted by William Faulkner's imperative for the South: what do people do here and why do they live here at all? The high civility of the North has become entangled here with the South's sensuousness in a deferred annuity with no redemption date, funding the search for Ponce de Leon's legendary Fountain of Youth. The sadness of the Everglades and the bitterness of that betrayal spill out into the ocean and drift onto the life-raft line of knitted islands known as the Keys. Here are the last traces, the final hallmark of the South on this peninsula. It's altogether fitting that the islands be tenuous in their connection with the mainland; it would probably be better were there no highway at all, that travel among the Keys had to be by small boat and ferry—it would suit the ambiance better, fulfill the psyche of Florida. For this is Papa Hemingway Country; it's easy to close your eyes and see Humphrey Bogart, Edward G. Robinson, and Lionel Barrymore on Key Largo.

They filmed *P.T. 109* just off Ramrod Key; the navy sent in a barge to dredge a channel for the island sequences. Some of the Peace Corps kids of the 1960s trained here in the sand, the salt-warm breezes, and as one of them, Larry Bracken, says, "in the general horniness of that generation." Bracken had one of the longest tenures ever in the Peace Corps. He served many years in the Pacific—on Pago Pago, Truk, and various Micronesian islands. Afterwards he was a folk singer on the Holiday Inn circuit all over the South. He was a gonzo journalist and never quite gave it up because today he is the premier gonzo college administrator in America, winner of the National Communicator of the Year Award in 1994. Bracken works as the executive director at Pensacola Junior College and his job is to get grants for the school (which he does to the tune of millions).

"The Keys didn't secede in the Civil War," Bracken avers. "But they sure want to now. The whole chain is as Southern as the French Quarter and the Bonnie Blue flag . . . with Key West as the new Confederate capital."

It's not that they're Lost Causers down here, refusing to forget; the folks on the Keys are just crackbrained crazies, not unlike their brothers of spirit in New Orleans. Henry Flagler's railroad connected the Keys all the way from Miami to Key West, but Flagler wouldn't approve of it now. The mayor of Key West is a bartender and it is he who flies the flag of secession for the would-be Conch Republic. Hemingway's conch people, desperate saltwater white trash, claim the Keys. Back in the Depression these folks made a living any way they could. They were no good at regular jobs, pumping gas or bell-hopping or caddying for the rich. The Conch ran contraband from Cuba or deckhanded on the fishing boats or took the long haul to Nicaragua on the banana boats.

"Years ago," Bracken tells, "they had huge salt beds here where they let the seawater in and then let it evaporate so they could scrape the salt up . . . before the discovery of the big salt mines out West, this was a booming business for Key West. Today a few of the old-timers say that Key West just scrapes the psyche of people and rubs salt in the wound."

Key West is not isolated unto itself with its streets, shops, tourists, the famous bars and hotels. The aura of the town and island spreads out toward the other Keys and you can prove it by walking on the beach in search of locals. They're easy to recognize—they all have ten-thousand-mile stares.

"Little Munson just north of Key West still has an old open house on it," says Bracken. "It's a summer place with a hidden dock. It was here in this idyllic setting where much of the dope from El Salvador came on its way up the Gulf. Back on Key West, the Casa Marina Hotel has just recently been restored. It was immortalized by shrimp boat rocker Jimmy Buffett, who has his own bar and his own crazies who go into a feeding frenzy about every night."

A lot of people come to Key West looking for Monley. "It was Clark Gable's favorite watering hole. Nearby is the incomparable Bottle Cap Bar, a great old place full of drunks playing shuffleboard with baggy-faced barflies and sad, pretty women 'wounded in their sex,' as Lawrence Durrell wrote. In the Bottle Cap the regulars keep repeating the standard island dream—'We all go to the Grand Cayman when we die, don't we?' "

Key West has a somber quality, and it has everything to do with the women. "The real women," Bracken adds as Hemingway devotee and authority on the way of life in the Keys, "not the tourists or the latter-day gold diggers. The women of Key West are beautiful but they're not larger than life, they're smaller. Down here they can't ever seem to get beyond the barriers. Somehow they're more basic and sadder than the men, emotional waifs ready to resign themselves to bad marriages and short-fused careers. You can see in the women's intelligent eyes they know they've lost their real chances . . . if they were up East, they'd be special."

If Key West were up East, it wouldn't be special at all, just another used-up Atlantic City or Coney Island. The beaches would be the same, but what are sandy beaches without tropical sun? And that, after all, was the reason Henry Flagler opened up this paradise in the first place.

So here it is, the final Irony Line of the South, tacked onto this curving horn of island outposts called the Keys. A total of 75 percent of Floridians today are immigrants, and the real irony is that they have never been aware of the Irony Line any more than were those legions of brave souls who first traveled down the Great Philly Road to find the South. Irony is the burnt ring around every redneck's heart, and the great hope for these new immigrants is that they will someday achieve the spiritual awareness of this Southern gift. "Life" was the so-called Greek gift; it could never be taken away if one had illumination. Southern irony can't be taken away either; it can only be misunderstood, as all true Southerners know.

This journey—call it pilgrimage or hegira—meandered through thousands of miles of the Southlands to come home not to the haunted hallows of the Old South but to the manners of the Old World as measured by A. J. Liebling's interrupted sea. It takes a little time to adjust to the peculiar ambiance of the Keys—to the memories of Hemingway's false-macho imagery and Tennessee Williams's orchidlike sweetness and to the frenzy of the Buffettheads' engrossment with cheeseburgers in paradise. Taken together, these nuances of the Keys don't sound Southern, but they are, for we have now come to the last vestige of the alchemist's dream that started at the Mason-Dixon Line, and we're abiding here for that final Grand Cayman prayer meeting.

Background Sources

Chapter 1. *Ancien Régime*

In addition to the works cited in the text, further detail and information may be found in the works of the seventeenth-century memorialist Richard Hakluyt, particularly his *Virginia Richly Valued* and *Divers Voyages Touching the Discoverie of America.* Selections from the original were imprinted at London in 1600. Material on the Jamestown colony can be examined in *American Genesis: Captain John Smith and the Founding of Virginia,* edited by Oscar Handlin; Carl Bridenbaugh's *Jamestown, 1544–1699* gives additional information on the early American settlement.

Although Hakluyt's work includes general assessment of Sir Humphrey Gilbert and his ill-fated expedition, more depth on Gilbert and his dream of empire is furnished by William Gilbert Gosling's *The Life of Sir Humphrey Gilbert;* Gosling details Gilbert's rise to favor with Queen Elizabeth and his brutal defeat of the Irish. For examples of Gilbert's learned demeanor and personality, see his own work, *Queene Elizabethes Achademy.*

Chapter 2. *Lost Causes, Old and New*

Although the principal source on the life and times of Thomas Jefferson remains *Notes on the State of Virginia,* a prime study is *The Life and Selected Writings of Thomas Jefferson,* edited by Adrienne Koch and William Peden. Another valuable source is Nathan Schachner's *Thomas Jefferson,* a fair and straightforward account. W. S. Randall's *Thomas Jefferson: A Life* is a revisionist view and challenges long-held assumptions.

By far the best analysis of slavery is to be found in Kenneth Stampp's *The Peculiar Institution: Slavery in the Ante-Bellum South.* The most complete analysis of Nat Turner's rebellion is found in S. B. Oates's *The Fires of Jubilee,* though William Styron's *The Confessions of Nat Turner* continues to stand as one of the finest works of its kind.

Chapter 3.   *New Magic in a Dusty World*

In his biography of W. J. Cash, Bruce Clayton points out that the chief detractor of Cash's *The Mind of the South* was the now noted Southern historian C. Vann Woodward. Woodward has recanted his early negative assessment of the book, and with such works as *Origins of the New South* and *The Burden of Southern History* Woodward has earned his status as perhaps the foremost Southern historian of the twentieth century.

The geographic story of the development of the Great Philadelphia Wagon Road through North Carolina and the Deep South is told in *Land of the South,* edited by J. W. Clay. Two noteworthy books—Theda Perdue's *Cherokee Editor* and Angie Debo's *And Still the Waters Run*—describe the ancestral lands of the Cherokee Nation. Not incidentally, the whole sweep of the South's settlement is painstakingly documented in the U.S. Department of Commerce's *Historical Statistics (Colonial Times to the Present)*. Noah Andre Trudeau's *Out of the Storm* gives much detail on the final months of the Civil War, including General Johnston's surrender in North Carolina. And not so incidentally, two other works shed light on North Carolina's heritage along Thunder Road: *Moonshine: Its History and Folklore* by Esther Kellner and *A Life in Pursuit of White Liquor* by Alec Wilkinson.

Chapter 4.   *The Grandees of God's Little Acres*

The definitive book on James Oglethorpe and his egalitarian experiment in the South is Phinizy Spaulding's *Oglethorpe in America*. C. J. Milling details the destruction of the native tribes of South Carolina in *Red Carolinians;* R. S. Cotterill gives further insight in *The Southern Indians*. Julia Floyd Smith's *Slavery and Rice Culture in Low Country Georgia* discusses the class system that developed in the 1750s and continued until the Civil War.

Among many worthy works, perhaps the best description of the firing on Fort Sumter that led to the Civil War is W. A. Swanberg's *First Blood*. The essential empiricism of John Locke is to be found in *Two Treatises of Government* (complete title: *In the Former, The False Principles and Foundation of Sir Robert Filmer, And His Followers, Are Detected and Overthrown. The latter, is an Essay Concerning The True Original, and Extent, and End of Civil-War Government)*. This work, which formed much of America's principles and government, was published in 1698 in London.

Chapter 5.   *"Just an Old Sweet Song"*

A study of the Southern economy from Colonial days to the present is available in Frank Levy's *Dollars and Dreams: The Changing American Income Distribution*. The theory of American capitalism is best expressed in John

Kenneth Galbraith's *The Affluent Society;* Galbraith's work continues that of Thorstein Veblen, and these theories are supported by statistical evidence in Levy's work. But no leisure for the descendants of slaves in Georgia is evidenced in Charles H. Martin's *The Angelo Herndon Case and Southern Justice,* a brilliant exposé of the Jim Crow era.

The illusions of Tara and *Gone With the Wind* are commingled in Edward D. C. Campbell, Jr.'s, *The Celluloid South: Hollywood and the Southern Myth.* A real Georgia is revealed in John Ransom's *Andersonville Diary,* a poignant account of a young soldier's suffering and survival in the macabre death camp. An almost surreal illusion of the South during the Civil War is shown in J. S. Silver's *Confederate Morale and Church Propaganda.* Silver's thesis is substantiated by several other works of the modern era that view the War Between the States as something akin to a holy war; notable among these revisionist theories are Thomas Connelly's *Army of the Heartland* and *Autumn of Glory.* For an understanding of the rise of populism and demagoguery in the South after the Civil War, see C. Vann Woodward's *Tom Watson: Agrarian Rebel,* a biography of the volatile senator from Georgia.

Chapter 6. *"Let Us Now Praise Famous Men"*

Frederick Law Olmsted's *A Journey in the Seaboard Slave States,* first published in 1856, reveals the sociologic and economic strata of Alabama's Black Belt, particularly the regions of the Tombigbee and Warrior rivers. This work clarioned the angst of Reconstruction and the subsequent Great Depression. In their chronicle of Alabama's poor white sharecroppers, James Agee and Walker Evans transformed Olmsted's overview into the stark reality of the South's relative deprivation. A. F. Raper's *Preface to Peasantry: A Tale of Two Black Belt Counties* was set in the same time and parallels Agee and Evans's work.

The Great Depression produced a wealth of artistic work through the WPA's Writers' Projects in every state, specifically in the South. Carl Carmer's *Stars Fell on Alabama* was of this era, as was Erskine Caldwell and Margaret Bourke-White's *Say! Is This the U.S.A.?,* but perhaps the most memorable work was John Steinbeck's *Grapes of Wrath.* In the 1940s the spirit of such works continued with Lillian Smith's *Strange Fruit* and Richard Wright's *12 Million Black Voices;* perhaps the epoch culminated with the civil rights movement, punctuated with such works as Pete Daniel's *The Shadow of Slavery: Peonage in the South, 1901–1969.*

The rich side of this deprivation is portrayed in Florence King's *Southern Ladies and Gentlemen,* an extravagant treatment of the rich and famous when compared to Lee Israel's biography, *Miss Tallulah Bankhead.*

Chapter 7. *Why We All Live at the P.O.*

The white man's view of classical Mississippi can be found in William Alexander Percy's *Lanterns on the Levee: Recollections of a Planter's Son.* The contrasting view is John Dollard's *Caste and Class in a Southern Town.* Percy sought to put a human face on Dollard's exposé of the rigid social structure in Mississippi's racially divided class system; James W. Silver's *Mississippi: The Closed Society* deals most convincingly with the same subject, as did the many journalistic works of Hodding Carter in his *Delta Democrat* newspaper.

The celluloid image of Deep South Mississippi is belied somewhat by W. R. Hogan and E. A. Davis's *William Johnson's Natchez.* Johnson, an educated black man in the mid-1840s, was murdered by a white plantation owner for being "uppity." The murder was witnessed by dozens, but the planter was never put on trial; Johnson's case set the standard for the denial of due process to African Americans in the South. The body of Richard Wright's works encompasses the malevolent intent of the closed society, yet one rather obscure oral history, Theodore Rosengarten's *Auto-biography of Nate Shaw,* truly authenticates the everyday deplorable nature of the black man's life in a white man's world.

The color of Mississippi today is neither white nor black but blue, for it was in Mississippi that the new American folk art of blues music had its origin. An expanding archive of works on and about the blues now exists, and besides Robert Palmer's *Deep Blues,* a valuable study is Paul Oliver's *Blues Fell This Morning: The Meaning of the Blues.* One of the most valuable sources overall about the South is *The Encyclopedia of Southern Culture,* a massive four-volume opus by writers, thinkers, and scholars throughout the South.

Chapter 8. *The High-Toned Old Christian Woman Weds the Horse Trader*

Though he was a Southerner by birth, H. L. Mencken and his High Church Episcopalian sensibilities were offended by the vigor of his homeland's apostolic creeds, as venomously exhibited in his *Prejudices, Second Series.* Mencken was the causal force for the Fugitive movement and its *I'll Take My Stand* of 1930. The Fugitives were offended by Mencken's slurring "Sahara of the Bozart" and they took pen in hand to counter him. The result was a literary outpouring from the likes of Allen Tate, John Crowe Ransom, Robert Penn Warren, and John Gould Fletcher, among others. What they managed was to lead literature into the New Criticism (which lasted until deconstructionism).

These so-called agrarians favored the preservation of old traditional values, and consequently the literature that came later fairly focused on tradition. Family life in Tennessee is poignantly depicted in James Agee's posthumous novel, *A Death in the Family.* W. E. B. Du Bois's *Souls of Black Folk* had its genesis at Fisk College, and the conscience of this high-toned state is buoyed by Will D. Campbell's *Brother to the Dragonfly.* J. S. Bassett's *The Life of Andrew Jackson* remains the definitive work on the man who so shaped the world of the Southlands.

The giant public works system that is the TVA actually had its impetus in the sociologic and statistical underpinnings of Howard W. Odum and his *Southern Regions.* Odum's unique approach became the heart and soul of the New Deal's regeneration of the South and has become something of an icon for the new breed of scientific sociologists. Odum's work is being continued and expanded by John Shelton Reed in his Center for Southern Cultural Research at Odum's home University of North Carolina.

Chapter 9. Outlanders

The unique approach to fundamental religion in the Outlander South can best be understood by a reexamination of the works of Jonathan Edwards, including *Freedom of the Will, Original Sin, The Great Awakening,* and *Apocalyptic Writings,* though Edwards's stature stands in the modern world on his dissertation concerning spiders.

Outlander life and lore can be found in the works of an overlooked and almost forgotten company of writers who lived and worked in the hills and valleys of the Great Meadow and Appalachia. A partial list of these works includes Jesse Stuart's *Men of the Mountains,* Harriet Arnow's *The Doll Maker,* James Still's *River of Earth,* and Elizabeth Madox Roberts's *A Time of Man.* Special consideration should be given to Davis Grubb's *The Voices of Glory,* a novel about West Virginia that is dedicated to the spirit of Mother Jones. The story of West Virginia's four major coal mine wars is told in Howard W. Lee's *Blood-letting in Appalachia,* in which Mother Jones, as always, is a major figure and fighter.

Chapter 10. The Latter-Day Phoenicians

Edward King, the Scribners travel writer, was for all practical purposes the first non-Arkansawyer to write about the state. King's book *The Great South* was published in 1875 and is a perfect companion volume to Olmsted's antebellum descriptions of the South. (An interesting publishing note is that King's book was brought out by the American Publishing Company, Samuel Clemens, publisher and editor.)

Mark Twain himself wrote about Arkansas and used the port town of Helena as the model for his Shakespearean Revival in *The Adventures of Huckleberry Finn.* Charles Portis provides uncanny insight into the Arkansas psyche in his *Norwood* and *The Dog of the South,* and Dee Brown's many volumes about the American frontier provide a wealth of accurate background on this anomalous region. Curiously, the author who bridges Edward King and his modern-day counterparts was another Southerner, Jonathan Daniels, who toured the South during the Depression and produced *A Southerner Discovers the South,* one of the better examinations of the Southlands. The state of Arkansas has no good work of history on itself, but Bob Lancaster's *The Jungles of Arkansas* offers many reliable insights and historical interpretations.

Chapter 11. Little Dixie

Washington Irving wrote in some depth about the Badlands in Little Dixie, notably in *A Tour of the Prairies* and *The Adventures of Captain Bonneville.* Irving's companion while touring the prairies was Albert, Count Pourtales, who later published a journal of his travels in the wilds of the Arkansas Territory: *On the Western Tour with Washington Irving.* A translation of this German work is available from the University of Oklahoma Press.

Dee Brown's memoir, *When the Century Was Young,* deals in part with the American Indians and their plight in the early twentieth century. Also on Indian affairs, Kenny Frank's *Stand Watie* and *The Agony of the Cherokee Nation* give an unbiased appreciation of the era from the Trail of Tears through the Civil War. Olmsted traveled through Little Dixie and wrote *A Journey Through Texas: Or, A Saddle Trip on the South-Western Frontier.* Brad Agnew's *Fort Gibson, Terminal on the Trail of Tears* provides good historical background for the region. John Fingers's *The Eastern Band of Cherokees* provides little-known information about the Cherokees who were first relocated in this region during the time of President James Madison.

Chapter 12. The Saltwater Way

The first explorers of the Gulf Coast were the Spanish, and innumerable works exist, among them *The Gentlemen of Elvas, The Relation of Núñez Cabeza de Vaca, The Account of the Narváez Expedition (1528–1536) as Related by Gonzalo Fernández de Aviedo y Valdéz.* Of all the Spanish journals and diaries, Cabeza de Vaca's has proven to be valuable, if not trustworthy.

Of works about the French presence in the Gulf, Francis Parkman's *La Salle and the Discovery of the Great West* has proven to be the most reliable, for the reason that Parkman himself proves exemplary (Parkman set the standard for historians who followed by actually going to the sites of his chronicles). La Salle's expedition to Texas in the 1680s was by then an old dream of empire, but by far the most bizarre dream of all was that of the "Golden Circle" held by George Fitzhugh, the archpropagandist of the slave-holding South. Details on the Golden Circle may be found in Robert E. May's *The Southern Dream of the Caribbean Empire,* but to understand these delusions the reader is advised to consult the primary source, Fitzhugh's *Sociology for the South,* and his sequel concerning slaves without masters, *Cannibals All!*

For local color and realism along the Saltwater Way, see the following: James Frank Dobie's *A Vaquero of the Brush Country,* Lyle Saxon's *Lafitte the Pirate,* George Washington Cable's *The Grandissimes,* and James Soda Pitts's *Life and Confession of the Noted Outlaw, James Copeland.*

Chapter 13. The Sunbelt South

The tragic fate of the Florida Seminoles is depicted in Edwin C. McReynolds's *The Seminoles.* Certain collected works on the settlement of Florida have appeared periodically, among them an 1881 tract published by Harper and Brothers entitled *A Century of Dishonor,* that deal with the betrayal of the Indians throughout the South. Recently Crown has published a collection of old articles, tales, and lore entitled *Tales of Old Florida.* Sharon McKern's *Redneck Mothers, Good Ol' Girls and Other Southern Belles* reveals the lighter side of the cliché of Southern womanhood, in much the same manner as Larry King's *Of Outlaws, Con Men, Whores, Politicians, and Other Artists.*

For in-depth treatment of Florida's environmental problems, see again Clay's *Land of the South.* As for the Florida Keys, the most enduring vision of its unique psyche is still contained in various works of Ernest Hemingway, namely *To Have and Have Not, A Moveable Feast,* and *The Old Man and the Sea.*

Index

Printed in the United States
By Bookmasters